Praise for

Pukka's Promis

"With his trademark attention to detail and descriptive abilities, Kerasote delves into the crucial factors affecting a dog's life — breeding, diet, environment, spaying and neutering, living conditions — as he chronicles his hunt for and acquisition of Pukka."

—*Austin American-Statesman*

"This might be the most important book about dogs written in a decade. Kerasote tells us early on that Pukka means 'first-class' in Hindi, and first-class is a perfect description of *Pukka's Promise*. It's a brilliant integration of speculation, cutting-edge science and story, and will keep you up at night wanting to read more. Every dog lover needs to read this book."

— Patricia B. McConnell, **author of** *The Other End of the Leash*

"Ted Kerasote gently and intelligently questions our fixed notions about living with dogs. Anyone who reads *Pukka's Promise* can't help but become a better dog person. I'd like it to be compulsory reading for all practicing vets and veterinary students."

— Bruce Fogle, DVM, **author of** *The Dog's Mind*

"Here's a dog lover who actually teaches his dog using modern training entirely: communication, observation, and now and then a clicker — not just to build a bond and a working relationship but also to create a running conversation between man and animal. This book also investigates kibble (Is it really good for dogs?) and vaccinations (Why so many? Why so often?) and other commercial pressures on our best friends' well-being. What a good read."

—Karen Pryor, **author of** *Reaching the Animal Mind*

Pukka's Promise

BY TED KERASOTE

Pukka's Promise

The Quest for Longer-Lived Dogs

Ted Kerasote

MARINER BOOKS
HOUGHTON MIFFLIN HARCOURT
BOSTON · NEW YORK

First Mariner Books edition 2014

Copyright © 2013 by Ted Kerasote

For information about permission to reproduce selections from this book,
write to Permissions, Houghton Mifflin Harcourt Publishing Company,
215 Park Avenue South, New York, New York 10003.

www.hmhco.com

Library of Congress Cataloging-in-Publication Data is available.
ISBN 978-0-547-23626-1   ISBN 978-0-544-10253-8 (pbk.)

Printed in the United States of America
DOC 10 9 8 7 6 5 4 3 2 1

"When We're Gone, Long Gone" © 1997 Sony/ATV Music Publishing LLC and Kieran Kane
Music. All rights on behalf of Sony/ATV Music Publishing LLC administered by Sony/ATV
Music Publishing LLC, 8 Music Square West, Nashville, TN 37203. All rights reserved. Used
by permission.

"The Lost Son," copyright 1947 by Theodore Roethke, from *Collected Poems of Theodore
Roethke* by Theodore Roethke. Used by permission of Doubleday, a division of Random House,
Inc.

Photos on the following pages are reprinted with permission: page 46: Copyright by Hoflin
Publishing, Inc., www.hoflin.com; page 47: Corbis/Yann Arthus-Bertrand; page 48: Mary
Elizabeth Thurston; page 49: AP Images/Seth Wenig; page 51: *Brehms Thierleben: Allgemeine
Kunde des Thierreichs;* page 52: Alamy/Life on White.

THIS BOOK PRESENTS THE RESEARCH AND IDEAS OF ITS AUTHOR AND
A GREAT BREADTH OF PROFESSIONAL VETERINARIANS. IT IS NOT IN-
TENDED AS A SUBSTITUTE FOR CONSULTATION WITH A VETERINARY
PROFESSIONAL WHO IS FAMILIAR WITH THE LATEST ADVANCES IN THE
FIELD. THE AUTHOR AND THE PUBLISHER DISCLAIM RESPONSIBILITY
FOR ANY ADVERSE EFFECTS RESULTING DIRECTLY OR INDIRECTLY FROM
INFORMATION CONTAINED IN THIS BOOK.

For my mother, who gave me her love of telling stories

A Note on Pukka's Name

It's pronounced PUCK-uh, the first syllable stressed and sounding like Puck, the mischievous nature sprite of English folklore. The word *pukka* itself comes from the Hindi and means "genuine" or "first-class."

Contents

And when we're gone long gone
The only thing that will have mattered
Is the love that we shared
And the way that we cared
When we're gone, long gone.

— Kieran Kane and James Paul O'Hara,
"When We're Gone, Long Gone"

CHAPTER ONE

Too Soon Over

WHEN MERLE THE DOG of my heart was dying, he rallied one morning, going outside on his own to take a pee. The sun had just risen; robins sang; geese called from the river. The snowy Tetons stood pink in the clear May sky.

Merle squatted and relieved himself. Then, walking to the spruce trees on the edge of our land, he had a bowel movement, holding himself in a perfect crouch. Just as had been the case when I tended my dying father, and any small sign of renewed vigor in him had given me hope of a recovery, these indications of normalcy in Merle buoyed my spirits. As the rising sun gilded his fur, I could for a moment deny the inevitable: that he would soon pass from this life and our remarkable partnership would end. His dying simply wasn't possible. After all, only thirteen years had gone by since we had met on the San Juan River, I a forty-one-year-old writer looking for an adventurous whitewater run, Merle a ten-month-old, half-wild pup living a very real adventure on his own in the Utah desert.

Golden in color, shading to fox red, Merle was of indeterminate ancestry and had strong Lab features—the tall rangy Lab, the field Lab—with perhaps a bit of hound and Golden Retriever thrown in. I liked his looks, and I very much liked his manners: no frenzied barking, whining, or licking. I gathered that he liked me as well, especially how I smelled, for he'd stick his nose against my skin, breathe in deeply, and sigh.

We went down the river together, and at the end of the trip he leapt into the truck and came home with me to Jackson Hole, Wyoming. Over the next thirteen years, we hiked, horsepacked, and camped throughout the Rockies, running rivers in the spring, hunting elk in the fall, and skiing the Tetons from October until June. We were partners in the outdoors as well as in our small village of Kelly, where Merle had his own dog door so he could come and go as he wished. Each day, as I went to my home office to write, he, too, would set off to work, visiting his friends in the village, both canine and human, exploring the surrounding countryside, and making sure that everyone and everything in his domain was in order. He was called "the Mayor" and was as collected, calm, and independent a soul as one could wish for, yet he always came home, bonded to me, as I was to him.

Now, almost fourteen years old, Merle finished relieving himself and trotted across the grass, his tail swishing happily. Jumping onto the deck with a surprising bound despite his arthritis, he gave a joyful pant: "Ha-ha-ha!"

I couldn't mistake his meaning: "Can you believe it, Ted? I'm feeling really good this morning!"

"You *do* look good, Sir!" I replied. "Like your old self. What do you say? Do you want to come with me and do the recycling?"

"Hah!" he exclaimed. "You bet!"

As we drove south along the Gros Ventre River in our big blue truck, he sat erect on the front seat, puffed up as he always was when he wore his dog seat belt. He looked out the window at the snowcapped Tetons with a grin of idiotic pleasure.

"They sure are pretty, aren't they?" I said.

He panted twice, deeply — "HAH! HAH!" — which I translated as: "Yes! Yes! It is *so* good to be alive and looking at them!"

"Yes, it *is* good to be alive!" I replied, putting my hand on his ruff and thinking, "Here we are, still together."

I was so grateful, for only two weeks before, most of our friends and all of Merle's vets except one had suggested putting him down after twenty-four hours of seizures. The one exception had been a canine neurologist who had counseled patience and prescribed two medications that had ended the seizures and allowed Merle to begin his recovery.

The neurologist had given us a stay, and we were making the most of it, unwrapping each day as if it were a gift. We dumped the trash bags at the landfill; we sorted the bottles and papers at the recycling center; and on our way back through Jackson I stopped at Valley Feed and Pet, which was having its annual spring sale, rows of booths set up under a pavilion-like tent that had been erected in the parking lot. I could see friends milling about and eating barbecue as their dogs sat alertly at their feet, noses pointed upward, their eyes saying, "Excuse me, I could use a bite of that."

"You want to meet and greet," I asked Merle as I parked the truck, "or stay and have a nap?"

He lay down on the seat and gave a soft pant: "I think I'll stay right here."

"Okay," I said. "I'll be back in a few."

I closed the door, gave him another pat through the open window, and walked toward the booths. Just then, a young, athletic-looking couple came out of their car and intersected my path. They were in their midtwenties, both of them dressed in baggy chinos, running shoes, and fleece jackets. The man held a small puppy, a chocolate Lab, with a broad, wrinkled face and bright yellow eyes that looked keenly at everything going on around him.

"Seven weeks old?" I asked as I stopped before the couple and reached out to pet the puppy.

"A little bit more," said the woman. "We just got him."

I leaned close to the puppy so I could touch noses with him. His breath smelled like milk and vanilla and young teeth. I made a smooching noise with my lips; he squirmed in delight. The man put him in my arms, and the puppy wriggled against my chest and licked my neck madly.

"Oh, you are a beauty," I told him, kissing his head. He squirmed again in happiness.

I had the sudden feeling of being watched and turned toward the truck. Merle was sitting up, looking out the window at me, his deep red fur not nearly as red as when we had met, his face as white as snow.

"Hah!" he panted. "I see you petting that puppy! Just remember who the main dog is."

I blew a loud kiss to Merle and held the puppy for one more moment—young and warm and delicious in my arms—before handing him back to the man, who snuggled him against his chest.

The couple walked toward the booths, and as I watched them go I thought: "In fourteen years, perhaps sooner, certainly not much longer, he'll break your heart. Your entire life from now until then will be colored by him: his woofs, his wags, his smells, how he swam, his yips while he dreamed, how he rode your first child on his back, and how he began to slow down just as you were hitting your stride."

I looked back to Merle, grinning at me from the truck. Like everyone's dog, he had been all that and more, and I thought: "Why do they die so young?"

I'm not alone in asking this question. In the months following the publication of a book I wrote describing Merle's life and what he had taught me about living with dogs, I received hundreds of e-mails from readers who had lost beloved dogs and closed their letters with a variation on this theme: "Why must our dogs die so young?"

Naturally, when most of us say this, we're not expecting an answer. We're expressing a rhetorical complaint: why do our best friends in the animal kingdom live so much shorter lives than we do, only about an eighth of our life span?

However, I also received more specific questions from many readers, many of them heartrending: "Why is my dog going blind from progressive retinal atrophy?" "Why has my dog come down with Cushing's disease?" "Why wasn't I told that my dog might become arthritic after being vaccinated?" "Why did my dog have to die of cancer at three, at four, at six years old?" "Why," as one person wrote, "have four of my five Golden Retrievers died of cancer?"

Some of these questions hit very close to home. Merle's best friend Brower, a Golden Retriever, was diagnosed with a malignant cancer of the snout when he was six. Another of Merle's good friends, a black Lab named Pearly, died at seven of a neurofibrosarcoma that began in a nerve root at the base of her neck. Merle himself, though no young dog at fourteen, finally succumbed to his brain tumor.

As more of these letters came in, I couldn't ignore them. I did a bibliographic search and discovered that no extensive and rigorous exploration of these questions could be found in any one place. Thinking that these questions deserved a book-length treatment, I began to investigate, and not merely because I'm perpetually curious about our closest animal friends. I knew that at some point my heart would heal and I would long for another dog with whom to share my life. I wanted to make sure that the care I would give my new dog helped him to live a long and healthy life, longer than Merle's, if possible.

It was with these two goals in mind—learning about the healthiest ways to raise our dogs and finding my own new dog—that I set out on a quest, combing the veterinary literature and interviewing veterinarians, dog breeders, and shelter workers about the factors that affect dog health and longevity. Six factors were on almost everyone's list: inbreeding, nutrition, environmental pollutants, vaccination, spaying and neutering, and the shelter system in which too many dogs end their days. One factor that wasn't frequently mentioned, but which I believe is also important, is the amount of freedom dogs enjoy.

This book is based on that peer-reviewed veterinary literature (referenced in the notes), as well as on the work of progressive thinkers in the worlds of veterinary medicine, dog breeding, and animal welfare, whose advances and reforms may not have appeared in your local veterinarian's office, kennel club, or shelter. It was with the help of these out-of-the-box thinkers that I began to question many of the outdated notions that surround our living with dogs, everything from yearly vaccinations to the idea that dogs need consistency in their diet. Indeed, since Merle and I met on the banks of the San Juan River in the spring of 1991, the way our culture raises dogs has changed considerably, as has mine. This book is about that evolution.

One thing hasn't changed in my thinking. I still believe that dogs are individuals as well as members of a class. Even though we can make generalizations about their nurture and training, we can't ever forget that each dog is unique, both physiologically and psychologically, and capable of making its own choices in complex and personalized ways, if only given the chance.

Merle, of course, led me on this journey of understanding from the start, helping me to see the richness of a dog's mind, a mentoring that Pukka has taken over, adding an insight that Merle was unable to provide. Pukka, being a very young puppy, helped to reopen my eyes to the ever-present newness of the world.

Sitting on my lap a few days after I brought him home, he watched a training video with me, paying close attention to the demonstrator dog's every move and pricking his ears when the dog barked. Then, when the video was over, he climbed onto my desk, and, quite sensibly for someone who had never seen a computer monitor before, peered behind the darkened screen to find where the barking dog was hiding. Glancing over his shoulder, he gave me a startled look: "That dog's not there."

Many people soon learned that I had a new puppy and sent Pukka gifts, a menagerie of stuffed animals that we stored in a wicker basket beneath the large windows overlooking the Tetons: a quacking duck, a howling wolf, a growling bear, a neighing horse, a barking dog, a laughing monkey, a wailing yak, a bellowing moose, and a squeaking hedgehog, as well as an assortment of rubber rings, stuffed cloth bones, knotted ropes, Frisbees, and balls.

Pukka would take them out one by one during the day, and I would put them away at night, and he would remove them again in the morning after breakfast, starting always with his favorite, the quacking duck, trotting across the room, and presenting it to me.

"We're going to town," I reminded him on this particular morning.

"Oh, please," his black button eyes implored, "toss it just once."

I launched the duck across the room, and he bounded after it, returning it to me smartly. Ten weeks old and he was already quite the retriever.

"Let's go," I said, "or we'll be late."

He looked at me coyly, furrowing his golden brows: "Just one more time."

There is a good evolutionary reason for puppies being cute. Few can resist their demands.

"Okay," I said, giving in. "One more time." I tossed; he fetched.

"That's it." I took the duck from him and walked it to the wicker basket, where I placed it on top of the other animals. "Let's go."

The instant I turned my back and took a step toward the door, he grabbed the duck and squeezed it — *quack!* — and dropped it at my feet.

"*Pukka*," I chided him gently, "we need to go." I put the duck in the basket. He plunged his snout in after it, snatched up the bear, and gave it a shake. *Grrr*, the bear growled.

I took it from him and placed it in the basket as he snagged the neighing horse, biting it and making it whinny.

"Enough, Pukka," I said, trying to sound firm. But he could see me smiling.

He dropped the horse and lunged for the yak. It wailed.

"Pukka, enough, let's go!" Dropping the yak, he snatched up the barking dog — *rau-rau-rau!* — and immediately tossed it aside for the squealing bone. Twice he bit it — *squeal! squeal!* — then flung it at me, only to grab the squeaking hedgehog. He was now laughing a big puppy grin as I put each stuffed animal into the basket and said, "Everyone back in place. Neat and tidy. There we go."

"Hah!" he panted, dropping the hedgehog and grabbing the wolf, who howled. Flipping it aside, he picked up the laughing monkey, the

Frisbee, the chirping ball, the bellowing moose, tossing out every single toy in the basket and running from one to the other, biting them, so as to keep his wildlife chorus going. Quacks, howls, barks, neighs, and squeals pealed around us. I fell to my hands and knees, laughing.

Pukka's eyes lit with joy: I really did want to play! He began to dash in mad circles around me, scooping up his toys and flinging them at me, his tail helicoptering.

Sitting upright, I held my belly, and he skidded to a stop before me. Placing his paws upon my shoulders, he looked me in the eyes. "See," he grinned, "there really was enough time to play." Then he licked me on the mouth, just once, sealing our deal.

Laughing, I shook my head in wonder. How many other animals will so consistently play with a member of another species? And then I shook my head wistfully, despite Pukka's young age. Why should these humorous, tender, and congenial spirits be granted such short lives when the standoffish grizzly bear lives into its twenties and many a cranky parrot into its seventies? Why has nature decreed that our friendly dogs are already ancient in their teens while giving the unhuggable tortoise more than a century of life and some whales two hundred years to swim through the polar seas?

CHAPTER TWO

The Clocks of Danger

ECAUSE THE TWO grizzly bears were young, just coming into their third year, and on their own for the first time in their lives, they were afraid of nearly everything. This was the reason that they were constantly looking up from the elk carcass upon which they were feeding. The elk had been killed by a pack of wolves in the Lamar Valley of Yellowstone National Park, and though there wasn't much meat left on its spine and ribs after the wolves and the scavengers had taken their fill, it was nonetheless a rich find for the two young bears, who were chocolate-brown in color, with black humps and paws. Only a week before, they had been run off from their mother's care by a big male grizzly bear interested in mating with her, and left to their own devices hadn't caught anyone larger than a mouse to supplement their diet of roots, grasses, and forbs.

On high alert, the two young grizzlies continued to look around and saw the approaching wolf a few seconds before Merle and I did. The wolf was coming out of the aspen trees at the bottom of the grassy hillside on which the elk had fallen, and it was black and younger than the bears. By its limber stance and not-quite-filled-out shape, I guessed it to be entering its second year. Like many young wolves, it was doing an exploratory walkabout away from its pack so as to learn the lay of the land on its own before returning to report what it had seen: "Bison in the next valley. Elk on the other side of the ridge. There are two grizzly bears on our carcass whom we could easily chase away." Unlike the two bears, who would soon split up and lead relatively solitary lives, the wolf would spend the next year or more with its pack. In fact, if it decided not to disperse, mate, and raise its own young, it might spend the rest of its life with its family.

Perhaps it was this knowledge—that its brothers, sisters, mother, and father were nearby—that bolstered the young wolf's confidence. No doubt the wolf had also read the furtive glances of the bears, their hunched body postures, their tenseness and fear, all of which made it decide to take matters into its own paws. It walked directly toward them with an attitude that said, "You better leave 'cause that's my elk."

At that moment, I felt Merle shiver by my side. I looked down to see his eyes riveted on the unfolding scene, one that I hardly needed binoculars to witness. The two grizzlies, the elk carcass, and the approaching wolf were about 120 yards from the shoulder of the road on which we stood next to our car.

There was no other person or vehicle in sight, for it was a weekday morning and still in the early years of the Yellowstone wolf reintroduction, when relatively few people had discovered that a great wildlife spectacle was transpiring in this little-visited corner of the park: wolves and grizzly bears hunting elk across the valley floor, bighorn sheep standing upon the nearby cliffs, and sandhill cranes dancing among thousands of grazing bison. Merle and I would drive up from Jackson Hole in the late spring, make camp in the valley, and cruise the Lamar road, stopping to set up a spotting scope and glass the greening hillsides.

As the black wolf continued toward the two grizzlies, Merle stared at them with rapt attention. Just as people have unique emotional responses to different species of wildlife so, too, did Merle, and these varied not only by the species we were watching, but also by where we were. In Yellowstone National Park he paid only scholarly attention to elk and antelope, lying on his belly along the shoulder of the road and observing their behavior with a quick snapping motion of his head—"Hmm, grazing. Hmm, bedding. Hmm, so that's how an antelope swims." He had quickly figured out that we didn't hunt elk or antelope on these trips, and so there was no need to display his usual excitement over them: obviously, they weren't going to be turned into meat.

If he spotted a grizzly bear, he became very grave, like the chairman of the Federal Reserve Board considering an oncoming recession, his sober face saying, "This could turn into a dangerous situation." On the other hand, he found black bears amusing, and he seemed to be able to distinguish between the two species easily. One day he even touched noses with a black bear as the bear put its paws against the side of our car and sniffed at Merle through the cracked window, both Merle's and the bear's nostrils going like bellows — *phoo-ah, phoo-ah, phoo-ah* — as they took in each other's scent. The bear's eyes suddenly grew worried, and it pushed away from the car and bounded off as Merle began to dance his paws up and down and pant, "Ha-ha-ha! Let me at him!"

This was very similar to his reaction upon spying coyotes, though his "Let me at 'em!" was hardly filled with the gleeful anticipation he had displayed toward the bear. It was filled with rage. A pack of coyotes had chased him in his youth, and he had never forgotten it. Every time he saw a coyote, he'd emit sharp whines and growls, telling it what he'd do if he ever caught it, which was no idle threat, I discovered. Surprising a coyote in an irrigation ditch near Kelly, he lit out after it in a determined sprint, doing nothing more, however, when he caught it than knocking it off its feet with a dramatic blow from his shoulder. Then, having counted coup, he returned to me at top speed and began to twirl madly in the air as he barked in jubilation, one of the few times I ever heard him bark.

He never acted in these ways toward wolves. In fact, from the first moment he had heard a wolf howl in Yellowstone and his eyes had widened in astonishment — "Wow! That's one big dog!" — he had treated them with respect mingled with awe and more than a bit of envy. Watching them course after elk, he would quiver with pent-up longing and expel feverish little breaths — *Phfooof! Phfooof! Phfooof!* — so that his lips fluttered: "Oh, oh, oh! To be doing that!"

This is exactly what he now did as the black wolf came closer to the bears. Glancing up at me, Merle blew out a heartfelt breath — *Phfooof!* "Can you believe it?"

"Yes, yes," I whispered to him, laying a hand on his ruff. "I've never seen anything like it either. That wolf's going to take on those bears, don't you think?"

A huge shiver ran through him.

"Let's watch."

The wolf continued to walk steadily up the hillside without mincing its steps or coming at the bears sideways. Walking directly at them, it hunched its shoulders, shoved its head forward, and glared at them.

The bears, who were at least twice the size of the wolf, gazed at it for a second, then whirled and ran up the hill, only stopping and turning when they had put a good eighty yards between themselves and the carcass. Seeing the wolf begin to gnaw at the elk's spine, the two young grizzlies sat down in disappointment. They had found this elk – an incredible windfall of protein for two youngsters on their own – and it had been stolen from them. Their faces were a study in loss.

They watched the wolf eat for a few moments, then they slowly turned their heads and glanced at each other without looking into each other's eyes. Rather, they examined each other's bodies. It appeared that they were making a comparison: "Here's my sibling, who is twice as big as that wolf over there, which has to mean that I'm also twice as big as that wolf. And there are two of us."

They looked back to the wolf; they looked to each other; and it was amazing to see the knowledge of what they were seeing pass between them: "That wolf is smaller than we are." Their agreement as to what to do next was simultaneous. They rose to their feet and – shoulder to shoulder – charged.

The wolf, who had its head buried in the elk's ribs, must have heard them coming. It looked up and its eyes bugged. Jumping as if electrocuted, it leapt around and fled down the hillside, ducking into the aspen trees with its tail between its legs.

"Hah!" Merle exclaimed. "Did you see that!"

"I did!"

The grizzlies reclaimed their elk and began to eat. A minute or so went by, and then we saw the wolf poke its head out of the trees and watch the bears. It stared at them for a very long time, and I could see its mind working, just as I had seen the bears' minds working. With each passing moment, its face became more resolved and its posture erect, as if to say, "I've seen bears like this before. They've just left their mother and are afraid of everything. I chased them off once. I bet I can chase them off again."

And in another moment that's exactly what the wolf did. It began to walk, head out-thrust menacingly, toward the elk carcass.

The bears looked up with a start. The wolf was back! They glanced at each other: "What should we do?"

The wolf saw their reaction, which fueled its determination. It sped up.

The grizzlies cast a glance at the oncoming wolf and caved. Turning, they ran . . . but they didn't flee as far as before. Stopping after about forty yards, they sat down and watched the wolf begin to gnaw at the elk's backbone. They exchanged a look, and it was as understandable as that of two human children: "Didn't we just chase that wolf off?"

We're way bigger than it is. We can do it again!" And with that they barreled down the hill.

The wolf, now knowing the bears could be intimidated, would have none of it. It raised its hackles and bared its teeth over the top of the carcass. The bears kept coming. The wolf waited a heartbeat longer — nope, the bears weren't stopping! Turning, it fled, but its second retreat, like that of the bears, was shorter than its first.

Stopping halfway to the trees, the wolf turned and watched the two grizzlies, ripping and tearing at the elk's rib cage and lifting if off the ground with their great strength. It sat down and cocked its head, and I saw it make the same mental calculation as had the bears: "I chased them off once. These are teenage bears. They're afraid of their own shadows."

The wolf stood and stalked back toward the bears, coming within twenty yards of them before one of the bears sounded a warning — a breathy *huff!* — and threateningly slammed its front paws into the ground. The bear and the wolf were now in profile, and it was painfully obvious how big the bear was compared to the wolf, even though it was a young bear.

The wolf sat down, looking very deflated. For a good thirty seconds it watched the grizzlies with a forlorn expression on its face. It was apparent that the bears weren't moving — at least not for one wolf.

Several minutes went by. Finally the wolf stood, turned, and took a few steps away. Pausing, it looked over its shoulder. Yes, the bears were still there. Hesitating, the wolf thought things over, but apparently no matter how it analyzed the situation, it came to the same conclusion: "I'm not going to get that elk." Turning away, it broke into a lope and descended the hillside, where it vanished into the trees.

Merle stared after the wolf, and then stood and panted with great excitement, "Ha-ha-ha!" Dancing his paws up and down, he continued to pant: "That was amazing!"

To see what he might do if I gave him the chance, I motioned to the two grizzlies with my hand and said, "Have at 'em, Merle, go ahead. Show 'em what a real dog can do."

Merle gave me an incredulous look and sat down.

"Go ahead," I said again.

He pulled his head back in concern, his golden-brown eyes asking, "Are you okay?"

I broke into a laugh and crouched by his side. "I'm kidding," I told him, putting an arm over his shoulder. "But I had you going, didn't I?"

He broomed his tail across the grass in relief, then returned his gaze to the two grizzlies, happily gnawing on their hard-won elk carcass. A few seconds later, he turned his head and stared down the hillside to where we'd seen the wolf vanish into the aspen, as if fixing the incidents of the last few minutes in his mind.

I always wondered if what we had seen was as unforgettable for him as it was for me: the most dramatic interaction between wolves and bears I had ever witnessed and one of the most telling demonstrations of why bears live so long and dogs do not.

This has not always been the case. Once, wolves and bears had the very same life span. In fact, they were the very same animal. About 40 million years ago their common ancestor was a weasel-like creature named *Miacis*. It had five toes and retractable claws with which it climbed trees, and it was only about a foot long. But over the next 15 million years *Miacis* evolved into many of the carnivores alive today, from the diminutive jackal to the giant polar bear, its many descendants adapting to various niches around the globe — forest, savanna, and ice edge — as they changed in size and shape.

During this time their prey also evolved into a variety of forms, one of the results being that different families of animals developed unique strategies to cope with environmental challenges. If you were a mouse-size animal, for instance, and the chances of your being eaten were high, it would make good sense, so to speak, to mature quickly and get on to the business of making more mice, so as to get your genes into the next generation. Those mice who had a predisposition to act in this way passed on their genes, and those who deferred reproduction did not. Today field mice are born, become sexually mature, and create a new generation in as little as two months.

On the other hand, if you were the ancestor of a grizzly bear — armed with sharp teeth and long claws — very few animals could harm you when you became an adult. While you were a youngster, you had your mother to protect you. An animal like you, as opposed to an animal like a mouse, could wait five to seven years before reproducing, and the chances of your genes being lost would be extremely low. Consequently, delayed reproduction was repeatedly selected for in grizzlies because it enhanced their survival: a mouse could get by happily in the corner of a meadow; confined to the same meadow, a grizzly bear would starve. A bear needed time, years, to learn all the different foods in her territory and pass that knowledge on to her children.

Ecologists have named these two different ways of meeting environmental challenges "r-selected" and "K-selected." The r-selected species, like mice, are small, reproduce early, have many offspring, and do not live very long. K-selected species, of which grizzly bears are a prime example, are big, reproduce late, have few offspring, and have long life spans. If you happen to be a wolf, your strategy lies somewhere between the two, but is much closer to mice than to bears.

This is because your life is very dangerous. Unlike a bear, who can live pretty handily on roots, grubs, and grasses, none of which fight back when they're being eaten, you, as a wolf, take down big animals to survive — elk, moose, and bison — who are five to twenty times larger than you and armed with horns, antlers, and slashing hooves. Not only do you have to make your living in this perilous way, but you also have to defend your territory against rival wolf packs many times during the course of your lifetime. Furthermore, if you run into a grizzly bear on your own, there's no way you're going to come out the winner in a scrap, as the wolf whom Merle and I had watched found out in short order. Is it any wonder that wolves live in packs? It's the only way they can take down animals much larger than themselves or successfully steal kills from large predators like grizzly bears: numbers and teamwork count.

The short life span of wolves, and that of domestic dogs, their descendants, clearly reflects these dangers: in the wild, the average wolf lives no more than three or four years, although in the safety of captivity a wolf can live as long as a big domestic dog, twelve to fourteen years. This means that if most wild wolves waited as long as grizzly bears to reproduce, there'd be no more wolves. Consequently, wolves start to breed when they're between two and four years old, and they have lots of pups because not all that many of them will survive to breed.

What's interesting to note is that the wolf's major prey in Yellowstone National Park, the elk, is much more like a grizzly bear in terms of longevity than the wolf itself. If an elk doesn't get injured, and if it obeys one of the key rules of elk society (stay in the herd, where there are many eyes to look out for danger), and most important, if it's a female, it can live about eleven years, having just one calf a year. Not infrequently, a cow elk will live to twenty and sometimes even thirty years of age. Bull elk, on the other hand, often die by the time they're seven and a half years old, worn out and wounded from their mating battles. Still, a bull elk of this age is living twice as long as the wolves who hunt him.

This directly proportional relationship between the size of an animal and its life span not only is true for elk, wolves, and grizzly bears, but is also generally true across the class of mammals: the bigger you are, the longer you live. There are some exceptions: small dogs live longer than big ones, and humans are quite a bit smaller than many mammals, yet we live longer than any other mammal except whales, our longevity being a function of our having invented tools to help us hunt and then — starting in the 1800s — our rapid advances in sanitation and medicine, which have greatly extended our life span.

If we include other classes of animals besides mammals in our sample, the inconsistencies between longevity and size multiply dramatically. Consider long-lived parrots. They're tiny compared to elephants, yet their life span is as long as that of the largest elephant — seven to eight decades.

For years, scientists puzzled over these anomalies, trying to discover a common factor that determined longevity for all species. Initially, some researchers thought that brain size correlated with life span: the bigger your brain, the longer you live. But why then do giant tortoises, with their comparatively small brains, live between 150 and 200 years?

Some biologists then suggested that life span is a function of metabolism. After all, rodents, with their little hearts racing away as they constantly eat to keep themselves alive, survive at best three years, even in risk-free laboratory conditions, whereas elephants, whales, tortoises, and humans, their hearts thumping slowly, live for many decades and sometimes even a century. But here, too, outliers crop up. Brandt's bat weighs but six grams, two-tenths of an ounce, yet lives for forty years.

To make matters even more puzzling, many small birds live longer than small mammals even though their metabolic rates are two and a half times higher. The tiny hummingbird, for instance, as well as songbirds such as vireos, warblers, and orioles, can live five years in the wild. The albatross, though far smaller than a horse, lives twice as long as most horses, gliding across the waves for half a century. Clearly, the metabolic theory of longevity had many problems facing it.

To be perfectly honest, I wasn't thinking about any of this as Merle and I sat peacefully under a Douglas fir tree one hot July afternoon. Along with our friend Benj Sinclair, we had been on a horsepacking trip in the wilderness between Yellowstone National Park and Jackson Hole and were on our way home. Merle was lying comfortably on his belly in the cool duff, gazing up into the tree over our heads, while Benj sat in the grass nearby, eating a sandwich. Gringo, Tinker, and Whisk, our three horses, were grazing at the forest edge, their tails swishing away flies.

A scurrying of clawed feet made us glance up. A squirrel had flattened itself on a branch and was staring down at us.

"Hah!" Merle snorted, jumping to his feet. "I knew you were there!" He gazed at the squirrel with undisguised longing. At this point in his life, four years old, he had become so adept at catching ground squirrels around Kelly that he had grown bored with pursuing them. Instead, he had directed his efforts toward capturing red squirrels, who live in trees and whom we often saw while walking in the forest. So far he had been unsuccessful in realizing his dream since red squirrels are extremely alert, agile creatures, having been pursued by pine martens — a large voracious weasel — from time out of mind.

Now, tail erect and every muscle taut, Merle studied the squirrel carefully, while the squirrel studied him back, a wary look in its dark little eyes. Without another moment's hesitation, the squirrel leapt into the air, taking us all by surprise since the nearest tree was thirty yards away, far too distant for the squirrel to reach before Merle would grab it. The squirrel, however, knew exactly what it was doing.

Spreading its four limbs, it extended its patagia — the lateral skin folds that gliding mammals have on each side of their body — and sailed swiftly through the air, disappearing into the distant forest before Merle could move a paw.

We were all astonished, for none of us had ever seen a northern flying squirrel before. They're uncommon in Wyoming, and they're also nocturnal. It was therefore a great stroke of luck to have seen one, and in flight no less, its Houdini-like escape providing a wonderful example of how each of our longevity clocks has been set by the hazards our species has faced during the course of its evolution. Animals who have evolved the ability to fly or glide can escape the environmental hazards – a dog named Merle, for instance – that strike down their earth- and tree-bound cousins.

Longevity records from around the world back up this premise: gliding species live 1.7 times longer than their nongliding counterparts. In addition to helping an animal escape predators, having the ability to fly or glide also allows an animal to find food that terrestrial members of its genus can't reach. This is the reason that bats live so long compared to flightless mammals of the same size, hummingbirds live longer than small rodents, albatrosses live longer than horses, and earthbound ostriches – eight feet tall and weighing two to three hundred pounds – live only half as long as parrots. Even though they are small and fragile, bats and flying birds can wing their way to safety.

Two other physiological attributes have functioned in a similar way to flight. The first, hard shells – like those worn by clams, lobsters, and tortoises – protect their owners from predators. And the thicker the armor the greater the life span: hard-shell clams tend to live longer than soft-shell ones, and tortoises live very long indeed. The second attribute, great size, has also contributed to extremely long life, in fact the longest lives on the planet. One of the best illustrations of this survival strategy is the life of the bowhead whale.

Spending their entire lives in arctic seas where the density of prey is low, bowhead whales must filter thousands of tons of seawater each day through their baleen – the comblike plates in their upper jaws – to strain out enough plankton to sustain themselves, mature to adulthood, and then reproduce. Consequently, they don't grow quickly, taking years to reach an adult size of forty to sixty feet. Over the course of their evolution, natural selection repeatedly favored those bowheads who matured a little more slowly than their peers and thus reached reproductive age a little later, when they were larger. Their larger size at sexual maturity allowed them to bear a calf with greater blubber stores, and it was these thick layers of fat that gave these calves a better chance of surviving the frigid conditions around the polar ice cap. Today newborn bowheads are fifteen feet long and weigh a ton. Immune from predation because of their giant size, and with delayed maturation having steadily extended their life span, bowheads are the Methuselahs of nature.

In fact, if mice are on the left edge of the longevity scale, dogs are somewhat to their right, and we're in the middle, then bowhead whales are on the scale's extreme right-hand side. Just how far to the right was only discovered at the beginning of the twenty-first century, when geochemists at the Scripps Institution of Oceanography in San Diego, California, began to age individual whales by measuring the changing levels of aspartic acid in their eyes. The ages of the whales that emerged from this study are mind-boggling: 135, 159, 172, and 211 years old. Like other long-lived bowheads, this last individual – the oldest living animal ever recorded – was a male, killed by Inuit during their annual subsistence hunt off the coast of Alaska. In the scientific record he is known only as 95WW5 – the fifth whale taken by the village of Wainwright during the 1995 season – but his number hardly describes what a mystical being he was.

As a newborn calf, he was swimming in the Arctic Ocean when the American Revolutionary War came to an end and George Washington retired to Mount Vernon. He was sending his young spout toward the midnight sun as Lewis and Clark began to pole up the Missouri River and Napoleon marched across Europe. He was barely middle-aged when Louis Pasteur discovered a vaccine for rabies. This whale was an elder of his tribe during the decades through which both world wars were fought and was still going strong as the twenty-first century approached and he met the only peril a mature bowhead has ever faced: a two-legged hunter armed with a harpoon. Through all of his two-hundred-plus years, he was peacefully swimming through the polar seas, eating a tiny crustacean known as a copepod. No doubt there are other bowhead whales older than this one, swimming – right now – off the far side of the world's longevity scale while we walk a good century to their left, and our dogs wag their tails another seventy years from us.

Or at least some of our dogs do. Since not all breeds have the same life span, the Miniature Poodle would be much closer to us on the longevity scale than the Great Dane. This large variation in the canine life span has been closely studied in Sweden, a result of the pet insurance industry having been in place longer than anywhere else in the world, the first Swedish dog having been insured in 1924. (For comparison's sake, the first British dog was insured in 1947 and the first American one in 1982.)

In the late 1990s, several university-based researchers began to use these insurance records to confirm what most of us already know:

small and medium-sized dogs tend to live longer than large ones. However, the researchers put hard numbers to this common observation while revealing some unsettling facts about the life spans of large dogs.

If you were a Miniature Poodle or a Miniature Dachshund, the researchers discovered, and you were eight years old, you had only a 10 percent chance of being dead by your tenth birthday. It was much the same for Golden and Labrador Retrievers and mixed-breeds: if you were a dog from one of these breeds and you made it to eight years old, you had only a 10 to 13 percent chance of sitting on a mantle in an urn by the end of your first decade.

But if you happened to be a very large dog, it was clear that you should make hay while the sun shone, for your chances of living a long life were poor indeed. By the age of ten, 75 percent of the insured Saint Bernards were dead, and so were 75 percent of the Bernese Mountain Dogs. Eighty-three percent of the Great Danes had also passed away, as well as a depressing 91 percent of the Irish Wolfhounds. Another study I looked at showed the average life expectancy of Irish Wolfhounds to be only six and a half years.

These are important statistics for anyone contemplating getting a puppy from one of these large breeds. As the authors of the Swedish study wrote, "Considering that for some breeds over 50% of dogs are dead by eight years of age . . . whereas in other breeds less than 25% have died . . . it is inappropriate to consider them as having equivalent biological age." Put in emotional terms, figures such as these mean that if you fall in love with a large-breed puppy when you graduate college, you have a one-in-two chance of losing it by the time you reach thirty, and, if it's still alive then, it will more than likely be an old dog, unable to accompany you on a run, a long hike, a ski, or a bike ride.

In fact, no matter what study I looked at—and in no matter what country the dogs happened to reside—the slopes of the graphs that plotted a dog's longevity against its size were remorseless in their angle. Even though there are outliers—the Saint Bernard who lives to fifteen, the Irish Wolfhound who reaches thirteen—the general and inescapable pattern of dog mortality is that big dogs die young, often before they are ten years old. Since the general law of mammalian longevity is that big animals live longer, the fact that big dogs live rather short lives remains puzzling for everyone who has thought about the incongruity.

In the mid-2000s, scientists unraveled this mystery. They discovered that a gene called IGF1 plays a role in controlling the domestic dog's great variation in size. A tiny mutation of this gene evolved very early in the domestication of dogs and led not only to smaller dogs but also to lower levels of insulin-like growth factor-1. This protein, called IGF-1 for short, is produced by the IGF1 gene, and today all small dogs possess a mutated form of it, whereas nearly all giant breeds do not. Other research has demonstrated that IGF-1 is crucial in determining an organism's life span. In species from worms to mice to dogs, it has been found that as an animal's cells produce less IGF-1, its insulin levels fall and its life span increases. This is why small dogs live longer than large ones.

The association between IGF-1 and longevity may extend to people as well. Similar gene mutations that promote reduced insulin levels have been found in a wide range of centenarian populations around the world, and a population of dwarf Ecuadorean Indians, who have a gene mutation that produces low levels of IGF-1, has an almost zero incidence of cancer. Geneticists are now trying to tease out exactly what biochemical template allows these unique individuals to resist disease and age more slowly, while other scientists are exploring the possibilities for achieving the same end through diet.

Over the ages, selecting for certain characteristics in dogs – whether it was size, coat color, or behavior – not only produced dogs with differing life spans. It also caused dogs of every size and shape to be more inbred and thus prone to a variety of genetically linked diseases. About four hundred of these conditions have now been cataloged in purebred dogs, and they take a toll on millions of dogs and their people. Forty-three percent of American households have at least one dog, and there are between 60 million and 77.5 million dogs in total in the United States, depending on whose figures you consult. About half of these dogs are purebred (four hundred breeds are officially recognized around the world), and in some European countries the majority of people live with purebred dogs.

Finding out how many years of companionship to expect from any one of these dogs is difficult. Death certificates aren't required for dogs; many people euthanize their dogs long before they would have died naturally; and the records of large pet hospitals, which do keep track of when their patients die, are skewed because their patients are so seriously ill. Consequently, the life spans of various breeds that are documented on the Internet and in dog encyclopedias are good-faith estimates at best.

A better place to get a sense of how long certain breeds live is from the surveys of breed and kennel clubs. Although such surveys suffer from the failings of all surveys—small population size, insufficient participation, faulty memory, and potentially biased recall—they give a more accurate view of canine longevity. Until 2007, this information wasn't readily accessible to the public. Then Dr. Kelly M. Cassidy, a biologist and the curator of the Conner Vertebrate Museum at Washington State University in Pullman, Washington, collected it in one place.

Cassidy was thorough. She looked at every health and longevity study done by kennel and breed clubs as well as by veterinary schools in the United States, Canada, the United Kingdom, and Denmark between the years 1980 and 2007. Cassidy averaged the information in these surveys and weighted the data according to sample size. Importantly, she makes no claim that the data she presents is a randomized sample. Indeed, the breed and kennel club surveys she consulted cover only a small part of the world. She also forthrightly states that the conclusions on her website, Dog Longevity, are her opinions. Given these caveats, what she has found in terms of life spans for certain breeds is instructive. It corroborates what longevity studies in the veterinary literature have found: certain breeds don't live as long as the popular imagination believes they do.

Take German Shepherds. If you do an Internet search for "German Shepherd life span," you will find many hits that push the average life span of the breed to thirteen years. But the breeder surveys that Cassidy averaged show a life span of a little under ten years. American Cocker Spaniels are said to live twelve to fifteen years on a website called Dog Breed Info Center. But the breeder surveys consulted by Cassidy brought that age down to 10.7 years. Boston Terriers are given thirteen to fifteen years on many websites. Breeder surveys show a life span of a little under eleven years. Is it any wonder that people believe their dogs are dying young? They are.

Cassidy opines that this credibility gap—between what popular literature cites as the life expectancies for certain breeds and what the surveys actually show—has been in part created by breeders of short-lived dogs. "The shorter-lived a breed," she writes, "the greater the reluctance among breed fanciers to accept how short-lived the breed really is." Instead, she speculates, they remember longer-lived dogs and take their life spans as representative of the breed. "The combination of vocal owners of long-lived dogs," she continues, "and quiet owners of short-lived dogs could give the impression that long-lived dogs are the norm."

Amid Kelly Cassidy's sobering data were also some welcome surprises. She found that some small breeds—Miniature Poodles, Tibetan Spaniels, and Lhasa Apsos—may live, on average, a year longer than dog encyclopedias and websites suggest: fourteen years compared to thirteen. She also demonstrated that sometimes our perception of a breed's life span and the survey data from breed clubs are in close agreement. For instance, Golden and Labrador Retrievers—two of the most popular breeds in North America and the United Kingdom—are thought to live ten to twelve years, and the club data shows that they live to 12.04 years on average. The popular literature tells people buying a Beagle puppy to expect twelve to fifteen years with their new companion, and Beagles live 12.3 years according to the clubs' surveys. Dachshunds are similarly believed to have a life span of twelve to fifteen years, and the surveys show that Dachshunds live until about thirteen.

In every study that Cassidy looked at, she found that mixed-breed dogs live, on average, a year longer than purebred dogs, an observation confirmed by five other studies I found in the veterinary literature showing that mixed-breeds suffer from fewer genetic diseases and live up to 1.8 years longer than purebred dogs of equivalent weight. Even so, it's the rare mixed-breed who lives beyond its late teens.

This enormous difference between the life span of human beings and every single breed of dog is the result of domestic dogs still sharing 99.9 percent of the wolf's DNA. It doesn't matter that tens of thousands of years have elapsed since humans began to domesticate wolves. Tens of thousands of years are but a finger snap in the course of evolutionary time. Dogs are still mostly wolves. The loyalty of a dog to its family is the loyalty of the wolf to its pack. The dog's need to roam and explore on its own is the wolf's curiosity and vast energy. And the dog's single-minded focus during the chase is also the wolf's, as Merle's exclaiming "Hah-hah-hah!" while he watched wolves course elk in Yellowstone so clearly indicated: "Oh, oh, oh! To be doing that! To be doing *THAT!*"

Most significantly, all the accumulated dangers of the wolf's evolutionary history — taking down animals far larger than itself with nothing more than its mouth — have been passed on to our dogs and are encoded in the clocks of their genes. This has made them who they are: a short-lived species compared to many other mammals. And although we may be able to extend their life span by improving their nutrition, breeding, and care, it's almost certain that dogs will never live as long as we do. Yet, across this bittersweet divide, which separates us so finally from them, we reach out — again and again and again.

CHAPTER THREE

Loaner Dogs

I, HOWEVER, COULDN'T reach out again—at least not right away. When Merle died, a world ended for me—the world he and I had shared, which belonged to the two of us and to no other: the hidden hanging valley on Sheep Mountain; the deep dark forest along the Gros Ventre River; the buried gray days of powder skiing on Teton Pass; and a dozen out-of-the-way summits that no other mountaineer would climb with me, but he was happy to. There were also the thousands of miles we drove—two-tracks, gravel, interstates—I listening to an audiobook, he gazing out the window at the passing scenery, each of us sending the other a glance if we spied a deer, an elk, or a moose: "Did you see that?" So much wordless time we spent together, so much time in a world before the power of language overwhelmed the subtlety of gesture and the reaffirming touch of skin on fur, fur on skin: *I am here, so am I . . . forever.*

Of course, it wasn't forever, and the briefness of his life was one of the keenest parts of my grief. This was the cost, I came to realize, of having fallen in love with a member of a short-lived species. Others felt differently.

More than a few of my friends and acquaintances suggested that I could snap out of my mourning by getting a new dog. In fact, some of them told me that when their dog had died they had gone to the animal shelter the very next day and gotten another one. It was a sure way, they counseled, to stop thinking about Merle, for I'd be too preoccupied with the new dog to grieve for him.

The thought made me ill. "I'd only feel worse," I told them. To which a surprising number replied, "How can you stand not having a dog in your life? I couldn't."

But it wasn't *a* dog I wanted; it was *the* dog named Merle. The type couldn't replace the individual, and I wasn't ready to open myself to a new dog yet. Besides, I still had a dog. I saw Merle constantly: hiking by my side on the trail, coming into my office to lay his chin on my thigh, and pressing his cheek against mine while riding in our car. I saw him reclining on his green bed in the corner of our bedroom, our eyes locked together as I reached up to turn off the light and said, "Good night, my lightfoot lad, and may flights of elk sing thee to thy rest."

And if there was pain in these recollections — and there was — the pain was too sweet to dampen. Instead of pushing it away, I hugged it to me as if it were Merle himself. Making the decision to write his biography, I replaced, word by word, the grief of losing him with the joy of reassembling the tender details of who he had been. And as I wrote I met other dogs who loaned themselves to me, leaning their paws against my chest and, with a soft push, opening the door to my heart once again.

There was the young reddish Lab wagging his tail at me from the rear door of a truck's camper shell as I walked through the parking lot of the Brew Pub one summer afternoon in Jackson. I was sun-parched and thirsty, having just finished a mountain bike ride, and had Merle been with me he would already have been on the pub's deck, greeting customers as they entered and left.

This young dog's ears were long and silken, as Merle's had been, and his skin was still loose around his flanks and shoulders, waiting for his body to grow into it. He had big paws, and he put them on my shoulders and licked the dried salt off my face, wagging his tail in delight at the taste.

Gripping his shoulders, I buried my nose in the top of his head and breathed in his scent, which, just like Merle's, was clean and nutty and had a distant whiff of musk and lanolin, as if a wild dog were still living inside the domestic one. "Oh, you are a sweetheart," I said, keeping my face pressed to his neck because my eyes were so full of tears. We hung on to each other for a few more moments, and then, wiping away my tears, I glanced down. The truck had Maine license plates, and a crazy thought crossed my mind: "Just carry the dog quickly into the Subaru, drive back to Kelly, and no one will ever be the wiser."

I gave the pup a hard hug, and he wiggled his body against my chest. Kissing him on the cheek, I went inside and had a pint with friends. When I came out, the truck was gone.

About a week later, I made a recycling run in the big blue truck, looking over to the empty seat, which was still covered with a spray of Merle's golden hairs. I had been unable to vacuum it. As I sorted green bottles into one bin and brown bottles into another, I heard Merle bay from up the hillside, where the animal shelter was located. I stopped dead. He was right there, brought back to life, but not quite. The timbre of his voice was right; the pitch was wrong. The baying went on and on, with a mean hard edge that Merle's voice never had.

Walking the hundred yards up the road, I saw a Bluetick Coonhound behind the outdoor kennel's chain-link fence. He was bouncing on his front paws and baying at people as they entered and left the main building. I went to him and knelt so we were at the same level. He backed up suspiciously, curling his lip at me and continuing his tirade. And though his voice was fierce, it was underlain by lament, the same lament I could see in his sad and wilted body: "Why am I here? Why am I here? Why am I here?"

Wishing to help him, I went inside, even though I didn't want a barking dog, and he appeared to be a dog who, even in happier circumstances, would like to bark. The woman at the counter confirmed my suspicions when she said, "You better not have any close neighbors."

I thanked her and leafed through the adoption book, looking at the photos of the dogs and reading their thumbnail biographies — "My family went out of town and couldn't take me"; "I'm very friendly, but also scared of being left alone"; "I'm getting on in years, but still love a good walk." I felt crushed by what I couldn't do: take all of them home at once. At least the knowledge that the Jackson shelter doesn't kill dogs consoled me.

The hound's baying worked on me, though. In the months that followed, I took to walking dogs, going on what amounted to blind dates with them. Like so many blind dates, they were awkward. I didn't act like their past human; they didn't act like my past dog. One night, as I returned from one of these walks, I stopped at the movie theater and saw *The Chronicles of Narnia: The Lion, the Witch, and the Wardrobe*. Just before dawn the following morning, I dreamt that I was in a rural house, talking on the phone as Merle lay at my feet. Suddenly, he leapt up and dashed out the door, crossing a nearby field and heading toward the river.

Dropping the phone, I ran after him, wondering what he had smelled and suddenly afraid that he might disappear, which even in my dream state seemed strange, since I had never been afraid of his going off and not returning when he'd been alive. When I got to the riverbank, I saw him lying on a large rock, his hip pressed against the hip of Aslan, the great lion king of C. S. Lewis's novel. Merle and the lion king were the same rich golden color and looked perfectly at ease with each other. Turning their heads, they smiled knowingly at me.

I awoke and felt the same smile on my face. Like Aslan, who had saved everyone, Merle had made everything right with the world.

As dawn brightened the windows, I looked over to the corner of the bedroom where his spirit form still slept and asked him, "How did you do that?"

"Hah," he said softly. "You know how."

And I did. After passing through the steep learning curve of his puppyhood, he began to temper his high spirits with a calm and steady approach to life that let him solve problems cleverly and with an admirable lack of fuss. There was the time I couldn't get a stubborn llama to move and Merle did so by biting it on its butt. There was the time he began to chase a very pale coyote, but—in midstride and going full tilt—he realized that the coyote was in fact a white wolf. Did he continue to chase it? No. He skidded to a stop and watched the wolf run away, turning to give me a stocktaking glance over his shoulder: "Now that would have been a tactical error." On still another occasion, he and I were skinning up a peak in the North Cascades of Washington with a friend of ours. Arriving at the rocky summit block, my friend and I took off our skis and left Merle with the gear. It was easy fifth-class climbing to the top, but too difficult for a dog. As my friend and I went out of sight, Merle began to bay in mournful indignation: "We came all this way together and now you're leaving me! I can't believe you'd do this!" I turned and called down to him, "It's too steep for you. I'll be back in a few minutes. Just hang out." We continued up; he stopped baying.

Shortly, we reached the summit and were able to look across all of western Washington and southern British Columbia, range after range of snowy peaks, marching down from the distant horizon to—I nearly jumped out of my skin.

Merle was walking toward me – but not the way we had come up. He had circled the summit block and found his way onto the steep north face, where he was tiptoeing across a narrow ledge, barely four inches wide, placing one paw directly in front of the other. There was nothing but empty space to his right – a two-thousand-foot drop to the glacier below.

I said not a word. I didn't want to distract him. He looked up, caught my eye, and grinned hugely. "Ha-ha-ha!" he panted smugly. "See, there was an easy way up!"

Unfazed by the drop, he continued his cool, measured padding across the ledge, bounded onto the summit, and cavorted around me in glee.

Yet, not long afterwards, as I crossed an icy log that stood above a rushing stream, he balked at going across. On the far bank, I turned and looked back at him, studying the slick of ice, which I had negotiated by using my ski poles, fore and aft, for balance.

"Come on," I said, "it's easy. Your claws will hold you."

He gave me a reproachful look, one that I had come to recognize: "You're wrong about this, you know. You're really wrong."

Glancing left and right, he spied a place where the stream was less swift, but still deep. Running to it, he swam across, shook himself heartily, and dashed up to me. "Hah!" he exclaimed. "Much safer!"

"Just two months ago," I told him, "you crossed that tiny ledge. Had you fallen off, you would have plummeted to your death. Now you won't cross this log" – I extended a hand to it – "which is far wider and only six feet above the stream. You puzzle me, Sir."

"Hah!" he replied. "Don't tell me what I can or cannot do. It's icy."

And with that, he trotted out ahead of me, his reddish-gold back, his waving tail, moving surely down the sunlit path.

I missed his survivor's knowledge and his quiet self-confidence. In the way in which some of us repeatedly gravitate toward the same breed, I wanted another dog from the breed called Merle, but I wasn't sure if more of him had been made.

So I waited, seeing dogs here and there whose fur had that certain shade of butterscotch and honey, lambent as September light, which I had come to associate with Merle's steady demeanor. It was the color of elk in their end-of-summer sleekness; it was the color of fire in our woodstove when the pine was full of resin; it was the color of shelter.

But they were always someone else's dogs. We touched noses; we shared a moment — skin on fur, fur on skin — and they went on their way.

A year went by, and then my next-door neighbors, Jess and Eric, got a dog. "Next door" needs to be understood loosely. Between our two log homes stood my lawn, then my aspen trees, then a sagebrush field, then their spruce trees, and finally their house.

Their dog, who was only about eight months old when I met him, was named A.J., a pale yellow Lab descended from field-trial specialists. Every bit of that breed's racy, wired energy was brought to its ultimate expression in A.J. He would burst from his front door and negotiate the trees and sage like a Stinger missile. Heat, light, and explosive energy, he'd streak onto my deck and drop a tennis ball at my feet. No matter how far I threw it, he'd almost always catch it after its first bounce. And if he misplaced all of his tennis balls, he'd bring me a stick.

He was shorter and more compact than Merle, but had the same intelligent, golden-brown eyes and an endless variety of facial expressions, including the ability to move his eyebrows independently, which had been one of Merle's most charming features. In particular, A.J. used his eyebrows to express his despair when I'd stop throwing the ball.

"Enough, A.J.," I'd say.

His right brow would go up, the left down: "Nooo! You can't mean that! You'll break my heart, and I'll die of sadness."

"You think you will," I'd tell him, "but you won't. Promise." I'd turn to go into the house. "I have to get back to work."

He'd stand on the deck, his head cocked plaintively to the side: "But isn't playing with me your most important work?"

I'd wave to him and say, "Later, A.J."

He'd wait about thirty seconds, just to make sure I wasn't going to change my mind, then pick up his ball and trot smartly home.

I enjoyed A.J.'s visits. His energy reminded me of Merle's when he had been a very young dog, playing endlessly with the love of his life, Zula, a Vizsla. But unlike Merle, A.J. had only one speed — top speed. He could rarely sit; he could barely lie down; he'd never accept more than the briefest pet from me. He'd slide away from my hand, pick up his ball, and drop it insistently at my feet. If I offered him a biscuit while I held on to his ball, he'd grab the biscuit, spit it out, and leap up and down on his four paws as he panted, "Throw it! Throw it! Throw it!"

Fortunately for all of us, Jess and Eric got another dog to keep A.J. company, a Golden Retriever named Burley. He was as reddish-gold as Merle had been in his early days and only six months old, with a happy-go-lucky disposition and a snaky wiggle when he greeted me. A.J. was ecstatic. He had finally found someone who was as tireless as he.

Now there were two Stinger missiles who launched themselves across the field and aimed themselves at my deck door. But whereas A.J. could barely be petted, Burley would fling himself sideways into my arms as I knelt on the deck at their approach. Turning over, he'd gaze up at me with a blissfully calm expression and snuggle himself deeper into my lap, making little groaning noises that said, "Oh, this is so nice. I could stay here forever." In the meantime, A.J. would be dropping his tennis ball on top of us and whining, "Stop this cuddling! Throw it!"

I'd fling the ball away, and A.J. would zoom off the deck with Burley at his heels.

I had been lonely for dog company, and now I had it—in spades. Eight, ten, twelve times a morning, A.J. and Burley would woof to come in, then ask to go out, shortly woofing to come back in, always at the southern deck doors. One morning, I'd had enough. They were disrupting my writing.

"Okay," I said to them, "today you learn how to use Merle's door." Walking over to the north entry of the house, I pulled out the foam blocks that I'd inserted to keep out the cold and held the flap open for them. They peered through the inner door to the mudroom with expressions that said, "So, a hole. Now open the door for us."

"No," I replied. "This is your new door. It was Merle's door, the dog whom you smell here. He came and went on his own and was in charge of his own life. Now you're going to learn how to do the same thing so I can work and you can visit and leave whenever you want. Sound like a good idea?" I pushed open the flap for them and gestured them through.

Together, they stuck their noses into the opening, then backed up leerily, just as Merle had done when first introduced to the door. So

I demonstrated, turning sideways and squeezing myself through the door.

"See." I held the flap open and looked back at them.

Their eyes lit up with comprehension: "Wow! You just went through the door!"

"Come on," I said, and they barreled through, first A.J., the older, then Burley, the younger.

"Okay," I said, "let's go back inside." And back through the door I crawled, and back through they crawled.

"Now on your own," I told them. "Out you go."

No one moved.

I held the flap open a bit, and after a moment's hesitation, A.J. exited into the mudroom, followed by Burley.

"Come back inside," I told them.

I saw A.J.'s face through the blurry plastic, hesitant, wary, and sniffing. "Good boy, A.J. Do it."

He lifted the flap and scrabbled through, followed an instant later by Burley. They began to spring wildly into the air, A.J. barking in excitement, "We did it! We did it!"

"Well done!" I shouted.

A.J. and Burley had inherited Merle's door.

No matter how many times they visited, though, and no matter how many games of toss and fetch we played, no matter how many times I got down on my hands and knees and doggy-bowed to them, eliciting twirls, growls, and cuffs ("A human who knows how to play like a dog!"), and no matter how many biscuits and elk bones I gave them, A.J. would not allow me to pet him. That's not literally true. He would let me pet him for three-quarters of a second.

Then, one summer evening, after a very long day of writing about Merle's declining health, I went out to the deck as the sun set. Having just revisited those sad weeks for the past ten hours, I was exhausted, wrung out, and missing him more than ever. I lay down on my back and closed my eyes.

A few moments later, I heard the thud of paws coming across the grass, followed by the tearing scrape of nails on the deck. A second later, I felt a ball and a stick simultaneously drop onto my chest. I opened my eyes. A.J. had brought the ball, Burley the stick.

"Please, not right now," I told them, pushing the ball and stick off of me. A.J. immediately picked up the ball and dropped it on my chest again. But Burley cocked his head and studied me with a quizzical gaze: "What's wrong? Are you all right?"

"Come here, Burls," I said, opening my right arm. Without a moment's hesitation, he lay in my arm and put his head on my shoulder, licking me once on the cheek.

"Thanks," I told him, "I needed that."

A.J. looked at us with disgust and continued to pick up the ball and drop it on my chest.

"Oh, A.J., come here," I said sweetly, opening my left arm. He danced away, grabbing the ball and flinging it back at me.

"Not now, A.J. Why don't you lie down? Come on, you'll like it."

Burley, in the meantime, had turned on his back and lifted his four paws in the air, while he rubbed his face against mine. I stroked his belly with my right hand while holding my left arm open to A.J.

A.J. studied us, his expression changing from impatience to curiosity.

"Come on," I cajoled, gesturing with the tips of my fingers.

He leaned closer. I reached up and stroked his shoulder. He shivered nervously and jerked away. I hooked a finger in his collar and said in a soft voice, "Easy, A.J. Join us. You'll like it."

Had he continued to pull away, I would have let him go. But he stood tensely in place, his front legs ramrod straight. Exerting a gentle downward pull on his collar, I said, "A.J., please lie down. Let me pet you just once."

He looked at me; then he looked at Burley, who appeared as comfortable as a dog could be.

"See, Burley's having a good time. Lie down. Just for a little."

Nothing happened.

Then Burley let out a sigh and snuggled closer to me. A.J. stared at him.

"Lie down, please," I coaxed him.

His front legs began to buckle — slowly, grudgingly — while he tried to keep his upper body in the air. It was like watching the abutments of a suspension bridge collapse while the cables still held up the roadway. His resistance, and his uneasy eyes, said, "This is the worst thing that can happen to a dog: to be still." Yet his friend Burley was lying quietly in Ted's arm and nothing bad was happening to him.

Slowly . . . oh, so slowly . . . A.J. let himself down. His belly touched the deck, and then—very tentatively—he leaned his left flank against my ribs. I stroked his shoulder and said, "See, it's not that bad." A moment later, on his own accord, he rolled onto his back and put his head on my shoulder.

Letting his head loll back, he opened his mouth and emitted a groan—a groan the likes of which I had never heard from a dog. It was the sort of groan—exhaustion mixed with relief—that people make after a week of final exams, after a marathon, after combat. I stroked his neck, and his chest began to rise and fall in a relaxed slow rhythm. A moment later, his tail swished several times, mixing happiness and surprise: "I can't believe how good this feels! Oh, this feels so good!"

I don't know how long we stayed there, for the three of us fell soundly asleep.

When I opened my eyes, the sky was incandescent blue. Over the Tetons, Venus hung, big and white and glowing. The two dogs breathed softly in my arms. Then I heard a whistle from across the field and Jess's voice calling, "A.J., Burley, dinner's on."

They leapt to their feet and like Stinger missiles, yellow and red, flew off into the night.

Over the next two years, I hiked and skied with A.J. and Burley, and they often napped behind my office chair while I wrote; sometimes they even had a sleepover and joined me in bed. But when Jess or Eric whistled from across the field, the two young dogs would raise their heads, wait for the second whistle—"Yep, our person's calling"—and hurtle down the stairs and out Merle's door to home.

Frequently, they were gone for weeks at a time, traveling with Jess and Eric, and though I missed them during these periods—the house empty of padding paws and panting grins—the sporadic nature of our attachment was fine by me. I was still attached to the dog who sat at the corner of my desk and whom I saw trotting across the field as he returned from his rounds. Still longing for him, I sifted through my memories and steadily wrote—week after week, month after month, over a period of nearly three years—snatching Merle from time's dissolution and turning him into story, the sweetest remedy I know for grief. And it worked. Reliving every time we shared, I had the chance to part from him on gentler terms than death had given us.

And when the writing was done, I traveled for another year on Merle's book tour, talking about him, showing images of his life, and answering every imaginable question about who he had been and how he had gone about his days, this extended road show—this public expression of grief for a dog on the part of people who hadn't met him—helping to bury my pain and lift Merle from the earth as surely as if he had been resurrected. He was no longer my dog; he belonged to all of us. He was every dog who had been loved and lost and mourned for dying too soon.

There was only one more step to take.

Returning from the last stop on the tour, I got into the Subaru, parked at the Jackson Hole airport, and turned the key.

"Ha-ha-ha," he said, stepping between the front seats and pressing his cheek against mine. "Home at last!"

I reached up and clasped our heads together.

"Home at last," I agreed.

His dancing eyes met mine. "See. Still here."

I put my hand on my heart. "Yes. Still here."

Our eyes locked, and he gave me the look he'd given me on the night we first met on the San Juan River so long ago: "You need a dog." But this time he didn't add, "And I'm it."

Several moments went by before I asked, "Are you sure?"

His golden-brown eyes stared into mine. "I'm sure."

"Maybe," I told him.

"No," he answered firmly. "It's time. It really is." He grinned.

I touched my heart. "But always here."

He leaned his body into mine. "Always here."

And with that, still pressed together, Merle and I drove home.

CHAPTER FOUR

Houndy Labs

W ITHIN A FEW DAYS of putting out the word that I was finally looking for another dog, I found no shortage of people willing to give me a hand. They sent me cross-postings about shelter dogs needing rescue; they recommended breeders; they showed up at my front door bearing puppies in their arms; and they e-mailed me countless suggestions, the most common being that my new dog should look nothing like Merle. In this way, I'd be less likely to make comparisons, which could only lead to my not accepting the new dog for who it was.

In this vein, one person suggested that I get a Husky. I was obviously a winter person, he observed, and it would be hard to find a better cold-weather breed than a Siberian Husky. Another person was adamant that a German Shepherd was the right dog for me; she had lived with German Shepherds her entire life, and they were superb, loyal companions. One friend, whose Beagle had just whelped, offered me pick of the litter; a second did the same for his new batch of Springer Spaniels; and a third suggested I try a Toy Poodle for my next canine friend. At the bottom of her e-mail my friend attached a photo of a little white dog, its fur combed up in a pompadour and circled by a tiara. Beneath the dog's photo she had written: "Be bold! Break with the past!"

I knew firsthand that such a small dog had the potential to live a very long life: one of Merle's friends, a Lhasa Apso named Toto, had lived until nearly twenty, but Toto had never skied deep powder with us. In a place where winter can last seven months, this was no small consideration. I had no interest in living with a dog whom I'd have to leave home from November until June. I also wanted a dog who would happily join me on hikes, climbs, and mountain biking trips in the summer and be big enough — about forty pounds — not to turn into coyote bait every time it left the house on its own. Dozens of mixed-breed and purebred dogs could fulfill this role handily, but where to look for them? A shelter or a breeder?

For many people, this question has only one answer. Given that 1.5 million healthy dogs are put to death each year in American shelters, a great number of people believe it's morally wrong to do anything but adopt a dog. More than a few of these folks now began a campaign, urging me to do the right thing and make my next dog another rescue. But having already spent some time researching dog health and longevity, I was confronted by several troubling facts. Compared to intact dogs, spayed and neutered dogs experience more adverse reactions to vaccines, a higher incidence of some cancers, and suffer more orthopedic injuries. They have a greater propensity to endocrine dysfunction and are more obese. In her dog longevity surveys, Kelly Cassidy found that dogs in the United Kingdom live a year longer than dogs of the same breed in North America, and one reason behind their longer life spans might be that far more dogs are left intact in Europe than is the case in the United States and Canada. I knew that if I got a dog from a shelter, it would almost certainly be spayed or neutered, potentially reducing my chances of giving it the longest life possible. Nor would I know much, if anything, of the dog's ancestry, particularly whether its forebears were healthy or plagued by illness. Yet I couldn't deny that millions of dogs were dying for lack of a home.

Deciding to set aside my concerns about spaying and neutering for the time being, I began to spend many hours on Petfinder.com, looking through the thumbnail biographies of dogs up for adoption, my surfing reminding me of my past Internet dating, with one crucial difference: the dogs weren't writing their own life sketches, nor were they receiving phone calls. There was no way I could call them and find out if we had anything in common. The photos of the dogs were sweet and appealing — there was no doubt about that — and part of me wished that I could adopt them all, but another part of me wouldn't get in the car and drive to Arkansas, Georgia, or Tennessee to meet dogs whose photos I had admired. Nor was I willing to adopt one of these dogs, as some advocates urged me to do, "sight unseen." I had been called too picky and overly careful in human romance, and I now was being called the same when it came to dogs. But ten or twelve years is a long time to spend with someone with whom you're not in love.

Feeling at a loss, I sat down one day and did what the Internet dating services always ask a subscriber to do: write a sketch about the person you want to find. "The dog I want to live with," I began, "would be both calm and intelligent. It would love the cold and high places and could navigate deep snow without its paws clogging." In my mind's eye, I could see my past and present Golden Retriever buddies, Brower and Burley, gnawing at their feet so as to remove ice balls, while Merle and A.J., their Labrador paws snow-free, waited patiently by their sides.

"My new dog," I continued, "would also love the water and have its original hunting drive intact; yet it could easily be convinced not to chase everyone with four legs. It would know the merits of silence, as do wild dogs, and it would bark infrequently. This dog would not be foolish; it would recognize danger; it would use finesse instead of force; it would be athletic and tireless and graceful. It would, of course, be Merle!"

I knew I was being silly, wanting his clone miraculously to appear, but there it was: I was still hopelessly in love with my old dog, the one who continued to press his cheek against mine as I drove down the road. And although I knew there was little chance of success in the endeavor I was planning, I got into the car soon after writing these words and drove all the way back to the San Juan River, 650 miles across the mountains and deserts of Wyoming and Utah, finally pulling into the campground where Merle and I had met on that long-ago April night. It was dusk when I arrived, and the campground was no longer as rustic as I remembered — new outhouses had been built, the parking lot had been expanded, and some handsome, educational billboards documenting the region's wildlife had been erected. The cottonwoods hadn't changed — they were still there, ancient and broad and overhanging the sandy beach across which Merle had trotted out of the darkness into my headlights. There, beneath one of the trees, was the exact spot upon which I had thrown my sleeping bag and the very place that Merle had dug a nest by my side. I walked over, crouched, and put my palms flat on the sand where we had slept.

It was after the river-running season, the water low, and there wasn't another soul around. I stayed perhaps an hour, sitting on the sand where we had first touched noses — watching the young Merle and the young Ted fall in love all over again on that spring morning. I kept hoping that he might reappear, or another dog like him would walk out of the cottonwoods and say, "You need a dog, and I'm it." But that would be too good a story, and, of course, none did.

Darkness fell, and I got in the car and drove to the nearby settlement of Bluff, stopping at an outdoor restaurant for dinner and showing some of Merle's photos to the waitress, who said, "He looks like some of the dogs who used to live around here." She recommended that I go over to the Recapture Lodge and talk to the woman who ran it, for she had been in town a long time.

After dinner I strolled down the road, and the manager of the lodge also confirmed that she had seen a few local dogs who looked like Merle. "But they don't last very long on the Res," she went on. "If people see stray dogs around their sheep, they shoot them, and the kids shoot them with BB guns." For a moment I thought of the slug Merle had carried on his right shoulder blade, which I discovered on X-ray when he was eight years old, then I returned my attention to what the woman was saying: "You might want to talk to Dora Benally in the morning. She's a Navajo woman who cleans here, and she knows all about the local dogs."

I spent the night and met Dora in the dining room at breakfast, where she was laying out fresh tablecloths. She was a short woman in her forties, with jet-black hair and a broad expressionless face that immediately brightened when she saw Merle's photos. "This looks like my Starsky," she said in a warm voice. "He disappeared in 1991."

That was the year Merle and I had met. Feeling uneasy, I said, "How old was he?"

"Five or six. And he had on a red collar. We always had him wear a collar. He loved people. He'd greet them over by the mission where we lived. One day he didn't come back. We figured someone took him."

I explained that Merle was about ten months old when we had met at the Sand Island campground about four miles south of Bluff and had been collarless. "These pictures," I added, "are from when he was about four years old."

"Then it wasn't my Starsky," she said, a little sadly. "Not him. But your dog looks a lot like the dogs from back in those years. Some people around here bred Labs, crossing them with dogs who had hound in them. I had yellow, black, and chocolate Labs, lots of dogs. But you know how it is. The dogs chase cattle, they get shot, they run away and get run over."

She held the photos, and I could see that she was thinking of Starsky. When she handed back the photos, she said, "If you want to see a dog who looks like Merle and is still alive, you should walk down that dirt road over there." She pointed across the main street. "A man named Larry lives at the end of the road, and he has a dog named Rodney. She's one of my dogs," she said with a touch of pride. "I bred her from a male Lab and a female with a lot of hound in her, and she could be Merle's sister."

I thanked her warmly, then walked down the lane. No one was home.

Several days later, after I returned to Kelly, I reached Larry by phone. We talked about free-roaming dogs on the Navajo Reservation and when I asked about the possibility of puppies, he said that Rodney had been spayed. However, he knew of another person in the Four Corners region who had bred a Lab with a hound and might have pups.

When I called this man in Blanding, Utah, he told me that, yes, he had a Labrador Retriever–Redbone Coonhound cross, but that after his dog had sired a couple of litters he had had him neutered. He gave me the name of a woman with a similar dog in Cortez, Colorado, but when I called her it was the same story—a Lab-Redbone cross, a female, one litter, then spayed.

Even though these leads didn't pan out, they did validate what I had come to believe about Merle's origins. One of my friends had given me a book about a Redbone Coonhound named Blender. He lived on the Colorado River above Moab, Utah, and swam out to meet rafts running the river. At the end of the day, after socializing with tourists and sharing their sandwiches, he would swim to shore and wait on the highway until someone picked him up and drove him the twenty miles upriver to his home. From the book's photos and text, it was easy to see that Blender and Merle had similar looks and mannerisms, most particularly a love of roaming.

A few months went by, and then I received a letter that gave me another trail to follow. It was from Denise Hamel, an editor at *Labrador Quarterly*, who wrote that Merle reminded her of the English field-trial Labs of the 1930s. I shouldn't confuse these dogs with some of the modern-day, American field-trial Labs, she cautioned, who were being bred for intense speed and drive and who had taken on the wispy, tucked-up appearance of Greyhounds.

My curiosity piqued, I started reading about the history of Labrador Retrievers, noting that they weren't originally from Labrador at all, but from Newfoundland, evolving from dogs who, starting in the early 1500s, were brought across the Atlantic by fishermen from the west coasts of England and Scotland. Sometime in the early 1800s, the Second Earl of Malmesbury began to import these dogs to Poole on the south coast of England, and it was his son, the Third Earl, who took to calling them "Labradors," the name passing into common usage despite the fact that most of the dogs came from Newfoundland.

Many retrievers went on to contribute their genes to the Labrador line – not only the black ones, whom the Third Earl favored, but also the Flat-Coated Retriever and the Curly-Coated, the Liver-coloured and the Golden, as well as yellow Labs themselves, all of them leaving their marks and creating dogs who were reddish, golden-yellow, and butterscotch. Even foxhounds were bred to Labs when the steady supply of fresh bloodlines from the New World became a trickle after Newfoundland passed a sheep protection act, allowing the killing of many dogs on the island, and Britain imposed a six-month-long quarantine on any imported dog in 1897 to stop the spread of rabies. Turning to foxhounds, and increasingly to Golden Retrievers, iconoclastic breeders brought the genes of these two breeds into the Labrador line, and some of their traits – feathering on the legs, a longer snout, uplifted tails, a baying voice, and a more streamlined frame – can still be seen in some Labs today.

Fascinated by this history, I continued to read along, looking at photographs of dogs who had been dead for over a century. I turned the page and stopped in astonishment. Before me was a photo of Merle himself – a lean, golden, houndy-looking dog, trotting in profile with a bird in his mouth. Born in 1933, this near-twin of Merle's was named Ming, and he became famous for being the first Labrador Retriever of any color to win both the English and American field-trial championships.

It was this type of rangy, athletic Lab who intrigued me, a dog who might bay instead of bark, who could track as well as retrieve – who could make his way through the world with versatile grace. Thoughtfully, I closed the book on my finger, marking the place where Ming trotted into history and emerged as Merle. Here was the sort of dog I had fallen in love with almost two decades before on the San Juan River. It was exactly the sort of dog I was still in love with now.

Finding him was no easy matter. First I revisited the shelter world, combing ads and following up on e-mail recommendations about houndy-looking Labs. I saw good dogs. I saw happy, clever, and athletic dogs. But I saw no dogs with whom I fell in love the way I had fallen in love with Merle.

Still, I persisted, getting in my car and driving through Wyoming and Colorado, across Arizona, and back through Utah, where I ended my tour at the Best Friends Animal Society outside of Kanab. There, on thirty-four thousand acres of red rock canyon and piñon-juniper forest, hundreds of dogs, cats, horses, birds, and rabbits live out their natural lives, if no one adopts them.

Going from one dog condo to another, I must have looked at thirty dogs, all of them living in spacious quarters with dog doors opening onto backyards. Then, in the condo called the Fairway, I had a sudden change of heart. I saw a red-and-white foxhound named Clyde — young, trim, and muscular — with rust-colored ears and a tail like an uplifted scimitar. He looked ready for anything the world could throw his way, and he smelled my fingers three times — *sniff, sniff, sniff* — before lying down with his back to me. Obviously, he wasn't very Labby, but I couldn't take my eyes off of him.

He had been a free-roaming dog, had been picked up while on his rounds, and had been left off at Best Friends. Whatever he had endured while being on his own, it had given him that special presence I was looking for — that collected air that said, "Watch out, I'm my own dog." There was only one problem with Clyde's attitude. He took it to the extreme: he not only turned his back on me — he wanted nothing to do with me.

I knelt and tried to talk with him. He ignored me. I took him for a walk, and he consented to it stoically. I petted him; he turned to stone under my hands. I play-bowed to him. He gave me a sideways look that said, "If I could cry, you would bore me to tears. Please go away."

When I took him back to his outdoor run, his kennel mate, an exuberant Weimaraner, mobbed him with affectionate kisses. He turned his back on her as well and lay down under a shady tree, where he stared at the distant ridges of red rock with the air of a mountain man whose best friend is the sky. Crestfallen, she walked away. I felt sorry for her, but at least I had gotten some perspective on Clyde's rejection of me: he was an aloof soul.

I headed home and on the long drive mulled over how I had been searching for my new dog. Given that I wanted some very specific attributes in him, that same enticing admixture I had found in Merle — a large dose of Lab, a pinch of hound, and a dash of Golden — it seemed that I was going about my search in a hit-or-miss sort of way. In addition, I was still concerned about the long-term effects of sterilization. Even in Merle's day, I knew that there were alternative procedures to spaying and neutering, vasectomies and tubal ligations, which prevented pregnancies yet allowed a dog to retain its beneficial sex hormones. But no shelter I had visited did these procedures or would allow an adopter to find a vet who would do them. The dogs were universally sterilized before they went out the door.

It was somewhere between Kanab and Spanish Fork that I decided to change my search strategy. "Why not," I thought, "turn to the people who are creating the very canine characteristics I'm looking for, and who'll hand over my new dog intact?" These people were, of course, breeders.

CHAPTER FIVE

Sifting the Genes

WITHIN DAYS OF searching their online directories, I was disappointed. I couldn't find a single breeder turning out the kind of dog for whom I was searching – a bespoke dog if you will, tailored to a customer's precise needs – and the reason was straightforward. The major kennel clubs won't register such amalgams, and unregistered dogs don't make breeders very much money. Indeed, even if both a pup's parents are registered purebred dogs, but are from two different breeds, their offspring have no cachet and are known as "mongrels," a word often full of derisive overtones, or "mutts," derived from "muttonhead," a word that became popular in the early 1900s and meant a stupid, dull-witted person, a fool.

In these politically correct times, "mongrel" and "mutt" have been softened to "mixed-breed" or "crossbreed," labels that in certain cases have been elevated to "designer dog." The latter term signifies the off-spring of two different purebreds who have been deliberately mated in the hopes of capturing the best qualities of each breed and producing a dog with fewer genetically transmitted diseases and more of what the breeders of these dogs call "hybrid vigor," a characteristic that one website devoted to such dogs defines as "the burst of fertility, good health and growth that is seen in the progeny when two unrelated breeds are mated."

Cockapoos, a Cocker Spaniel–Poodle cross, were the first designer dogs, created in the 1950s. They were followed in the 1980s and 1990s by the Labradoodle (a Labrador Retriever–Poodle cross) and the Gold-endoodle (a Golden Retriever–Poodle cross), both of whom are adver-tised as combining the friendliness and tractability of the retriever line and the high intelligence and nonshedding coat of the Poodle.

People have found designer dogs both fashionable and friendly, and as a consequence their breeders have turned a profit on them. Such fusion breedings, though, have elicited the same reaction in the traditional world of purebred dogs as fusion cooking has in the world of haute cuisine: a raised eyebrow, a disapproving sniff, and the dismissive labeling of the resultant mélange as "confusion." Worse, the US Labrador Retriever Club contends that "crossbred dogs are prone to all of the genetic disease of both breeds and offer none of the advantages that owning a purebred dog has to offer."

Yet when I read the scientific literature — genetic, biological, veterinary, and horticultural — I found it full of examples of the first generation of hybrids being bigger, healthier, and more fertile. What is far more accurate to say than "hybrid vigor doesn't exist in dogs," as some breeders told me, is that it doesn't occur reliably. This is because many of the traits we value are polygenic — they're produced by genes acting in consort. Thus, people who buy a Labradoodle for its nonshedding coat are occasionally disappointed.

Despite such letdowns, hybridization has been one of the techniques that breeders have repeatedly used to create today's purebred dogs, one of the most outstanding examples being the 1868 creation of the Golden Retriever by Lord Tweedmouth in the Scottish Highlands. Tweedmouth mated Nous, his Wavy-Coated Retriever, to Belle, his Tweed Water Spaniel, combining what he considered excellent retrieving ability with a love of water. He then mated Nous and Belle's offspring to Irish Setters and Bloodhounds, bringing some of their looks and scenting ability into the line.

Once such present-day, well-known breeds as the Golden Retriever were established, however, the two kennel clubs that largely oversaw their creation — the Kennel Club of Great Britain (founded in London in 1873) and the American Kennel Club (founded in New York City in 1884) — put a stop to such interbreed liaisons. They tried, in the best tradition of eugenics, to enforce the opposite of fusion — breed separation. And by and large, they've been successful. Few recognized crossbreeds have been created since the early part of the twentieth century. And this, it may be argued, is when the health problems of purebred dogs began.

We now have hundreds of unique and useful dogs who can match just about anyone's tastes, personality, and needs, but because a great deal of inbreeding has gone into heightening the particular characteristics of some of these breeds, they can also have a multitude of debilitating and sometimes fatal genetically transmitted diseases. Some of these diseases are simply canine ones. By default, if you're a dog, you have a chance of getting cancer or having hip dysplasia. On the other hand, if you're a Bernese Mountain Dog, your chances of getting systemic histiocytosis, a multi-organ form of cancer, are far greater than in the dog population in general, or even in other purebred dogs. If you're a German Shepherd, your chances of having hip dysplasia are high; if you're a Greyhound, they're close to zero.

Two factors have contributed to the phenomenon of certain illnesses plaguing certain breeds: first is the small number of dogs who have been used to found these breeds, and second is the decreasing number of male dogs who, as time has gone by, actually contribute their DNA to their gene pool, a practice called the "popular-sire syndrome."

For example, using data from the Kennel Club, researchers discovered that only 5 percent of male Golden Retrievers in the United Kingdom get to pass on their genes. Think about this for a moment. What would the human population look like if only 5 percent of males were allowed to have children? It is this tiny number of dogs who are actually breeding that has narrowed the funnel of the purebred canine gene pool and led to dogs who may look unique but who are sometimes functionally crippled.

For a long time critics of purebred dog breeding have raged against such practices, vilifying breeders and calling them thoughtless, selfish, benighted, and greedy. Ever more frequently, they're called uncaring about the health problems they create for their dogs. The first person to level such criticism may have been Charles Darwin himself, a dog lover if there ever was one, and one of the more acute observers of dog behavior in his time. In 1868 he was already saying that some dog breeds had achieved an "almost monstrous character."

Three decades later, the social economist Thorstein Veblen echoed and expanded Darwin's sentiments in his landmark book *The Theory of the Leisure Class*, saying that the greater "the degrees of grotesqueness of a dog" the more social worth it had because of its consequent scarcity and expense. Numerous other critics — including *Time* magazine and *The Atlantic Monthly* — weighed in on the subject of unhealthy, inbred, pedigree dogs during the following century, and so did the BBC.

In 2008 the BBC aired a documentary called *Pedigree Dogs Exposed*, produced by the British filmmaker Jemima Harrison. The film shows Cavalier King Charles Spaniels suffering from syringomyelia, an excruciatingly painful condition in which a dog's skull remains too small for its growing brain. The footage is so graphic and heartrending that it prompted a parliamentary investigation of the British Kennel Club, which eventually announced that it would no longer register puppies from closely related parents — mother and son, father and daughter, and sister and brother — and that it was also changing some of its breed standards for dogs with exaggerated anatomical features, like the Bulldog with its pushed-in face, so that these unhealthy features would be penalized in shows.

The tsunami of public outrage that the film spawned made its way across the Atlantic, much diminished, but nevertheless nudging the staid American Kennel Club to begin a certification program for its breeders, called "Breeder of Merit." It was modeled after the Kennel Club's "Accredited Breeder Scheme," but like the British program, it remains voluntary, without any oversight to ensure that breeders so named on the clubs' websites are in fact performing the recommended health screenings for their particular breeds.

And so the breeding of unhealthy dogs has continued, two of the most notable examples of famous, widely admired, but dysfunctional dogs being the winner of the 2012 Westminster Kennel Club Dog Show, Malachy the Pekingese, who gasped for breath on his abbreviated circle of the ring and had to sit on an ice pack after his victory, as well as one of the runners-up, the German Shepherd Captain Crunch, whose hocks nearly touched the green carpet when he ran.

Not all that long ago, dogs from both breeds looked quite different, the German Shepherd, for example, having a level spine until the middle of the twentieth century, a conformation that even the most casual observer of dogs would call normal, as in the photo on the previous page of Beowulf, born in 1899 and one of the founders of the German Shepherd line.

But starting in the early 1950s, the interpretation of the breed standard was increasingly altered to favor German Shepherds with drastically sloping rear ends, as seen in this photo of a German Shepherd born in the twenty-first century.

The makeover was done to create a German Shepherd with what is called a "flying trot" in the show ring. However, some German Shepherd breeders dispute this standard. They point out that such low-slung dogs now have chronic balance problems, lower rear legs that actually touch the ground, and an increased incidence of osteoarthritis, often caused by hip dysplasia, a condition in which the ball-and-socket joint connecting the top of the femur to the pelvis is abnormally formed. Data from the Hip Improvement Program at the University of Pennsylvania's School of Veterinary Medicine supports these critiques: modern German Shepherds have a 60 percent chance of having osteoarthritis in their hips once they pass the age of two, whereas Labrador Retrievers, with their normal-looking rear ends, have only a 20 percent chance.

The Pekingese was similarly made over during the twentieth century. Photographs of the founder of the modern Pekingese, Ah Cum, who was born in the Imperial Palace and imported to England in the late 1890s, as well as photos of other Pekingese from that time, reveal a dog who might not be recognized as a member of the breed today. These early Pekingese, like Dimple II, shown in this photo from 1913, were taller than modern ones, with longer legs, shorter hair, and a longer snout that wasn't so markedly flattened.

But over the next one hundred years, the Pekingese was made over so as to shorten and broaden its skull—a trait called brachycephaly—which has made these dogs appear wide-eyed, childlike, and cute. The breed's coat has grown much longer and now trails on the ground.

Malachy, in this photo from the 2012 Westminster show, is the culmination of these changes, which began in earnest when the Kennel Club of Great Britain approved a cross between the Pekingese and the Shih Tzu in 1952 so as to modify what some Shih Tzu breeders perceived as faults in their breed: a dog who was too big, too leggy, and too long-nosed.

The resulting crossbreeds not only lacked these so-called faults; they also had longer coats. Steadily, they made their way into the

hands of Pekingese breeders, giving them what one historian of the breed calls "a competitive edge" in the show ring. Over the next half-century, longer coats, shorter legs, and flatter faces became the norm in the Pekingese, the overriding reason for this transformation being what John French, the president of the Pekingese Club of America, told me is "the glamour factor."

But breeding for what is thought to be glamorous and fashionable in the appearance of a dog, especially a flattened face that resembles a human child's, has resulted in a variety of health problems. Three-dimensional CT-scanning done at the University of Leipzig's Department of Small Animal Medicine has shown that such shortened facial bones cause a dislocation of the nasal conchae – the thin scroll-like bones at the sides of the nasal cavity – pushing them into the respiratory duct and impeding the flow of air. The deformation of the typically longer canine snout not only gives such short-faced dogs breathing problems; it also causes them to overheat easily, for dogs don't pant only through their mouths when they're hot.

Researchers at Duke University in North Carolina put air flow–measuring masks on dogs and discovered that dogs in fact inhale through their noses and exhale through their mouths when they pant, the incoming air being evaporatively cooled as it's drawn through the nasal mucosa. Later experiments have shown that during increased heat stress a dog inhales and exhales through both its nose and mouth while also producing increased amounts of saliva and increased flows of blood in its tongue. The dog's oral cavity then acts in tandem with the nasal mucosa to help reduce its temperature. Consequently, a dog with a short nose – or no nose at all – cannot cool itself as efficiently as nature designed it to, as canine airline deaths have shown. Between 2005 and 2010, half of the dogs who perished while being shipped by air were members of short-faced breeds.

Selecting for brachycephaly isn't the only way we've changed the archetypal shape of the dog, creating ill health. Until about the middle of the twentieth century, breeds like the Chow Chow, the English Setter, the English Springer Spaniel, and the Labrador and Golden Retriever were functional dogs who could run, jump, hunt, and pull sleds. They've been steadily transformed into little tanks and furry peacocks who can no longer perform these activities as well as their ancestors.

One Chow breeder who has rebelled against this trend and tried to restore the health of her dogs through selective breeding — particularly by X-raying her dog's hips and elbows to reduce her line's incidence of hip and elbow dysplasia — is Kathy Beliew of Imagine Kennels in San Bernardino, California. She remains an outspoken critic of her fellow breeders, who she says have reduced our dogs' ability to work by emphasizing style over functional conformation, the problem being especially prevalent in breeds that no longer have any real work to do, like toy dogs, whose ancestors once pulled carts and turned spits. "Go back to the old breed standards," she told me, "and take a look at those for hounds. Today hounds still look like hounds from the 1800s. Why? Because they still have to function. But in so many nonsporting dogs, function doesn't matter anymore. It's been lost."

One way to restore such function would be mandatory fitness tests administered before a dog is shown in the ring or allowed to breed. I heard of this idea from the Austrian canid geneticist Dr. Hellmuth Wachtel, who believes that all breeds, including toy breeds, should pass what he calls "vitality tests." These would include running and swimming races and pulling weights so as to eliminate physiologically compromised individuals.

To emphasize his point, Hellmuth opened a photo album — we were sitting in his living room in Vienna — and showed me some old photos of his black Miniature Poodle Pearcy. Although Pearcy had weighed only fourteen pounds, he had accompanied Hellmuth on bike rides of up to thirteen miles in length; he had hiked in the Alps; he had swum through icy rivers. "Just because a dog is a toy dog doesn't mean that he can't be active," said Hellmuth, who at eighty-six remains lean and fit.

To be sure, it may be some years before we see a Pug competing against a Pekingese in the four-hundred-meter dash, since, as Hellmuth went on to say, "Their present conformation would prevent it."

Unfortunately, the smaller the breed, the less the likelihood that its conformational problems will be addressed, since most breeders no longer think that toy dogs can be athletes. No better example of this mind-set can be found than in those who breed Pugs.

In the late 1800s, Pugs had a noticeable snout through which they could breathe when they ran, as shown in this engraving from the nineteenth-century German classic *Brehm's Life of Animals*.

Mops (Canis familiaris molossus fricator). ¼ natürl. Größe.

But a modern Pug, whose face complies with the breed standard, has no nose at all. It has been completely eliminated by selective breeding—the thoughtless kind, as shown in the photo on the next page.

Despite the gross disfigurement of these dogs, the Pug Dog Club of America gives only a brief mention on its website of the fact that Pugs have breathing problems. Nor does the club discuss the possibility of correcting the underlying cause: a breed standard that includes as one of its hallmarks a pushed-in face. Instead, the club recommends surgically correcting pinched nostrils and elongated soft palates (both of which can make Pugs gasp for breath), thus giving the impression that such respiratory problems are flaws in individual dogs rather than

flaws in the breed standard itself. The club's short and cheery health page says that "Pugs tend to be a healthy, hearty breed that can easily live into the mid and upper teens."

The Pug Club of the United Kingdom is just as bubbly. On its website, it minimizes the Pug's difficulties with running, breathing, and thermoregulation and asserts that "fifteen or sixteen year old pugs are no rarity." Kelly Cassidy's review, using data from the Kennel Club of Great Britain, found that the average life span of the breed is eleven years.

Breeders of large dogs — breeds that are still expected to run and jump and be active — are not this sanguine about the health of their dogs and have been more proactive in trying to extend their lives. The Newfoundland Club of America, the Bernese Mountain Dog Club of America, and the Golden Retriever Club of America have asked their breeders to share information about the diseases that afflict their dogs by contributing health records to centralized databases so as to prevent matings between dogs whose health is known to be impaired. The Golden Retriever Club of America has also partnered with the Morris Animal Foundation in a study designed to identify the heritable mutations that predispose Goldens and other breeds to hemangiosarcoma and lymphoma. If these genes can be identified, the hope is that through selective breeding the incidence of these cancers can be reduced.

As of 2012, there was no proof that such efforts have helped to extend the life spans of these breeds. Studies in the 1990s found the life span of Bernese Mountain Dogs to be between seven and eight years, and when the Bernese Mountain Dog Club of America repeated its surveys in 2000 and again in 2005, those numbers had remained unchanged:

seven to eight years. Lori Littleford, a member of the Newfoundland
Club of America's Health and Longevity Committee, told me that she
thought the Newfoundland's life span had gone from about seven years
in the 1980s to between ten and twelve years in 2011, but she could not
prove it. And even though the Golden Retriever cancer study is a welcome step toward finding out why so many Goldens die of the disease,
the study doesn't address whether the knowledge it produces—that a
particular gene leads to cancer in Golden Retrievers—will convince
breeders to employ that knowledge to create healthier dogs.

And that's the rub. The health committees of some breed clubs
are made up of savvy, concerned, scientifically minded individuals
who have a good idea of what's wrong with their breeds and how to
correct it. Even the health committees of some small breeds like the
Cavalier King Charles Spaniel have tried to be proactive in addressing their breed's maladies, recommending that breeders test dogs for
genetically transmitted diseases, not mate close relatives, and reduce
exaggerated anatomical features. Yet these recommendations have no
regulatory teeth. Breeders are free to ignore them and go on producing
unhealthy, crippled dogs.

Why would they do so? As I continued my search for a new dog, I
had to ask myself why breeders who claimed to love their dogs kept
on producing animals who by most commonsense measures—Can the
dog breathe? Can the dog walk?—were disasters. After speaking with
many breeders in both North America and Europe, I began to develop
a theory. I noticed that a considerable number of breeders involved in
the show world share two characteristics: a strong competitive drive
to win blue ribbons and a love of how a dog looks instead of how it
performs. I suspect that it is these two qualities that begin to take
some breeders down a slippery slope, one dog at a time, overriding
first caution, then common sense, and finally compassion. To appreciate how this can happen—incrementally and without malice—come
along with me on this thought experiment: for the next few minutes,
become a dog breeder who loves a dog named Sam.

Sam is a warm, friendly fellow with a narrow regal nose, which
you've admired since he grew out of his puppyhood, especially because
he likes to lay his nose over your shoulder when you sit on the floor
with him. So, wanting Sam's most noticeable and fondly regarded fea-
ture to live on after he's gone, you mate him with a dog named Sweetie,

who has a somewhat narrow and regal nose as well. Sam and Sweetie have seven puppies, and you take the brother and sister who have the narrowest noses and you mate them to each other, and then you mate their offspring back to Sam and Sweetie, occasionally finding one of Sam's or Sweetie's close relations, whose noses you admire, to mate to as well. And all the while, you're making sure that you don't breed those puppies who have three eyes and two tails. In other words, you don't pass along the obvious genetic defects that arise from mating these close relatives.

Pretty soon you have stunning, long-nosed dogs whom you love and who are the pride of your life. Have you done anything malign or thoughtless? Not in the least. All you've done is what horse breeders and cattle breeders and pig breeders have done throughout history as they've selectively bred their stock to produce horses who run faster, cows who produce more milk, and pigs who yield more ham. This is what selective breeding does, and it works in humans as well. Masai look like Masai and Swedes look like Swedes because like has mated to like.

Human nature being what is, though — covetous of the novel as well as simply admiring it — your friends and acquaintances who have admired your dogs now want to buy some of them. Of course, you sell them puppies because you believe your dogs will make them happy. And they do, and your friends tell others about these unusual, magnificent, long-nosed dogs, and pretty soon people from all over the country, and perhaps even the world, want to buy Sam's services. Sweetie, of course, can have only so many litters, but Sam's supply of sperm is nearly endless.

If Sam happens to have won a few blue ribbons during this time, more and more people will want to have his sperm for their bitch in the hopes that they, too, will have pups with Sam's looks and mettle, and who will eventually win them some championships.

So you begin to ship Sam's semen around the country — chilled and by overnight delivery. But something has changed. You can no longer control which of Sam's offspring will be allowed to breed in the hope that their pups will have ever-longer noses, and, well, if having three eyes and two tails is the price of such wonderfully long noses, so be it.

Here is where the real problems begin. You're now Sam's business manager, and as his manager it's easy to mate him hundreds of times, forgetting that he (really you) may be passing along some of his hidden time bombs along with his many wonders – time bombs that are far scarier than having three eyes and two tails because you can't immediately see them. In fact, you don't have a clue as to what they might be, or in what grim ways they might combine, or at what stage of life they may appear. In fact, what you haven't realized is that attached to the gene for Sam's long nose is a gene for some nasty condition and that the two of them are inherited together.

It is this inattention, denial, or ignorance that begins to merge your love of Sam's unusually long nose with what can be justifiably called a disregard for the welfare of his descendants, especially considering that warnings about breeding for extreme anatomical features appeared not long after the Kennel Club began to register dogs in 1903. In 1911, for example, Judith Blunt-Lytton published a book, called *Toy Dogs and Their Ancestors,* in which she excoriated her fellow breeders for "the artificial preservation of that which is unfit and unsound." An outspoken woman with the clout of her position behind her – she was the Sixteenth Baroness Wentworth and the great-granddaughter of Lord Byron – she also inveighed against the Kennel Club for creating standards that forced judges to award championships to dogs who were "feeble" and "deformed" and, "as a consequence of their artificiality," were struck down by "ghastly diseases" that "would not have existed . . . had our pet stock been less inbred and unsound." She could not have been clearer. Yet, despite her impassioned prose, her peerage, and the irrefutable evidence before everyone's eyes, hardly anyone listened to her.

And if perchance you missed reading Lady Wentworth when you began to breed Sam, you might have seen the work of Captain Max von Stephanitz, who developed the German Shepherd from German sheepherding dogs in the 1890s and published one of the more sensible books on dog breeding and training, *The German Shepherd Dog in Word and Picture,* which saw its first English edition in 1925. Like Lady Wentworth, von Stephanitz did not pull his punches about breeding for looks instead of health. If one breeds for "exhibitions," he stated, "it is not done for the sake of the dog, nor does it make him more useful, but is done only for the vanity of the breeder and the subsequent purchaser."

If at this point you still hadn't realized what might happen if you bred Sam too many times for his looks, the dangers of his being a popular sire were described in perfect clarity by the geneticists John Paul

Scott and John L. Fuller in their 1965 book *Genetics and the Social Behavior of the Dog:*

> If a male becomes a great champion, everyone wants one of his puppies, and he may be bred to several hundred females. If he carries even one recessive gene, it will be spread throughout the whole breed in such numbers that it will be almost impossible to eliminate when his descendants eventually begin to be mated with each other, and it is finally recognized as a serious problem. Thus current dog breeding practices can be described as an ideal system for the spread and preservation of injurious recessive genes.

And by the early 1970s our little parable of Sam and Sweetie is exactly what happened to the North American Golden Retriever. One field-trial dog, Holway Barty, and two show dogs, Misty Morn's Sunset and Cummings' Gold-Rush Charlie, won dozens of blue ribbons between them. They were not only gorgeous champions; they had wonderful personalities. Consequently, hundreds of people wanted these dogs' genes to come into their lines, and over many matings during the 1970s the genes of these three dogs were flung far and wide throughout the North American Golden Retriever population, until by 2010 Misty Morn's Sunset alone had 95,539 registered descendants, his number of unregistered ones unknown. Today hundreds of thousands of North American Golden Retrievers are descended from these three champions and have received both their sweet dispositions and their hidden time bombs.

Unfortunately for these Golden Retrievers, and for the people who love them, one of these time bombs happens to be cancer. To be fair, a so-called cancer gene cannot be traced directly to a few famous sires, but using these sires so often increases the chance of recessive genes meeting — for good and for ill.

Today, in the United States, 61.4 percent of Golden Retrievers die of cancer, according to a survey conducted by the Golden Retriever Club of America and the Purdue School of Veterinary Medicine. In Great Britain, a Kennel Club survey found almost exactly the same result, if we consider that those British dogs — loosely diagnosed as dying of "old age" and "cardiac conditions" and never having been autopsied — might really be dying of a variety of cancers, including hemangiosarcoma, a cancer of the lining of the blood vessels and the spleen.

This sad history of the Golden Retriever's narrowing gene pool has played out across dozens of other breeds and is one of the reasons that so many of our dogs spend a lot more time in veterinarians' offices than they should and die sooner than they might. In genetic terms, it comes down to the ever-increasing chance that both copies of any given gene are derived from the same ancestor, a probability expressed by a number called the coefficient of inbreeding. Discovered in 1922 by the American geneticist Sewall Wright, the coefficient of inbreeding ranges from 0 to 100 percent and rises as animals become more inbred.

As my search for a new pup continued, I thought a lot about this number. It had become perfectly clear to me that no one was going to put together a composite Merle for me — that athletic Lab, that focused hound, that happy Golden — whom I had loved to the bottom of my heart. But there were Labs out there — slim and houndy Labs with darkly rufous coats — whose pictures I was browsing on websites and to whom I was attracted. How inbred, how potentially disease-prone, were they?

It was easy to find out. I could calculate their coefficients of inbreeding longhand, as Sewall Wright had done, or I could download a computer program that did it for me. I chose the latter, using one from PedFast Technologies that cost $11.59. My goal was to find litters who had COIs of less than 6 percent. I could find no definitive study showing that lower coefficients of inbreeding led to longer life spans, but several health-conscious breeders told me that they tried to keep the COIs of their litters at less than 6 percent. I did find one nonrandomized survey of Standard Poodles that contained 349 records, and it showed an interesting correlation between COI and longevity over ten generations. The Poodles in this survey who had a COI of less than 6.25 percent lived nearly four years longer than those dogs whose COI was greater than 25 percent.

I had also begun to study a growing body of evidence demonstrating an association between general genetic diversity and the diversity of a particular gene cluster known as MHC, or the major histocompatibility complex. In both dogs and people, MHC helps to differentiate an individual's own tissue from foreign material, and as coefficients of inbreeding go up, the diversity of MHC declines, leading to an increased susceptibility to a variety of autoimmune diseases: endocrine dysfunction, dermatitis, diabetes, and rheumatoid arthritis, all of which have begun to affect increasing numbers of dogs. Whether you're a dog or a human, this is why it's not a good idea to have children with your parent or sibling.

As the months went by I found myself putting more study into finding this new pup — genetics, math, biochemistry — than I had ever invested in buying a car, a camera, or a pair of skis. And I persevered — looking at pedigrees and trying to find out what a prospective litter's grandparents and great-grandparents had died from — not because I'm particularly dogged, but because I was scared.

Every few weeks I continued to get e-mails from readers who had bought their dogs sight unseen on the Internet, or driven over to a local pet store, and now their best friend — their inseparable companion, the partner of their heart — was going blind . . . was becoming crippled . . . had an autoimmune disease . . . had been diagnosed with cancer. In some cases, the diseases their dogs had contracted had been absolutely preventable, but the breeders had not done a simple DNA test on both parent dogs, needing only a blood sample or cheek swab, to see if either of the breeding pair carried a recessive gene for progressive retinal atrophy (causing blindness) or centronuclear myopathy (a muscle-wasting disease).

The importance of these tests cannot be overemphasized: they show a prospective puppy buyer that even though two parent dogs are healthy, they are nonetheless carriers of the recessive gene for that condition. If they are mated, there is about a 25 percent chance that their recessive genes will meet, producing the actual disease in about one-quarter of their puppies.

My heart broke for these dogs and their people, and I took their stories to heart: I did not want to find myself in their straits within a few years. I also had to wonder why in an age when products such as electrical appliances, automobiles, pharmaceuticals, home furnishings, and toys must meet safety standards before being sold to the public, dogs are still sold without any regulations concerning their quality and health. Or so it is in North America and much of Europe.

Sweden, which led the world in insuring pets, has also led it in trying to certify the health of dogs. Unlike most North American and European kennel clubs, the Swedish Kennel Club has instituted health regulations, top-down, to its breeders. In 1976 it began to require that any dog who was to be used for breeding and whose breed had been identified as being prone to hip dysplasia had to complete a health screening for the condition before its progeny could be registered with the club.

These facts were related to me by Dr. Åke Hedhammar, a widely published veterinarian researcher in the fields of genetics and breeding and a professor at the Swedish University of Agricultural Sciences in Uppsala. He had picked me up at the airport outside of Stockholm and was driving us through the forested countryside toward the capital. He went on to explain that there were now 122 breeds in this hip dysplasia category and hip screenings weren't the only test required. The club maintained an open health registry on which it displayed each dog's genetic tests for the particular diseases that affected its breed. This rich mine of health information – including both positive and negative test results and health profiles of parents, grandparents, and great-grandparents – went back to 1976.

To see how anyone could use this website, instead of having to call individual breeders as I had been doing, Åke drove us on to our destination, the Swedish Kennel Club, where we were met by one of the club's breed consultants, Karin Drotz. Her job was to advise breeders on the health consequences of prospective matings. In addition to personal consultations, she used the public website that Åke had mentioned. Leading us into a conference room, she illuminated a digital slide projector attached to a computer. She then virtually mated two dogs, both of whom had the recessive gene for the blinding disease progressive retinal atrophy. Their affected progeny – which on average would be one in four pups – were represented by the internationally recognized red STOP sign.

Karin then pointed out that I could choose another dam or sire from the database, one without the recessive PRA gene, and that if I mated this dog to either of the two affected parents, their progeny would be of two sorts: completely clear of the gene or carrying only one copy of it. In either case, these puppies would never be affected by PRA. By selectively breeding in this thoughtful way, a dog's sought-after characteristics – Sam's long and lovely nose, for instance – can be passed down with a greater degree of safety, so long as future breeders have access to this kind of information and avoid mating two dogs who have both been identified as having recessive genes for the same harmful condition.

The Swedish Kennel Club had now gone far beyond creating a virtual mating website, Åke and Karin explained. It had asked the nation's show judges to identify those breeds whose health had been compromised by exaggerated anatomical features. After identifying fifty breeds, they had sent this list to the breed clubs in question for their input on revising these standards.

Was there any proof that these efforts had worked to create healthier dogs? Yes and no. From 1976 to 1988, screening the seven most affected breeds in Sweden for hip dysplasia saved $2 million in veterinary care. But by the end of the 1990s, the data was less encouraging. The Finnish Kennel Club also tied registration to health tests, but this extra decade of statistics showed that improvement in the incidence of hip dysplasia had stalled or been inconsistent. These findings led researchers to theorize that other factors besides a gene for bad hips were contributing to the development of the disease — for instance, selecting for exaggerated anatomical features, as has been the case for the German Shepherd with its low-slung back end.

Åke and Karin also told me that fewer dogs with exaggerated anatomical features were now competing in Swedish dog shows, the operative word being *fewer*. Flat-faced Pekingeses and Bulldogs, as well as Pointers with upturned snouts, were still winning blue ribbons when I checked in 2012. These dogs were allowed to compete because they had passed all the required health certifications for their breed. Yet, as anyone with an eye for a functional dog could see, they still had conformational problems, demonstrating how difficult it is even for a strong kennel club like Sweden's to enforce reasonable breed standards when judges remain swayed by fashion.

Despite the inconsistent performance of mandatory health tests, other Scandinavian kennel clubs have tied registration to health certification. So have some individual breed clubs in Germany, and in 2011 the British Kennel Club took an important step to improve the genetic diversity of purebred dogs: it began to open its stud books to permit unregistered dogs who look like a particular breed to mate with dogs who are already registered in that breed, allowing those breeds with seriously narrowed gene pools to be infused with new blood. It also added a virtual-mating webpage to its website, a "doggie dating service" patterned after the Swedish model.

In the United States, the American Kennel Club has also taken a stab at improving the health of purebred dogs. In 1995 it spun off the AKC Canine Health Foundation, which has contributed $25 million to research grants that have directly resulted in the development of genetic tests that identify canine diseases, and a year later it inaugurated a compliance program through which it inspects breeders who register twenty-five or more litters per year. Some of these operations would fit the legal definition of a puppy mill — "a dog breeding operation in which the health of the dogs is disregarded in order to maintain a low overhead and maximize profits" — and in this regard, the AKC has brought some oversight to what has been a freewheeling business that abuses dogs.

The AKC's compliance program also educates breeders about puppy socialization, genetic health screenings, grooming, exercise, and adherence to breed standards, some of these breed standards being the very ones that are increasingly being called into question by other major kennel clubs. However, the AKC has steadfastly refused to revise such dysfunctional breed standards, claiming that, unlike the Scandinavian and British kennel clubs, it doesn't own them and thus can't alter them to create healthier dogs. In the United States, these standards are supposedly owned by the more than 170 breed clubs affiliated with the AKC. That's the letter of the law according to the American Kennel Club. In practice, the AKC has ignored it.

In 1991 and 1994 the AKC recognized the Australian Shepherd and then the Border Collie as official show breeds, over the objections of both breed clubs. Members of these parent clubs repeatedly told AKC leaders that Aussies and Border Collies had no need for a show-ring standard since they were herding dogs whose most salient quality was performance, not appearance. Their wishes were ignored, and the AKC went so far as to pressure breeders to get its way, telling them that their dogs would be barred from competing in AKC performance events if they continued to resist the creation of a show-ring standard. The reason behind these strong-arm tactics was money — the AKC makes about half its revenues from registrations. Thus, when it suits the club's bottom line, it seems to be more than willing to meddle with breed standards.

The sole North American organization attempting to certify the health of dogs is the Orthopedic Foundation for Animals, which was created in 1966 to combat canine hip dysplasia through X-ray evaluation. During the last half-century, the OFA has expanded its mission to include health certifications for many other canine diseases, and with over a million public records, it's the world's largest canine health database. But a million records are but a tiny fraction of the number of dogs registered in the United States and Canada. Participation in the OFA system is voluntary, just as it is for the AKC's Breeder of Merit Program, and breeders who do participate are under no obligation to reveal abnormal findings.

Calling Eddie Dziuk, the OFA's chief operating officer, I queried him about the limitations built into such a voluntary system, and he readily acknowledged their existence, conceding that some of the European kennel clubs were helping to create healthier dogs by making health certification a mandatory prerequisite of registration. He doubted, however, that such a system could be instituted in the United States. The US organization that had the most reach, the American Kennel Club, wasn't designed to be a registry of health test results, and enforcement would be difficult. More important, he wanted me to appreciate the cultural differences between the United States and Europe.

"Even though I'm a dog breeder," he told me, "and canine health is really important to me, I'm also enough of an American that I don't want some outside regulatory body mandating what I can or cannot do in terms of my breeding decisions. At the end of the day, I want to be the person who bears responsibility."

This is the heart of the matter when it comes to improving the health of dogs in the United States: there is a deep American distrust of regulating the private sector, until it does something egregious, like poisoning the food, water, or air. Then Americans ask government to step in. Today the federal government regulates all three because the private sector has done such a poor job of protecting the public's health. Eventually, a combination of state and federal supervision may do the same for the health of dogs, although kennel and breed clubs that find such oversight repugnant could forestall this eventuality by exploiting a lucrative niche that is waiting to be filled.

The public — and not merely the dog-buying public — knows that there is an inbreeding problem with purebred dogs, just as most of us have noticed the issues of rising gas prices and the increased use of pesticides in foods. The free market hasn't stood idly by. The Toyota Prius and Whole Foods — along with their numerous look-alikes — have been the free market's response. Niche filled.

The British Kennel Club's Accredited Breeder Scheme and the AKC's Breeder of Merit Program are similar attempts at filling a niche — the public's desire for healthier dogs — but both have proved inadequate.

Nor has either kennel club embraced the idea of radical outcrossings: mating two completely different breeds so as to improve the health of one of them — for example, mating Greyhounds, who have excellent hips, with German Shepherds, who have poor ones, to reduce the incidence of hip dysplasia in the latter.

The only kennel club in the English-speaking world that has promoted such radical outcrossings is the United Kennel Club, whose headquarters are in Kalamazoo, Michigan. Serving as a meeting ground for breeders interested in the performance of their dogs, the UKC was founded in 1898 by the dog fancier Chauncey Bennett, who launched the club out of dissatisfaction with shows that emphasized looks over physical fitness. More than a century later, the club still promotes the notion that all dogs, no matter their size, can be physically sound, something I saw firsthand when I attended the club's Premier Event and watched every manner of dog, from terriers to Irish Wolfhounds, coursing after lures, running head to head in races, doing long jumps off of docks, pulling weights, and competing in field trials.

The club's president, Wayne Cavanaugh, a trim man with auburn hair and a Celtic complexion, showed me around the sprawling fairgrounds, and as we went from one venue to another, he said, "You're not going to compete in these events with bad hips or without an airway."

I remarked that he and the Austrian geneticist Hellmuth Wachtel had much in common, an observation with which he readily agreed. Then I asked him why, given his obvious concern for canine health, had he not followed the lead of the Swedish Kennel Club and tied registration to health certification.

He gave a resigned shrug and said, "I'm envious of the Swedish model, but we don't control the dog population the way the Scandinavians do. In America, if you tie health certification to registration, people won't register with your club."

In a small way, he was trying to follow in the Swedes' footsteps. At the urging of the breed clubs that oversaw the Anatolian Shepherd, the Chinook, and the Silken Windhound, he had now tied a variety of health screens and DNA tests to the registration of these three breeds. He remained unconvinced, however, that mandatory health registration alone would solve the challenges facing purebred dogs. He continued to see dogs who had passed all their genetic health screenings yet were functionally crippled. When such dogs won blue ribbons, they went on to become popular sires, seeding their unhealthy genes throughout the breed.

He believed that dog show judging was at the root of the problem. Hoping to change how show judges visualized dogs, he was now traveling around the country, giving seminars where he pointed out the differences between the historic standards of many breeds, which emphasized good biomechanics, and the dysfunctional conformations of dogs who won in today's shows. Attendance once every three years at such judging seminars was now mandatory for all judges who wanted to officiate at a UKC event.

Having crossed the fairgrounds, we came to a quiet grove of trees where Wayne introduced me to Francie Stull, a friendly woman with curly blond hair. A geneticist as well as a dog breeder, she sat in a folding chair, surrounded by several members of the new breed she had created, the Silken Windhound: slim, racy, long-snouted, black-and-white dogs, standing between eighteen and twenty-four inches at the shoulder.

Lying on the grass between them, I listened to Francie recount how during the 1970s she had grown despondent over seeing her Deerhounds die at ten years old. Vowing to produce a longer-lived sighthound, she began to cross Borzois with Whippet-based lurchers in the early 1980s, knowing that she would have to reduce the size of her dogs in order for them to live longer. She was disciplined in her DNA testing, removing dogs with genetically transmitted diseases from her breeding program, and when she formed the International Silken Windhound Society, she insisted that other breeders do the same.

Thirty years later, the results lay around us — calm, friendly, aerodynamic dogs who looked like they could run forever. As of 2012, there were about eight hundred Silken Windhounds in the world, the majority of them only eight to twelve years old, too young to prove anything about Francie Stull's efforts to create a longer-lived sighthound. However, the longevity of her first dogs — some lived into their late teens, and two made it to twenty years old — holds out the promise that their descendants might also have long lives.

Perhaps other kennel club leaders besides Wayne Cavanaugh will support and recognize such carefully done outcrossings as essential for reversing 150 years of unhealthy breeding practices in purebred dogs. These leaders might also recognize the public's desire for healthy dogs as one of the better marketing opportunities that has come along since the invention of purebred dogs themselves. Maybe then we will see German Shepherds with sound back ends, Bulldogs who can breathe, new breeds with longer life spans, and a Pekingese and a Pug — with the longish snouts of their ancestors — running down the homestretch of a fitness test, neck and neck, and grinning with glee.

In 2012 the British Kennel Club took a historic step in this direction. It introduced veterinary checks for "Best of Breed" winners at all its competitions, beginning with its premier event, Crufts, the world's largest and most widely watched dog show. Fifteen high-profile breeds with exaggerated anatomical features were designated by the Kennel Club for health screenings, and six dogs among them — a Basset Hound, Bloodhound, Clumber Spaniel, Mastiff, Bulldog, Neapolitan Mastiff, and Pekingese, all of whom had won "Best of Breed" — failed their screenings and were stripped of their wins by independent veterinarians and not allowed to compete further. It was similar to an athlete having failed a drug test.

Ironically, the Pekingese who was barred from competing further at Crufts had been bred in the very same kennel as the Pekingese who won "Best of Show" at Westminster the month before. In fact, the two dogs looked almost identical, but the British dog was thrown out of the competition and the American one honored as a champion.

Around the world, critics of the purebred dog fancy praised the British Kennel Club for finally taking a stand against canine fashion and overruling judges who awarded form over function. In practical terms, stripping blue ribbons from these six dogs made them less likely to pass on their genes.

Many American breeders watched these developments with horrified disbelief. Within hours they began to unleash a blogstorm of criticism against the British Kennel Club, their anger prompted by a common concern: "Could such disqualifications happen in American dog shows?"

Dennis Sprung, the president of the American Kennel Club, assured American breeders that it would not. From Crufts he wrote: "Our parent clubs own their respective standard and we support them 100 percent. Furthermore, a judge's decision is final and we respect that as well. . . . I will never allow this wrongful practice in America. Never!!!"

In early 2012 the American purebred dog world received yet another surprise. Wayne Cavanaugh announced that the United Kennel Club was revising all its breed standards to prioritize health over appearance, calling the endeavor "our moral duty to the canine world." Changing breed standards to emphasize the function of a dog was not a panacea, he admitted, but it was a beginning, and there was no better place to start than with the crippled German Shepherd. Henceforth, German Shepherds with low-slung back ends and hocks that touched the ground would not be permitted to win awards in UKC shows.

Another blogstorm erupted, some breeders saying that "breed clubs should be responsible to make these change, NOT the UKC!!!," while others replied, "I am beyond thrilled to read this." The majority of the mail supported Cavanaugh, as have dog registrations during the last decade. Since 2000, registrations at the UKC have climbed 10 percent, while those at the AKC have fallen 40 percent. In this corner of the canine world, a new dog has begun to run.

CHAPTER SIX

On a Farm in Minnesota

OVER THE COMING decades, the advances made by progressive breeders and kennel clubs — more widespread genetic testing, revised breed standards, and judging for physical fitness rather than looks — will no doubt improve the health of purebred dogs. Yet none of these developments will eliminate the need for a dog buyer to investigate breeders personally. Who, after all, buys a car just because it has air bags and seat belts? Virtually all of us do more research and eventually test-drive a few cars ourselves. This is exactly what I now did as I continued my search for a new dog.

I looked at the websites of Labrador breeders, found photos of dogs I liked, downloaded their pedigrees from a variety of online data banks, and then telephoned the breeders, asking them a long list of questions: What can you tell me about the health of your dogs' ancestors? Who bred Charger and Bonnie, and how can I get in touch with them? What did grandparents Ace and Mattie die of, and how old were they? What kind of socialization do you give your pups? What do you feed them? Do you vaccinate them before they leave for their new homes? What sort of temperament and personalities do your parent dogs have (temperament being what a dog is born with and personality being the result of how that temperament is modified by socialization)? If the breeders had not posted their dogs' health certifications on their websites, I asked if these tests had been done, and if they had not, I scratched these dogs from my list.

Then I went for "test-drives." I found kennels that were run like fine country inns, a few that were people's homes, and one that evoked images of a concentration camp, the skeletal dogs stacked in crates, the stench of urine and feces burning my nose. On this kennel's website I had seen photos of beautiful dogs in gorgeous rural settings, and seeing the facility in person reminded me of the advice that every kennel club gives to potential puppy buyers: do not buy a pup unless you've visited the place where it was bred. This remains good advice even as radiographic screenings and DNA tests become more the norm, for these tests – done on parent dogs – can give a false sense of security. Such tests say nothing about a puppy's temperament, nor are they necessarily indicative of a puppy's biomechanics; moreover, they won't reveal a thing about its first weeks of socialization. Interacting with the parents of your prospective puppy as well as its breeder can tell you more about what sort of dog you're going to live with.

During my travels I met breeders who used additional tools to improve the chances that their puppies were healthy. Rhonda Hovan, a longtime breeder of Golden Retrievers in Akron, Ohio, told me about one of her favorites: the vertical pedigree. Unlike traditional horizontal pedigrees, which show the most recently born dog on the left and its ancestors stretching away to the right, vertical pedigrees stretch up and down and include a dog's extended family: not only the parents of the dogs in question but also its siblings, aunts, uncles, and cousins, as well as the siblings of these relations. Such an in-depth look at a dog's ancestry gives a breeder, and a dog buyer, a much better idea of whether good hips, for instance, are really prevalent in a family or might only be appearing in a dog's immediate forebears. If comprehensive records have been kept, one can also see how long a dog's relations have lived and whether certain diseases run in an extended family.

Debby Kay, a Labrador breeder from Harpers Ferry, West Virginia, and the author of *The Labrador Breeders Handbook*, was also a breeder who carefully screened her breeding stock by looking for dogs who had had long-lived ancestors. She then augmented their good genetics by feeding them organic meats and vegetables that she seasonally rotated. In addition, she pointed out to me a frequently overlooked aspect of canine longevity – a dog's emotional environment. She believed that dogs, being great empaths, collect their people's positive and negative energy. Even if a dog received excellent nutrition and exercise, its health might suffer, she explained, if its person was angry, pessimistic, or depressed.

Debby had been employing these longevity-promoting techniques, including minimal vaccinations, in her breeding program for the last thirty years, and her results were impressive. The average age at death of the ten Labrador Retrievers who had remained under her care since 1976 was 15.02 years, three years longer than the average life span for the breed. Four of her dogs had lived to over sixteen — dying when they were 17.7, 17.9, 18.2, and 18.7 years old — a remarkable achievement.

Had Debby been breeding the type of houndy Lab for whom I was looking, I would have been standing in line for one of her puppies. But since she wasn't, she pointed me to the website of Holzinger Kennels in Prior Lake, Minnesota, where I found photographs of rangy dogs, with complete health certifications. One of them, Cash, had Merle's looks and color and flair and had recently sired several litters in the southern part of the state.

And so, in this roundabout way, I found myself driving through Minnesota one bleak February morning, the thermometer pegged at ten below zero. I visited one of Cash's litters outside the Twin Cities, but his seven pups had already been weaned and their mother moved away. Discouraged not to have met her, and also by the fact that none of the pups had their father's rufous coat, I continued south a few more hours, finally pulling into a farmyard outside the hamlet of Essig. A two-story, yellow clapboard house stood in a grove of trees, with a long, low shop opposite it. Snowy fields — corn stubble and windblown furrows — stretched away into misty gray clouds.

Walking to the door of the shop, where the breeder had asked me to meet him, I knocked. Through the glass I could see a big reddish Lab uncurl himself from the floor where he had been sleeping. He strolled to the door, stared up at me through the window, and gave his tail a swish: "Hi."

I opened the door and called, "Anyone home," while the big reddish dog, who looked uncannily like Merle, calmly pressed his head against my left thigh and gave me a warm greeting. Another large dog — a pale yellow Lab — got off his rug in the corner, padded over to me, and put his head against my right leg, wagging his tail in the same polite way as had his friend.

"Just went over to the house." A deep pleasant voice, full of Minnesota lilt, sounded behind me.

I turned around and saw a big man — big as a professional football player — filling the door with the same welcoming good cheer his dogs had given me. He wore a sweatshirt, jeans, and a blue ball cap, and

shaking my hand warmly, he said, "Doug Radloff. And this is Casey."
He nodded to the reddish Lab. "And Jake." The yellow one. Four and
fourteen years old.

Jake hardly looked fourteen years old, and when I remarked upon
it, Doug told me that many of his dogs lived into their teens, and that
one of them, Trapper, had lived to seventeen and died in the yard,
where she liked to sleep with the cats on top of her. He tossed his head
to indicate the snowy drive between the yellow clapboard house and
the shop. "I found her there one morning, passed away on her own,
with the cats still sleeping on top of her."

Beyond the drive, the winter fields stretched away into the clouds,
a windbreak of trees on the horizon like a faint line of ghosts. I kept
my hands on the ruffs of the two dogs as Doug spoke. There was a
quiet unhurried freedom about the place, the dogs unkenneled and
unfenced – a freedom I had rarely seen in the facilities of other dog
breeders – and it reminded me of home.

"But I guess you came to see Abby," he said.

We walked through a door into his taxidermy shop, followed by Casey, while Jake went back to his rug. Deer and bear skins lined the
walls, and here and there hand tools and fiberglass animal forms lay
scattered on long wooden workbenches. A large particle-board whelping box had been placed in the back corner of the shop, with a rug
pulled aside from the cutout door. In it sat a russet Labrador Retriever,
her head attentively cocked to our approach. I stopped in midstride.
She could have been Merle's sister. In fact, she was Casey's.

When I approached, she came out of the whelping box and gave me
the same warm greeting Casey had, laying her head against my knee
and wagging her tail gently. I put my hand on her cheek, and after a
few moments, she turned and walked back to her whelping box and
looked in. Then she gazed up at me pointedly, her shining eyes saying,
"Pretty good, eh?"

"It is," I told her, kneeling and admiring her eleven puppies. Abby
watched with a soft smile as I picked up one of her little balls of reddish-gold fur and held the tiny puppy to my chest. Casey came over to
me and stood by my side, giving his tail an appreciative swish, clearly
pleased with everything that was going on.

I had met so many dogs during my travels – dogs who were too
aloof, too effusive, too small, too large, too just not my kind of dog, and
who had ranged from the half-crazed to the wonderfully mannered.

None of them seemed to have quite the attributes of the dog whom I had known. Yet here on this Minnesota farm — as far from the desert of Utah where I had met Merle as I could imagine — were two dogs who seemed calm and conversational, their golden fur like a talisman under my hands. We have all known this moment — when we are drawn to a person or a dog and connect with them just like that. I would have taken Casey or Abby home in a heartbeat.

It was a while before I could turn around and ask Doug, "How come your dogs are so mellow?"

Pushing back his ball cap, he shrugged and said, "I spend a lot of time with them. On day one — the very first day of their lives — I take them for a ride in the truck, to the vet's, for their first checkup. Then I take them on errands with me, and they're free to come and go as they want." He gave a nod toward the door. "They know where the road is, and they don't go there. A lot of people come into the shop every day, and I have two kids as well, four years old and nine, and they're in here all the time, too, right in the whelping box."

I placed the pup back on the rug next to his brothers and sisters, and Abby stepped through the door, lay down, and nursed.

Doug and I walked to his desk. He pulled out a chair for me, and Casey settled himself at my feet, staying there for the better part of two hours, as I asked questions and Doug answered them.

He told me that his dogs were great athletes, but calm in the house. He believed that it was part of their hereditary line. Casey and Abby's father, Drake, was very laid-back and a great family dog, even though he had been the 2004 National Field Trial Champion. Their mother, Minni, was also sweet-tempered. But heredity alone couldn't make puppies into well-socialized dogs. It was how they were raised as puppies. "By the time my puppies are seven weeks old," he concluded, "they've been handled every day, met dozens of people and children, heard all sorts of noises, and met other dogs."

I was happy to hear this. Studies done since the 1970s have shown that puppies handled from infancy are better learners, better socialized, and perhaps healthier than those who are not. As for his dogs' diet, Doug fed them NutriSource chicken-and-rice. "Made right here in Minnesota," he said proudly, sounding like Garrison Keillor, "so you know it's fresh." He showed me Abby's health certifications. She had normal elbows and hips; she was clear for progressive retinal atrophy; and he considered her clear for centronuclear myopathy "by parentage" — in other words, both her parents were clear, but she in fact had not yet been tested. This was a potential red flag, since parentage in dogs, as in humans, is not always verifiable without a DNA test. However, since Cash had been tested for CNM and he was clear, none of his and Abby's puppies could actually be affected with the muscle-wasting disease, and I was willing to go on listening.

Doug also told me that in his kennel he had never had a case of coccidia — puppyhood diarrhea caused by a protozoan that can live in the mother's feces. He washed out the whelping box and changed the rugs in it twice a day, first thing in the morning and last thing at night. Once the last pup had gone off with its new family, he burned the whelping box to make sure that the next litter would start fresh.

The afternoon wore on; the daylight faded; on we talked. I had met other breeders who had done as much homework as Doug, but their style of dog hadn't appealed to me as much as those I was now seeing. Unfortunately, none of these pups could be mine. Just before I had left on this scouting expedition, my publisher had asked me to go on a second book tour for *Merle's Door*. I'd be on the road when these puppies were ready to go to their new homes.

When I mentioned this to Doug, he suggested an alternative. He was going to mate Casey to a nearby rufous Lab named Lizzie, and I could look at their litter in the fall. If none of their pups were suitable, I could take a look at Abby and Cash's next litter. He was planning on mating them again the following winter.

It seemed like a very long time to wait, but before meeting Merle I had spent a year and a half looking for a dog. Glancing up, I saw Casey and Abby watching me. It would be wonderful to have a pup from either one of them. It would be like having bits of Merle back in my life. What was another six to twelve months of waiting, when I might be spending ten to fifteen years with my new dog?

"Let's see what happens," I said to Doug. "For the time being, I'll wait."

He beamed. "We'll keep in touch then," he answered. "We'll keep in touch."

We stood and grasped hands. I walked to the back of the shop, where I gave Abby a long pet while gazing at her puppies. Casey and Jake followed me to the door, and I stood a moment with a hand on each of their ruffs before driving off into the snow.

Doug and I had talked much longer than I expected, and it had grown late. The roads were snowy, and dinner and old friends were waiting in Minneapolis. Just a few hours away, though, in the little town of Eyota, lived Cash, who next year might be contributing half of my new pup's genetic legacy. I hesitated at the highway junction. At this point, Cash was no more than some attractive photos, the glowing recommendations of Doug and Terry Holzinger, and a clean bill of health. What of the dog himself?

I turned east and well past dinnertime found Cash in the finished basement of a suburban home where he lived with his family and his number-one person, a slim, athletic-looking man named Rob Ramer, with whom he traveled around the country, competing in field trials.

Cash had a reddish-gold coat, a Merlish face, and not one ounce of Merle's, Casey's, or Abby's calmness. He greeted me with tornado-like exuberance, twirling in my arms before sprinting off to lap the room — again and again. He was A.J. raised to the second power, and I could see one reason he had such a string of championships beneath his name: he was a force; he had the energy for his high-performance job; and his son, Chase, whom Rob let out of another crate, was even more wired.

Their over-the-top exuberance worried me. I had been around enough highly athletic Labs to know that they could also be well mannered in the house, and I wondered what such unbridled energy and Abby's collected nature would produce in the way of puppies. All of a sudden I had doubts about Cash being the father of my new pup — I wasn't interested in living with a super-hot field-trial dog.

Driving off into the night, I decided to mull things over while I continued to investigate the other factors that influence canine longevity. And, as it turned out, the dogs themselves decided who my new puppy would be.

CHAPTER SEVEN

Duration of Immunity

W HEN MERLE WAS ALIVE, I took him to the vet at least
once a year, reminded of his annual visit by a postcard.
His vets looked into his eyes, ears, and mouth, listened to
his heart and stomach, palpated his gut, declared him sound, and then
gave him his shots. I never bothered to keep track of how many vaccinations he actually got. His veterinarians recommended them, and I
followed their advice.

Much later, after Merle had passed away and I was looking through
his medical records, I counted the number of vaccinations he had received and was startled to discover that he had gotten ninety of them
between his arrival in Kelly and his twelfth year. Seven of them were
given annually: distemper, hepatitis, leptospirosis, parvovirus, and
parainfluenza (in a multivaccine cocktail called DHLPP); there were
also bordetella and coronavirus, to prevent two forms of kennel cough;
and every second year he got a rabies shot. Such a vaccination schedule
is hardly a thing of the past. To this day millions of dogs continue to be
vaccinated almost exactly as Merle was.

To be fair to Merle's vets, far less was known about the adverse effects of vaccinations in the early 1990s than has come to be appreci-
ated in the following two decades. Merle's vets, like thousands of others — then and now — were following long-established protocols and
believed that vaccines were benign. One of Merle's vets did not. In
Merle's twelfth year, his holistic veterinarian, Marybeth Minter, suggested that I ignore the advice of his other vets and stop vaccinating
him.

She noted that the duration of immunity for some of the vaccines
he had been receiving for life-threatening diseases, such as distemper

and parvovirus, was known to be in excess of a year and was perhaps even lifelong. Undoubtedly, Merle had achieved armor-plated immunity to parvo and distemper — he didn't need any more shots to protect him. As for his two yearly kennel cough vaccinations, she asked me if I ever boarded Merle in a facility with a large number of dogs, where canine respiratory diseases flourished, or did I take him to dog shows? My answer was no. Why then, asked Marybeth, should he receive two kennel cough vaccinations annually? Not only was it a waste of money, but I should also consider that this extravagant load of vaccines might be causing his itchy skin as well as overly challenging his immune system to the point that he had been unable to fend off a louse attack and now needed an anti-louse shampoo.

What she said made sense to me. After all, humans aren't vaccinated every single year. We get childhood vaccinations and are subsequently protected into young adulthood. We also receive far fewer vaccines than do dogs, approximately thirty-five vaccinations by the time we're twelve years old. Once we've been given our childhood vaccines, we're vaccinated only if we're exposed to certain diseases during travel.

In this vein, I took a closer look at Merle's exposure to leptospirosis, a disease that is caused by a spiral-shaped bacterium carried in the urine of rats, mice, and many species of wildlife, including deer. The disease attacks the kidneys and liver and causes vomiting, fever, and thirst. If leptospirosis sounds serious, it is. It can kill a dog — or a person for that matter — and Merle received twelve inoculations for it during his lifetime. Yet Merle's risk for contracting leptospirosis was extremely low, as it's a disease that typically occurs in mild and tropical climates, in warm wet regions, and in places where it rarely freezes. This is hardly the description of Jackson Hole, Wyoming. Why then did Merle need a vaccine for a bacterium that was unlikely to survive where we lived?

I not only stopped inoculating him against leptospirosis. I stopped his other vaccinations as well. Fortunately, I didn't have to face any legal consequences for not giving him another rabies shot, which is periodically mandated for all dogs in the United States. When Merle passed away at fourteen, his last rabies vaccine was still current.

Marybeth Minter wasn't alone in having noticed that some dogs exhibit a downturn in health and a variety of skin, joint, and autoimmune complaints after being vaccinated. Starting in the late 1980s, other veterinarians began to note these same adverse reactions, and one issue of the *International Vaccination Newsletter* published a selection of their comments online. "The most common problems I see that are directly related to vaccines on a day to day basis," wrote Dr. Pat Bradley, "are ear or skin conditions, such as chronic discharges and itching." Another contributor, Dr. Pedro Rivera, added that in his practice he saw hypothyroidism, joint problems, and chronic yeast and ear infections. And a third veterinarian, Dr. Nancy Scanlon, summed up the experience of many other DVMs when she wrote, "Every veterinarian who has been in practice long enough has seen reactions to vaccines, ranging from lethargy, mild fever, sore neck to vomiting and sleeping for 24 hours, to total collapse and shock."

These reports were anecdotal, of course, and despite the pithy remark of the Nobel Prize–winning ethologist Nikolaas Tinbergen – "many anecdotes make a statistic" – countless veterinarians remained skeptical that vaccinations could be negatively affecting the health of their patients. That attitude began to change in 1987 when Pennsylvania required that all cats be vaccinated against rabies. Within a short time vets began to notice sarcomas growing directly at the site where the vaccine had been injected. These cancers were extremely aggressive, and the likelihood of a tumor developing at the injection site increased with the number of vaccines that were given simultaneously at that location. Some studies found as many as ten cats per ten thousand developing injection-site sarcomas. These were no longer mere anecdotes, and in response to this unassailable evidence, some veterinarians began to vaccinate cats in a rear leg instead of at the nape of the neck so that the leg could be amputated if the cat developed an aggressive sarcoma.

Soon veterinarians also began to see dogs developing cancers at the site of their vaccinations, though the number of dogs affected has remained small compared to the number of afflicted cats. In addition, researchers have seen cancers forming around microchips in hundreds of laboratory mice and rats, leading them to suggest that some of the components in the vaccine, or the wound itself – the prick of a needle or the insertion of the microchip – leads to inflammation, and the inflammation then triggers changes in the DNA of genetically susceptible individuals, initiating the growth of tumors.

Nor are injection-site cancers the only serious diseases that vaccinations seem to cause. During the 1990s, researchers from Purdue

University and the University of Pennsylvania followed up on veterinarians' reports of autoimmune diseases occurring on the heels of vaccination. Using dogs of different ages and breeds, these scientists found a postvaccination increase in immune-mediated hemolytic anemia, a disease that results in the destruction of red blood cells. In addition, there were ever more reports of adverse reactions to the rabies vaccine, everything from muscular atrophy to autoimmune diseases to seizures, the fatality rate of these adverse reactions higher than those associated with other vaccines.

In response, vaccine manufacturers have asked veterinarians and the public to report all adverse reactions to the Center for Veterinary Biologics at the US Department of Agriculture. But what does "adverse" really mean? A dog who goes into anaphylactic shock a moment after being injected has apparently had a very bad reaction, but has the dog who becomes stiff and lame a month after receiving a vaccination also had an adverse reaction?

Trying to assign cause and effect in such cases can be tricky, as this real-life incident, reported by a physician, points out. Meeting with their pediatrician, a mother and father were discussing the pros and cons of a vaccine for their baby. Unsure about what to do, the parents continued to hem and haw, asking more questions about the vaccine's side effects, and in the fifteen minutes they were talking with their doctor their baby had a seizure. Now, had their baby gotten its vaccination, it's likely that the parents, and possibly the doctor, would have been forever convinced that the vaccination caused the seizure. In other words, correlation doesn't imply causation — just because B happens after A doesn't necessarily mean that A caused it.

For this reason, many veterinarians have been circumspect about reporting adverse reactions to manufacturers and the USDA's Center for Veterinary Biologics, and the scarcity of the data reflects that. Between 1999 and 2005, the CVB received only 5,740 reports of adverse reactions for dogs, cats, and ferrets, while hundreds of millions of them were being vaccinated. This means that either vaccines are very safe or many adverse reactions are going unreported.

In the early 2000s, someone finally decided to take a run at the growing number of statistics that had accumulated in another location, veterinary data banks, to see if there was a pattern to what were being called "vaccine-associated adverse events." Dr. George Moore and his colleagues at Purdue University and Banfield Pet Hospital looked at the medical records of 1.2 million dogs who had received 3.4 million vaccine doses between 2002 and 2004. They uncovered four very important facts: smaller dogs, weighing under twenty-two pounds, had twice the number of adverse reactions to vaccines — swelling on the face, welts, severe itching, vomiting, and soreness — as larger dogs; neutered dogs had a much higher risk of having an adverse reaction to vaccines than dogs who were sexually intact; the risk of an adverse reaction increased with the number of shots administered in a single visit to the veterinarian; and dogs who were one to three years old had the greatest risk of all.

The researchers theorized that it was the antigen and adjuvants in the vaccines that might be causing these adverse reactions. This was not a new observation. Antigens — modified viruses, for example — are the operative substances in vaccines that create an immune response in the body and are responsible for the production of antibodies against a disease. Tenth-century Chinese physicians may have been the first to note that sometimes the use of antigens backfires: occasionally some of the healthy people they inoculated with the discharge of smallpox pustules died. Learning from these experiences, Chinese doctors dried the scabs of smallpox victims, and also used the scabs of people who had survived their inoculations, to create weakened and safer forms of antigens. Today the antigens in the canine parvovirus, distemper, and adenovirus vaccines are similarly attenuated so as not to kill the dogs who receive them.

Adjuvants, on the other hand, are substances added to a vaccine to make the antigen more powerful. They provide a signal to the immune system to initiate a stronger response than the antigen might create on its own. The man responsible for pioneering the use of adjuvants was the French biologist and veterinarian Gaston Ramon, who in the early 1920s observed that horses who developed abscesses at the site of their vaccinations produced more antibodies than those horses who did not. He theorized that if a similar response could be artificially induced, vaccination would be more effective. Tapioca, agar, lecithin, and saponin were employed to this purpose, all of them soon overshadowed by aluminum, which became one of the most effective and frequently used adjuvants in vaccines despite emerging evidence that ingesting too much aluminum could cause a range of ill effects in both mice and people, especially children, including reduced muscular strength, anemia, and bone disease.

Why, though, did some dogs and cats sail through their yearly vaccinations without blinking an eye and others became ill? Researchers came up with a partial answer when they discovered a genetic susceptibility to vaccine-induced sarcomas in certain cats, irrespective of whether the vaccine contained an aluminum adjuvant, a non-aluminum one, or no adjuvant at all. It was also seen that dogs who developed hemolytic anemia after being vaccinated had a genetic predisposition not to tolerate the cocktail of antigens and adjuvants, whereas those who remained unaffected lacked this suite of genes.

Even with a substantial amount of evidence showing that adverse reactions to vaccines occur in genetically susceptible dogs, many veterinarians have remained wedded to the practice of annual vaccinations for three very good reasons. The first is that the benefits of vaccinations outweigh their costs. Vaccines save lives directly, as they protect vaccinated dogs from deadly diseases such as rabies, parvo, and distemper. Widespread vaccination also saves lives indirectly, for even if some dogs remain unvaccinated, they live among dogs who have herd immunity. Herd immunity is conferred when enough individuals in a population are vaccinated, making it less likely that an unprotected dog or person will come in contact with an infected one.

As Dr. Marian Horzinek of the veterinary faculty at Utrecht University in the Netherlands has noted, "Vaccination is the most successful medical and veterinary measure: More lives have been saved by immunization, more animal production safeguarded than through all other medical and veterinary activities combined."

Anyone who doubts the truth of Dr. Horzinek's contention should consider that in the developing world a little over three million children die every year from infectious diseases such as diphtheria, measles, mumps, polio, and whooping cough, which have been eliminated by routine vaccination in developed nations during the last century. This astonishing achievement has become such an ordinary part of our lives that few of us give a second thought to the fact that we no longer have to bear three children so that two of them will survive to adulthood.

A similar phenomenon has occurred with dogs. Before vaccines for rabies and distemper were developed, seeing dogs dying by the side of the road from these infections was an unremarkable part of daily life. Only recently has the toll from these diseases been markedly reduced.

Louis Pasteur began to vaccinate people bitten by rabid dogs in 1885, Japan started to vaccinate the dogs themselves in 1919, and the United States did the same in 1922. In 1947 the United States mounted a public education campaign about the disease and the need to vaccinate all canines. Free or low-cost vaccination clinics were set up throughout cities, educational materials were handed out in schools, and eventually universal rabies vaccination for owned dogs became required by law. This campaign has been enormously successful. In 1947, 6,949 rabid dogs were reported in the United States; in 2006, there were 71.

Western Europe has had even more success in eliminating rabies: many of its countries are now completely free of the disease because the major vector species, the red fox, was vaccinated by dropping vaccine-laced baits from airplanes. As a result, dogs are no longer required to have a rabies vaccination in many western European nations. Scandinavia, Iceland, Australia, New Zealand, Japan, Malaysia, and Papua New Guinea are now also free of rabies except in bats.

Similarly dramatic reductions in mortality occurred with canine distemper beginning in the 1950s, and with canine parvovirus in the early 1980s, the latter disease having only first appeared in the world's dog population in 1974. Today few of us will ever see a dog suffering from rabies, distemper, or parvo unless we work in a shelter or in the veterinary field. This, then, is the major reason that countless veterinarians counsel their clients to continue vaccinating their dogs.

In addition, veterinarians promote the notion of annual vaccination because it provides an easy way to encourage clients to bring in their dogs for a yearly wellness check during which a dog's health can be monitored and potentially harmful conditions diagnosed and treated. Last, and certainly not least, veterinarians continue to give annual shots because they make a lot of money from them.

As one veterinarian in a rural western town told me, he marks up his vaccines between 100 and 150 percent. Another veterinarian told me that in the North American clinics in which she had worked, rabies vaccines were bought for between $1 and $2 and administered for between $10 and $20, exclusive of the accompanying exam. Still a third veterinarian, this one in Rome, Italy, confided to me that it was standard practice to buy a vaccine for three euros and charge thirty for its administration. One clinic in New York City told me that a rabies vaccination for my dog would cost $43. A few minutes after speaking with the clinic, I found the same rabies vaccine online at Wholesale

Kennel Supply for $1.39. In short, the clinic was marking up its rabies vaccine 3,100 percent.

Obviously, the practice of annual vaccination has become a cash cow for some veterinarians, and I had to wonder how the practice became so entrenched. Did a veterinarian once upon a time say, "Let's vaccinate dogs every year and make lots of money"? Not initially.

The American Animal Hospital Association points to one influential veterinarian who started the convention: Dr. James Baker, the director of Cornell University's Veterinary Virus Research Institute during the 1950s. But the AAHA report was secondhand, and I wondered if Baker himself—the éminence grise of the mid-twentieth-century veterinary world and the head of the team that developed the first vaccine against canine infectious hepatitis—might have said something more nuanced. In fact, he did.

After much searching through Cornell's archives, I found his original October 1959 "Message from the Director," a letter published in *The Institute Report,* which contained his official recommendations about vaccinating dogs. Baker observed that about one-third of all puppies who had been vaccinated and achieved immunity subsequently lost that immunity within twelve months. Their immunity was determined by a blood test that measured antibodies and was called a "titer."

Baker went on to suggest that "two procedures are possible to help prevent disease." The first was to titer dogs every year so as "to check their level of immunity." Those who had lost their immunity could be revaccinated. "Or," as Baker went on to write, "an alternate procedure would be to vaccinate all dogs annually." Because some dogs were known to lose their immunity two years out from their puppy vaccinations, Baker then made a suggestion that would have profound implications for hundreds of millions of dogs in the coming decades: "To insure continued protection, annual vaccinations of all dogs is recommended as a routine safety measure."

Dr. James Baker and Cornell University were enormously respected. They were Moses and the mountaintop. Veterinarians latched on to Baker's recommendation to vaccinate dogs annually and forgot that he had also suggested a viable alternative to yearly shots: titering to see if immunity has been achieved after one round of vaccination. Of course, in the 1950s veterinarians thought vaccinations were relatively harmless, and they also believed that clients wouldn't want to pay for a titer and then also pay for a second booster shot if the dog was found to be unprotected. Since the true duration of immunity for these vaccines was not then known, it appeared to be far cheaper to give all dogs shots every year.

Thus, the principle of annual vaccination became enshrined – medically and fiscally – and yearly vaccinations now contribute a significant amount to some veterinarians' incomes as well as to the bottom line of the pharmaceutical companies that manufacture canine vaccines.

Fifteen years had to go by before researchers understood that the duration of immunity for vaccines was considerably longer than anyone had imagined. It wasn't until the late 1990s and early 2000s that actual challenge tests (vaccinating dogs and then waiting years to infect them with the disease against which they had been immunized), as well as estimates from blood titers, verified the substantial duration of immunity provided by the four primary canine vaccines, which have become known as the "core vaccines." The DOI for the distemper vaccine was found to be nine to fifteen years, depending on the strain. For the parvovirus vaccine, the DOI was seven years; for adenovirus-2, it was seven to nine years, and for rabies seven years.

The man behind much of this research was Dr. Ronald Schultz, one of the world's preeminent immunologists and the chair of the University of Wisconsin–Madison's Department of Pathobiological Sciences. During the 1970s, when he was working at Cornell University, he noticed that those dogs who had been vaccinated for distemper or who had recovered from a distemper infection could be "drowned," as he told me, in a vat of distemper virus but could not be reinfected. "The dog would die of drowning," he repeated, his blue eyes twinkling, "but it could not get distemper."

We were sitting in his book-lined conference room; it was a warm July day in Madison; and Ron's neat, snowy-white beard, his equally white and bushy eyebrows, and his shining bald crown looked sun-kissed and aglow, as if he had been spending long hours outside. It was a good guess. He had been on his sixty-acre farm, restoring himself with his livestock, two black Labs, a Blue Heeler, and an assortment of Beagles and Pugs. "You can take the boy away from the farm," he told me, smiling broadly, "but you can't take the farm out of the boy."

Trying to drown dogs in distemper virus – at least figuratively – gave Ron Schultz the notion that the duration of immunity for the distemper vaccine was far longer than anyone had previously suspected, a fact that he also discovered about the adenovirus-1 vaccine then in use. His years at Cornell also revealed that vaccinating a dog who was already protected by a vaccine didn't increase its antibodies against the disease in question, as many veterinarians then believed and still do. On the contrary, the dog could become sensitized to some of the vaccine components – for instance, the fetal bovine serum on which the vaccine was cultured – and then have an adverse reaction.

By the turn of the millennium, Ron's three-decade-long campaign to reduce vaccinations, along with the hard evidence from challenge tests, led the American Veterinary Medical Association to issue a report noting that there was increasing evidence that some vaccines provide immunity beyond one year and that unnecessarily stimulating the immune system through repeated vaccination doesn't result in enhanced resistance to disease but in fact can expose dogs to unnecessary risks. In 2006 the American Animal Hospital Association's Canine Vaccine Task Force went even further, rescinding James Baker's advice and the tradition of annual vaccination. It recommended that veterinarians give the core vaccines no more frequently than once every three years, a sea change from what was in place.

Nonetheless, Ron Schultz believes that a triennial vaccination protocol is still excessive, since it doesn't increase immunity while exposing dogs to vaccine components with inherent risks. The least risky among the core vaccines, he now explained, were the modified live vaccines such as those for distemper, parvovirus, and adenovirus-2. These vaccines contained the live virus itself, attenuated so that it couldn't cause clinical disease. Such vaccines therefore didn't need an adjuvant.

The rabies vaccine had also once been a modified live virus vaccine, but in the late 1970s some severely immunocompromised cats in California developed rabies subsequent to being vaccinated. To prevent this happening again, and to reduce the risk of a vaccinated but suddenly rabid cat biting people with potentially fatal results, a killed-rabies vaccine was developed. However, as the virus was now killed, it had to be potentiated with an adjuvant to cause an immune response. That adjuvant was aluminum, and the adjuvanted rabies vaccine continues to cause noticeably more reactions than its non-adjuvanted counterparts.

Ron therefore felt it important to help prove that the rabies vaccine's duration of immunity was longer than currently accepted. If a longer DOI could be proved, dogs could forgo being vaccinated every three years, as is legally required in the United States. Some municipalities even require dogs to be vaccinated against rabies every single year. To accomplish this end, he and his longtime colleague, the immunologist and hematologist Dr. Jean Dodds, were now overseeing the Rabies Challenge Fund, designed to determine whether the duration of immunity for the canine rabies vaccine is in fact five to seven years, as French research and titers from Ron's own work have shown.

Jean Dodds supervises the project from Santa Monica, California, where she runs Hemolife, a laboratory she founded that provides sophisticated blood, endocrine, and immunological diagnoses for pets, including titer tests. Ron Schultz has also volunteered his time to conduct the research at the University of Wisconsin's School of Veterinary Medicine, which has donated the facility and covers operating expenses.

Two groups of Beagles are being kept at the vet school, one group having received a rabies vaccine, one not. In 2012, and then again in 2014, the two groups will be "challenged" — infected with rabies — and though the members of the group that has not received a vaccine will almost certainly die, the ones in the vaccinated group should, according to the best available evidence, live, proving to the satisfaction of the USDA — the licensing agency for canine vaccines — that dogs can be vaccinated for rabies only once every five years, and, if the 2014 group remains protected, once every seven years. If successful, Ron and Jean's experiment should fundamentally alter the health of US dogs for the better. No veterinarian or municipality will then be able to recommend or require that dogs be vaccinated against rabies more frequently than every seven years.

Given that the duration of immunity for the other three core vaccines — parvo, distemper, and adenovirus-2 — has been shown to be in excess of seven years, but the Canine Vaccine Task Force recommends that they be given every three years, I wondered if Ron might be able to advise people on how to safely vaccinate their dogs, reducing the likelihood of adverse reactions while also giving them adequate protection.

"If you vaccinate at sixteen to eighteen weeks of age with distemper, parvo, and adenovirus," he told me, "then titer the dog three to four weeks later and demonstrate that you have antibodies to these diseases, I would feel very good about those vaccines having worked. A very high percentage of these dogs will then be immune for life."

Once puppies passed into adulthood, Ron went on, he would advise people to titer their dogs every three years, and if they saw a dog's titers fall off, it would be wise to revaccinate it. "This is exactly what I've done with my own dogs since 1974," he added. "Once they receive an immunizing dose of parvo, distemper, and adenovirus-2, I never vaccinate them again for the rest of their lives." He added that of course his dogs received their rabies shots on the mandated, three-year schedule, beginning when they were puppies of twelve to sixteen weeks old, and that they would continue to do so until the Rabies Challenge Fund proved otherwise.

Ron did want me to appreciate that dogs with severely depressed immune systems, such as those suffering from an autoimmune disease or cancer, could still have an adverse reaction when given the non-adjuvanted parvo, distemper, and adenovirus-2 vaccines. Even though these vaccines were the safest currently available, an immunocompromised dog could react to the fetal bovine serum in which they are grown. Such immunocompromised dogs should not be inoculated.

I had recently visited with Jean Dodds, a no-nonsense woman with blond hair and resolute brown eyes, and she had largely agreed with Ron's recommendations for minimally vaccinating dogs (see the notes for her recommendations). However, she had disagreed with him on two important issues. The first was the need to vaccinate dogs against adenovirus-2. As she told me, adenovirus-2 was not present in the United States. Why then should we vaccinate for it? She also believed that small dogs — those weighing less than twelve pounds — should get half the normal dose of vaccine given to larger dogs. I now broached these subjects with Ron, starting with adenovirus.

Touching his index fingers together and settling back in his chair with a warm smile, as if embarking on a very fond subject, he said, "Adeno is really two different viruses, and two different diseases." Adenovirus-1 produced fever and congestion and was also known as infectious canine hepatitis, while adenovirus-2 caused a variety of respiratory infections. The vaccine for adeno-2 protected against both.

Inclining his head soberly, Ron added, "Adeno-1 is on our southern border. We've got it on our northern border as well — the wild canids of Canada — and foxes die in the wild from infectious canine hepatitis. If we were to stop vaccinating and got a population of dogs that was susceptible, it could come into the United States without any trouble at all." This was no small concern, as adenovirus caused about a 25 percent puppy mortality, and in adults it could be very severe, about 10 percent of the dogs who contracted the disease dying from it. "That's why I think we should continue to use the adeno-2 vaccine in the core," he concluded, "even though Jean doesn't."

"What about small dogs?" I asked. "Jean claims that a Chihuahua should get far less vaccine than a Saint Bernard because a small dog has fewer receptor cells."

Over the previous few months, I had interviewed veterinarians who employed this practice, either splitting the dose for smaller dogs or giving what they called a "tickler" dose of rabies vaccine — just a tiny bit when a dog, no matter its size, needed its rabies certification revalidated. Such veterinarians believe that the rabies vaccine did in fact have a much longer duration of immunity than three years, but felt legally obligated to inject a bit of the vaccine so as to sign off on the paperwork with a clear conscience.

Ron's blue eyes lit up as I mentioned such dose splitting. "You cannot determine receptors — the number of cells that are capable of being infected — based on the size of the animal," he said unequivocally. "You cannot. There are some Saint Bernards, for example, that need only a tenth of a dose, and there are some Chihuahuas that would need the same tenth of a dose. But no one knows which dogs these are, and so we try to give everyone the minimum immunizing dose for the species — not for the Saint Bernard, not for the Chihuahua, not for the teacup Poodle, but for the species."

Pausing, he held out a hand to me. "Think about it this way. It may take, say, ten thousand infectious doses of measles to infect me, but it may take only one hundred to infect you. This is the reason why everyone in a room with a sick person doesn't get the flu. That's the genetic difference between us. In a similar way, the dosage of a vaccine is not based on body mass. It's based on the immunogenetics of the animal."

He regarded me steadily and added, "So I tell veterinarians, 'Don't even think about splitting doses.' And I especially tell them this when it comes to the rabies vaccine. 'Oh my God,' I say, 'if you are going to reduce the dosage of a rabies vaccine, don't ever write it in your records. And you'd better make sure that you get those dogs titered, and if they don't have antibodies to rabies, get them a full dose of the vaccine.'"

In fourteen states (listed in the notes), it has become easier for veterinarians and their clients who are worried about the adverse reactions associated with the rabies vaccine to avoid the practice of splitting doses. If a veterinarian in these states verifies that a dog will be endangered by the rabies vaccine, the legal requirement to vaccinate the dog can be waived.

Jean Dodds pointed out to me that seeking such an exemption might be the wise course of action for people who have dogs known to have high incidences of adverse reactions to the rabies vaccine – any breed with a white or dilute-colored coat, especially American Eskimos, Samoyeds, Malteses, and white, cream, silver, or apricot Poodles. Jean also mentioned that certain Akitas, Weimaraners, Old English Shepherds, Kuvasz, and Great Pyrenees could be particularly prone to having an adverse reaction after being vaccinated. This was an especially good reason, she added, to titer these dogs once they had received their first immunizing dose of the core vaccines rather than risk giving them triennial booster shots. Perhaps in the not-too-distant future, genetic tests will be developed that reveal an individual dog's genetic predisposition to having an adverse reaction to a particular vaccine, thus allowing us to make more accurate decisions about which dogs to vaccinate.

It was growing late, and as I packed my things Ron Schultz brought up an important point that he wanted to make sure I understood: dogs could not be made to live longer simply by eliminating all vaccines. "The reason that the Bernese Mountain Dog has an average life span of six years," he said, "is not because they're being overvaccinated. It's because the average life span of a Bernese Mountain Dog is six years. I don't care whether you vaccinate that Bernese Mountain Dog once in its lifetime, say at sixteen to eighteen weeks of age, and never vaccinate it again, you're not going to make it live an average of ten years. In fact, if we don't vaccinate that Bernese Mountain Dog, it might not live even to six years because the likelihood of its coming across parvo or distemper is so great that it would die as a young puppy."

Bidding Ron good-bye, I headed back to Wyoming, thinking that in light of what I had learned from him, Jean Dodds, and Marybeth Minter, I would give my new puppy a minimal course of vaccines: rabies, parvo, distemper, and adenovirus-2. I'd then titer my pup to see if it had sufficient antibodies to protect against these diseases, and call it done.

Marybeth Minter gave me another suggestion in lieu of annual vaccinations, which I eventually followed. She recommended that I send a blood sample from my new pup to Jean Dodds's lab and have her run a complete blood panel so that I'd have a baseline for my dog's blood chemistry. I could then give the dog annual blood screenings (costing about $150) instead of annual vaccinations, and in this way I'd be able to monitor its ongoing blood profile and perhaps address any changes that occurred before they became serious. As Marybeth told me, "We do this for humans. Why don't we do it for dogs?"

I still had one question about vaccines that these experts hadn't addressed: should dogs who live where Lyme disease is prevalent be vaccinated against it? To provide an answer for veterinarians as well as the public, the American College of Veterinary Internal Medicine surveyed forty-five small animal diplomates from around the United States in 2006, discovering that thirty-nine of these vets did not recommend vaccinating dogs against Lyme disease, four vaccinated only rarely, and only two recommended that the vaccine be given.

The overwhelming consensus not to vaccinate against Lyme disease even in endemic areas was founded on three facts: 95 percent of exposed dogs remain asymptomatic; the disease was self-limiting in some cases; and when it wasn't, it could be effectively treated with the antibiotic doxycycline. Dogs who spend their lives in a house, get walked on concrete, and don't frequent areas inhabited by white-tailed deer (the deer tick is the main vector of the disease) have an extremely low risk of contracting Lyme disease. Suburban and rural dogs, on the other hand, have a much greater risk, and it is for this reason that the ACVIM recommended tick treatment for such dogs.

The health risks of tick and flea collars, however, as well as tick-and-flea shampoos and spot-on treatments, are not insignificant. In 2008, forty-four thousand adverse reactions to spot-on treatments were reported, including six hundred deaths. The Environmental Protection Agency and Health Canada issued a joint health and safety advisory in 2010, asking for public commentary, and in 2011 both agencies reported that they would develop more stringent testing procedures for the inert ingredients in these products. They would also ask that warning labels be put on flea-and-tick products, notifying consumers of possible adverse effects. As of 2012, the changes had not gone into effect, but even when they do, they won't eliminate pesticides from flea and tick collars.

There are healthier alternatives for dogs who live in flea and tick country. They can be sprinkled with cedar oil or, even safer — since cedar oil can cause an allergic response — food-grade diatomaceous earth. The latter is a sedimentary rock created by the accumulation of ancient diatoms, single-celled algae whose cell walls are made of silica. Food-grade diatomaceous earth is benign to dogs, cats, and people, but not to a wide variety of insects, according to the USDA. Sprinkled on a dog or cat, the diatomaceous earth absorbs moisture and fat from the bodies of fleas and ticks, killing them. Having a dog who likes to swim also helps to control these pests. Fleas and ticks can withstand quite a bit of mashing, crushing, and squeezing, but they do drown, though it takes a while. A short dip in a pond won't kill them.

Heartworm, a small threadlike worm, is also an infection for which some veterinarians advise periodic treatment — every month for dogs who live in geographic areas where mosquitoes are prevalent. However, such monthly treatments are rarely necessary because of the unique temperature requirements needed for the heartworm larvae to become infective. These larvae begin their lives when adult female heartworms, living in a dog's heart, release their offspring into the dog's bloodstream. When a mosquito then bites the infected dog (coyotes, wolves, and cats can also be affected by the disease), it ingests these infant heartworms, called microfilariae. In about two weeks, if the ambient temperature remains above 57 degrees Fahrenheit, the microfilariae develop into mature infective larvae within the mosquito. These are then injected into another dog when the mosquito stings it, starting the cycle anew.

Given the narrow temperature range necessary for the heartworm microfilariae to become potent, the disease is endemic year-round only in warm regions such as the southeastern lowlands of the United States and the Gulf Coast. If the ambient temperature drops below 57 degrees, even for a few hours, the microfilariae living in the mosquito cannot become infective and the life cycle of the heartworm is broken.

Consequently, the recommendation of many veterinarians and the American Heartworm Society to treat dogs every month for heartworm must be examined with a critical eye, taking into account that the American Heartworm Society isn't a neutral body. Eight of its ten corporate sponsors, including Bayer, Merial, Pfizer, and Merck, produce monthly heartworm treatments.

We also need to be clear that what is typically called "heartworm prevention" is really "heartworm treatment," for monthly heartworm drugs are parasiticides, neurotoxins designed to kill any larvae that your dog may be harboring. Like veterinarians who continue to give the core vaccines every year, ignoring the triennial vaccine schedule of the Canine Vaccine Task Force, those vets who insist on giving dogs a monthly dose of heartworm treatment may not be reading their own peer-reviewed literature. As Dr. David Knight and Dr. John Lok of the Department of Pathobiology at the University of Pennsylvania's School of Veterinary Medicine note in their study of heartworm, "The practice of some veterinarians to continuously prescribe monthly chemoprophylaxis exaggerates the actual risk of heartworm transmission in most parts of the country and unnecessarily increases the cost of protection to their clients." Knight and Lok also point out that because veterinarians, unlike human doctors, are permitted to sell the drugs they prescribe, their prescriptions may not always have a sound medical justification.

A healthier and far more nuanced way to address the risk of heartworm is to calculate the first date that the local temperature consistently stays above 57 degrees and when it once again dips below that. For the mid-Atlantic states and New England, this would mean giving your dog its first monthly heartworm treatment around June and the last one in November – six months of taking a toxic chemical instead of twelve. This is still a very aggressive treatment schedule and unnecessary since, if your dog gets stung by an infected mosquito on June 1, the larvae will not grow into adult heartworms for a couple of months. Therefore, if you live in these areas, you can treat your dog with invermectin (a common heartworm parasiticide marketed as Heartgard) in September, and once again in December, and call it done. Even on the Gulf Coast, where the ambient temperature may not ever dip below 57 degrees, dosing your dog with heartworm treatment once every three months should protect it. For many parts of the United States and Canada, no heartworm treatment at all is required. Nonetheless, a yearly heartworm test is a good idea, especially if you travel to warmer climes with your dog. If you then discover that your dog has contracted heartworms, it can be treated with an injectable drug called Melarsomine. All but the most advanced cases can be successfully resolved, though the treatment is unpleasant for both the dog and its people since the dog must be restrained from all exercise for at least a month.

• • •

Back from my travels, I was sitting at my desk one morning, organizing my notes, when the phone rang. It was Doug Radloff, telling me that a new genetic test had been developed at the University of Minnesota for a condition known as exercise-induced collapse. Labrador and Chesapeake Bay Retrievers as well as some Pointers, Spaniels, and Corgis were prone to the disease. After as little as five minutes of strenuous exercise, dogs with the condition became weak in their rear ends and collapsed. They remained alert and conscious, and the majority of them recovered within twenty-five minutes, but a few had been known to die during an attack. Of course, an attack while swimming could be fatal.

The important personal news for me, Doug went on, was that both Abby and Cash had been tested for EIC and both were carriers of the recessive gene. Neither of them was affected, but those puppies who had received a recessive gene from each of them — potentially up to 25 percent of the litter that I had seen that past winter — could be.

As bad luck would have it, one of these puppies eventually developed exercise-induced collapse. Even though the test for the condition hadn't been available when Abby and Cash were mated and Doug couldn't have known that they were carriers, he gave the family a new puppy from Abby's next litter. This dog became the family's hunting dog, while the EIC-affected puppy went on to enjoy a comfortable life as their house dog — not the perfect outcome for an energetic Labrador Retriever, but certainly a testament to the power of such genetic tests to avoid such outcomes in the future.

Abby and Cash would never be mated to each other again or to any other dog without first knowing that the dog was clear of the EIC gene. Casey and Lizzie had also been tested for EIC — neither of them was a carrier — and Doug hoped that I would still be interested in one of their puppies. I told Doug that I was still very interested in one of Casey's puppies.

A few months passed, autumn came, and Lizzie went into heat as expected. Then I got another cheerless call from Doug. Lizzie had not liked Casey enough to mate with him. Hearing this news from Doug, I laughed aloud and thought, "Man proposes and Lizzie disposes." Dogs, I reminded myself, do have their preferences, just like us, or perhaps Lizzie had been a day or two on either side of her prime ovulatory period when she was with Casey and therefore not interested in sex.

I had now invested a considerable amount of time and emotion in

Doug's dogs, and my spirits were low. It seemed that I would have to look elsewhere for my new pup. Maybe all these setbacks – not finding a dog in a shelter, Abby and Cash no longer being able to have puppies together, Lizzie not liking my hero Casey – were omens. Perhaps I was not meant to have another dog after Merle.

Another month went by before Doug called once again, telling me that he had taken Abby up to Terry Holzinger's kennels to meet and hunt with Terry's own dog, a Labrador Retriever named Taylor.

"Did she like him?" I asked immediately.

"Oh yeah!" Doug replied warmly. "Oh yeah. She liked him a lot. And he's a great dog, a real athlete, but very calm. Take a look at his photo on Terry's website."

I did and I liked what I saw: a rangy dog with an alert, studious air and a golden coat with rufous highlights. I was in too deep at this point not to go see the dog himself. I flew back to Minnesota and met Taylor and Terry in a field adjacent to Terry's kennels and office, a long low building set among woods and fields. Terry looked comfortably laid-back, a big, placid, soft-spoken man dressed in khaki field clothing, with a whistle around his neck. Taylor, on the other hand, bounded from the truck, ripped and ready to go, a lean yellow Lab who sat by Terry's side and gazed up at him with rapt attention, waiting for instructions.

"First say hello," said Terry, gesturing to me, and Taylor relaxed at once. Grinning, he walked over to me, smelled my hands, and gave his tail a thump – "Okay, you smell good." Then he let me rub his shoulders and scratch his rump even though a moment before he had been focused on the retriever dummies Terry was holding. I liked that. He had both speeds: on and off.

"How about a picture?" I asked him.

Taylor sat and smiled at the camera. "Okay," I said. "Thanks for humoring me." A moment later he was charging after the dummies Terry threw, stopping instantly at his whistle, changing direction by 180 degrees at Terry's hand signals, and returning the dummies with merry laughs: "Oh, this is so much fun!"

It was obvious that Taylor was a trained and focused athlete, but he also had a very relaxed air about him, and in fact he lived at home with Terry and his wife. In addition, his health certifications were perfect. Any puppies from him and Abby would not be blinded by PRA, crippled with CNM, or keel over from EIC. Moreover, when I went to the PedFast website and calculated the coefficient of inbreeding for their prospective litter, it turned out to be 1.5 percent going back five generations and 2.2 percent going back ten. This was a low COI, and I hoped that it was another indication that Abby and Taylor's pups would be healthy.

I also approached Doug and asked him if he'd forgo vaccinating Abby's puppies at six weeks of age, an antiquated practice that his veterinarian continued to recommend despite the fact that many puppies still have maternal immunity at this age and cannot be effectively vaccinated. I wanted to wait until they were older and vaccinate them just once with the minimalist vaccination protocol that Ron Schultz had recommended. Doug, as I had hoped, said this was fine by him.

And so, at last, we were on our way, or almost. Abby still had to like Taylor enough to dispose her favors upon him when she came into heat. But as Doug had said, she liked him a lot: they tied twice during the two days they spent together.

Over the following two months, Doug kept me apprised of Abby's pregnancy, and I made arrangements to be at the farm a day before her scheduled date of delivery so as to see the puppies being born.

I was at my desk early one March morning when the phone rang. It was Doug, sounding both excited and tired. "Abby went into labor last night," he said, "and I delivered all the pups by this morning."

I sagged. I had so wanted to see the birth of the puppies, and I knew that I should have been in Minnesota several days ago, but having been on the road far too much, I was enjoying being at home. I had reasoned that Abby, having given birth on schedule last time, would do so again. My mistake. Still, here was the moment I had been waiting for. Yet I hesitated.

Leaning away from my desk, I gazed out my office door, through the hallway, and into the living room to the dedicated quadruped couch, where on so many snowy afternoons I had seen Merle lying with his chin on the arm of the sofa, one eye closed, the other open and meeting my gaze: "Are you finally ready for a ski?" For one sentimental moment, I thought, "Why not keep those memories undiluted?"

Doug was waiting patiently, and I took another moment to titer my heart, going down into it, far down, and measuring the emptiness I found. Merle's death had inoculated me against any other dog for years, but my immunity was over at last. I wanted no empty couch. I wanted no silent house. I wanted another dog in my life.

CHAPTER EIGHT

At Our Start

HE FOLLOWING AFTERNOON I walked into Doug's shop and knelt by Abby's whelping box. Eleven puppies—their coats pale yellow, deep gold, and rufous—lay between her legs, their pink noses pressed to her belly as they nursed. Abby raised her head and gave me a huge grin.

"Well done, Abby!" I told her.

She thumped her tail.

I was immediately drawn to a reddish-gold pup, the darkest of the males, and picked him up. Cupping him in my palms, I sat outside the whelping box and gazed down at his wrinkled forehead, his eyes still closed. He was thirty-three hours old, and in addition to his little pink nose he had tiny pink paws and a round pink belly. He was motionless and silent while his littermates made contented "ungh, ungh, ungh" noises.

Holding the puppy, I thought, "Yep, this is the one!" In almost the same breath, I reminded myself to keep an open mind and not get attached to this one pup at such an early age. However, I really wanted a male dog, another brother dog, and a reddish-gold one at that. I had never had a brother, and Merle had been that brother for me: a trusting, joking, forgiving, ready-for-anything (well, almost anything) brother, with whom I had shared some of the best times of my life. I wanted another brother dog like him, and one who had his looks. Hearts have made lifelong choices for less.

Soon Doug and I weighed the puppies. They were about one pound each, an ounce heavier than their birth weight. As we admired them, Doug showed me the list of their birth order. The male whom I had been holding had been born second in line, ten minutes after his eldest sister.

As we spoke, Abby reclined on her rugs, nursing the puppies on one side of the whelping box. On the other side of the box were wood shavings, where the pups would soon learn to do their business. "I'll give you a bag of shavings when you take your pup," Doug told me. "It's an easy way to get them home. You put down the shavings and they know where to go."

We talked until well after dark; then I went to my hotel for the night. Early the next morning I was back, sitting outside the whelping box and watching the pups nurse and sleep. An hour went by, then another, and still I sat, unable to leave, watching Abby and her puppies with a deep, calm, satisfying joy. For the longest time – ever since I had been a teenager – I had enjoyed knowing firsthand the roots of what supported me: fishing and hunting for my food, eventually planting a vegetable garden, and helping to fell the trees that made my home. Now I was seeing the dawn of the puppy who would become my partner. I was sad that I would miss his next seven weeks, but I felt lucky to have been with him at his start. So few of us who live with dogs get to see that part of their lives anymore.

At home in Wyoming, I could hardly forget him. Doug sent me photos documenting the pups' rapid growth, and I was occupied with buying all the paraphernalia that I hoped would make my puppy's introduction to his new home as smooth as possible: a small crate to use in the motels on the drive back from Minnesota; a seat-belt harness, even though he would ride in the back of the Subaru, for I had now heard of too many dogs going through the windshield when their person had braked hard; collars in graduated sizes since the pup would be growing quickly; stainless steel bowls for food and water, not plastic ones, so he wouldn't be eating the contaminants that plastics contain; a pile of old beach towels and a spray bottle of deodorizer for cleaning up accidents; bitter-tasting apple spray to prevent him from chewing furniture and electric cords; and three dog beds – one for the car, one for my office, and one for our bedroom.

In the first week of May, I left for Minnesota, scheduling my arrival for the pups' forty-ninth day of life, a time that many dog behaviorists believe is a good time to begin a puppy's bonding and socialization with its new family. Before walking out the door and beginning the drive, I paused, gazing back at the great room where Merle's laughing photo hung on the far wall, overlooking the house he'd helped to build. I motioned with my head — "Let's go" — and I saw him bound across the room to join me.

I closed the door — closing it on our past, and beginning our future. Standing on the console, Merle lay his face against my cheek and stared eagerly down the road, as he always had, as I knew he always would.

A day later I pulled off the small farm road and into the yard of the now-familiar yellow farmhouse. As I got out of the car, Abby, Casey, Jake, and Doug's new chocolate Lab pup, Chloe, came running to greet me, surrounding me with beating tails. Doug came out of the shop in his summer work clothes: T-shirt, jeans, ball cap. We shook hands warmly: this was a day we had anticipated for more than a year. We walked around the side of the shop, with its dog door opening to the attached fenced-in kennel, allowing the pups to enter and exit the shop on their own.

Inside the enclosure they tumbled over each other in a molten heap of wriggling tails and laughing tongues. They had grown remarkably in seven weeks — fourteen ounces to fourteen pounds — and white, yellow, gold, and rufous, they pressed their paws against the wire, yipping, barking, and whining. All except the reddish male puppy whom I had held and admired as an infant. He hung back on the edge of the litter — square-faced and black-nosed — sitting quietly with a look that said, "I'm going to watch you a little before deciding if I want to say hello."

I sat down away from the fence and watched the litter for about half an hour. Some of the pups continued to plead for my attention at the fence; some went back into the shop through their dog door; one plopped down for a nap; the reddish pup and two of his littermates, both of them with slightly lighter coats, wrestled.

After a while I began my puppy aptitude tests. These temperament tests were originally developed in the 1930s as a way to choose guide dogs, and over time they've evolved into tests designed to sort dogs into dominant and subordinate individuals and reveal an inkling about their future personalities. The dog trainer Wendy Volhard is the developer of a well-known ten-point puppy aptitude test that includes the degree of social attraction a pup has to people, its willingness to follow them, how much it can be restrained, how dominant or submissive it is, whether it likes to retrieve, and how sensitive it is to sounds, touch, sight, and being startled.

I had done my best to ensure the litter would be healthy, and now, faced with nine candidates from that litter (two of the females had already been taken), I was hoping that these aptitude tests would help me choose a well-adjusted pup who would fit my lifestyle.

I gazed at the puppies for a few more moments, then opened the gate and waded in. Six of the pups were not my first candidates. They clawed at my trouser legs, leapt up at my knees, and fell on their backs, only to leap up and mob me again — typical puppy behavior — but I was waiting to see if there might be some quieter ones. By coincidence, or maybe not, the three darkest brothers were a bit calmer — not in the first circle of attackers — and one by one I took them out of the kennel and into the grassy meadow away from the litter, where I began the tests.

First was the darkest pup, whom I had held as a newborn. When I knelt and called to him — a test that measures social attraction and confidence — he ignored me. He wandered away and sniffed the grass. I gave him a rating of six on the puppy aptitude test's scale of one to six, one being a dominant and aggressive puppy, six being a subordinate and fearful one who lacks confidence.

On I went, holding the pup aloft, having him follow me, throwing a crumpled ball of paper for him to retrieve, jerking a towel before him, making a loud noise by knocking on a pot, then repeating the tests with the other two pups. All the while, Doug leaned against the side of the shop, his ball cap pushed back on his head as he watched me with patient amusement. When I was done, he said. "I've had people test every puppy in the litter, taking all day, before they decide. And you know what, if you come back this afternoon, and do it over again, it'll be different. Those tests don't mean that much."

"You think?"

He raised an eyebrow, meaning, "I know."

I decided to take his advice and returned after lunch. Just as he had predicted, the pups' test results were very different on the second go-around. The dark pup was far less willing to be restrained than during the first round and now retrieved like a field champion, bringing me crumpled paper balls with prancing delight. But when I offered him the jerked towel, he went to my clipboard and began to tear up my notes, as if to say, "I'm so tired of your tests. This is a lot more fun!" The brother with the slightly lighter coat also showed a different side of himself. He was now far calmer than during the first round, and just as reluctant to retrieve as Merle had been: "Me, fetch? No way!" Pup number three, the lightest of the three, seemed tired of the whole business and took a nap. I was now thoroughly at sea, though I did comfort myself with something that the dog behaviorist Patricia McConnell mentioned about puppy aptitude tests in her book *For the Love of a Dog:* "They are just probability statements, like a weather forecast."

I took my three candidates inside the shop to the whelping box in which they had been born, and there they fell asleep. The dark pup was the first to wake, standing up and putting his paws on the box's wall. He made a deep play bow to me along with a tiny whine whose meaning was obvious: "Pick me up."

I did and carried him outside, where I sat on an overturned bucket. Leaning against the wall of the shop, I let him snuggle in my arms. He touched noses with me and licked my mouth.

I placed him on the ground, and he followed me across the grass, breaking into a run as I did. The sun was setting, the light was long and gold, the air warm and full of the scents of budding trees. Scooping him up, I sat back down on the overturned bucket. He settled in my arms with a ready comfort, turned his little mouth up to mine, and gave me a kiss. His breath was sweet, and his face looked like a tiny version of Merle's.

I made one more test. Lying on the grass with my two leading candidates—the rufous puppy and his slightly lighter brother—I put my nose into their ruffs. The darker pup smelled rich—like lanolin with a hint of nuts—a faint remembrance of Merle, of hounds, of Golden Retrievers. The lighter pup smelled clean and white, bordering on scentless. I wondered if on some unconscious level, some pheromonal level, I had been drawn to the darker pup for this very reason. I've always trusted my nose when it comes to decisions of the heart, and it's one of the reasons I so admire dogs and the shameless priority they put upon smell, among all our senses the most difficult to fool.

Closing my eyes, I lay on my back in the small field and let the two puppies mill about me. After a while, the lighter pup sprawled at my feet, while the darker pup settled against my ribs and put his chin in the crook of my neck, his nose against my cheek. A few moments later, the lighter pup made a move that clinched my decision. He got up and walked to the kennel, trying to get inside with his littermates. The darker pup sat up, watched him go, then glanced at me. I gave him no hint as to what I wanted him to do. Once again, he looked to his departing brother, but instead of following him, he flopped comfortably against my side, snuggling along my ribs and giving a sigh that said, "Touch. Together. Here is where I want to be."

We drove away the next morning, the seat belt harnessed around his little gold chest and buckled into a piece of overhead webbing that stretched from one side of the car to the other behind the front seats. He could move around, but if I hit the brakes he wouldn't go flying. As we headed down the farm lane to the main road he stood on the passenger seat, put his paws on its back, and gazed intently at the receding shop and farmhouse. Up until this point — when I took him from his brothers and sisters, when I let him say good-bye to Abby and his uncle Casey, and when I held him while Doug and I finished the paperwork — he had been entirely composed, participating in every one of my moves with curiosity and only a little concern: why are my sisters and brothers, and my mom and uncle, on one side of the fence and I'm on the other? But as the farmhouse disappeared behind a windbreak of trees, his face took on a look of surprise, then worry, then shock. A second later, he began to cry, yelping plaintively and turning to me with a look of despair. A stab of guilt went through me: I was taking him from his family to come live with me.

"Oh, Little Sir," I said softly, trying to comfort him. "It'll be fine." I reached over and held my palm against his chest. "Just you wait and see. You're going to Wyoming where you'll have room to roam."

He gave me a skeptical look: "I'm not sure I understand what you're saying."

"I'm sure you don't," I replied.

Nonetheless, he came over to me and settled on the console between the two front seats, giving an anxious yawn before putting his head on his paws and dozing. A few moments later, he opened his eyes, looked around, and let out a whine that sounded like, "Oh my goodness, where am I going?"

"You're going to the big mountains, with lots of snow, and skiing, and elk to eat. Mmm-mmm-mmm," I hummed. "And rivers to swim in, so many dog friends to play with, and people who will love you."

He followed everything I was saying, looking directly into my eyes.

Apparently satisfied with my happy tone of voice, he crawled into my lap and put his chin on my left wrist. As we drove along, he slept, awakening now and then to cry out, "Oh, where am I going?" Then he'd close his eyes and begin to dream, paws twitching. I wondered if he was dreaming of his brothers and sisters, of his mother and his uncle Casey, of Doug and the kennel. Or might he be dreaming of something so ancient that I couldn't even imagine it?

We stopped in Worthington, Minnesota, for gas before getting on I-90 and starting the long haul west. It was pouring rain, pouring so hard that I decided not to put down the shavings Doug had given me to indicate to the pup where he needed to go. Holding an umbrella over the two of us, I led him onto a strip of grass behind the gas pumps, he scampering along happily by my side.

"Have a pee," I said matter-of-factly. As the words came out of my mouth, he squatted and peed. He, of course, didn't know what my words meant. He simply had to go. It was a fortuitous training opportunity.

"Excellent!" I cried and gave him lavish pets.

He wriggled in delight and scampered back to the car with me. I lifted him onto the passenger seat, then moved the car to the entrance of the convenience store. I went in and bought a sandwich. When I came out, he was sitting where I had left him, but he had pointed his nose to the roof of the car and was howling mournfully. In fact, I could hear him fifteen feet away even with all the windows closed: "Awooo! I'm lost! I don't know where I am! I'm all alone! I miss my family! Awooo! Woe is me! Awooo!"

It seemed extraordinary that so small a dog could emit such incredible howls. I opened the door, and before I could sit down in the driver's seat he mobbed me with kisses and excited whines, "You're here! You're back! I'm not alone!"

"You're not alone," I said, hugging him. "I'm right here, and we're off on a great adventure!" I raised my voice into its "Oh boy, aren't we having fun?" register.

I felt him relax in my arms. He nestled himself on my lap, and with my sandwich wrapper spread over him, he fell asleep as I drove away.

Once on the interstate, I picked him up and placed him on his golden fleece rug. He lay there sleeping — tiny and jowly, round and soft, with a dreamy smile curving his black lips. I could have stared at him for hours, but I forced my eyes back to the road, and as I did Merle stepped onto the console, his laughing eyes full of approval. I cupped his cheek, and he pressed his head against mine. Down I-90 we drove, the three of us in the perfect privacy of our car.

In Rapid City, I found a pet-friendly motel where the puppy walked with me to the check-in. I placed him on the counter to be fondled by the two young female clerks, and then, continuing his socialization, I walked him around the swimming pool, full of squealing children adorned in orange life preservers, purple dragon floats, and masks and snorkels. They jumped out to greet him, and he seemed unfazed by these new sorts of creatures, accepting their wet pets with wiggles and little laughs.

Nor did the full-length mirror in our room give him pause. Thinking it another room, he trotted directly into it, smacking his head soundly. Backing up, he noticed the other puppy in front of him and play-bowed to it, growling and wagging his tail. Suddenly, he noticed me in the mirror as well, and he looked from the real me to the reflected me in bewilderment. I knelt by his side and said, "That's you, and that's me." I pointed. "And this is you, and this is me." I touched his head and then my chest. He looked to the dog in the mirror, play-bowed to it once again, and growled happily.

Needing to answer a backlog of phone messages, I gave him a toy — a stuffed white dog — that a friend had sent me in anticipation of my getting a new dog. When shaken, it barked the tune of "Take Me Out to the Ball Game." He now shook it mightily, and the barking tune repeated over and over as I sat on the bed and listened to my voice mail.

So far we'd had an uneventful day, he peeing and pooping like a champ on the grassy berms of gas stations. But now a major challenge awaited us: bedtime. The last time I had had a puppy, I was almost a puppy myself — my parents had done the job of house-training her — so I had read extensively in the puppy training literature, noting the varied advice on what to do with a crying, lonesome puppy on the first nights away from its mother and littermates, the common denominator being: don't give in to the puppy's demands and let it sleep in your bed or you'll be sorry, unless you relish sleeping with your dog for the rest of your life. This is not an insignificant consideration when small puppies grow into seventy-pound dogs.

So I pulled the pup's large dog bed next to my own and placed him upon it, saying, "Oh, is this ever so nice and comfy." I patted it. "What a wonderful night's sleep you're going to have! Sleep well." I kissed the top of his head and turned off the light.

He began to cry. I said nothing. A few moments later he put his paws on my bed and tried to crawl up. I lay there a moment, thinking about the crate on the other side of the room. I had bought it without enthusiasm, for I'm not a fan of crates. In fact, I think that they've gotten far too much praise as a way to manage dogs who must be left alone. Instead of defaulting to the crate, I was convinced that it was better to take the time to teach the dog manners so that it behaved while under its own supervision. This approach — leaving well-mannered dogs under their own recognizance — had worked well with Merle and Brower, with all their friends, and in the last two years with A.J. and Burley. Not once in nearly two decades of all these dogs being at liberty to enter and leave my house on their own through the dog door, and then being allowed to go anywhere in the house even when I wasn't there, had a single object or piece of furniture been destroyed.

That said, crates can be a godsend for house-training puppies quickly, since no dog likes to foul its own bed. If the crate gives the puppy just enough room to turn around, the pup can't find a place far enough away from its bed in which to pee and poop. Having to go, it will cry out, "Hey, let me out so I can keep my space clean!" In this way, you can quickly train a pup to go in a designated area, and then, once the pup is house-trained, you can pass the crate on to someone else who is getting a new puppy.

I got up and fetched the crate, padding its floor with a thick towel and placing the crate directly next to my bed where the pup's bed had been. Fondling him, I said, "Oh, boy, a little house of your own, right here on the prairie. You and Laura Ingalls spending the night together! Won't that be fun?"

He wagged his tail, "That does sound like fun!"

I put him in the crate and closed the door.

He waited until I got into bed and pulled the cover over myself before he started to cry, warming up with a little whimper and getting louder and louder until he was crying pitifully, "Aaaaooooo, I am dying of loneliness! Urrrrrrr, my heart is breaking! Warrrrrrr, I can't stand this!" I touched the grate of the cage and whispered, "Oh, shh, shh, shh, shh, shh. Talk to Laura. Talk to Laura." Then, as he continued to moan, I gave a loud "Shhh!"

Instantly, he stopped crying. I waited. Five seconds went by. I could hear the hum of the bedside clock. Then he began to cry again. I said nothing. He cried for two more minutes as I watched the clock, not making a single sound myself, and then he stopped, just like that, and went to sleep. Miraculous.

Two hours later, I heard him whine, but this was not a cry of loneliness. Not in the least. He was saying, "Hey! I gotta pee!"

I threw on my clothes and hustled him out the door. The instant he got to the grass on the other side of the parking lot, he squatted and let out a long stream.

"Well done, Sir!" I praised him. "Anything else?"

He didn't seem interested in anything else, so after letting him nose here and there on the grass I led him back to our room and put him in his crate, where he immediately began to cry and I immediately shushed him.

He continued to whimper, "This is so hard. Please hold me." I said nothing. He cried for another half-minute, and then he stopped. I didn't dare move. A few moments later I heard his sleeping breath.

"What a good fellow you are," I thought.

He slept for three hours straight before waking me with a soft insistent whine, "Wake up! I have to go. And I mean now!"

"I'm coming," I called, rubbing the sleep from my eyes. It was a little after three in the morning. He whined with ever-greater anxiety. "I'm coming," I called again, a smile crossing my face as I thought of the role I had played at the end of Merle's life — tending to his eliminations — and now, at the beginning of this pup's life, I was doing the very same thing, albeit under happier circumstances.

"Hang in there," I encouraged him, pulling on my clothes and opening the crate. He shot toward the front door, and we ran across the parking lot together. When we got to the lawn, he stopped short, squatted, and peed for a preposterously long time. At last he stood. Not for long. He hustled a few steps away and pooped.

"*Ah, monsieur!*" I said admiringly. "*Tu es un champion des toilettes canines.*" And I picked up his deposit in a plastic bag.

He stood, placing his front paws on my knee. I bent down and rubbed his shoulders, which delighted him.

"How about some more shut-eye?" I asked, and at once he followed me back to the room, walking directly between my legs while I stepped away from him and he scurried back underfoot. Trying to avoid him, I stepped right and he followed me right. I feinted left; he darted left.

Hopscotching to avoid him, I stepped on his right front paw. Instantly, I took my weight off of it.

Sitting, he whined pitifully, "I'm hurt! I'm hurt so bad!" He held up his paw in a pathetic gesture.

I was almost certain that I had put very little weight on his paw, but I knelt, gently picked it up, and kissed it. "Oh, I'm so sorry," I crooned, examining his paw as he watched with big, round, limpid eyes. "I think it's fine," I told him softly. "I really do. Come on, let's go."

Carefully, I let go of his paw and took a few steps toward the room. He remained seated, holding his paw in the air and moaning, "It's broken. I know it is. I can't move."

I doubted this was the case, and I decided to use the strategy I had once seen a mother grizzly bear adopt with one of her cubs who had fallen off a log and was playing at the same game — "I can't move. I'm crippled for life. You have to carry me." She simply walked away. When she was a hundred yards off, the cub leapt to its feet and galloped after her.

I kept walking. The puppy looked at me a moment, then came right along, trotting with a perfect gait, as if nothing had happened.

On the other side of the parking lot, we walked along the line of rooms.

"Can you find which one is ours?" I asked him.

He stopped at the one next to ours, sniffed at the crack beneath the door, and continued, pausing at ours, giving it a sniff, and then glancing up at me with a look that said, "I think this is the right one."

"Very good!" I exclaimed, opening the door for him. "What a nose!" We went inside, and before I had gone four steps he grabbed my trouser cuff and began to tug it vigorously. I knelt on my hands and knees, and he ran under my chest, doing laps around my extended arms. Grabbing him, I kissed the top of his head and rubbed his belly, and he panted, "He-he-he! This is so much fun!"

It was 3:15 A.M., but what else did I have to do?

Leaning against the bed, I placed him on my thighs. "Oh, you are quite the pup!" I told him. "I can see that already. You tell me when you need to go. You pee and poop like a champ, and you find our room. I think you may be the best puppy on the planet. No doubt about it, the best!"

He gazed up at me with trust and love and joy.

"Yes, in fact I think you're a pukka dog." It was the old Hindi word that I had heard on so many climbing expeditions in the Himalaya, its meaning capturing the notions of "genuine," "first-class," and "the best," as in, "What a pukka meal!" or "He's a pukka sahib!"

The name felt right as I said it. "Will Pukka work for you, my lad?" I asked him.

Reclining on my legs, he gave me a sleepy smile and closed his eyes in contentment.

In the morning, after two trips to the lawn with him, I sat outside our room with my back against the door as I ate the leftovers of the walleye I had had for dinner. Little Pukka stood next to me, making "I want food" noises and trying to lick my mouth. I considered telling him, "No begging," but decided to take a different approach. Picking up a little piece of fish between my thumb and forefinger, I waited until he decided to sit down. The instant his butt touched the concrete, I said, "Sit," and gave him the fish. I ate some more. He begged. I ignored him. Eventually he sat, and again, the instant his butt touched the ground, I said, "Sit," and immediately gave him some fish. Proceeding like this, I would say "sit" every time he sat, and give him a morsel. We were on our way to learning manners.

I finished my breakfast and he lay against my right hip in the fine May sunshine, his head facing toward my feet. Growing sleepy, he rolled on his side, and I reached down and petted his round firm belly.

He looked very peaceful. Giving a big sigh, he turned on his back, his paws hanging limply over his chest like those of a bunny rabbit. I rubbed his chest and then gently scratched his ears, saying, "Oh, ears are so important for a dog, aren't they? Yes, they are. Very important. And the chin. What about the chin? How important is the chin for a dog to get scratched? Yes, just like this, when he's in the sunshine and his black nose is glistening and his ears are so very reddish-gold. What could be better?"

He flung his head back in ecstasy and stretched his front legs over his head, holding his paws next to each other so I could see his ten jet-black pads arranged in two perfect semicircles. Suddenly I saw him, perhaps fourteen years from now, stretching in just this way, and I could hear myself saying, "Remember that day in South Dakota, Pukka, when you ate your first walleye, and you had your first sitting lesson, and we were new and at our start?"

It was all too short — far too short — and I didn't want to miss a single second of it. I was glad I had driven to Minnesota to get him instead of having him shipped by air.

"What do you say?" I asked him. "Shall we go to Yellowstone so we can see some bison and elk and maybe even some bears and wolves?"

By way of an answer, he stretched his legs farther out: "I think I'll stay right here."

Of course, as soon as I got up, he did, too, following my every move as I carried our gear to the car. When it was loaded, I said, "What about a little walk before the drive?" He was not interested. He had seen his gear go into the car, and he wasn't taking any chances.

He slept on and off all the way to the northeast entrance of Yellowstone National Park, where I said, "We're here, Pukkacito."

He lifted his head and yawned, his tongue curling neatly as he exclaimed, "Yow!" Shaking his head, he woke up, pushed himself into a sitting position, and looked around at the soaring peaks. Twisting his head this way and that, he gazed at them, his expression seeming to say, "Hmm, we're not in Minnesota anymore."

We continued down into the park and emerged on the sprawling meadows above Soda Butte, the prowlike remains of an old hot spring. Just beyond its chalky dome, I saw a herd of bison grazing alongside the road, and I stopped. Rolling down the window, I took Pukka into my lap. He put his right paw on the top of the window and rested his chin upon it, watching the huge shaggy animals intently, his nose chewing their scent out of the breeze.

"Bison," I said. "Bison."

He glanced at me.

"They're called bison, Pukka. Bison."

Looking back to them, he furrowed his brows in concern: "They look very big."

"They are," I said. "That one there"—I pointed to the shaggy head of an enormous bull that stood only ten feet from the car—"I bet he weighs a ton."

Pukka followed my pointing finger and stared at the bison. Apparently, he had already grasped what pointing meant, something that the puppies of domestic dogs comprehend at between two and four months of age. By contrast, wolf pups don't understand the meaning of an extended finger until they're a year and a half old, and then only if they've been intimately raised by a human keeper.

"What do you think?" I asked Pukka. "Enough bison?" Having seen thousands of bison over the years, I was ready to go. But this herd was Pukka's first, and he continued to gaze at them in awe.

"Okay," I said. "Let's watch the bison some more."

In about fifteen minutes the herd moved on, and so did we. Heading downriver, we soon spied a black and then a grizzly bear, both of whom I named for Pukka. He wagged his tail at the black bear — "That looks like a big black dog" — but at the sight of the grizzly, he nestled deeper in my lap, his entire body language saying, "I'm really glad I'm in the car. That looks like a very serious animal."

"It can be," I said. "But if you don't chase grizzlies you'll be fine."

The dusk fell, and although it was only a three-and-a-half-hour drive to Kelly and home, I wanted to spend another day in the park, introducing Pukka to more of the animals around whom he'd spend his life. So I drove up to Cooke City in the growing dark, and Pukka had a violent dream. He was curled in a fetal position on the seat, his legs churning and bucking, and I wondered if he was dreaming of bison and bears.

We passed another motel night — he whining every three hours to go out and I rising to accompany him — and by sunrise we were back in the park. Near the entrance, I showed him two moose in a willow patch, their almost-black coats shining in the newly risen sun. He appraised them with a steady regard — no anxiety yawn, no burrowing deeper into my chest. Even at this tender age, did he understand that these were ungulates, the animals his lupine ancestors ate, whereas the grizzly bear he had seen was a competitor and at times an adversary? An interesting question.

At the turnout above the confluence of the Lamar River and Soda Butte Creek, I found many of my old wolf-watching friends with their spotting scopes set up and trained beyond the creek. One of the gray females of the Druid Wolf Pack stood only a few hundred yards off, clearly visible in the grass, and when I turned my scope upon her, I saw her staring our way with big yellow eyes. She threw back her head and opened her mouth to the sky. A second later her low, drawn-out howl floated over us. I rushed to the car and got Pukka. The wolf was too far off for his inexperienced eye to spot, but he could certainly hear her. As I held him in my arms, the wolf howled again. A few seconds later several of the other females in the pack answered from the hillside above us, their howls going back and forth in the crisp May air. Ears pricked, Pukka snapped his head in the direction of the single howl, then to the answering chorus.

"Wolf," I said. "Wolf."

He began to tremble in my arms. Obviously, he had heard something in the howls that I had not. Perhaps the wolves were singing, "Let's go kill some coyotes," an age-old practice of theirs, since they consider coyotes competitors. Maybe they were only singing, "What a nice morning, see you in a bit," but, being wolves, their song was underlain by the power of their pack, which had no inhibitions about chasing and killing strange dogs who came into their territory.

Whatever the case, Pukka continued to listen carefully and soon stopped trembling. He began to squirm, and I put him on the ground, where he ran to the grass at the edge of the parking lot. I thought that he had to pee, but he raised his nose into the air and smelled the breeze, his lips slightly parted. After a few moments, he began to sniff the tall bunchgrass and the sage, cocking his head and closing his eyes while taking in the scents of his new world.

Firing up my camping stove, I brewed some tea, keeping a close eye on him as he made little forays into the sagebrush. They were very short. He immediately hurried back out to gaze in my direction: "Yep, you're still there." Satisfied that I was where he had left me, he mouthed small rocks; he chewed the grass; he stopped to sniff the air and listen to the wolves — now with composure.

Suddenly, out of the corner of my eye, I saw a park ranger drive into the turnout and jump out of her vehicle. She was a slip of a girl, pretty and dark-haired, but as she ran toward Pukka she looked determined, her "Smokey the Bear" hat clapped on her head and her gun belt bristling with a Glock, a Taser, and handcuffs.

"Uh-oh," I thought. "Better get him on the leash."

I knew, of course, that I had been breaking the law: all dogs must be leashed along the roadways of Yellowstone and Grand Teton National Parks and are prohibited — leashed or not — in the backcountry. However, what harm, I had reasoned, could come from a seven-week-old puppy wandering at the edge of a parking lot, thirty yards from me?

The ranger seemed to think otherwise. She grabbed Pukka, scooping him up in her arms, and I imagined her locking him in the caged rear half of her SUV and driving him down to park headquarters, where I'd have to pay a fine to recover him.

"Oh my God!" she began to moan. "He's so cute! I can't stand it! I miss my dog so much!"

I stopped in my tracks, watching in relief as she nuzzled Pukka and told him what a beautiful puppy he was. He squirmed in delight and washed her mouth with kisses.

She waved away the leash that I'd brought over. "He's just a puppy," she said. "Let him play."

On the spot, I canonized her: "Saint Ranger of the Lamar."

We chatted about her dog, left behind because of her job in the park, and about my finding Pukka in Minnesota. Then the crackle of her radio summoned her away. Off she drove; I drank my tea; and we watched the wolves — or at least I did. Pukka was going from person to person, introducing himself.

The morning warmed and we headed downvalley, passing herds of pronghorn as the meadowlarks sang. I showed Pukka a bison pie and bison fur, both of which he smelled studiously as I pointed to the bison nearby and said their name once again: "Bison."

At last it was time to go, but there was one more treat in store for us: a bighorn ram grazing by the side of the road near the Yellowstone River, with many people photographing him. I got out of the car and walked to within fifty feet of the sheep with Pukka in my arms. Tan, with a white muzzle and piercing amber eyes, the bighorn had nine annular rings on his sweeping horns. I had seen him at this spot for the past few springs, and he was very habituated to people, paying them no mind.

"Bighorn sheep," I said. "Pukka, look, bighorn." Alertly, Pukka examined the sheep, his head ticking this way and that as the sheep reached down and plucked off mouthfuls of grass.

"Bighorn," I repeated. "Very exciting to be this close!"

Behind me, from across the road, I heard someone say, "Did you ever see anything as stupid as that? He's telling the puppy it's a bighorn."

Perhaps it did look stupid, but what I was doing with Pukka on his first trip through Yellowstone — pointing out wildlife and repeating their names — was exactly how I had taught Merle the English words for what he was seeing, smelling, and hearing. Soon, Merle knew the names of virtually every big mammal who lived around us: a greater taxonomic knowledge of the region's fauna — tied to unique odors, shapes, sounds, and their English designators—than many people possess. I had no doubt that Pukka would soon also share that rich knowledge and that most of our dogs could do so as well.

Of course, most of us don't live on the edge of a national park. Yet cities and suburbs can be equally full of life: pigeon, squirrel, deer . . . car, bus, bike . . . beach, park, river. The opportunities to teach a dog the names of the inhabitants, objects, and destinations of its home turf are nearly endless. The truth is, if you're excited about the world, your dog responds with equal excitement, its brain soaking up the new with remarkable precociousness. Rico, a smart Border Collie, was able to learn hundreds of words, and Chaser, another brainy dog of the same breed, knew more than a thousand.

There's also an important side benefit to giving dogs such a broad education, especially in their early months. It helps to socialize them. One of the main reasons that the life spans of some dogs are painfully short is that they're surrendered to shelters for behavioral issues — everything from peeing in the house to barking, to biting, to chasing — and then they're put to death when they're not readopted. Exposing dogs to every stimulus imaginable—from grizzly bears to squealing children in dragon floats, to the grizzled man selling pretzels — gives them a better chance of developing good manners: dogs who won't snap, run at cars, chase wildlife, or be nuisances; dogs who, in other words, are good citizens.

Exhausted by his day of new smells, sights, and sounds, Pukka slept the entire way home while I savored the drive up the Firehole River and down the Gibbon—over Craig Pass with Yellowstone Lake frozen in the distance, its fumaroles smoking into the sere blue sky—and through the lodgepole forest of the Continental Divide. Then down, down, down we coasted, leaving Yellowstone's high plateau and descending into Jackson Hole, where we drove under the great snowy spires of the Tetons, welcoming us home.

We turned off the main road at Antelope Flats Junction, drove under Blacktail Butte, turned right at Mailbox Corner, where the Gros Ventre Mountains began to rise before us, went past the Science School turnoff, and came down the long hill, seeing the green roof of the house snuggled among its spruce trees and Merle's prayer flags waving in the field beyond. We had not seen a traffic light since Billings, Montana, 284 miles behind us, a long sweet run of wild country.

In the grassy fields not a half-mile north of the house stood a herd of about fifteen elk. I stopped the car, turned off the engine, opened the window, and woke Pukka. Picking him up, I pointed his nose in the direction of the herd. He didn't see them until one bull tossed his head and did a circle: "Why are you watching us?"

Instantly, Pukka fixed on them, his ears perked forward.

"Elk, Pukka," I said. "Elk, they're the best. We're home, Pukka, we're home."

CHAPTER NINE

Outward Bound

IN A FEW MINUTES we were—literally—home. I pulled into the drive, unharnessed Pukka from his seat belt, and placed him on the ground, where he glanced around: the Subaru, the woodpile, the aspen trees, the two-story log house. He looked a bit dazed.

"Let's stretch our legs," I said, leading him around the house and across the lawn. At its far end stood Merle's prayer flags, flapping in the breeze, and Pukka bounded to them and leapt upon Merle's grave, where he play-bowed to me. Before I could respond with a play-bow of my own, he flopped on his belly, front and back legs extended, and rolled a complete circle, then stretched lavishly. Coming upright, he gave me a self-satisfied look that said, "Very nice to be out of the car!" He appeared restored.

"Welcome home, Sirs," I said, seeing the spirit Merle laughing behind Pukka, but I didn't have time to add more.

A.J., Burley, and Goo spied us and came sprinting across the field to say hello. Goo was their new housemate, a compact English Setter with a white coat and auburn ears. Pukka, seeing these three large dogs charging him, dropped his tail and pressed himself against my legs. My inclination was to pick him up, but I stifled it. Placing a hand on his shoulder, I said in my most reassuring tone of voice, "No worries, Pukka, these are friendly dogs."

Coming up to us, the three dogs didn't know what to do first—say "hi" to me, whom they hadn't seen in a few days, or say "hi" to the new arrival. They decided to check out Pukka, taking turns smelling him.

A.J., now a stocky, brawny Lab the color of straw, gave a laughing pant and a steady wag of his tail: "He's a nice little guy." Burley, who had turned into a very shaggy, henna-colored Golden Retriever, gave Pukka several aloof sniffs and then ignored him: "Just a puppy; beneath my notice." Goo—a nervous rescue who still refused to use the dog door no matter how many times he saw his buddies go through it—skittered away, unsure of this unfamiliar dog, even though he was three times his size.

Neighbors, always on the stroll during fine weather, began to stop by with their dogs, and Pukka—lifted, dandled, kissed, and cuddled—soaked up the greetings with a madly beating tail. When at last everyone had said hello and resumed their walks, we took our own stroll across the sagebrush to the Landales: April and Scott, their two daughters Tessa and Eliza, whom Merle had babysat, now grown into rangy girls of fourteen and twelve, and Buck, their ninety-pound yellow Lab. He was a giant of a dog who could knock me off my feet with a friendly swipe of his head, but who was now exquisitely gentle with Pukka, lowering his long snout to sniff Pukka's nose.

The sniff lasted no more than three seconds, but when it was done Pukka was a different dog. He raised his front paw and affectionately held it against Buck's face, saying, "I really like you, Buck."

Giving a gracious nod of his head, Buck returned the compliment: "I like you, too, but I've got things to do." And with that he marched off across the grass toward the willows that bordered his unfenced yard. Pukka was not about to break off their meeting so quickly. Following Buck along the trees, he sniffed where the big dog sniffed, and peed where the big dog peed, all the while wearing a starstruck look that said, "Here's a dog I can learn something from!"

It being May, the light was long, and lazily we strolled back across the field as the sun set above the Tetons, Pukka dashing through the sage for ten yards before returning to my side. He'd brush against my leg—"Touch, that's better, all is well"—and set off again.

I could see Merle running before us, and gazing at the dog who had opened the door to my heart and the dog who was now stepping through it once more, I thought about how I might help Pukka, this small, innocent puppy, become the sort of collected, freethinking dog Merle had been.

The experiment was made more difficult because my natural tendency was to protect Pukka from the school of hard knocks that had helped to shape Merle and so many other stray dogs into the durable souls they are. But only a sadist would knowingly expose a dog to what

Merle had endured and risen above: probably being beaten, certainly being shot, starving, scrounging trash, and surviving on whatever small animals he could find. The trick then was to expose Pukka to the sort of adversity that builds character, instills steadiness, and develops a problem-solving ability without intimidating him in the process. In fact, I wanted to do the opposite: make the adversity fun. I had considerable practice in doing this.

In my twenties I had worked for a school called Outward Bound, which was founded in Aberdovey, Wales, at the beginning of World War II. In those dark days, Sir Lawrence Holt, the president of the Blue Funnel Shipping Line, faced an ever-mounting loss of seamen. When their ships were torpedoed by German U-boats, his sailors perished in their lifeboats despite having spent their entire lives in the merchant marine. Holt believed that they lacked the training and resourcefulness to survive in open boats, a knowledge that had been lost since the days of square-rigged sailing ships.

At this critical moment, he was approached by Kurt Hahn, a German-born educator who had denounced Hitler, emigrated to Great Britain, and founded a school in Scotland that combined traditional education with rigorous outdoor activities emphasizing adventure, curiosity, and enterprise. Hahn needed funding; Holt provided it; and Hahn moved to Aberdovey, where he opened a training school for mariners called Outward Bound, the term used by sailors to signify the moment a ship leaves its moorings, committing itself and its crew to the hazards of the open sea.

The school became so successful in saving the lives of mariners that the basics of its curriculum — hard physical challenges, navigation, problem-solving, and group cooperation — were applied to the education of young people and exported to Africa, Asia, Australia, and North America, coming to Colorado in 1961. I landed in the school's embrace in the mid-1970s — in my midtwenties and only five to ten years older than my students — but I had something they did not: a great deal of world travel; some high cold mountains under my belt; and the Chilean coup d'état, during which, as an innocent traveler, I had nearly lost my life. Arrested, interrogated, and marched up against a wall, I was nearly shot. That event left me with the same quality that I had noticed in Merle from the start: a seventh sense about dangers lurking just beyond the edge of his perception, not a constant anxiety about unforeseen peril but an attention to peril's possibilities. That attention is what I had tried to instill in my students, as well as the knowledge of how to backpack, cross rivers, rock climb, ski bad snow, avoid lightning, avalanches, and rockfall, sleep comfortably in a tent when it was thirty below zero, eat wild plants, and, equally important, how to rescue their own ass when things went wrong. For many of these students, those three weeks in the Colorado backcountry were some of the most memorable of their lives.

Now it was Pukka's turn to go outward bound.

Not taking my eyes from him, I let him roam big circles through the sage. He, of course, constantly returned — after all, I was the center of his universe.

I continued to give him his head when we got home, letting him follow me in and out of the house and explore on his own as I unloaded the car. The great room — containing living room, dining room, and kitchen, all without walls — has a twenty-foot-high ceiling and many large windows that look out to the Tetons, dissolving the boundary between inside and outside. Pukka gazed around him, trying to gain perspective on this unusually bright and airy space. Then he poked his nose under the couch, sniffed the end table, and crawled beneath the dining room table, searching out the places where Merle and the other dogs had left their scents. He stopped at the empty kitchen trash can, sniffing appreciatively: "Good stuff's been in there." At last, he followed me into my office, where he watched me reattach my laptop to the desk monitor with the fascinated attention that comes from seeing everything for the first time.

I sat down, powered up the computer, and heard him leave. A few moments later, I heard a plaintive whine, which I translated as "Come quick!" Rising, I went to the office door, but I wasn't quick enough. He was already squatting. Calling a sharp "No!" I rushed to him, scooped him up in midstream, and chanted, "Outside, outside, outside's the place to go." I hustled him out the door and deposited him on the grass.

Here he squatted and resumed his pee. "*Excellent, monsieur,*" I told him. "Anything else before we go back in?"

He nosed around the grass, and I said, "Come out to the sage. That's a better place for your poop. Come on." I patted my thigh with my palm and led him into the sagebrush where, after sniffing around a bit, he crouched and had a bowel movement.

"First-class," I complimented him. "Remember, here's the scoop on your poop: outside is fine, inside is not."

He scampered to me, wagging his tail and giving it an emphatic little exclamation point in the air: "Wow! Did I ever have to go!"

My approach to Pukka's house-training was another facet of giving him freedom to learn on his own or, more accurately, freedom with some boundaries. He would have the run of the house during the day — the dog door sealed during his first weeks to protect him from wandering off — but he'd be crated at night. This method is hardly my own. It's a mix of what two well-known dog experts recommend. The first is Elizabeth Marshall Thomas, who, in her book *The Social Lives of Dogs*, points out how intimidating it must be for a young puppy, clumsy and unsure of itself, to have a large and authoritative person looming over it, constantly fuming about its eliminatory habits and making it ever more fearful.

"Just as we cannot learn when we are jittery and unsure of ourselves," she writes, "neither can the dog." She then offers a bit of sage advice: "A laid-back attitude is therefore very important on the part of the owner."

If Thomas is at one pole of the puppy training world, the veterinarian and animal behaviorist Dr. Ian Dunbar is at the other. In his book *Before and After Getting Your Puppy*, he recommends long-term confinement of one's new puppy in a crate and taking it out only hourly so it can do its business. According to Dunbar, such confinement prevents a puppy from making any eliminatory mistakes and keeps it from chewing anything that the human doesn't want it to chew. In other words, the crate makes the puppy's house-training errorless, which for Dunbar is paramount. As he writes, "Allowing a single housesoiling mistake is a disaster since it sets the precedent for your puppy's toilet area and signals many more mistakes to come."

Obviously, it's a good thing that Elizabeth Marshall Thomas and Ian Dunbar aren't married: they'd have a hell of a time raising their dogs. I, of course, was with Thomas, as are those hundreds of millions of people who, without ever resorting to long-term crating and despite the fact that their dogs made numerous mistakes, have successfully trained hundreds of millions of dogs not to go in the house.

Nonetheless, Dunbar makes an important point: the crate works wonders at night. The puppy, after all, is used to sleeping by its mom. It'll like sleeping by you, and wanting to keep its small crate clean, it will whine when it needs to go out, as I had discovered on our drive back from Minnesota. This is a sweet way to teach a puppy to vocalize when it wants to do its business — here was Pukka, whining to go out after only two nights in the crate — and after a couple of weeks you can set the pee- and poop-wise puppy free.

Back inside the house, I asked him, "Will you please help me roll up the throw rugs? That way they'll stay safe while you're a puppy." I hadn't had time to put away these potentially expensive blotting mats and chewing temptations before leaving for Minnesota. Getting down on my hands and knees, I rolled up the rugs while he chased their amazing disappearance, pouncing on them as I rolled them ahead of us.

"That's right," I said. "What a help you are, Pukka, very good. One more."

We stored the downstairs rugs in the guest room, and then I climbed the stairs on my hands and knees as he galumphed by my side.

"Oh, excellent!" I told him. "You're a climbin' dog. There's no doubt about it. I can see that already."

"He-he-he," he panted happily.

In the bedroom we rolled up the two large throw rugs on each side of the bed and stored them in a closet. Turning back to the room, we stared at oceans of easily cleaned wood flooring on which he could now make his mistakes without any serious consequences. Moreover, instead of being in a crate with a chew toy while I had done these necessary tasks, he had helped me. He was a participant in our world, not an observer. We were on our way to becoming a team.

At first light, he woke me — he had woken me only once during the night — and we took our morning constitutional. I fed him and carried my toast and coffee to my office, saying, "Okay, my lad, the party's over. I have to go to work, and so do you."

I had placed his bed in the corner by the bookshelves, and I now put his barking dog toy upon it and gave the bed a pat. "Here you go — you at your workstation and I at mine." I went to my desk, and he leapt upon his bed and began to chew his toy dog.

I was lucky to have my new puppy by my side while I worked, but not everyone is so fortunate. For those people who work away from home, Doug Radloff recommends scheduling a two-week vacation to begin on the day they pick up their pup from his farm in Essig, Minnesota. In this way the puppy can bond with its person or people, be house-trained, and be well on its way toward becoming socialized before it has to be turned over to doggie day care. If you or a responsible family member is unable to devote a couple of weeks to your new dog before it can be turned over to day care — or, as a second-best alternative, hire someone knowledgeable to socialize the pup while you're at work — you shouldn't be getting a dog, much as you want one. Consider that for a month or so after a seven-week-old puppy is brought home it's almost the equivalent of a human infant, and virtually everywhere on earth, leaving an infant home alone in a crib is considered bad form. Too many crated, left-alone puppies end up without manners, are surrendered to shelters, and are then killed because people underestimated the time required to raise a dog properly.

Turning on my computer, I began to catch up on my research. In a few moments I heard a noise below me. I glanced down. With a coy look at me — "Here I am" — Pukka was chewing the corner of my desk stool. I pried open his mouth and said, "Leave it." This forestalled him for about ten seconds. Turning to the phone cord, he began to gnaw it. "Why fight this?" I thought.

I went to the pantry and got the bottle of bitter apple spray, he following me with eager curiosity. He then watched me spray every potentially chewable object in my office as I said, "Let's see what you think about this." He tried to taste each object as I sprayed it, following me from the stool to the power cords, to the USB cords, shaking his head after each taste and giving me a look of doleful disapproval: "That is really horrible stuff. And you ruined my fun!"

"That's the idea," I said gently. "Now let's try this instead."

Going to the refrigerator, I fetched one of those acclaimed beehive-shaped rubber chew toys with a tube through its long axis. Mushy dog food is stuffed into the tube, and dogs have to work to get it out, keeping themselves occupied. I had never before had any experiences with such chew toys since Merle had no use for them. He found bones around Kelly, and I gave him the uncooked bones of elk and antelope. But Pukka was a blank slate, and I wanted to see his reaction to such a chew toy. To make it especially enticing I had stuffed it with organic bison pâté, especially formulated for dogs.

"Look at this, Pukka!" I said breathlessly. "A chew toy stuffed with bison! Mmm-mmm-mmm. Could anything be better?"

Eyes wide, he took it from my hand and carried it to his bed, where he lay with it between his paws as he worked his tongue into the opening and tried to suck out the bison pâté, occasionally drawing back his head to look into the tube.

"Perfect," I thought and returned to my computer, where I discovered that my e-mail program had crashed. After fiddling with it to no avail, I called my software consultant and asked her advice. Just then, I heard Pukka's sucking stop. Glancing at him from the corner of my eye, I saw him trotting to my wastepaper basket. He put his paws on its top edge, peered inside, and turned it over on top of himself. The software consultant said she would remotely manipulate my computer and call back. Hanging up, I picked up the bison-stuffed chew toy and inspected it. It was still mostly full of pâté. "So much for hours of distraction," I thought, watching Pukka thrashing in the wastepaper basket. I wondered if I'd get any work done.

Suddenly Pukka became still. For a few seconds he didn't move a muscle, seeming to consider his situation. Then he quickly backed out of the trash can and gave me a look that said, "I don't think I'll go in there again."

I held out the chew toy to him. He sniffed it, took it without interest, and immediately dropped it. Glancing around, he spied the books on the lowest bookshelf and bounded to them. "Ah," his bright eyes said, "this is better to chew on," and he began to gnaw on the spine of the nearest book.

Stifling the immediate "No!" that was rising in my throat, I said nothing. Instead, I went to the fridge and got the elk bone that I had defrosted for this eventuality. It was the top of a femur, about ten inches long, with a lot of meat on it. Such bones had distracted virtually every dog with whom I had been acquainted over the last four decades, but in today's veterinary world, giving a dog a bone has become controversial, despite the ancient rectitude of the phrase. Some veterinarians point out that bones can splinter and, if swallowed, puncture an intestine, or a dog can crack its teeth while chewing a bone, or the bone can produce inflammation of the GI tract, or it can carry bacterial contamination, not only for the dog, but also for the person who handles it. "Why take the risk?" the anti-bone contingent asks. Far better to give a chew toy or an artificial dental bone that a dog can work on safely.

The problem, though, as I had just seen, is that chews aren't interesting enough for some dogs—even ones filled with bison pâté. The other confounding factor is that the risk associated with dogs eating bones is highly dependent on the type of bone they're given. There isn't good, peer-reviewed, veterinary data on the danger of bones according to type, and therefore we must turn to the evidence of the ages, which is fairly robust: cooked bones tend to splinter and can cause injuries, while raw bones are safer; pork bones tend to splinter more than beef, bison, or elk bones; and chicken and turkey bones are notorious splinterers when cooked, but pliant when raw. In fact, as an older dog, Pukka would eventually eat entire raw pheasants and chickens—all the meat, bones, guts, feathers, and feet—crunching away with delight and leaving nothing more than a circle of primary feathers that so exactly resembled what a coyote leaves when it consumes a grouse that the similarity made the point: domestic dogs, given the chance, can handle food in its original form, particularly coarsely textured food, which cleans their teeth.

Research has shown that most dogs don't chew such foods often enough, and consequently 60 to 75 percent of them over four years of age are afflicted with periodontal disease (a disease of both the teeth and gums); the smaller the breed, the higher the risk of periodontal disease, since small dogs have the same number of permanent teeth as large dogs, forty-two, but they're packed together in a tiny mouth instead of having spaces between them. Even if a small dog chews coarse food, its teeth aren't completely cleaned and plaque accumulates.

The immediate signs of periodontal disease are ugly yellow teeth and bad breath. Far less apparent is the connection between periodontal disease and serious diseases that can follow upon its heels—hepatitis and heart, kidney, and lung disease—the bacteria that accumulate in the gums causing inflammation that eventually becomes systemic and contributes to the pathogenesis of these other conditions.

Hence, giving your dog a bone, a dental chew, or a good toothbrushing is cheap prevention, and the smaller the dog the more dental care it needs. Studies done at the Waltham Centre for Pet Nutrition in Leicestershire, England, and at the University of Pennsylvania, show that for small dogs chewing a real bone or a dental chew plus daily brushing is the way to keep periodontal disease at bay.

Bigger dogs, with wider spaces between their teeth, may not need quite so frequent brushing as do smaller breeds, and they may not need any at all if they eat the right sorts of bones. For small dogs, uncooked chicken wings and chicken necks are ideal, and for bigger dogs raw turkey necks serve the same purpose: the soft tendons and ligaments that these sorts of bones contain act like doggy dental floss, the mechanical shearing, as the dogs chew through them, removing tartar. Eventually this is the strategy I used for Pukka, and I found that, unlike the hard leg bones of elk and bison, which wore the ends of his canine teeth, poultry necks produced no wear at all.

Some people may find the notion of feeding their dogs bones messy and offensive, daily toothbrushing tiresome, and dental chews expensive, and for such people the pet food companies have created dental kibbles, which contain abrasives that help to remove plaque. But research — again done at the Waltham Centre — has shown that such kibbles are unable to maintain healthy gums. Waltham's veterinarians recommend brushing if such a diet is fed.

I myself have remained a fan of real bones. My childhood dog, Tippy, ate real bones; Merle and Brower chewed real bones; and so do A.J., Burley, Goo, and Buck, as well as dozens of other dogs who have stayed at my house, all without cracking a tooth, puncturing an intestine, or having GI problems. Nor have I ever gotten sick from *E. coli* or *Salmonella*. I defrost the bones; I hand them to the dog; I wash my hands. With the bone in its mouth, the dog — no matter how energetic it was a few moments before — turns meditative, addressing its bone to the exclusion of everything else in the world. Could anything be better for a rambunctious puppy? I thought not.

Carrying the elk bone into my office, I pried Pukka's mouth off the book he was gnawing, and said, "Please leave that," and as I did, I showed him the bone, adding with great enthusiasm, "Look at this, Pukka! An elk bone. Mmm-mmm-mmm. I think you'll like it." His eyes widened at his first sniff, and his face took on an expression of open-mouthed wonder.

"Come now, Little Sir," I said as I led him away from the bookshelf to the center of the office, with the elk bone in front of his nose. "Here it is. Your very first elk bone. And may there be many more." I handed it to him. He took it reverentially, and it being too heavy for him to carry, he dropped it on the floor, where he began to gnaw it, first with subdued little groans and then with loud yips of pleasure.

I went back to work, listening to him chew on the bone behind me. Fifteen minutes passed; a half-hour went by; a full forty-five minutes elapsed, and still he gnawed, moaning and whimpering with joy. "Yes!" I thought, remembering wolves bringing elk bones to their puppies. "This is how wolf parents get some rest."

Apparently for Pukka the elk bone was orders of magnitude more engrossing than the chew toy stuffed with bison pâté. On and on he chewed, at last carrying the bone — now diminished in size and weight — to his bed. Putting one paw under it and one paw over it, he continued to gnaw at the bone, eyes half-closed in rapture.

A few minutes later, I heard A.J.'s bark in the mudroom, the dog door having been closed to keep Pukka inside.

I went out, opened the human door, and A.J. followed me into my office just as my software consultant called me. Speaking to her about my e-mail program, I glanced behind me and saw A.J. staring sternly at Pukka. I took a step toward him. "Good boy, A.J.," I said and gave him a pat. He wagged his tail stiffly and lay down on the right side of my desk, turning his back to Pukka and me.

Standing up from his bone, Pukka walked over to A.J., wagging his tail in a warm greeting: "A.J., how are you!"

I saw it coming, but couldn't move fast enough.

With a savage growl, A.J. pounced on Pukka and mauled him on the head. Pukka screamed in terror and dashed around me, shrieking and leaving a trail of pee. He hid behind my desk.

"I'll call you," I said to the software consultant and hung up. Lifting Pukka, I turned him over in my arms, which were immediately covered in blood, gushing from a deep gash under his right eye. I snuggled him against my chest, and he went silent. Whirling, I stared in disbelief.

A.J. — my friend, my ski partner, the dog who had slept in my arms, the one who had helped me get over Merle's death — glared back in hatred. But he wasn't glaring at me; he was glaring at Pukka.

"Bad," I said to A.J. "So bad! Out." I pointed. "Out." As he began to pad from the office I booted him in his behind with my moccasin-shod foot, more of a shove than a kick. He skulked across the great room, and I followed him, holding the door open for him. "Way bad," I said. He walked across the porch, shoulders hunched and head hung.

Pukka watched with stolid composure.

"Oh, that bad A.J.," I said to him soothingly. "But I'm right here." Tenderly, I kissed him on the head and took him upstairs and sat him on the bathroom vanity, where I washed out the gash with soap and warm water. "Oh my goodness," I said, "what a brave dog you are. Not a peep out of you, and I bet that stings. I'm so sorry this happened, so sorry."

With relief, I saw that his eye seemed fine — mobile, alert, and shining — but the gash beneath it was long and wide and looked like it would need stitches. "I think you'll survive," I said, "but let's call Theo."

The bleeding stopped and I took Pukka downstairs, where I called Merle's old vet Theo Schuff. He said he could see Pukka in an hour. I didn't want to wait in his office, where there would be other dogs, so I sat on the dedicated quadruped couch, cuddling Pukka in my lap, kissing him on the top of the head, and saying, "It'll be fine. Not to worry. Theo will sew that right up."

Pukka looked at me stoically, but suddenly grew very tired, and in a few minutes he fell asleep in my arms. Once he was asleep and I had a moment to myself, I felt the pit of my stomach go even more hollow than it had been, and I noticed that I was shaking slightly.

Pukka was barely eight weeks old — just entering the developmental period that lasts through ten or eleven weeks of age and during which puppies are very sensitive to a trauma. Indeed, they can be scarred for life by a single bad experience. Somehow, I had let A.J. — whom I had envisioned as being one of Pukka's mentors — maul my new puppy. Yet (I was now defending myself), how many times had I given Merle, Brower, Buck, A.J., Burley, or Goo a bone and another dog had appeared, sometimes A.J. himself, and the dog without the bone had simply watched the dog with the bone eat? I hadn't given a thought to A.J.'s being jealous. I had seen no reason to. In over a quarter of a century in Kelly, I had seen a dozen puppies raised alongside all manner of adult dogs and had never witnessed an incident like this one. Yet there is a first time for everything, and after trying to cover so many bases, and allowing my puppy the freedom I believed he deserved, I hadn't covered this contingency. I now had to face the nightmare of every Outward Bound instructor: a student who's been hurt on one's watch. I hadn't protected him.

I heard a bark at the sliding-glass door. A.J. was standing on the south deck, staring at Pukka and me. He barked again, a very mean-spirited bark underlain with despondency: "I hate that you have that new dog. I thought I was your dog!"

I put Pukka on the couch — he remained asleep — and I went outside.

"That was totally uncalled for," I told him. "You were very bad."

At my words, he hung his head. I said nothing. I just stood there, scowling at him. He softly pushed the side of his head against my knee and held it there, saying, "Please pet me. I'm not happy."

I scratched his ears. "A.J., I'll still love you, even with Pukka. But I'm really mad at you. I've got to take Pukka to the vet."

Turning, I went inside. Picking up a very sleepy Pukka, I carried him to the car and placed him on his bed, buckling him in. A.J. came to the driver's-side door, looking hurt, apologetic, and as unhappy as a dog could look. "What you did was really terrible," I told him out the window. His head fell, and dejected he walked away.

Driving to Theo's, I replayed the morning. If only I had been a better reader of A.J.'s stern look at Pukka. If only I hadn't let him in. If only I had thought to defrost a bone for him. If only I hadn't been preoccupied with the crashed e-mail program. If, if, if . . . "Damn," I thought, "what a rotten way to start Pukka's life in Kelly."

Theo — a tall, lean, eternally good-natured man — was gentle with Pukka, just as he had been with Merle, calling him "partner," just as he had called Merle "partner." He cleaned out the gash with saline, dyed Pukka's eye, and saw no scratch on the cornea. He declared stitches unnecessary: the gash would close on its own and stitches might create a bigger scar. Pukka remained absolutely calm as Theo examined him, not a wiggle, not a squirm. He seemed to be aware that we were trying to take care of him.

Handing Pukka back to me, Theo said, "A.J. was probably trying to give Pukka a side knock with the flat of his eyeteeth. He must have missed slightly and caught a loose piece of facial flesh." At his words, I recalled Merle mauling Brower in exactly the same way when Brower, as a young puppy, had foiled one of Merle's stalks for a squirrel. Merle had growled horrifically, savaging Brower around the head, but he was simply reprimanding Brower in the noisy but harmless way that adult dogs often correct annoying puppies: Brower didn't have a scratch on him. What if Merle had missed, though, and had done this to Brower? Had A.J. had bad luck, bad aim, or bad intentions? I'd never know.

Enough drama had occurred for one morning. I wanted to put some normalcy in Pukka's day and not blow A.J.'s attack out of proportion. Driving back through town, we did errands — the pet store, the bank, the bike shop — and Pukka strolled around the stores, met people, and was petted. When we got home, I fed him, and he seemed suddenly happy, licking his bowl clean and wagging his tail. I left him alone a moment to answer the ringing phone, and while I was talking he peed on the floor of the great room. I cleaned it up without a word, took him outside through the sliding glass doors, placing him on the grass and saying pleasantly, "Here we go. This is the place. Outside is fine, inside is not."

Spying us from across the field, A.J. and Burley came running toward us, and Pukka immediately put his tail between his legs and looked at them warily. I did not scoop him up. I stood next to him, pressing the side of my leg against his flank as I said, "I'm right here." Calmly, A.J. sniffed Pukka from head to foot as if nothing had happened. I kept a hand on his collar and said firmly, "You be nice, A.J."

At my words, he stood erect, his confident grin saying, "I showed him who's boss." I expected Pukka to cringe, but he didn't. Poker-faced, he stared back at A.J.

"Let's go inside," I told Pukka and let him back through the sliding glass doors, which I closed on A.J. and Burley. Burley left, but A.J. stayed on the deck, looking forlorn once again. Eventually, he walked around the house and whined at the sealed dog door. I ignored him, and when I glanced out my office windows, I saw him walking back to his house, head lowered, shoulders hunched, for all the world looking like a rejected suitor. "What a sad situation," I thought. I had so wanted him and the other dogs to be Pukka's friends. Feeling low, I went to my desk, and a moment later I heard "Take Me Out to the Ball Game" floating from the great room.

Pukka had picked up his barking white dog and was shaking it. He trotted into the office, bearing it proudly, and I reached down and grabbed it. He braced his front paws and began playing tug-of-war with me.

"Rrrr," I said, play-growling to him.

"Rrrr," he replied.

I let go and got on my hands and knees. Dropping the white dog, he scooted beneath me, rolled on his back, and pawed the air between us, laughing open-mouthed, his black eyes dancing.

"Oh, he's back!" I exclaimed. "You can't keep a pukka dog down!" I mouthed his belly, and he pawed at my face with joy. "Yes, he's back!" I cried.

· · ·

But he wasn't.

Over the next few days, his eye swelled, sealed completely shut, and crusted over with a hard scab. Holding him in my lap, I put hot compresses on it, irrigating it with saline solution and wiping away the accumulated yellow pus with a Q-tip. Warmed and swabbed clean, his eyelid was able to blink, and the shining black orb emerged. Pulling his head back and bringing my face into focus, he would stare at me for a long time — his little face very sober, very reserved — then he'd lean forward and tenderly lick my mouth and rub his cheek against my chin before putting it on my shoulder and emitting a sigh that said, "This has been hard. Thank you for taking care of me."

"I wish I could have done a better job," I told him.

His lacerated eyelid wasn't the only part of him that was injured. He would no longer follow me away from the house, gamboling with head and tail high. He'd sit on the deck, looking in the direction of A.J.'s house, his little jaw set in an attitude of mortal concern. Using a Ziploc bag of elk jerky, I would cajole him off the deck, and lured by food, he'd prance after me, but only to the long grass at the edge of the firebreak, where he'd sit down.

"Come on," I'd say, running from him, kneeling, patting my hands against my chest, and shaking the bag. He wouldn't move, his look saying, "You are such a fool, my friend. Here on the lawn at least I can see A.J., if he comes for me. Out there in the sage, he could ambush me just like that."

His point was well taken. So I'd pick him up and carry him the hundred yards through the sage, placing him down on the old dirt road that cuts through Kelly's central field. By his lights, he was now safe. Without an instant's hesitation, he'd follow me to the Landales, to the post office, and to points beyond.

Upon our return, he'd be high-stepping along and would follow me into the sagebrush, either having forgotten that it might be hiding A.J. or having a different estimation of its danger when we were approaching our house. On more than one occasion, A.J., Burley, and Goo would come racing off their porch to greet us, A.J., back to his old form, carrying a ball or stick for me to throw.

Pukka would shrink against my legs as the big dogs sniffed him, and I would firmly tell the three of them, "Be nice! He's just a puppy!" Burley and Goo would wag their tails — "We know that! We like him!" — but A.J. would growl: "I don't like him at all!"

I would point a finger in A.J.'s face and say, "You stop that."

He'd drop the ball or stick at my feet, grin up at me, and wag his tail: "It's not that I don't like you, Ted. I don't like him. Now could you please throw that."

"Pukka now comes with me, A.J.," I'd remind him.

He would sit down and look up at me plaintively, his head cocked: "Why does it have to be this way?"

I'd pick up the ball or stick and fling it as far away as I could, and with the three dogs sprinting after it, Pukka would trot directly ahead of me, putting my body between himself and his persecutors, until we got to the house.

If this scene happened once, it happened a dozen times. But not once in all those times — when we left or returned to the house — did I lift Pukka off the ground when the three big dogs surrounded us. I continued to put a comforting hand on his shoulder as he leaned into my leg, saying through the calm pressure of my hand, "I am here for you — right here — and I will do a better job of protecting you this time around."

Merle had had his school of hard knocks, and Pukka was having his. I hoped that Pukka would graduate from Camp Kelly with as much confidence as the desert had given Merle.

The days grew longer, and on our morning walks we would loop over to Buck's house and ask him to go along. The joy with which Pukka greeted Buck, and the deep care with which Buck responded, helped to lighten my sadness over A.J.'s attack. Unleashed and uncollared, Buck and Pukka roamed ahead of me, Buck leading and Pukka following with keen concentration: smell this bush, paw this turd, mouth that grass. If something scared Pukka, he would dart under Buck's belly and stare out at the world from between the big dog's legs. At these moments, Buck did not ignore Pukka and trot off, nor did he condescend to him by panting, "Oh, that's just a ruffed grouse," or, "That's only a cow elk barking." Staring into the distance at the sounds that he had heard many times before, he would say by his attentive body language, "Don't worry, Pukka. I'll take care of everything."

At these times my affection for Buck spilled over the tops of the Tetons. Walking back to our house, Pukka would be a new pup, tail high as he capered ahead of me. Then the terrible trio would rush across the sage to greet us. Tail down, Pukka would huddle against my legs.

"I'm right here," I'd say as I petted all four dogs at the same time. A.J. — thoughtfully smelling Buck's scent on Pukka — would keep his growls to himself.

One morning after we had run the gauntlet of the big dogs and came into the house, Pukka immediately trotted upstairs. Sunlight was shining through the skylight, laying a golden swath on the landing, and Pukka went directly to it as if he had remembered that it would be here at this time of day. He lay in the patch of sunlight, and looking very pleased with himself, he thumped his tail at me: "This is where I want to be."

For the next few weeks, Pukka would come in from our morning walks and go directly to his patch of warmth and security. From it, he could look down the stairs up which no dogs could come without his seeing them. To his back was the second-floor bedroom, whence no dog could approach him unless it could fly through the windows. He had chosen his redoubt; he had decided on his own where he needed to be.

Naturally, he made mistakes during these first few weeks. Indeed, he made some of them right in the bedroom near his patch of sunlight, not wishing, it seemed, to go down the stairs where A.J. might be waiting, at least in his imagination.

Sometimes, first thing in the morning, he'd sit at the top of the stairs, gazing down them with a concerned expression on his little golden face. "Come on, Pukka," I'd say to him. "I know you have to go. I'll be right there with you. Come on, that's a good boy. Let's go down the stairs and I'll walk right by your side."

Teetering on the top step — "Oh, I've got to go so bad, Ted, but I don't want to go down there!" — he'd begin to pee, and I'd scoop him up, saying, "Outside! Outside's the place to go."

Fortunately, none of these mistakes were on the scale of the Gulf oil spill or Chernobyl. Paper towels and a bottle of organic spray deodorizer took care of them, the latter proving such an effective odor remover that Pukka never returned to the same spot twice.

Soon, he grew too big for his crate — he could barely turn around in it — and I borrowed a much larger one from a friend who used it for his two English Setters while traveling. In the bottom of this enormous crate was a comfortable gray rug. Placing the crate near my bed, I said, "Look at the size of this dog bedroom, Pukka. It's not even a bedroom. It's a trophy home, and you can really stretch out in style."

He walked into the crate, sniffed the rug, and I closed the grate behind him. Instantly, he began to whine, then cry out loud. He pawed the grate. This was unprecedented behavior. He was now sleeping seven hours straight through the night. Unthinkingly—or rather, thinking only about the old advice not to give in to a puppy's demands at night—I told him to shush and got into my own bed. He continued to cry, more and more loudly, and no amount of shushing would quiet him.

I lay there, listening to his cries, and I didn't hear what I had heard on the first night I put him in his crate, in the Rapid City motel: "My heart is breaking. I'm so lonely. I miss my brothers and sisters." Instead, I heard, "I don't like this crate. I really don't like it."

It had been a long day: writing before dawn, walking and training with Pukka, driving to puppy play dates, more walking and training, and then editing the several hundred digital images I had taken of him and his friends until midnight. I was dead tired. But in a mixture of altruism and self-interest—I wanted him to be comfortable and I wanted to sleep—I went downstairs and out to the porch where I had placed his small crate.

Bringing it upstairs, I put it by the door of the bigger crate, and opened both doors. Pukka sprang from the larger crate and into the smaller one as if getting into a lifeboat. Barely managing to turn around, he settled himself and went to sleep.

Shutting off the light, I lay there and thought of what I had just witnessed. Pukka had been sleeping happily in his small crate for days. I had given him a bigger one, much more comfortable, and yet he didn't like it. What had he been whining? "I don't like these big dog smells. They frighten me." Or: "I don't like where this crate was. It has a bad smell to it." Or: "The dog who was here before me was sad when he had to stay in here." The possibilities were numerous, but had a common theme: "I am not happy."

The next day I laundered the big crate's rug and scrubbed out the crate itself. That night I reassembled it in our bedroom, and Pukka gave it an exploratory sniff. I had also placed his own towel alongside the laundered gray rug to sweeten the pot. He flopped across both of them and gave me a look that said, "Well done, Ted! I didn't like that rug." Within a minute, he was asleep.

As for what smell the rug contained, I do not speak good enough Dog to offer an opinion. I did lie there, though, listening to Pukka's calm sleeping breath while thinking of the millions of puppies across the globe — crying in their kennels, in shelters, in crates by people's bedsides — and of how by changing one small thing we might make them happy, if we could only understand them better.

Toward the end of May, the aspen finally bloomed, and Pukka's eye healed, leaving a crescent of black scar beneath the lid. We lengthened our walks, venturing along the Gros Ventre River, the wet morning smells heavy in the air and the trumpeter swans honking as they flew upstream. In the adjoining fields, the Canada geese yakked their warnings, protecting their nests, while the bluebirds, robins, and magpies hopped across our lawn. Unlike Merle, who had little use for the avian world, Pukka paid constant attention to all these flying creatures, listening to me carefully as I would say, "Those are swans, Pukka, trumpeter swans, our biggest waterfowl. And those are bluebirds, not good to eat, though I've never tried."

His ornithological interests didn't stop at birds. One afternoon, as a jet went by, making its approach to the Jackson Hole airport behind Blacktail Butte, Pukka stared at it with rapt attention from the deck and then looked at me inquiringly: "That's a strange bird."

"It's a jet," I said.

Not two minutes later, a helicopter came overhead, heading toward the airport as well, and Pukka gave me the same look: "What's that?"

"Helicopter," I said. "Another kind of plane. They're not birds, though, like swans or geese. People fly in them."

He considered this. A few days later, as we were walking along the river, he chanced to look up and saw the three-quarter moon in the sky. He stopped dead, looking directly at it with wide eyes as if seeing something truly miraculous. Then he looked to me for what he had come to expect — a name.

"Moon," I said, wondering how to convey to a dog the notion of a planetary body circling the earth 240,000 miles away. "It's the moon," I repeated. "It's far, far away."

Apparently, this satisfied him.

The weather turned colder and I went back to building fires, bringing in an armful of kindling as Pukka watched me. The second time I brought in a load, he picked up a piece of kindling from the woodpile and carried it into the house, where he dropped it in front of the woodstove.

"*Que bueno,* Pukkacito!" I complimented him, quite impressed at how he was miming my behavior. "But you must put it inside the stove." And holding his shoulders, I helped him drop it on the growing flames.

That night, after his evening constitutional, he stood on the deck and listened to the coyotes singing from across the road, his ears pricking in time to their yips as he gazed into the darkness.

"Coyote," I said. "Coyote. The little big dog."

He looked at me with the thoughtful expression I had come to recognize: "I have it: *Coyote* belongs to that sound."

Just before we went to bed, the long spring rains began. I opened the front door for Pukka so he could have his last evening P&P, and he tentatively stuck his nose outside. As he gazed at the sheets of water falling from the eaves, his face took on a look of distaste. He planted his butt on the floor.

"Oh, come now, Little Sir," I urged him. "A bit of rain is not going to make you melt."

He remained seated.

"I *know* you have to *go,*" I sang.

Mincingly as a cat, he walked to the edge of the deck and stepped off, pressing his flank against the deck's fascia so as to keep himself just under the eave and out of the rain. He squatted, peed, and turned in a flash to race inside. Closing the door before him, I blocked his way, "Uh-uh, not so fast," I said. "How 'bout a poop? Out there. Go ahead." I motioned to the sagebrush.

He looked miserably at the falling rain, not budging, so I picked him up and carried him into the sage, where he stepped with exaggerated care, as if the wet ground might be laced with land mines. At last, he crouched and quickly did his business, hurtling back to the house when he was done and waiting for me to open the door so he could shoot into the great room and gallop toward the woodstove. Laying his front paws under the glass window, he stared into the flames as if gazing at the face of the divine.

"Oh, Little Sir," I admonished him gently, "you are very delicate for a Labrador."

One night, after having gone through this routine for the last three rainy evenings, he remained planted by the woodstove when I said, "Time for bed."

I walked to the hall; he didn't follow; and I said again, "Time for bed."

He put his head between his paws: "I think I'm going to stay right here."

"Are you sure you don't want to go up to bed?"

He scrunched his head farther down between his paws and flattened his body on the floor.

"He's a baby," I thought. "I should just pick him up and carry him to his crate." Then I checked myself. He was following me around Kelly; he obeyed simple commands; he knew the names of the local animals; and he had been beaten up by a bigger dog and was meeting him every day with his own four paws on the ground. Obviously, at this moment, he knew what he wanted. So I left him there, saying, "Sleep well."

I went upstairs, and before long I heard him pick up his barking white dog. He brought it upstairs, walked into his large crate, and lay down. I didn't close the door. If I was willing to let him sleep downstairs on his own, should I really be closing the door of his crate anymore?

Six hours later, I awoke to the barks of "Take Me Out to the Ball Game."

"Good morning," I said. "Did you sleep well?"

He came out of his crate, put his paws on the edge of my bed, and wagged his tail with great pleasure: "Terrific!"

Then he walked to the landing, looked back at me, and started down the stairs on his own.

Over the next few nights, he slept with his crate door open, and then, as an experiment, I brought his round green bed upstairs, putting it in the corner where Merle had slept. Pukka settled on it straightaway, as if he'd been sleeping there his entire life. I got into my own bed, saying "'Night, Sir," as I had said so many times to Merle.

I didn't have a chance to turn off the light. Pukka stood and walked across the room and into his large crate, which was still by the head of my bed. I thought about what he had just done. "Does he want to be in the crate?" I thought. "Or does he want to be closer to me?" Without a single word to him, I got up and placed his bed next to the crate. Then I got back into bed.

As I was pulling up the covers, he got out of the crate and lay on his bed, looking at me with appreciative eyes: "That's exactly what I wanted — not the crate, but my bed close to you."

"Sleep well, Pukka," I said. "I love you," and I turned off the light.

Pukka received his vaccinations at sixteen weeks of age, and three weeks later Marybeth Minter drew a blood sample from him and sent it to Jean Dodds's laboratory to be titered. A few days later, we had the results. Pukka had more than adequate immunity to distemper and an insufficient immunity to parvovirus. Marybeth boostered him with another parvo shot, and his immunity proved fine when we subsequently titered him. In another few weeks, he got a rabies shot, and we titered him for that as well, to make sure he had sufficient immunity. He did, and that was that. He received no vaccines for leptospirosis, Bordetella, or coronavirus. According to his titers and Drs. Marybeth Minter, Jean Dodds, and Ron Schultz, he was immunized. And that was good enough for me. In the years to come, I would continue to use titers to make sure he had retained his immunity.

I also had Pukka tested for centronuclear myopathy and progressive retinal atrophy, and he proved clear. Not so for exercise-induced collapse. Abby was a carrier, and Pukka had inherited her recessive gene. Although he would never exhibit symptoms of the condition — collapsing during hard exercise — he could never be mated with another dog who was a carrier, lest one of their puppies inherit a gene from each of them and be afflicted.

In addition, I had Pukka tested for several other heritable eye diseases by a board-certified veterinary ophthalmologist. His eyes proved normal, and I registered the results with CERF, the Canine Eye Registration Foundation. Later, when Pukka was two years old, I also had his elbows and hips X-rayed for dysplasia. His elbows proved to be "normal," and his hips were "good," which I had hoped would be the case, given that his parents' elbows and hips ranged between normal and excellent.

All his test results can be found on the website of the Orthopedic Foundation of America and the Centronuclear Myopathy International Central Registry. If I ever breed Pukka, I would make sure that his mate has been similarly cleared of genetically transmitted diseases and has a low coefficient of inbreeding. I would also ensure that the COI of their litter was low. Anyone interested in one of their puppies would be able to find Pukka's and his mate's test results on these websites and would then have a guarantee that the pups were, at a minimum, beginning life with a clean slate, at least to the extent that current veterinary technology allows us to predict.

There proved to be no titer test, however, that was able to measure an increase in Pukka's immunity to A.J. My hope had been that through our walks and his meeting other dogs and their people—by exposing him to crowds and cars and to A.J., Burley, and Goo themselves—I'd help to build up his resistance to their intimidating presence across the field. But he continued to shy from them.

Then one day, as Pukka and I were returning from the post office, the three big dogs came running over to meet us. As usual, A.J. held an object for me to throw, this time a ten-inch-long plank, a two-by-four, that he had snagged from my kindling pile. He dropped it at my feet as Pukka scuttled between my legs, getting out of his way.

Picking up the piece of wood, I threw it into the field, and as was almost always the case, A.J. got to it before Burley and Goo and brought it back to me. I threw it again, but this time Pukka peered inquisitively from between my legs. The third time I threw the two-by-four, Pukka stepped a few feet away from me, sat down on the deck, and watched A.J. and Burley scuffling for the wood as Goo ran around in frantic circles, barking.

A.J. emerged with the wood and pranced smartly back to me. But as he placed the two-by-four in my hand, Pukka—without the least warning—jumped up and grabbed it. Planting his front paws, he began to tug it from A.J.'s mouth.

I stared in wonder. Perhaps his many experiences with friendly dogs and people had finally had their effect; perhaps his having me by his side, my hand on his shoulder as I said, "I'm right here," had given him the self-confidence he needed; perhaps the maturing biochemistry of his brain had connected a synapse that had suddenly brought him out of his period of fear. Whatever the case, he was tugging hard at the two-by-four, the determined look in his eyes saying, "I'm going to get this from you, A.J."

A.J. appeared suddenly rattled and confused, as if he didn't recognize who Pukka was. Only for a moment. Then his face become hard, and he glared down at Pukka with an expression that said, "Didn't I beat you up a while ago? Give me the stick! Now!"

Pukka would have none of it. He growled loudly and tugged harder, front legs stiff, tail erect, brow furrowed in concentration.

I stood transfixed as Pukka and A.J. set their front paws and yanked each other around, their expressions very serious.

To prevent another incident, I pulled the two-by-four from between them and flung it into the field toward Burley, who was hanging out there like a center fielder. A.J. shot off, and putting on an extraordinary burst of speed shouldered Burley aside.

Meanwhile, Pukka followed the throw, the dash, and the scuffle with electric attention. As A.J. ran back with the wood, Pukka — his little tail straight up in the air — intercepted him on the fly, gleefully snagging the end of the two-by-four once again.

A look of grave doubt crossed A.J.'s face, and his brows pumped up and down with apprehension: "This puppy is more than I bargained for."

Pukka was tugging mightily, and I took the two-by-four from them, saying, "Well done, Pukka, well done!" Throwing it far into the field, I added, "Let's go inside now. I think you gave A.J. something to think about."

This was not the end.

Several days later, as Pukka and I came back from our evening walk, A.J., Burley, and Goo met us on the deck, A.J. carrying a softball. He offered it to me and I threw it toward Merle's prayer flags.

The three big dogs ran after it and to my astonishment Pukka leapt off the deck and followed them. They outdistanced him in a flash, and he stopped halfway across the lawn, staring after them wistfully. Glancing over his shoulder, he regarded me, then he turned to watch the three dogs scuffling over the ball. Once again he looked back to me, this time his expression asking, "Is it okay to go out there?" He was only fifty feet away, but he had decided to leave the mother ship.

Gently I swept my hand toward him and lifted my chin toward the distance: off you go. Reassured, he took a few steps toward the three older dogs, but they were already on their way back, A.J. bearing the ball.

Instead of going to them, Pukka lay in the grass and crouched like a little lion waiting for its prey. A.J. saw him and sidestepped. Pukka sprang up, bumped his shoulder into A.J.'s flank, and raced alongside him back to the deck. A.J. continued to ignore him — "Puppy? I don't see any puppy" — and dropped the ball at my feet.

Mistake.

Pukka pounced upon it, flattened his belly on the deck, and lay with the softball between his paws, looking up at the much larger dog with steady eyes that now seemed more challenging than playful. "Sorry, A.J.," they said, "this is mine now."

Burley and Goo had joined us. They looked on, both of them very still. A.J. looked on as well. There was not a soul among us, except Pukka, who did not think, "This little dog does not have a clue as to what he's doing."

I stood at the ready to grab A.J.'s collar, to step in front of him, if he so much as dared make an aggressive move. Instead, he cocked his head at me, his golden eyes saying, "Please get my ball back. This puppy's turned into a monster."

I couldn't help it. I burst out laughing. A.J. looked crushed.

"I'm sorry, A.J.," I said, sympathetically. "But you're going to have to share the ball, and you're going to have to share me."

Looking deflated, he sat down. The world he had known — A.J. owns the ball — had come to an end. Pukka was happily chewing on the stitching of the softball, and A.J. glanced up at me. "He's here to stay," his resigned eyes said, "isn't he?"

"Yes, he is, A.J.," I replied. "Pukka's here to stay."

CHAPTER TEN

Building the Dikes

PUKKA'S CONFIDENCE GREW rapidly, and soon he was venturing into the sagebrush by himself. Sitting on the deck, I'd watch him cross the lawn and make a shallow arc into the low green jungle, raising his head frequently to make sure that I was still in sight. I'd wave to him and go into the house, keeping a constant eye on him as he smelled bison pies and coyote trails and the myriad birds, rodents, and garter snakes who made the sagebrush their home.

Within a couple of more weeks he was exploring two hundred yards from the deck, I now watching him through binoculars, a smile lighting my face as I saw him get to his farthest-reached point. There, like a mariner seeing the great ocean before him, he'd gaze back to the house, deciding if he should go farther. Ten yards, twenty yards, thirty yards he'd venture. Surely it must have been like this for the Phoenicians, the Norsemen, and the Polynesians setting off in their small boats—a gaze back to the fading shore, to the disappearing house, a gaze ahead, too far!—and he would turn and dash in mad puppy gambols back through the sage, onto the deck, and through the open doors, rushing at me and rubbing himself against my leg, reaffirming our bond—"Touch, there, that's better"—and then panting, "He-he-he!," telling me what he had discovered.

Finally, on a sunny July morning when he was four months old, I watched him disappear into the far edge of the sagebrush meadow, like a ship fading into the offing, his golden tail sinking below the horizon, outward bound and on his own at last. I thought of following him—just to make sure that he was okay—but I remembered how annoyed I had been when my parents appeared out of nowhere, checking up on me as I was in the midst of my childhood adventures. So I waited patiently, and about twenty minutes later I saw him returning from the south—only his golden back and uplifted tail visible in the sage and yellow flowers, like a ship reappearing over the rim of the sea. He had left on a southwesterly course, and his return from a new direction must have meant that he was already confident enough to take a different route home. And, in fact, he did seem to be navigating perfectly, heading directly for the house even though he couldn't see it. He stepped into the open fields by the horse corrals and gazed around to take his bearings. Spotting the house, he broke into a run—a long, lean, golden puppy streaking by the horses and through the aspen—bounding over the grass, onto the deck, and into the great room, where he twirled before me and laughed with happiness: "Heh-heh-heh"—his voice was getting deeper—"I walked everywhere on my own!"

"What an explorer you are!" I cried.

"I am!" he panted joyfully. "And you won't believe what I found!"

Standing on his hind legs, he began to wave his front paws at me, yipping and woofing and recounting his triumphant adventures. There was no ticker-tape parade, but he could have been Lindbergh after having crossed the Atlantic or Glenn returning from space.

Then one fine summer morning, as I was drinking my coffee at the picnic table on the deck, one of the potential costs of having a free-roaming dog—even in a place like Kelly, Wyoming—came walking along the edge of my land. I saw my neighbor Ron on my property boundary, a backpack sprayer on his back, a hose snaking to the long wand in his hand, his gaze intent upon the ground as he hit plant after plant with bright green jets of herbicide. Ron—a fair, redheaded man—married into the Kent family, which owns the twenty-acre sage field in the midst of the village. The Kents had maintained the land as open space, allowing everyone—people, dogs, horses, and wildlife—to cross it at will, and Ron, who lived on the north side of the field (we lived on the east), had taken on the responsibility of eradicating the spotted knapweed that had begun to overwhelm this parcel of land, as well as many other lands in Jackson Hole, during the early 2000s.

He wasn't alone in this mission. Each summer Grand Teton National Park sends spraying crews across the valley floor, targeting the spotted knapweed, a Eurasian plant that is believed to have arrived on the shores of British Columbia and Washington in the 1890s, hidden among alfalfa, with which it grows indigenously in the Eastern Hemisphere. It is a beautiful plant, I must admit, its thin green stems branching to three feet in height, each stem topped by showy purple flowers, the petals long, slender, and profuse, like a punk rocker's spiky hairdo.

Spotted knapweed also happens to be an extremely aggressive plant: it crowds out native forage for wildlife and livestock, increases surface water runoff, and causes hundreds of millions of dollars of lost revenue across southwestern Canada and the northwestern United States. There is increasing evidence that biological controls – specifically herbivorous insects – may eventually be able to control spotted knapweed, but in the meantime most people and most agencies spray it to death.

I put down my mug of coffee, walked out into the sage, and bid Ron good morning, asking him what he was spraying this year. "Milestone," he replied. He was wearing no respirator, no HAZMAT suit, not even gloves. "It's so mild," he added, "you could drink it."

We had had this conversation several times before because I'm not a fan of toxic chemicals being sprayed on my land and didn't want Ron, in his zeal, to stray over my property boundary. However, if one person controls knapweed and another doesn't, the knapweed seeds simply blow from the untreated to the treated ground, defeating efforts to eradicate it. When Merle was alive, I had asked Ron not to spray my land (something he had graciously offered to do without cost to me), and in return I had handpicked the knapweed on my land, trying to pull it out by its taproots.

It had been a never-ending and time-consuming task – soaking the ground to loosen the taproot and then spading. It was also an unrewarding job since the spotted knapweed would return the following year in other places on my land, the seeds having blown in from adjoining properties, the very factor that also makes spraying unrewarding. And this, of course, is the point that the champions of biological controls make: only a natural predator of spotted knapweed will finally control it.

I looked toward the house. I had closed the door behind me, so Pukka wouldn't come out and step into the newly applied herbicide, and I could see him standing with his paws on the back of the dedicated quadruped couch, his curious golden face looking at us through the window.

"It's perfectly safe," said Ron, following my glance. "Don't even worry about your dog. It has no known toxicity. Check it out."

I said I would, but in the meantime I asked him please not to spray my land. I would handpick the knapweed once again.

Back in the house, I Googled "Milestone," produced by Dow Agro-Sciences, and just as Ron had said, it was billed as having low toxicity to birds, fish, mammals, and aquatic invertebrates. It had low persistence in the environment, said the Dow brochure, and didn't contain the controversial compound 2,4-D, whose use has been associated with an increased incidence of non-Hodgkin's lymphoma in farmworkers in America and Europe. Non-Hodgkin's lymphoma is the same cancer that kills dogs the world over. However, when I turned to the "Material Safety Data Sheet" and the Milestone label itself, a slightly different picture emerged. True, no emergency medical treatment was necessary if you swallowed it, but you were supposed to flush your eyes and skin if either came in contact with it. The label did recommend wearing gloves.

These cautions made me think of Pukka romping barepawed through the bright green herbicide now splotched around my land, his unprotected nose snarfing up this new addition to the landscape. I decided that he wasn't going outside on his own for a while.

During the next two days I kept him in the house, accompanying him on walks as we wended our way through the green splotches of Milestone. I had learned that the half-life of Milestone exposed to sunlight was 0.6 days, and on the third day after Ron sprayed I let Pukka out on his own. Shortly, I heard several dogs barking and found Pukka across the road — along with A.J., Burley, Goo, and Buck — playing with the park spraying crew. The six college-aged men and women, on their summer jobs, had stopped for a break after treating the lands that the National Park Service owns within Kelly. They sat on the tailgates of two pickup trucks, their backpack sprayers laid aside, their jeans and shirts as well as their bare hands colored bright green with Milestone as they petted the dogs. Obviously, they hadn't been wearing gloves despite the label's warning. I said "hi" and told the dogs to go home.

"Don't worry," said one of the young men, holding up his green hands, "you could drink this stuff."

Like many of the people who were cheerfully applying the herbicide on their skin as well as on the spotted knapweed, he didn't seem troubled by what were its unknowns: What exactly was in the 59.4 percent of the compound – more than half of it – that Dow listed as "other ingredients"? Might there be toxic effects from minuscule quantities of Milestone, far, far below the quantities that had been tested, as had been found to be the case with other synthetic compounds that were once thought to be safe? Had anyone tested Milestone in combination with the other herbicides that the park had applied in past years – just a few of the thousands of chemicals to which we and our dogs are now exposed?

That my concerns weren't an exercise in paranoia was demonstrated in 2008 by a study done on twenty dogs and thirty-seven cats at a Virginia veterinary clinic. Their blood and urine were sampled, and the dogs and cats were found to be loaded with toxins: the dogs carried eleven carcinogens, twenty-four neurotoxins, and thirty-one substances harmful to their reproductive systems, and the cats had similar amounts. Moreover, two perfluorochemicals known as PFCs – those Teflon-like chemicals found in the stain-resistant and grease-proof coatings of dog beds and kibble bags – were found at levels in the dogs that were 500 percent higher than those found in the average American. Dogs also had the breakdown products of four phthalates at levels ranging between 110 and 450 percent higher than in people. When it came to PBDEs, the fire-retardant polybrominated diphenyl ethers that are found in carpets, furniture, and some dog beds, dogs had 1,700 percent more of them than the amount found in the average American, and their levels were 3,400 percent higher than in the average European. Cats fared about as badly as dogs when it came to PFCs and PBDEs, but didn't have the same burden of phthalates that come from plastics, a bit of circumstantial evidence that points to the fact that dogs may get more of their phthalate contamination through their chew toys.

The heavy toxic load borne by cats and dogs is a result of there now being eighty thousand synthetic chemicals loose in our environment. Since the passage of the Toxic Substances Control Act of 1976, the Environmental Protection Agency has tested fewer than 1 percent of these eighty thousand chemicals for their health risks. Moreover, in over three decades of regulatory oversight, the agency has issued regulations to control only five of these chemicals, four of them carcinogenic and one implicated in the destruction of the ozone layer. Some sixty-two thousand of these eighty thousand chemicals cannot be legally tested for their health risks by the EPA. The Toxic Substances Control Act grandfathered them, and until the law is changed they are with us — for good and for ill.

The upshot of this lack of regulatory oversight is that we, and our dogs and cats, swim through a vast chemical ocean. We swim through it each and every day of our lives, and our dogs and cats are far more affected by its harmful ingredients — carcinogens, neurotoxins, and endocrine disruptors — than you or I. There are two very good reasons for their increased susceptibility to pollutants.

First, dogs and cats wear no shoes and they put their noses to the ground, dogs more so than cats with respect to taking in the world through their nostrils. They walk on herbicide-treated lawns as well as on pavement and roads, which are covered with windblown pesticides, automotive exhaust, and airborne industrial pollutants. Dogs and cats are then exposed to these pollutants a second time when they ingest them by licking their paws and fur.

The other reason dogs and cats are more awash in the chemical ocean than we are is that they're smaller. Their exposure to environmental contaminants is larger per unit of body weight than it is for adult humans. But size alone doesn't make dogs and cats more vulnerable.

In its massive report *Pesticides in the Diets of Infants and Children*, the National Academy of Sciences points out that the metabolic pathways of children are not fully developed and so can't metabolize and detoxify pollutants as well as those of adults. Since the blood-brain barrier of children is more porous than that of adults, children may also stand a greater chance of losing brain function when exposed to pollutants. And everything that the National Academy of Sciences writes about children also applies to dogs and cats, especially when they're young. Indeed, the NAS goes so far as to say that we might expect the biological effects of pesticides and other chemicals to be more pronounced in more rapidly growing animals, and it actually uses the example of dogs to make its point. Dogs have achieved a tenfold increase from their birth weight when they reach 165 days of age, whereas humans don't reach the same mark until they're five thousand days old. With this in mind, the NAS authors write, "In the absence of other factors direct carcinogens are more potent in rapidly growing animals."

Given that this vast chemical ocean is not going to dry up in the near future, is there a way to reduce our exposure, and that of our dogs and cats, to its dangerous elements? I believe there is. It takes some thought, some time, and a bit of expense, but it can be done, not eliminating these compounds from the greater chemical ocean — it will take a change in governmental policy to do that — but rather keeping them from our own personal space much as the Dutch have kept back the North Sea. In short, we have to build some dikes, and in order to appreciate how this can be done on a household level, let's first consider what we're facing. There's no better way of doing this than by looking at a day in the life of an average dog — your dog, perhaps.

When your dog eats its breakfast of kibble, it's not just eating its food. It may also be ingesting some potentially toxic PFCs from the grease-proof lining of the bag in which its kibble is packaged. If your dog's kibble is corn-based, it may also be eating some glyphosate residue, the principal ingredient in Roundup, an herbicide that is now sprayed on about 85 percent of America's corn. In addition, your dog may be eating some atrazine, another common herbicide used on corn, and it may also be lapping up some of this popular weed killer in its post-kibble drink of water since the herbicide is widely used on parks, golf courses, lawns, and gardens, from which it drains into municipal water supplies.

Although atrazine's manufacturer, the Swiss corporation Syngenta, has long claimed that its flagship herbicide is harmless in the concentrations found in drinking water and in foods, its claims fly in the face of international peer-reviewed scientific research that links exposure to atrazine to a variety of cancers, disruption of endocrine systems, reduced sperm quality, and reduced reproduction and tissue abnormalities in fish. Another study done in the Midwest discovered that the use of atrazine along with several other common organophosphate insecticides increased the incidence of non-Hodgkin's lymphoma in farmers.

Despite these many cautionary studies, and even though atrazine is banned in the European Union, the EPA allowed it to be reregistered for use in the United States in 2006. To demonstrate what we're up against in trying to protect ourselves against such chemicals, reflect on the fact that during the EPA's deliberations for the reregistration of atrazine, the agency held approximately fifty private meetings with representatives from Syngenta without allowing any public representation.

A 2009 report by the US Government Accountability Office found the credibility and integrity of the EPA's procedures to assess the safety of chemicals to be seriously in question and to lack transparency. The GAO's strong critique of the EPA, along with continued pressure by scientists and citizen groups, has forced the agency to begin a new review of atrazine. As of 2012, the review was ongoing.

Having followed these proceedings, you remain worried about feeding your dog corn-based kibble. So you've switched to canned food. However, your dog may now be eating some BPA along with its meal, as this endocrine disruptor is used in many protective coatings such as those found in the linings of food cans. Bisphenol A, the full name of BPA, is also found in the fire retardants that are used in furniture and appliances, and it's incorporated into a wide variety of plastics, including plastic beverage bottles. So pervasive is BPA in our chemical ocean that it is present in the urine of 93 percent of Americans older than six. Children under the age of six have urinary concentrations of BPA twice that of adults, largely because they play on the floor, where BPA-laden dust is found, and then put their hands in their mouths. Dogs and cats also play on the floor – indeed live on it – and lick its dust off their fur. More than one hundred studies have shown that BPA negatively alters the function of the endocrine system, and there is strong evidence that it also increases the risk of cancer by reprogramming how genes are turned on and off.

In addition to getting atrazine in its kibble and water, and BPA in its canned food, your dog may be getting some nitrates in its water, if your water comes straight out of the tap without being filtered. These nitrates are a by-product of nitrogen fertilizer leaching into groundwater. Reacting with your dog's stomach acids and proteins, nitrates can form cancer-causing N-nitroso compounds.

Now finished with its breakfast, your dog runs to the bathroom, happily greeting you as you step from the shower, towel yourself off, and apply some body lotion, which your dog eagerly licks off your skin, getting a dose of phthalates to add to the ones that it may have gotten from eating out of its plastic bowl and by lying on your kitchen's lino-leum floor. Phthalates are used as softening agents in the manufacture of the vinyl plastic that goes into flooring, wall coverings, and food wrappings; they're found in medical devices like IV tubing; they're put into lacquers and varnishes; they're found in time-release capsules, perfumes, cosmetics, and lotions; and they've been linked to a dizzy-ing array of health problems: asthma, allergies, cancers, and ADHD in children, attention deficit hyperactivity disorder, which in dogs may express itself as excessive chewing, barking, and separation anxiety. Endocrine-disrupting chemicals such as BPA and phthalates may also be making both you and your dog fatter. Research from around the world indicates that a wide array of endocrine-disrupting chemicals can alter the body's normal controls over energy balance and what's called "adipogenesis," or the laying down of fat.

Researchers have begun to call this class of endocrine disruptors "obesogens" and have pointed out that they can create metabolic im-balances at unthinkably low doses — as little as two micrograms per kilogram per day — particularly during a narrow and critical window of fetal development. What does two micrograms per kilogram mean? It's like spreading a 44-pound bag of dog food through 22 billion pounds of kibble. Put into railway cars, that's a freight train stretching from Portland to San Diego or Hamburg to Rome. It is these minute amounts of endocrine-disrupting chemicals that may determine whether a child or a puppy is physiologically impaired, normal or au-tistic, fat or thin, bright or not so bright.

One of the most ubiquitous classes of these endocrine-disrupting chemicals is the fire-retardant PBDEs — the polybrominated diphenyl ethers widely used in textiles, building materials, and electronic equip-ment such as computers and televisions. Because the European Union has banned two out of three of the commercial mixtures of PBDEs, the concentrations of these chemicals are seventeen times higher in the bodies of North Americans than they are in Europeans, and the indi-viduals who are the primary collectors of PBDEs are those children, dogs, and cats who live in homes with carpets, which have been found to act as long-term sinks for environmental contaminants, holding them up to one year. Since PBDEs are also found in the foam used in dog beds and furniture, dogs who sleep for many hours on either get an especially large dose of these chemicals.

Done with your shower, shave, or makeup, you now take your dog for a walk before heading off to work. Your dog bounds across several of your neighbors' lawns – they don't mind, they have dogs, too, and you're all good friends. However, your dog has now picked up some 2,4-D on its paws, as the herbicide is used in hundreds of lawn care products to control broadleaf weeds. This herbicide is also used on agricultural crops, and many studies, done all around the world, have shown an association between the application of 2,4-D and non-Hodgkin's lymphoma. The National Cancer Institute believes that there may be a similar risk for dogs.

Even when people use no pesticides on their lawns, in their gardens, or in their homes, pesticide residues have nonetheless been found on their carpets, floors, windowsills, and furniture. The pollutants drift in through open windows and through cracks in the structure and are tracked in by adults, children, and most often by the dogs themselves. In fact, one study found that 60 percent of the residues on the floor could be attributed to the household's dog.

At work you have a busy day, while your dog – deep in doggy dreams – breathes in your home's off-gassing formaldehyde, a chemical that is used in the manufacture of plywood, particle board, and carpeting and is a known carcinogen. Elevated levels of formaldehyde are frequently found just above new carpeting, exactly where your dog is lying. In the short term, exposure to elevated levels of formaldehyde can cause burning eyes, sore throats, and difficulty breathing; in the long term, it can cause cancer.

With a big project to complete, you stay at work an hour longer than usual, thinking that at least you'll miss rush hour traffic. No such luck. There's been an accident on the interstate, two lanes are closed, and you're two hours late getting home to your dog, where you find that it's been unable to wait for you. It's left a deposit by the front door, and it gives you a look that says, "I tried to get outside." Feeling angry that your place of business won't allow dogs, even well-behaved ones like yours, you hurriedly clean up the mess without a reprimand or cross word to your dog, using a brand-name, all-purpose cleaner. You then freshen the air with a brand-name air freshener and launder your dog's bed with a brand-name detergent since it's tracked some of the mess onto it. In the space of a few minutes both you and your dog have been exposed to a mix of more than one hundred chemicals that you didn't have a clue existed since they're not listed on the packaging of these household products. But just because they're not listed doesn't mean that they're harmless.

In 2009 researchers from the University of Washington analyzed the unlisted ingredients in twenty-five common, fragranced products sold in the United States — laundry detergents, personal care products, cleaning supplies, and air fresheners. They found that each product emitted at least one toxic or hazardous compound; some emitted as many as eight. Eleven of these products made some claim to being "green," "organic," "natural," or "nontoxic." Yet every one of these green products contained at least two toxic or hazardous compounds.

Such common household products expose us to numerous toxic chemicals every day, yet it is nearly impossible to find out their contents since manufacturers consider their formulations proprietary. Nor are there any federal regulations that require manufacturers to disclose the ingredients of such products.

The European Union is ahead of the United States in this regard. It has mandated that the labels of detergents and household cleaners list all the ingredients they contain, and in 2007 it began an eleven-year phase-in of a program called REACH (Registration, Evaluation, Authorisation, and Restriction of Chemicals), designed to identify known carcinogens. REACH places the cost of adequate testing on the chemical industry instead of on government.

Such regulations are lacking in the United States, where the 1976 Toxic Substances Control Act doesn't require testing industrial and agricultural chemicals before they are released into the environment. Ironically, the American chemical industry must comply with REACH to sell its products in Europe. But on its home grounds it can continue to use Americans and their dogs as guinea pigs.

The EPA especially lacks the power to regulate so-called inert ingredients, which are not listed on the labels of American household cleaners, air fresheners, detergents, weed killers, and fertilizers. Such "inert" ingredients may be one of the culprits behind the increasing incidences of some forms of canine cancer. Researchers at Purdue University's School of Veterinary Medicine have noted that what are called inert ingredients frequently make up 95 percent of lawn care products, but these ingredients are not benign. They include toxic solvents such as benzene, toluene, xylene, and other petroleum distillates that have been associated with an increased risk of human bladder cancer. The Purdue vets found that the incidence of bladder cancer in dogs increased 600 percent between 1975 and 1995 and suggested that lawn care products might be the culprit. Inert ingredients are also found in hundreds of pesticides and household products, and they're lipophilic — stored in fat — which may account for heavier dogs being at higher risk for developing certain cancers.

Frustrated with how your day has turned out, you sag onto the couch and light a cigarette, even though you've been trying to quit. If your dog is a long-nosed one, and you smoke frequently, it has an increased risk of nasal cancer; if it's a short-faced dog — or if it's a cat — it has an increased risk of lung cancer. Furthermore, tobacco products aren't transferred only through the air; they're also transferred via your hands when you pet your dog: it licks its fur and ingests carcinogens.

Stubbing out your cigarette, you grab some of your dog's favorite toys — a Frisbee, a plush stuffed animal, and a tennis ball — and head outside. You throw them, and your dog, overjoyed to be playing, alternately fetches them and lies with them between its paws, chewing the Frisbee, disemboweling the stuffed animal, and demolishing the tennis ball. Fun though this is for your dog, the toys may add several more endocrine disruptors and carcinogens to its daylong feast of contaminants. But, just as is the case for household products, it is difficult, if not impossible, to find out whether any of these dog toys contain harmful substances, something that I encountered firsthand when I called Doctors Foster and Smith, the online pet supplier of some of Pukka's toys, and asked. Breezily, the phone attendant told me that "the manufacturers do rigorous testing on the stuff we bring in, to make sure they meet government standards."

I asked where I could find this information on the company's website. Unfortunately, he told me, it wasn't there; nor did he have any information on what the toys contained. Trying to be helpful, he said that if I had a specific toy in mind, Doctors Foster and Smith would be willing to research its contents for me. I told him the names of the toys, and when the answers came back, they proved a mixed bag.

Pukka's red football was said to be made from "nontoxic vinyl," and the squeakers inside some of Pukka's toys were "made from plastic." Doctors Foster and Smith apologized, but they were unable to obtain any further information from the manufacturers. So I was no further along in finding out what was actually in Pukka's toys, though I had seen a 2007 study done on German dog toys that found harmful levels of phthalates and other contaminants in nine of the seventeen toys tested, the worst offenders being vinyl balls, a vinyl Frisbee, and a vinyl retriever dummy.

Unable to find a similar test done on North American dog toys, I decided to do one myself. I chose a few of Pukka's toys and sent them to ALS Environmental, one of the largest environmental testing groups in the world, with over forty laboratories based on five continents.

A couple of weeks later, the results came in. As Doctors Foster and Smith had related, the red football, made of "nontoxic vinyl," did indeed contain no detectable amounts of lead or cadmium. It also met governmental standards for allowable levels of phthalates, as regulated by the children's products section of the 2008 US Consumer Product Safety Improvement Act.

Nonetheless, it had trace amounts of DEHP, bis(2-ethylhexyl) phthalate, which has been found to have profound and irreversible effects on the reproductive systems of male rats at very low doses. After reading such studies, I had to wonder if the amount of phthalates Pukka was getting from his toys could be within the range that causes endocrine disruption and abnormal sex changes. There was no way to tell, since Pukka, like millions of other dogs, was ingesting phthalates from the environment at large as well as from his toys, some of which contained a disturbing amount of phthalates. His orange retriever dummy, for instance, contained 99,000 parts per million of DINP, diisononyl phthalate, and his white one had 54,000 parts per million of the compound. The phthalate DINP has been banned in children's toys, pending further study. I decided to give the red football, the retriever dummies, and his other plastic toys a final toss — into the trash.

Some of Pukka's toys did test completely clean. A blue plastic ball with a large grip handle and a Frisbee made from Cordura had no detectable amounts of lead, cadmium, or phthalates. I kept these toys. I also tested one of Pukka's favorite stuffed animals, the squeaking hedgehog, which Burley found irresistible as well and frequently stole. The hedgehog's internal squeaker, sounding so much like the alarmed cry of a rodent, was free of lead, cadmium, and phthalates, and so was the toy's plush brown-and-white outer nap. However, its polyester filling had 194,000 parts per billion of antimony, a suspected carcinogen that is used as a catalyst in the production of polyester yarns. These yarns are then spun into a wide variety of products, everything from fleece jackets to the stuffing in dogs' toys.

Pukka's hedgehog contained nearly 10,000 times the maximum level of antimony recommended for drinking water by the World Health Organization, which is 20 parts per billion. How much antimony was Pukka actually ingesting by chewing on the hedgehog and other polyester-stuffed toys that he dismembered? ALS Environmental could not answer these questions for me; nor was I successful in finding anyone else who could.

I was also curious to find out what went into the making of tennis balls — for some dogs the most coveted toy of all — and my efforts to find out exactly how harmful tennis balls might be to our dogs' health is an example of how very difficult it is for any of us to gauge the safety of the products our dogs use day in and day out.

I began by calling Wilson Sporting Goods, whose customer relations person would not even address my question about what the company's tennis balls contained. "That's proprietary information," she told me. As for their potential toxicity to dogs who chew on them, she pointed out that Wilson did not make tennis balls for dogs, but for people playing the game of tennis.

So I called Chuckit!, the maker of dog fetch toys, one of which is the company's signature fetch ball that looks exactly like an orange-and-blue tennis ball. Pete Powell, Chuckit!'s operations manager, told me that the company periodically tested its products at independent testing facilities and that everything the company produced complied with the children's products section of the Consumer Product Safety Improvement Act.

"Does this mean," I asked, "that a child can put a Chuckit! ball in its mouth?"

"Now I didn't say that," Pete replied.

Was there any BPA in the Chuckit! balls? I continued. Pete wasn't sure. Could he tell me about the components that went into the rubber underneath the nap? I asked. He could not. That was proprietary information.

Not much further along in finding out what goes into tennis balls, I continued to poke here and there on the Internet and soon stumbled upon the website of the International Tennis Federation and its fascinating documentation of the fifteen-step process used to create tennis balls, starting with natural rubber, which is benign. Of more concern were the glues, vulcanizing solutions, and accelerants used in the process, two of the last being named on ITF's website — DPG, diphenyl-guanidine, and CBS, cyclohexyl benthiazyl sulphenamide. According to the material safety data sheets for DPG and CBS — which I found on the website of Merchem, their manufacturer, located in Kerala, India — both are "very toxic to aquatic organisms," and the first is "harmful if swallowed" and may cause "impaired fertility." But though I called and wrote Merchem over a two-month-long period, the person to whom I was directed — the expert who would answer my questions about the toxicity of DPG — was never available to speak with me. Nor would he answer my e-mails.

Surely, I thought, someone must be concerned about these potentially toxic accelerants besides me, and sure enough someone was — the National Cancer Institute as it turned out, because of the potential for human exposure to these compounds and the resultant form of contact dermatitis called "rubber itch" that afflicts workers in rubber plants. The NCI was also concerned that DPG could be metabolically converted into carcinogenic compounds, and in 1989 it asked the National Toxicology Program at the US Department of Health and Human Services to study DPG by feeding it to rats.

The animals on the highest-dosage diet showed clinical signs of toxicity — they salivated, staggered, and breathed with difficulty — and the majority of them died. But a pathologist who examined the rats' internal organs and tissues found no effects attributable to chemical exposure. He concluded that "the observed changes were indicative of reduced nutrient intake."

Perplexed about the seeming incongruity, I called the lead scientist, Dr. Richard D. Irwin, a chemist at the National Institute of Environmental Health Sciences, who told me that "clinical signs of toxicity didn't necessarily mean that the rats were being poisoned by the DPG." Rather, the rats' wretched appearance was a result of the DPG giving their food a bad taste or odor. As a consequence, they ate far less of it than did the control group.

"Given these findings, then," I asked Dr. Irwin, "would you say that there's no danger whatsoever to dogs who mouth or chew tennis balls, especially over long periods of time?"

"It would be difficult to answer that question," he replied. What one had to consider, he noted, was the bioavailability of these substances and how easily they were extracted by a dog's saliva. One would have to test each brand of tennis ball to ascertain its contents and their bio-availability.

I had asked ALS Environmental to do that very thing, but the lab had not yet developed a protocol to analyze accelerants in tennis balls, as it had done to analyze the phthalates and heavy metals in children's toys. ALS would be happy to create such a protocol, I was told, but it would cost me $8,000. Much as Pukka and his pals loved their tennis balls, $8,000 was more than I was willing to spend to encourage their habit. Instead, I gave them balls made from latex or a thermoplastic elastomer called TPE, the nontoxicity of both materials well established and the appeal of each kind of ball very high, according to my five tester dogs who sampled them. In fact, one TPE ball, made by a company called Planet Dog, was the only dog toy that Pukka, Burley, A.J., Goo, and Buck — the great chomper himself — could not destroy. I had been told by Planet Dog that its balls were entirely free of phthalates and heavy metals, but just to make sure I sent three of them — one red, one white, one blue — to ALS for testing, and all of them came back as had been billed: completely nontoxic.

I asked Dr. Irwin one more question: "Given that antimony leaches from plastic bottles into beverages, do you think that a dog's saliva would also leach antimony from the polyester in dog toys?"

"It's a very feasible thing," he said. "Very feasible."

And that was as much time as I cared to spend on seeing what went into dog toys, retriever dummies, and tennis balls. Obviously, my visual inspection of them couldn't reveal very much, and regrettably, no organization like *Consumer Reports* has yet conducted a comprehensive review of dog toys. Until one does, we can try to find organic or nontoxic dog toys through an Internet search, which will reveal quite a few. But it's important to follow up with a call or an e-mail to the manufacturer, asking to see its organic certification, issued by its home government, or, if a product is billed as "nontoxic," requesting a third-party laboratory certification substantiating that the product is indeed free of phthalates, BPA, and heavy metals. If the manufacturer can't provide such certifications, it really has no right to claim that its products are "organic" or "nontoxic."

Nontoxic toys may be particularly important for dogs who experience the stress of being left alone for long periods of time each day. Toxicologists at the University of Wisconsin–Madison have demonstrated that toxic responses to environmental pollutants begin to appear in stressed animals, whereas unstressed animals remain unaffected. What has been even more disturbing to learn is that the way in which genes are regulated by environmental pollutants is permanently incorporated into the germ line — sperm and eggs — and is then manifested in subsequent generations even in the absence of these toxins. In other words, if your great-grandmother was exposed to a pesticide or an endocrine disruptor during her pregnancy, her child, that child's offspring, and you and all your descendants can have altered physiologies, behaviors, and metabolisms, in particular being fatter than normal. These epigenetic changes, in other words genetic changes resulting from environmental influences and not from the DNA itself, have been shown to last for a minimum of three generations in animals; in plants epigenetic changes have been passed on for 250 generations; they may in fact be permanent.

Since stressed animals are more susceptible to epigenetic changes, reducing stress is now being seen as a key element in avoiding chronic diseases and enhancing longevity. One way is through companionship. It has been shown that hamsters and mice who form social bonds not only are less vulnerable to environmental stress but they also heal their wounds more quickly than those animals who are socially isolated. These findings provide a scientific underpinning for why dogs should not be left home alone day after day.

This, then, is the chemical ocean through which most of us, and most of our dogs, swim, its effects upon us made more powerful because its many pollutants work in combination, amplifying each other's potency in ways that are neither well understood nor commonly tested. The chemical ocean's vast extent, and its intrusion into our very homes, is so dismaying to many of us that we may throw up our hands and say, "What can we do? Better not to think about it."

Others find a brisk swim in the chemical ocean quite refreshing. Such optimism is best represented by groups like the American Council on Science and Health, whose spokespeople find the risk of eating pesticide-treated food "essentially zero." They also find no hazards whatsoever in the use of BPA and say that those of us who question the use of pesticides are "anti-technology, anti-business, anti-progress ideologues." This is certainly one view of the chemical ocean – and one that hundreds upon hundreds of scientific papers have discounted.

Still a third position to take is that the potential dangers of the chemical ocean must be considered and prudent people can use the knowledge of its contents, generated by peer-reviewed science, as a way to protect themselves and their loved ones. In short, they'll put up some dikes between themselves and the sea.

To give you an idea of how this can be done – in other words, to provide you with some bricks and mortar for your dike – I'd like to describe what I've done in my own home. Some of the dikes I've erected are easy and inexpensive to put in place, while others take time and are more costly. In either case, there's no better place to start than with breakfast.

Once I brought Pukka home from Minnesota, I switched him to a grain-free diet, eliminating the pesticides sprayed on corn, wheat, and soy. I also found canine diets whose bags didn't have grease-proof linings containing PFCs or aluminum foil. You can find foods sold with such packaging through an Internet search.

If you like the kibble you're feeding, but it comes in PFC-coated bags, you can buy the freshest bag possible and empty it into a galvanized trash can, sold in hardware stores for about $20. FDA regulations list galvanized steel (it has a zinc coating) as suitable for food storage so long as the food is not acidic. You can also use stainless steel, ceramic, or glass containers for kibble, but whatever type of container you use, wash it out between refillings to remove any grease that may have become rancid. If, on the other hand, you're feeding canned food, you can look for manufacturers that have switched to BPA-free cans. Do an Internet search for "Which pet foods have BPA-free cans," and you will find them.

Long before Pukka arrived, I also took a closer look at the contents of my water supply, which comes from a well that I drilled on my land. I sent off water samples to a nationally certified water-testing laboratory to be tested for heavy metals. I was disappointed to find that the water had trace amounts of lead, but it was easily removed by installing a $150 under-the-counter water filtration system that uses cartridges that are changed semiannually.

Most people in the developed world now get their water from a municipal supply, but that doesn't mean that such water is free of heavy metals, nitrates, pesticides, or chlorine. Indeed, if you get your water from a municipality, it almost certainly contains chlorine, and as the President's Cancer Panel noted in its report, *Reducing Environmental Cancer Risk: What We Can Do Now,* "chemical by-products are formed when disinfectants such as chlorine react with organic matter, and long-term exposure to these chemicals may increase cancer risk." A home water purification system is one of the most inexpensive and easiest-to-build dikes that you can erect between yourself and waterborne pollutants, and as an added benefit, your coffee, tea, and food will taste and smell better.

Another important dike that I put up while building my home was my careful choice of materials. I avoided pressed-wood products containing the carcinogen formaldehyde. Where I needed to use plywood, I chose construction-grade plywood that off-gasses its formaldehyde load within one month, long before Merle and I moved in. All the finishes, glues, chinking, insulating foams, and countertops were nontoxic and contained no volatile organic compounds or pressed-wood products. The only exception was the polyurethane finish on the floor—toxic while being applied, nontoxic once totally cured. Having pine floors also eliminated pollutant-trapping carpeting. I did put down throw rugs, but they were made of wool and cotton, untreated with formaldehyde, and wood is not the only nontoxic flooring one can find. Tile, slate, and concrete all make phthalate-free floors, and there are many carpets made from natural fibers, if you want wall-to-wall carpeting.

One thing all of us can do to make our homes less polluted from tracked-in contaminants—no matter what sort of flooring we have—is to leave footwear at the door. You may wish to break this rule if you occasionally give fashionable dinner parties, but as a daily practice it's an excellent way to keep the house freer of tracked-in toxic substances, not to mention a good way to keep it cleaner.

When it comes to phthalates, your own and your dog's daily dose of them can be reduced by replacing plastic bowls and food containers with stainless steel or glass ones. I've also reduced Pukka's and my exposure to endocrine disruptors by choosing body care and household cleaning products that don't contain them. In addition, I've kept antibacterial soaps out of the house. As noted by the Centers for Disease Control and Prevention, antibacterial soaps were developed for use in hospitals and have had no demonstrated health benefit in the average home. In fact, the opposite is the case: the widespread use of antibacterial soaps is now leading to the development of resistant bacteria.

Given that most household products don't advertise their ingredients on their labels, and many body care products have long lists of unfamiliar chemicals that may or may not be harmful, how can you tell which ones to buy? You can do an Internet search on the product in question, and some manufacturers, proud that their products contain no harmful substances, actually advertise the ingredients. One long-running Internet site that documents tests for thousands of body care and household products is hosted by the Environmental Working Group.

Still another healthful change you can make for your dog is to think about what goes into its bed and the furniture it sleeps on. Before buying Pukka's beds, I called around and found one that had no fire-retardant foam or PFC-containing, stain-resistant finishes. Happily, this bed proved to be the very same brand that Merle had slept on, and Pukka and the other dogs have found it to their liking as well. To buy furniture that's free of fire-retardant materials, check the product's hang tag. If it says, COMPLIES WITH CALIFORNIA TECHNI-CAL BULLETIN 117, it contains fire-retardant PBDEs and you may wish to look for an alternative. Even if you live outside of California, your furniture may still meet the state's fire-retardant standard, as hundreds of manufacturers comply with California regulations so as to be able to sell their products in a state that has the eighth largest economy in the world.

That remarkable twentieth-century invention — the perfectly green, single-species lawn — is also a substantial source of our dogs' exposure to toxic chemicals. With that in mind, consider a mower instead of herbicides. Although I have four varieties of native grasses in my lawn, as well as Kentucky Bluegrass, brome, three varieties of clover, ox-eyed daisies, quack grass, yarrow, foxtail barley, and dandelions, it turns into smooth lovely sward when mowed, easy on the eyes as well as on the feet. In a similar vein, there are healthier alternatives for tending trees and ornamentals than spraying them with toxic chemicals. They can be injected through their bark with insecticides, eliminating clouds of spray.

The final dike that I've erected has been dietary: Pukka and I eat fruits and vegetables grown without pesticides. There are no long-term, peer-reviewed studies showing that people and dogs who eat such fruits and vegetables have fewer chronic diseases or live longer lives. But given the preponderance of the evidence linking exposure to pesticides with increased cancer risk and endocrine disruption – and the recommendation of the President's Cancer Panel that we choose foods grown without pesticides or chemical fertilizers so as to reduce our risk of cancer – I decided to put up this additional dike, even though it's the most expensive one to build. These costs, though, will come down as more people choose to eat organic food. It's also important to note that as more people eat organic food, the total amount of pesticides in the environment will decrease, reducing everyone's toxic burden, since these pesticides reach us through nonfood sources: the air we breathe and the water we drink.

As for Pukka's three-dozen-odd puppyhood toys, I didn't have to put up a dike to keep them out of the house. Almost all of them disappeared in the natural course of things before I did my testing. They were left on walks, abandoned in the sage, and picked up by passing dogs. I did not replace them but found others that I could certify as nontoxic. One old favorite, though, miraculously reappeared.

On a cold winter day when Pukka was nearly two years old, he burst through the dog door, covered with snow. Leaping through the air, he tore across the room, shaking a bedraggled brown object in his mouth. Sitting proudly, he offered it to me.

I took it from him and examined it. The brown-and-white plush dog toy was faded from the sun and the snow; one of its legs was missing; its head was partially chewed off; and its polyester guts wisped from its stomach. Yet there was no mistaking the toy's identity: it was the original squeaking hedgehog given to Pukka by a friend when he was a puppy and lost long ago in the Pukka-Burley toy wars. I had bought another hedgehog, exactly like the first, for the tests run by ALS.

"The hedgehog itself!" I cried, holding it up.

With a huge grin, Pukka broomed his tail across the floor: "Yes, the hedgehog! I found it!"

"What a treasure, Sir!" I exclaimed warmly.

His eyes glowed: "You could toss that for me."

I hesitated, thinking of the hedgehog's 194,000 parts per billion of antimony, and then said, "With pleasure."

I threw the hedgehog halfway to the twenty-foot-high ceiling, and Pukka coiled low as he tracked it. Leaping into the air, he met the descending hedgehog higher than my head, shaking it mightily as he landed and growling in triumph, "Got you back! Got you back! I've got you back!" He cavorted around the room, bucking like a bronco.

At that moment Buck came through the dog door, as he often did first thing in the morning, a blanket of snow on his back. Running up to him, Pukka sat down, leaned his head forward, and offered him the hedgehog: "Look, Buck! I found it! The hedgehog is back!"

Buck didn't hesitate. He grabbed one end of the hedgehog, and Pukka growled: "Ready?"

Buck growled, "I am!" and they began a furious tug-of-war, both dogs throwing themselves around the room, smiling and growling, planting their paws, shaking their heads, and scattering throw rugs everywhere.

Giving the hedgehog a violent wrench, Pukka wrested it away from Buck, who for reasons known only to himself rushed out the dog door as if he needed to catch a train. Watching him go, Pukka gave his tail a faint wag: "Are you sure you want to leave?" Then he lay upon his bed, where he proceeded to rip open the hedgehog, completing the evisceration he and Burley had begun months before, scattering the toy's white polyester innards about him and finding its squeaker tube, looking so much like a real trachea, which he punctured with his canine teeth, making it emit a last mournful, dying cry before he spat it out. Looking at the surrounding carnage with an air of profound satisfaction, he put his head upon his paws and went to sleep.

Quietly, so as not to disturb him, I picked up the remains of his final puppyhood toy and put them in the trash.

These are the dikes I built around my dogs and me. Soothing in theory, they are admittedly not perfect. In the way previous generations had to face typhoid, smallpox, and polio, we have to face environmental pollutants. We can agonize over this, trying to live in a HAZMAT suit, or we can build reasonable dikes that allow us to move on to more important business, one of the most important being the reform of the Toxic Substances Control Act of 1976, now so antiquated and giving such preferential treatment to the chemical industry that it's worthless in protecting the health of Americans. The other important thing we can do is speak with our buying power.

When Rachel Carson published *Silent Spring* in 1962, the word *silent* in her title referred to the eerie spring silence that descended upon the world as birds fell from the sky, killed by dozens of newly introduced pesticides. At that time an innocent public was ignorant of the ill effects of these toxic chemicals, and so were many scientists.

Fifty-one years later, as this book is being published, that is no longer the case. You would have to have lived in a cave during the last half-century to have missed the news that pollutants can damage your health. But because such toxins are so pervasive, most of us tend to soldier on, since protesting falls on deaf ears and voting has little effect when representatives from all parties are so handsomely lobbied by the chemical industry.

Yet one powerful way of cleaning up a small bay of the chemical ocean is within our reach. We can vote with our purchases. It is the one thing to which industry pays attention. How many polyester dog toys, laced with antimony, would manufacturers continue to produce if none of us bought them? How many Frisbees, footballs, and retriever dummies full of phthalates would they make, if these toys sat on the shelves? How many fire-retardant dog beds and how many kibble bags lined with PFCs would any manufacturer ship, if they remained unbought? It is a powerful way to change silence into action. Our dogs, after all, have no say.

CHAPTER ELEVEN

In the Time of the Big Light

DURING PUKKA'S FIRST summer we spent most of our days outside, the dawn coming early, four in the morning, the dusk sifting into darkness at nearly eleven – not Arctic by any means, but a good long run of day. Often we played toss and fetch near the aspen tree under which Merle had spent his last weeks, and one evening, as we were lying on the grass after our game, the sky darkened over the Sleeping Indian – the mountain above Kelly – and a thunderhead began to tower. I hoped it would boom and give me the opportunity to thunder-proof Pukka at this young and impressionable age.

Snuggling against my side, he dozed, and soon turned onto his back so I could rub his belly. Just then the ominous sky let out a shattering crash. He flipped over. Wide-eyed, he stared at the great black roiling cloud.

"Thunder," I said in a happy voice. "Oh, so very exciting!" I stroked his shoulders.

The thunder crashed again.

"See, thunder!" I said enticingly, pointing upward. "Big boom! What fun!"

He stared at the dark clouds and thwacked his tail on the grass: "Thunder. What fun!" He wiggled against my side, his tail swishing happily while the sky crashed and the lightning flashed above us.

My lesson worked better than I could have possibly imagined. On the Fourth of July, we walked to the base of Snow King Mountain, where fireworks are shot into the sky above the town of Jackson. I knew of no dogs who liked fireworks, and I was ready to comfort Pukka and take him speedily away, but he sat down, his jaw hanging open in wonder as he stared at the red, white, and blue starbursts crashing over our heads. A great wave of white rockets rushed upward, and he leapt into the air as if to chase them, laughing jubilantly, "More, more, more!" his tail beating faster and faster and finally vanishing in a blur as the fireworks reached their monumental crescendo, ear-shattering detonations echoing from the mountainside. Then, as the sky darkened and the world slowly quieted, a look of disappointment crossed his young face. He stared into my eyes: "You mean that's it?"

"Till next year," I said.

He sat down, turned his face to the sky, and waited.

Some of his learning was far less noisy. He learned to lie quietly in cafés and on the decks of restaurants, considering patrons as they went by us and then slowly turning his face to mine, his expression as deadpan as a spy's: "You did notice that man with the turkey sandwich, didn't you?"

I raised my eyebrows: "I did notice him."

He declined his nose at me: "Why don't you get one?"

I shrugged in agreement: "Sounds good to me."

So many of our conversations were conducted in just this way—in silence, gesture carrying our meaning—a convention that I employed in his training, teaching him voice and hand commands simultaneously: sit, lie down, come, go left, go right, go away, wait. The last, indicated by an uplifted palm, is a very good one for a dog to have in its repertoire. You can employ it if your dog is on the far side of a road and cars suddenly zoom by. If there are a lot of distractions such as traffic noise, people, and other dogs, your dog may not hear your voice, but it can see your uplifted palm, and that signal, meaning, "Hey! Wait right there!" may save its life.

Finally, Pukka learned the meaning of "leave it," although this took a while. Holding him on a leash, I would tempt him with a small salmon nugget set on the ground before him, and when he'd make no move toward it, I'd reward him with a much larger piece of raw elk. Like "wait," "leave it" is also a useful command for a dog to know, for the command can be extended to unknown trash by the side of the road, to deer and poisonous snakes, and to other dogs. In one case, Pukka's having learned "leave it" quite possibly saved his life.

We were on our way home from a hike on the far side of the Gros Ventre River, and Pukka ran down the bank for a drink while I stood on the single-lane bridge gazing at the fast-moving current. It had been raining and the river was swollen.

Suddenly two otters rose up from the dark water, not five yards in front of Pukka, and chirped at him. In the middle of the current, three more otters appeared. The two nearer otters ducked under the surface; the three distant ones called to Pukka in their high-pitched cheeps. Without a moment's hesitation, he leapt into the river, for despite his initial dislike of rain, he had become an avid swimmer once I'd introduced him to the comforts of hot springs. Now there was no keeping him out of water. Swimming hard, he went after the otters, the brawny current immediately sweeping him downstream.

"Leave it!" I yelled.

At the sound of my voice, he glanced up to me, standing on the bridge, but all five otters had risen from the water only fifteen feet in front of him and were gazing at him while trading glances with each other as if to say, "Look at that dog, trying to be an otter."

Not far downstream lay the Gros Ventre's notorious, river-wide hydraulic, a deadly recirculating hole that just a few years before had trapped a father who dived into its raging white water to save his teenage son. The son had slipped off the narrow spillway while fishing. He survived; his father did not.

Again I shouted, "Leave it!"

This time Pukka held my eyes, but the otters chirped at him once more and porpoised downstream as if taunting him to chase them. The temptation was too great. He followed.

Cupping my hands around my mouth, I bellowed, "Leave it!" filling the command with every bit of authority I possessed and now some terror. Good swimmer though he had become, I didn't think that he could swim out of that ferocious hole — fast approaching — or that he'd know enough to dive to the bottom of the river's channel and crawl along its rocky bed until he could escape the hydraulic's fateful clutches.

There are times when the stentorian approach does work. As my voice thundered over the water, he glanced back at me, and I saw the light go on in his eyes: "Oh, it appears that Ted is really serious about this." Immediately, he turned toward shore. That's when he realized what a predicament he had gotten himself into. He now had to swim across the current instead of with it, and his eyes started in alarm: "Uh-oh, how did the river get so strong?"

He began to swim with determination, the water occasionally surging over his head, but he didn't fight it. Angling against the current, he ferried himself neatly across the river. But when he reached the shore and tried to land, he was swept away — once, twice, three times — until he found an eddy that let him scrabble through the willows and onto the bank. Shaking himself happily, he crashed through the underbrush and in high excitement met me on the bridge.

"Well done, *señor!*" I cried with passion and no small relief as he pranced about me, his tail helicoptering with glee: "I would have caught them, Ted, I really would have, if you hadn't called me."

I didn't bother to contradict him. "What a good 'leave it,'" I said, stroking his shoulders and praising him. It was no time to quibble over the fact that he was supposed to obey the first time he heard the command, not the third. As I petted him, he poked his head through the bridge railings and his tail increased its tempo.

I glanced to where he was looking and saw the five otters porpoising upstream, swimming effortlessly. Reaching the bridge, they stood out of the water and stared at us with their sleek and mischievous faces. It appeared that they had actually returned to see where the playful dog had gone.

"Otters," I said, now having a moment to name the animals for him. "The happiest animals in the world, Pukka. Well, maybe dogs might be as happy."

He gave his tail an appreciative wag as he stared down at the otters.

"Not to chase, though. No, no," I intoned. "Leave them be."

His tail slowed, then picked up its pace as he leaned out over the river, ready to take the twelve-foot leap: "I bet you I could — "

I put a hand on his shoulders. "Pukka, I don't think so. Leave it."

As if to reinforce my point, the otters chose that very moment to duck under the surface. Like brown torpedoes, they flashed downstream, arcing out of the river and disappearing beneath it. Just before being swallowed by the breaking rapids, they dove and vanished. Together, Pukka and I watched and waited . . . waited and watched. Had the otters survived? Ten seconds went by, fifteen, twenty . . . the otters burst above the surface, nearly back at the bridge, standing upon their tails and chattering at us, completely and magnificently at ease. It was like watching a flock of ravens slip and tumble through a tearing wind.

Pukka's tail stopped wagging, and he gave the otters a long considering look before turning to me with the same resigned grin he had worn when, as a very young puppy, he had tried to catch ravens walking on our lawn. Flapping their wings, they had easily escaped him.

"Otters," I said. "Very good swimmers."

"Huh!" He gave a soft pant and a wistful wag of his tail: "Well, maybe I won't catch one." And with that acknowledgment made, he turned and trotted jauntily off the bridge, his tail held high, otters now having joined that growing number of animals whose powers exceeded even those of a first-class dog.

He learned many other things during this time. He learned to ride in rafts and canoes, to leave chickens and cows alone, and to dance country swing, doing turns under my legs and prancing alongside me as we two-stepped across the room.

The days being long, there was much time to work on these things, as well as to walk most everywhere: along the river and on the flanks of the surrounding hills, along the Snake River Dike, and up the trail to the top of Snow King Mountain, where so many people like to walk with their dogs. On all these hikes he wore neither leash nor collar when he was away from roads, running freely on his own, and more than one person remarked, "Aren't you afraid he'll run away?"

"I feed him three times a day," I'd say. "He sleeps in my room. He lies under my desk when I work. We go almost everywhere together. Why would he run away?"

Later in the summer, when Pukka was older and could go on longer hikes, we would drop down the back side of Snow King, traveling cross-country through fields of wildflowers, and I would stop occasionally so I could tell him their names: silky phacelia, slender cinquefoil, shooting star, and my favorite, the demure harebell, its lilac petals as pure as the dusky sky over the Tetons, dividing earth and heaven.

He would taste them all, wild roses and columbines being his favorite, mine as well, as they are so sweet. Then, taste-test done, he'd bound off, leaping through the red and yellow petals, the blue and purple blossoms, before disappearing into a field of sunflowers, their hot-yellow pods swaying to mark his passage.

Although we hiked Snow King many an afternoon, our favorite outing was close to home — out the deck doors, across the sage fields, and along the privacy of the Gros Ventre River, with its multitude of interesting animals to smell and see: deer and moose, sometimes the small herd of resident antelope, and a newly born threesome of great horned owls, who peered down at us from their perch in a cottonwood tree, as inquisitive about Pukka as he was about them.

One sunny morning, as we walked along the river trail, he suddenly stopped, gazing toward the moving water, his nose twitching at a scent that wafted to him. He was wet, having just swum, and he breathed softly, his ribs showing faintly through his wet fur, the muscles rippling in his shoulders and haunches, while his tucked-in waist, his poised back legs, his forward-tipped ears were all on alert, his golden fur shining.

He gave me a sidelong glance to see what I would do.

"What is it?" I called to him. "Show me."

He ran through the low brush, over logs, and came to the river, where he put his nose to earth at the edge of the bank, eight feet above the moving water, tracing a narrowing circle with his nose, until he came to some scat, curled upon itself and the diameter of a small cigar. He sniffed it studiously. I crouched and picked it up – it was slightly dry – and I smelled it myself, leaning forward so we could smell it simultaneously, our noses on each side of the turd, which I held between my fingers. It smelled aquatic and plantlike.

"Muskrat," I told him, giving him the English word for the animal whose scat we were smelling.

"Do you think it came up the bank over there?" I nodded toward the water, where we could see a faint trail-like runnel.

Pukka peered down the bank and gave his tail a tentative wag: "I think it did come up there."

"Good find!" I told him, giving him a stroke on his ruff. "Excellent scenting, and thank you for pointing it out to me. I would have missed it completely."

I placed the scat where he had found it, and back to the trail we went, he trotting along with his head held high, the proud jut of his chin saying, "See, Ted cares about what I find, and he wants to smell it, too."

He learned to use his dog door effortlessly, having been brought up with one in Minnesota, and with the canine entrance now permanently open and the deck doors flung wide in the summer's heat, we had a constant stream of visitors from both ends of the house. Working at my desk, I'd feel a wet nose nudge my elbow, and I wouldn't know until I looked down whether it belonged to Pukka, Buck, Burley, Goo, or even A.J. Having decided to put his grudge against Pukka behind him, he now came in for pets, bones, and the company of the other dogs.

Human visitors, seeing four or five dogs stroll into the house, would start in surprise, and one woman declared, "It's as if they all just live here."

"They do," I replied. "Some more so than others."

Among all of Pukka's friends, it was Buck who lived with us the most, crossing the field in the morning as regular as a commuter, parking himself on Pukka's bed or behind my desk chair to await the magical noon hour when elk bones and turkey necks appeared from the fridge. Often, he'd spend the entire day with us, and Scott — tall, red-haired, and quiet — would have to fetch him at ten o'clock at night. Even then, Buck would only leave Pukka's bed with the greatest reluctance, following Scott grudgingly down the road. A minute later, Buck would charge back through the dog door, grinning madly as he swiped at my thighs with his head — "I'm back! I couldn't leave you!" He'd throw himself on Pukka's bed, and Pukka, adoring friend that he was, would go to the dedicated quadruped couch.

Scott would return a few minutes later, shaking his head at Buck's loyalty to his second family, and Buck would slam his tail on the bed, emphasizing his point: "It's the bed!"

"He really likes that bed," I told Scott.

Soon thereafter, and much to their credit, the Landales bought Buck a bed just like Pukka's — or so they thought. Having only looked at photos of it on the L.L. Bean website, April ordered Buck the company's Therapeutic Dog Bed instead of its Premium Dog Bed. And what did Buck do? He tore great gaping holes in his brand-new therapeutic bed, designed for older dogs, ripping it into shreds and marching across the field in a huff to sleep on Pukka's bed, which, it was now clear, he loved inordinately.

April was at a loss to explain his behavior until I pointed out to her that although the two beds looked exactly the same, they had different interiors — one made of foam, the other, the Premium, of polyester, and no doubt they felt and smelled different to Buck. She rolled her eyes. Nonetheless, he was a member of her family, and his preference needed to be respected. So she ordered him the Premium Bed, in precisely the same size and color as Pukka's so there would be no chance of his not liking it. And what did Buck do? He sniffed his new bed carefully before settling himself upon it with a satisfied sigh and a thump of his tail: "The Premium Bed at last!" Then he closed his eyes and blissfully went to sleep, without putting a single tooth mark in it.

It was also during this long light-filled time that Pukka learned something else, something that I wished he hadn't learned. He learned to bark, and not merely in surprise, but avidly, frequently, and, as he got bigger, with a bawling sonorous bay that rattled every window in the house and sounded far more like a hound's voice than a Lab's. His learning to bark did not happen incrementally. It happened over the space of one weekend.

I had gone to my niece's wedding in Chicago and had left him for three days with the Landales and Buck, who, among his many shining virtues, has one fault: he barks uproariously when someone comes to the door. It doesn't matter if he knows you; it doesn't matter if you're a family member; it doesn't matter if he has just seen you only a few minutes before. He believes that people coming to the door must be announced. I am certain that in a previous life he was a town crier.

Before I left for Chicago, Pukka's reaction to someone coming to the house had been to walk to the door quietly, wag his tail, and wait for it to open. But on the day after my return, when the UPS man delivered a package, Pukka leapt to his feet and roared his head off.

Although this was a wonderful confirmation of the many scientific experiments showing that dogs learn best by observing other dogs, I was hardly pleased to have the very proof before my eyes or, more accurately, my ears. I don't like barking dogs, or rather, I don't like dogs who can't distinguish between the UPS man and a burglar. Even when faced with such a potential threat, dogs can use methods just as effective as barking, if not more so, to let their people know danger is nigh.

Subdued and considered warnings, however, aren't what the majority of humans have reinforced over the ages, or at least they haven't reinforced them since the time when hunter-gatherers became farmers and herders. As a farmer or herder, you wanted to know if a leopard was slinking toward your cattle or if thieves were about to steal your chickens. A barking dog was very useful in these situations. On the other hand, as a hunter-gatherer, you kept no livestock and owned almost nothing but your weapons. You were more interested in learning what animal was slinking toward you in the night rather than scaring it away. After all, it could be a juicy oryx or a big fat water buffalo – a windfall of protein with very little investment of energy on your part. In such cases, you wanted your dog to be silent and to tell you about who was approaching in some other way besides barking: perhaps no more than an undercurrent of breath murmured in your ear, or a nudge of its snout against your shoulder, or the dancing of its eyes and the pointing of its nose, all mannerisms Merle had employed to let me know that elk were nearby. Villagers, in other words, wanted alarm and bluff; hunter-gatherers wanted silence and observation. Merle, having grown up in the desert partly on his own, among coyotes and herders with guns, knew all about the wisdom of silence. Pukka, with little danger in his life, and also with what I considered poor canine role models, needed schooling.

So began over a year of trying to convince Pukka that our house needed neither a security system nor a town crier. It was a task made especially difficult because of how much peer reinforcement Pukka was getting for barking.

Buck was not the only barker. A.J. barked, and Burley barked, and Goo barked, too. They barked at people walking across the field; they barked at the UPS man, the FedEx woman, the Lower Valley Energy man, bicyclists whom they didn't recognize, and wandering deer and coyotes. Given how much they barked, it's surprising that Pukka didn't start barking until he spent a weekend at Buck's, a circumstance that may have had to do with his admiration for Buck and his leeriness of A.J. and his crew.

The initial instigators in all this barking, as far as I could tell, were two American Black and Tan Coonhounds who lived on the east side of Kelly, chained to two telephone wire spools by their person, a teenage boy in love with hunting mountain lions. The telephone wire spools were turned on their sides and doors had been cut in them, creating little kennels, and night and day, summer and winter, the two hounds were chained to their small shelters, unless they were out hunting lions, which wasn't often.

Bored out of their minds, and wildly jealous of every dog in the village who had its freedom and walked by them, the hounds bayed endlessly in frustration, hour upon hour, while the teenager was in school. I had spoken to the boy, offering to keep his hounds at my house with the other dogs during the day.

"You couldn't let those dogs off a chain," he said flatly. "They'd kill a cat" — he meant a house cat — "just like that. Besides, they'll just run away."

So the dogs bayed on and on, and one afternoon I walked down the road and across the creek, upset at what I was hearing in their baying. It wasn't merely frustration; it was pleading: "We want to play with the other dogs. Let us off our chains."

No one was home — the dogs didn't bay when their people were at home — and the two coonhounds erupted when they saw me approach. Leaping against their chains, they rushed me, bawling at the top of their lungs and looking ferocious. Their vicious behavior was why everyone in the village gave them a wide berth. But they weren't growling in the least.

I knelt before them and said, "Oh, you poor buggers. You just want to play, don't you?" I made some kissing noises with my mouth, and the bigger dog, the male, pricked his ears, looked at me carefully, and then did a play-bow. Putting my hands on the ground, I play-bowed back to him. He wagged his tail exuberantly, and edging closer I cupped my palm low before him and let him smell it. He wagged his tail even harder; I stroked his chest; a few moments later he turned on his back and let me rub his belly, wagging his tail fervently.

I would have taken both of them home right then and there, but they were not my dogs. Around the world, dogs are still property, and I could have been prosecuted for stealing them, even though people are rarely prosecuted for treating a living being as these two dogs were being treated, chained night and day, eighty degrees in the summer, twenty below zero in the winter. The recent passing of anti-tethering legislation in some municipalities may finally bring this deplorable practice to an end.

The teenager left for college and took his hounds with him, but the damage to Kelly's dog culture had been done. There had been no barking dogs in Merle's time, in those halcyon days no dogs being perpetually chained. Now, having heard the chained coonhounds baying, A.J., Burley, and Goo decided that barking might not be a bad idea. Instead of being a passive observer, a barking dog could make things happen: he could make people move away; he could keep them at bay (baying dogs themselves having put this far-reaching idiom into the language); and, if the person was a dog lover, a barking dog could make that person kneel and talk to him sweetly, asking what was wrong, as I had done with the coonhounds. In all three cases, the dog was noticed, not ignored, and up and down the main road of the village dogs began to bark.

With this much peer pressure, it was enormously difficult to convince Pukka that I knew better than all of his buddies and that he alone among them should be silent. But I didn't want to live with a barking dog, and so I tried to teach him not to bark. In fact, I tried every technique I could find in the training manuals. I tried diverting him with other behavior — having him sit, for instance. Pukka soon learned to sit and bark simultaneously. I tried having him sit while feeding him raw elk burger for not barking, and I soon discovered that a dog can sit, eat raw elk, and resume barking all at the same time — at least Pukka could, strangled though his barks were. I tried the "going ballistic" technique, as some training manuals call it — yelling at the top of my lungs, "No barking!" This certainly frightened poor little Pukka, but had no lasting effect upon him except to make me feel despicable. Yelling is not my style — had it been, I might have lived happily with a barking dog — and I abandoned the going ballistic technique after a couple of attempts. I also found the offshoot of this advice — strike the dog sharply across its muzzle with an index finger — beyond the pale and did not so demean Pukka or myself.

I tried talking to him sweetly, kneeling by his side, putting an arm around his shoulders, and saying, "You really don't need to bark like those other dogs. It's unnecessary and raises your blood pressure." Hearing A.J., Burley, and Goo barking from across the field, he would tremble, rumbling in his throat, and the instant I would stand up from our tête-à-tête, he would join them in barking. I tried giving him timeouts in the bathroom. He would remember them for an hour or so and then resume his barking. I bought two bark boxes, which emit a high-pitched sound that dogs supposedly don't like, and placed them at the front door and at the sliding glass door, where Pukka habitually would bark. Within two days, he learned to walk fifty feet beyond each box and bark. When I placed the small rectangular black box on his collar, as it was meant to be placed, he was dismayed, but quickly adapted. He began to woof, just loud enough not to set the collar off. This was a step in the right direction, but hardly a solution. I didn't want to live with someone who was constantly grumbling under his breath.

At last the dog who began Pukka's barking career helped me to end it. One afternoon I was watching Buck and Pukka play. Buck was lying on Pukka's bed, where they had been mouthing each other and crying out in delighted playful yelps. After a while, Buck grew tired of the game. Not so Pukka. He leapt at Buck and backed off, and when he got no response he pawed at Buck's face, then bit his ears, Buck yowling in high-pitched annoyance, almost a plea, "Please stop. I'm trying to rest." This only fueled Pukka's exuberance: more biting, more pawing, more lunging, until Buck moved his head sharply against Pukka's face, not striking him with his eyeteeth, but rumbling furiously in his throat: "GRRRRR! Stop it!" Instantly, Pukka backed off and lay down a few feet away. That's all Buck had to do — emit one deep menacing "GRRRRR!" — and Pukka left him alone.

I considered what I had just seen and filed it away. Buck went home, Pukka had his dinner, and in a bit A.J., Burley, and Goo broke into a fusillade of barks when a cyclist went by. Pukka leapt up from the floor where he had been napping and raced out the dog door to join them, bawling, "AwRooo! AwRooo! Danger! Alert! Scramble for action!" Flinging open the door, I rushed after him, fell to all fours alongside him, put my cheek against his head, and said, "No barking." Then I growled dramatically, "GRRRRR!"

His shoulders fell. His tail went between his legs. He ducked his head and whined, pawing my face submissively and trying to lick me on the mouth. "We don't bark here," I said. "It's pointless. It's unnecessary. It disturbs the peace. And it hurts my ears."

He looked at me.

"Grrrrr," I added.

He pressed his head against my shoulder: "Oh, please don't growl at me."

"I won't have to, if you don't bark," I replied sternly.

Cowed, he lowered his head. Suddenly I saw his eyes brighten with an idea. Rushing through the dog door, he disappeared for about ten seconds before bursting back outside. He had a bone in his mouth. It was the one I had given to him at midday, and it was still filled with marrow. I had remained on all fours, and Pukka now leaned his shoulder against my upper arm and gently pressed the bone to my lips. His eyes looked into mine and said, "I'm sorry, and here's my bone to prove it."

It's difficult to be upset with a dog, and a young dog at that, who has developed such a refined sense of statecraft. I had spoken to him in Dog, and he had responded in kind, making reparations with the greatest treasure he owned, his still-juicy bone. Taking it from him,

I said, "Thank you, Pukka. It's a lovely bone." I sniffed it. "Mmm, it really is. And I'm touched that you would give it to me. Apology accepted, and please have it back." I handed it to him, and demurely he took it.

And that was that. I won't say that he no longer barked. But getting down on my hands and knees and growling at him — talking Dog to him — worked better than anything else over a period of months to make him a quieter dog. He had his relapses, to be sure, but more often than not, when Goo, A.J., and Burley barked, Pukka would sit on the deck, rumbling softly in his throat as he gazed across the field at them.

"No barking," I would remind him quietly.

Another soft rumble: "I'm not barking, I'm rumbling." And this, it proved, was his negotiated settlement with me: I was his person, but he had his peers — the canine culture surrounding him — and he would split the difference between the two of us.

The days went on; the sun lowered in the sky; the aspen turned gold. As often happens in the Tetons, it snowed while the leaves were still on the trees, and one night after sweeping the snow off the deck I came inside to find one of my sandals, a blue plastic Croc, lying in the middle of the great room, between the woodstove and Pukka's bed, upon which he was reclining.

He had occasionally teethed on my trail shoes as well as these Crocs without harming them since I'd take them from him right away. "No chewing please," I'd say and immediately give him a bone.

I glanced around. The other Croc was nowhere to be seen. Holding up the sandal, I said, "Pukka. Where's my other Croc?"

He gave me the offended look of the wrongly accused: "Croc? What Croc?"

"Pukkaaa," I said, stretching out his name, "where's the other Croc?"

He put his head between his paws.

"You find that other Croc, Sir," I told him, placing the remaining one on the mat by the front door. "You find it. Come on. I need that Croc."

His eyes went from mine to the Croc and back to me: "The Croc's right there. What more do you want?"

Shaking my head, I went upstairs, took off my clothes, and heard the *slap-slap* of the dog door as he went out for his now-ritualized last pee of the evening. I brushed my teeth, and as I pulled back the covers to get into bed, I heard his nails, *tok, tok, tok,* on the floorboards of the stairs.

Turning, I saw him walk into the bedroom: a slim golden puppy, bearing a snowy blue Croc. He came directly to my bed, put his front paws upon it, and placed the Croc next to my pillow, sitting down and looking at me with an expression that said, "Is this what you wanted?"

"Oh, Pukka!" I exclaimed, taking his face between my hands and giving him a kiss on the head. "Well done! I am so proud of you!"

He beamed.

I had a sudden thought. Just to make sure that I wasn't coming to a hasty conclusion about his ability to understand English, I walked onto the balcony that overlooks the great room. Turning on the light, I glanced down to where I had placed the other Croc on the shoe mat. There it lay, exactly where I had left it.

The sun continued its downward journey in the sky; the light at last waned — at least the light in the sky did. Pukka's light did not grow dimmer. For five years my life had been dogless, and now doglight was back in it, no matter how short the days. One afternoon, just after the winter solstice, we went up to Teton Pass and climbed the ridge called Edelweiss. I wasn't worried about the approaching evening. I had my headlamp, the sky was clear, and the full moon would soon rise.

At the top of the ridge, by a clump of white bark pines, I ripped off the climbing skins from the bottoms of my skis, Pukka watching me with glowing eyes and a softly swishing tail, for he knew what was about to come: the downhill run, where steep slopes and several feet of airy snow allowed dogs to fly. I buckled my boots, tightened my pack, and said, "*D'accord, monsieur, es-tu prêt?*"

Wag-wag went his tail: "Been waiting for *you, mon ami.*" He grinned.

"Let's go then!"

Over the edge we went, dropping like hawks through the gloaming, into the steep bowl that fell a thousand feet to the dark forest below. Much snow had fallen over the last few days and the bowl was smooth, deep, and trackless as we spiraled down into the dusk, turn after turn, the snow flying over my shoulders and making hushing whispers against my knees. Looking back, I saw Pukka bounding behind me, arcing from the snow like a golden fish from the darkening sea.

Where the slope momentarily eased back and he wallowed on the shallower ground, I snowplowed to let him catch up. Then the slope made its final plunge to the valley floor. Over the edge we went, swooping through snow so perfectly light, so perfectly smooth, so utterly diaphanous that it seemed the stuff of the first spinning creation.

Casting a look behind me, I saw Pukka, dipping and rising like a swallow, throwing up puffballs upon each landing. There was not a sound to be heard, not a light to be seen, as we flew down through the forest, down, down, down, on the long white nave of snow.

Then it was over and nearly dark.

"Ski dog!" I exclaimed at the bottom, applauding him as he bounded toward me.

He beat his tail against his flanks, pressing himself against my thigh and laughing from a face covered with powder: "What a run!"

"What a run!" I agreed, hooking an arm over his shoulders.

I put my skins back on and we climbed up through the trees on the opposite side of the narrow valley, up through the meadows, up to Teton Pass, Pukka leading the way. By the time we reached the parking lot at the top of the pass, it was perfectly dark and all the cars were gone except ours.

I stowed my gear and harnessed him into his seat belt in the back of the Subaru. As I fastened the buckles, he pressed the top of his head against my chest, pushed hard, and wagged his tail with great feeling: "Thank you for that wonderful ski."

"Thank *you*," I said, hugging him. "What a skier you've become, Sir. Simply the best."

We drove down the snowpacked road, and as we did the full moon rose from behind the Gros Ventre Mountains, floated over a rim of clouds, and lit the world.

CHAPTER TWELVE

Carnivore to Monovore

I N HIS DAY, MERLE ATE lots of wild game — elk, antelope, grouse, duck, goose, and pheasant — but by and large he ate commercial dog food, most of it kibble. Quite a few people, who believe that kibble is a bad thing to feed dogs, have taken me to task for feeding it to Merle. How could I have fed him this garbage, they've written me, with its artificial colors and preservatives, its rendered meals made from diseased livestock, and its heavy load of grains? But my reasoning was straightforward. Even though I believed wild game to be healthier for Merle, containing fewer additives, pesticides, and hormones than dog food made from grain and domestic meat, I couldn't legally shoot enough wild game to feed an active seventy-pound dog.

One also has to remember that when Merle and I met it was 1991. Dr. Ian Billinghurst, the Australian veterinarian who founded the raw-food movement, did not publish his first book until 1993. Ann Martin's eye-opening account of the questionable ingredients that have gone into kibble, *Foods Pets Die For,* did not appear until 1997. Dr. Marty Goldstein, the New York vet and champion of raw-food diets, did not publish his groundbreaking book about canine well-being until 1999. The Illinois veterinarian Dr. Karen Becker did not start talking about "species-appropriate diets" for dogs and cats on her widely read website Mercola Healthy Pets until 2009.

When Merle and I returned to Kelly from the San Juan River, the great variety of commercial dog foods that canines eat today — grain-based kibble, kibble with no grains and whole meats, frozen raw-food patties, dehydrated meat chips made from organic livestock, canned foods containing bison and venison — did not exist. We were still in the dark ages of dog food, and the vet who gave Merle his first checkup and vaccinations sold us the dog food that he carried in his office, Science Diet. Just as I accepted his advice on vaccinating Merle every year, I also took his advice on what to feed him. Within a month, Merle was scratching at night, scratching during the day—his neck, his shoulders, his flanks—and licking his paws frequently.

How curious, I thought, that when I had met Merle he was eating whatever he could scavenge, including ground squirrels, and wasn't itching. Yet after a month of eating kibble, he seemed to be a bundle of itches. On the recommendation of the same vet, I switched Merle to Eukanuba's lamb and rice kibble, which, like Science Diet, contained corn, but as its third ingredient, not its first. Presto! Within a couple of weeks, Merle was scratching and licking far less. However, his itching never completely went away until I switched him to Lamaderm canned lamb, with rice but no other grains, supplementing it with wild game.

As I searched for my new dog, I remembered these experiences, and I also read widely about canine diets and interviewed many veterinarians over the course of two years before deciding what my new dog would eat. Along the way I met veterinarians who passionately believed that a steady diet of kibble from a recognized pet-food company remained the most proven way to feed dogs healthily. I also met vets who with equal conviction maintained that canine health and longevity were best promoted by a diet of raw meat, bones, and vegetables.

I had hoped that the scientific literature would break this stalemate and point to a clear, evidence-based way to feed my dog. But I was disappointed. No scientific study has examined what constitutes a healthy diet for dogs over the long term. In other words, no one has compared dogs eating kibble to those on a more natural diet and then seen which group has been healthier and lived longer after a couple of decades.

Given this lack of data, I had to reason from less-specific nutritional research that has been done on canines—as well as the evidence accumulated by scientists working with human and other animal species—to learn what diets best promote health and longevity in dogs. I also followed the lead of those human nutritionists who have examined our historic diet and noted that we might be healthier if we ate foods made from whole ingredients that have been minimally processed. Likewise, when I delved into the scientific literature on dogs,

I immediately found an important fact about their historic diet that needs to be considered as we try to puzzle out what to feed them today.

When dogs were first domesticated between thirty-three thousand and sixteen thousand years ago not a single one of them was eating grain. Dogs weren't eating grain — corn, wheat, rice, oats, soy, or barley, the major ingredients in many present-day kibbles — because agriculture had yet to be invented. None of these grains existed in their domesticated forms until about ten thousand years ago. Nor were dogs yet in their domesticated form. They were just beginning to slip from their wolfdom, a process that has never been truly accomplished, at least genetically, since domestic dogs differ from the gray wolf by at most 0.1 percent of their nuclear gene sequence.

This is a tiny number, and if you'd like to visualize exactly how small it is — how small a portion of your dog's DNA is not a wolf's DNA — think of your dog as an apple pie with a diameter of twelve inches. To remove a slice of the pie that is not a wolf, you'd have to cut a sliver measuring just over one-thirty-second of an inch along the crust, less than a millimeter, a very tiny slice indeed. In other words, when it comes to their DNA, dogs are almost entirely wolves. And so the question naturally arises: should modern dogs eat like wolves? If so, then we ought to know how real wolves eat.

Wanting to find out, I visited with Douglas Smith, the head of the Yellowstone Wolf Project, catching him in his office at park headquarters in Mammoth Hot Springs, Wyoming, a tall, long-limbed man, with a graying Fu Manchu mustache and a plaid outdoorsy shirt, his walls covered with maps of the wolves' territories. In over thirty years of studying wolves, Doug had seen thousands of them kill and eat elk, moose, and deer, and he now told me, "Wolves eat the internal organs first — liver, heart, lungs, and kidneys — and the brains as well, which are a delicacy for them, if they can break open the skull and get to them. Deer and elk calves they eat entirely, including all the bones, and there won't be a shred left."

He went on to say that Yellowstone wolves rarely ate fish, but that wolves in other ecosystems did. Yellowstone wolves ate ground squirrels opportunistically, popping them down "like gum drops," and would eat "most any small mammal or bird, if they had the chance." The park's coyotes and foxes ate berries when they were blooming, and in great numbers, but wolves rarely consumed fruit. He had never seen wolves eat the vegetable matter in the stomachs of their large prey, a finding corroborated by another one of North America's respected wolf biologists, L. David Mech, from his own long-term studies of wolves on Isle Royale in Lake Superior. Wolves did eat a small bit of vegetation, Doug pointed out, grass in particular, as evidenced by his finding it in their scats. However, it comprised only a tiny portion of their diet, less than 2 percent.

In conclusion, he wanted me to know that wolves were not picky about the freshness of their food. "They have cast-iron stomachs," he added, "and will eat rotting animals. Once, on Isle Royale, I found a moose calf, bloated in the July heat. It stunk like you could not believe. I didn't want to pick it up right then, and I came back two days later. There was nothing left. The wolves had eaten it all. Another time, when the wolves first arrived in Yellowstone and were being kept in pens, I cut my finger on a dead bison that we were going to feed them. I almost lost my arm to the infection. But not a single wolf that fed on that rotting bison got sick. I have seen scats with nothing but bones in them; it's completely normal for a wolf. It's an animal that's 98 percent carnivore."

There can be little doubt that the wolves who first began to live with people were similarly carnivorous. After all, there was not enough high-calorie wild food on which to survive except meat. Based on skeletal artifacts that have been carbon-dated, this new canine-human partnership began in a swath of country from Siberia to Europe about thirty-three thousand years ago. However, it is thought that these wolf-dogs did not pass on their genetic legacy to present-day dogs. Instead, wolves in southeastern China sixteen thousand years ago and in the Middle East twelve thousand years ago began an affiliation with humans, and it is these wolves who are our dogs' ancestors.

The diet of these protodogs began to change with the invention of rice farming between nine and ten thousand years ago in China. Farmers, thinking that their wolf-dogs might be a ready source of food — one that didn't need to be hunted — began to keep them as livestock. As no other animals had yet been domesticated — no cattle, pigs, or chickens — meat for these wolf-dogs would have to be hunted, costing time and energy. Far cheaper to turn these carnivores into rice-eaters, a strategy that is still employed worldwide: feeding dogs grain is less expensive than feeding them meat, as anyone knows who has compared the price of a large bag of kibble to the equivalent amount of canned dog food. Thus, it has been theorized, carnivorous wolves began their journey toward being omnivorous dogs.

In the Middle East, wolves became similarly omnivorous with the domestication of wheat, whose cultivation turned hunter-gatherers into village-dwelling farmers. Attracted to refuse dumps on the outskirts of these villages, wolves grew increasingly habituated to people and were eventually tamed. Later, when people began to migrate, their dogs went along, taking their newly acquired omnivorous habits with them.

Thousands of years later, present-day wolves, as well as domestic dogs, haven't lost this ancient digestive flexibility — they are meat-eaters by preference, but turn into omnivores if presented with opportunity or struck by need. Biologists conducting research in very different landscapes have frequently observed such behavior. For example, Adolph Murie, in his 1944 monograph *The Wolves of Mount McKinley*, wrote that wolves visited the park's garbage dumps and that he subsequently found garbage in their scats. Also using scat analysis, the Italian wolf biologist Luigi Boitani has estimated that garbage makes up 60 to 70 percent of the diet of Italian wolves, whose hunting for wild prey is limited by large human populations, farms, and roads. Even so, Boitani discovered that these garbage-eating wolves were high-grading what they consumed, preferentially eating more protein than vegetables or grain. Trapping the wolves, he took blood samples, which when analyzed showed significant concentrations of the type of nucleic acids found in the internal organs of sheep and cattle. Italian butchers — cautious about infecting their customers with the tapeworms and flukes common to the liver and spleen of livestock — were discarding these organs in the local dumps, where the wolves feasted on them.

Until the early part of the twentieth century, what people fed domestic dogs reflected this historic smorgasbord. Dogs got meat, bones, vegetables, fruit, and grain — all the scraps that kitchens produced and dumps collected — supplemented with what the dogs caught on their own: mice, rabbits, birds, and snakes. If dogs happened to live on a farm, they often got the chance to eat the afterbirths of livestock — full of nutrients, which is why mother dogs eat their own. If they lived in a high-class kennel of hunting dogs whose owner had an eye for performance, they would have been fed stews of fresh vegetables and slaughterhouse leavings — the heads of sheep and cattle boiled up along with entrails. If one had a lot of dogs to feed and economy was a concern, experts of the nineteenth century, like the Scottish-born medical doctor and dog fancier Dr. William Gordon Stables, recommended mixing in rice, barley, or oats to extend the meat — oats being his favorite, especially for sporting dogs or those dogs who, as he wrote, "are much out of doors." Nonetheless, Stables cautioned against overfeeding grains, saying that rice should not be fed more than once a week and oats no more than two days running. Corn, which he called "Indian meal," was at the bottom of his list of grains to feed dogs. He was also adamant that in addition to meat and entrails, dogs needed vegetables at least three times a week: cabbage one day, kale the next, then turnips, and so on. And Stables was hardly breaking new ground.

As early as 1827, *The American Farmer* counseled its readers to feed their dogs almost precisely the same diet: soups made from sheep's heads, pigs' feet, vegetables, and oats. Strikingly, given my experience with feeding Merle corn-based kibble and his subsequent itching, James Watson, an American dog breeder and prolific writer on canine subjects, called cornmeal "our *bête noire*" in his 1905 ten-volume work *The Dog Book*. Unless corn is thoroughly boiled, he warned, "it will in a month set a kennel of dogs scratching themselves to pieces."

This knowledge about which foods made for healthy dogs — meat, vegetables, and a small amount of grains — began to disappear into the hopper of industrialized pet foods during the end of the nineteenth century. The man who did more than anyone to set this trend in motion was James Spratt, an American who sailed for England in the late 1850s. Upon his arrival, Spratt saw stray dogs lining the quay and gobbling the moldy hardtack that the sailors threw them. An electrician, he had come to Britain to sell lightning rods, and at that moment a lightning bolt of marketing inspiration struck him. Spratt conceived of manufacturing ready-made dog cakes that would contain all the food a dog needed in a handy, ready-to-eat package.

Much as he is credited with inventing modern dog food, Spratt was not the first to have this notion. Dog biscuits were already being made in America and England during the 1820s. Spratt, however, had the acumen to patent his product — a kind of baked shortbread made of wheat, beetroot, and vegetables, with beef blood as a binder — and christen it "Spratt's Patented Meat Fibrine Dog Cakes." He then advertised his new dog food with unflagging zeal and unsubstantiated claims, stating that the old ways of feeding dogs were dangerous while his was healthier. "Remember," warned one of his advertisements,

> diseases are commonest among meat-fed dogs. The safe, sustaining and health-fortifying food for your dog is SPRATT'S – be he large or small, young or old. It is a *balanced* food, providing meat and wheat in a form most readily digested and assimilated. That is why dogs thrive so splendidly on SPRATT'S, and why veterinarians praise it so enthusiastically.

Spratt advertised in the *Saturday Evening Post* and in the American Kennel Club's journal, and he also gave away free samples at dog shows, where he proudly noted that Queen Victoria's dogs now ate Spratt's. He soon had manufacturing plants in Newark, St. Louis, San Francisco, and London, having created an entire line of specialized dog foods: Patent Charcoal Dog Cakes for those dogs with sensitive tummies; Pet Dog Cakes for urban dogs; Cod Liver Oil Old Dog Cakes for canine geriatrics and those recovering from illnesses; Greyhound cakes; and Spratt's Puppy Meal, Puppy Biscuits, and Orphan Puppy Food. Sound familiar? Today virtually every large manufacturer of dog and cat food has taken its lead from Spratt, creating a variety of foods that are advertised as being specifically formulated for different age classes and even different breeds, but whose ingredients are often identical.

By the beginning of the twentieth century, many other manufacturers had jumped onto Spratt's bandwagon, producing a variety of dog biscuits – the F. H. Bennett Biscuit Company of New York City, for example, baked the first Milk-Bone in 1908 – as well as dry foods and canned meats. These dry foods could not yet be called kibble, but were instead a mixture of grain leavings and by-products of the meatpacking industry, presented as loose granular feeds or pressed into cakes. Canned dog food used horse meat as its main ingredient, since North America and Europe still moved goods and people by horsepower and horses were always dying.

Using what other industries considered their waste products – grain husks, meat trimmings, worn-out livestock, dying draft animals – the dog food industry became one of the outstanding examples of value-added manufacturing. It took cheap raw materials, added a minimum of capital and labor, and produced a product that could be sold for a high profit margin.

In the 1890s, William H. Danforth became one of the masters of this business model. A dapper, clear-eyed Missourian, he helped to found a livestock feed company—the Robinson-Danforth Commission Company—that eventually diversified into breakfast cereal, using the slogan "Where purity is paramount." Danforth, as much a marketing genius as Spratt, distilled the slogan into the more riveting "Purina" and branded his company with the name. He then partnered with Dr. Ralston, the pseudonym of the founder of an idealistic institution called the Ralston Health Club. Ralston preached the virtues of "good health, cleanly lives, purity of heart, and progressive existence" to 800,000 followers and gave Danforth's new breakfast cereal a testimonial as well as a customer base. He also provided the company with a new name, the merger creating what would become one of the largest agribusiness and dog food companies in the world: Ralston Purina.

During the decades that Danforth and his descendants were changing how Americans thought about food—creating products like Ry-Crisp, Wheat Chex, and eventually, in 1957, Purina Dog Chow—a New Jersey veterinarian named Mark L. Morris Sr. decided that the canine diet needed improvement. In 1928 he established the second small animal hospital in the United States, in Raritan, New Jersey, where he devoted himself to fighting canine diseases through nutrition. By the late 1930s, he had created a diet especially tailored for dogs with renal problems. Business grew, and in 1948 he contracted with the Hill Packing Company in Topeka, Kansas, licensing his canine dietary formulas to them so they could begin mass production. The partnership between Morris and a relatively obscure Kansas packing company also became one of the most widely recognized names in the dog food industry: Hill's Pet Nutrition.

In addition to being a good businessman, Morris was civic-minded and philanthropic, and in 1948 he established the charity known as the Morris Animal Foundation, which today funds a variety of research projects devoted to animal health. Then, in 1960, Morris became the president of the American Veterinary Medical Association, not an insignificant office for someone who was also selling dog food. One might say that through these moves Morris affianced the dog food industry and the veterinary profession, but before the marriage could be consummated, two more factors had to fall into place: an industrial process and a governmental policy, both of which have made corn the most widely used ingredient in modern dog food.

The process was named "extrusion," and it has given us a wide variety of well-known products: Fig Newtons, Cheerios, and pasta shells of all shapes and sizes. Extrusion was first applied to dog food in the 1950s, and the basic technology has remained unchanged. Raw ingredients are mixed into a moist dough that is cooked under pressure and forced through a die—the extruder—that shapes the individual pieces into their unique shapes, forming the kibble. But extrusion has a limitation. The process must use dough with a high starch content in order to expand the kernels. Corn was the leading candidate: it contained enough starch, it was cheap, and it would become ever cheaper during the next half-century as federal price supports were removed, subsidies were given to corn farmers, and the market was flooded with corn, making everything from dog food to Big Macs to Coca-Cola profitable for agribusiness and a bargain for consumers. Worth noting is that the man most responsible for initiating declining corn prices was Earl Butz, the secretary of agriculture under Richard Nixon in the early 1970s. Butz came to Washington directly from Ralston Purina, where he was chairman of the board.

It's doubtful, though, that price point and convenience alone would have created so many modern corn-eating dogs if the veterinary community itself hadn't also blessed corn as the proper food for canines. This endorsement was very much an effort of Dr. Mark L. Morris Jr., son of Dr. Mark L. Morris Sr. Continuing in his father's footsteps, Morris Jr. created a new line of corn-based dog foods for research facilities and called it Science Diet, making the kibble available in veterinarians' offices in 1968 and marketing it in a pure white bag to emphasize its medical and scientific underpinnings.

In 1983 the marriage between veterinarians and the dog food industry was finally consummated when Dr. Morris Jr. began to co-author and edit *Small Animal Clinical Nutrition,* now in its fifth edition and published by the Mark Morris Institute, an organization that is dedicated, as its website writes, to "a global program of support for veterinary nutritional education." Hill's calls this massive textbook "the most widely used source on the subject around the world" and gives it free of charge (it retails for over $200) to veterinary students across America. Many veterinary students on other continents also rely on the text, which states in one of its opening chapters, "Dry extruded dog foods typically contain 30 to 60% carbohydrate, mostly starch, and cause no adverse effects." This chapter has eight authors. Seven of them work for or are affiliated with Hill's. The eighth works for the veterinary pharmaceutical company Elanco.

The close alliance between the pet food industry and the veterinary profession is cemented in several other ways during the training of young veterinarians. Depending on the veterinary training college, Hill's supplies students with lab coats and book backpacks, throws parties for them, and gives them a free twenty-pound bag of dog or cat food for their pets each month while they're in school. Purina, IAMS, and Eukanuba also distribute free dog food at some vet schools. In addition, Hill's funds scholarships and educational initiatives at veterinary training centers in both the United States and abroad, but it was unwilling to disclose the amount it donated. Moreover, the twelve veterinarians on the faculty of the Mark Morris Institute teach nutritional courses at veterinary training colleges in the United States, Canada, and the Caribbean, again without charge. Nine of these veterinarians also work for Hill's Pet Nutrition, and another is employed by Royal Canin, another manufacturer of dog food.

Obviously, the outcome of all these activities is influence. Hill's Pet Nutrition and other pet food companies guide how future veterinarians think about what to feed our dogs and cats. Do the vet schools think this is a problem? To find out, I called twenty-nine vet schools in the United States. Twenty replied. Only two vet schools — at the University of Missouri and Ohio State University — thought that this sort of influence might be a problem. For a variety of reasons, all the rest of the schools didn't think that the influence of the pet food industry was anything to worry about. One school, the University of Wisconsin, had instituted a policy forbidding students to accept even such low-value items as pens from pet food companies. At the University of Tennessee, one veterinarian, echoing the sentiment of others, said that she remained neutral in her nutritional recommendations despite the fact that Hill's was funding her salary. Many of the institutions replied that Hill's Pet Nutrition wasn't the only pet food company represented on campus. Yet these other pet food companies — Purina, IAMS, Eukanuba, Royal Canin — don't offer a substantially different nutritional viewpoint from that of Hill's. They, too, make dog food from grain.

The lack of separation between the veterinary profession and the pet food industry has now influenced how tens of millions of dogs have been fed, including shelter dogs. Hill's and other pet food companies donate food to animal shelters, often for no more than the cost of shipping, a generous and meritorious act that keeps many shelters in business and many dogs alive. In fact, since 2002, when Hill's created its Hill's Science Diet Shelter Nutrition Program, the company has donated 113 million pounds of pet food to shelters. When a dog is adopted, a free bag of kibble frequently accompanies the dog to its new home so that it doesn't have to change its diet, a notion that has been widely recommended by veterinarians: dogs need consistency in their food.

This, of course, is a wonderful way to promote a particular brand of dog food, but it may not be the best way to raise a dog to eat eclectically and get its nutrition from a wide variety of foods, as many firsthand accounts and one notable study have shown. The psychologist Zing-yang Kuo took sixty newborn Chow puppies and divided them into three groups. The first group was fed an enriched soy diet, the second had fruits and vegetables with added vitamins and minerals, and the third ate cow's milk, butter, cheese, and a variety of meats, fish, fruits, and vegetables. After six months, eighteen out of the twenty puppies in group one would not touch any new food, even when starved for twenty-four hours. It was nearly the same for the puppies in the second group. Only the puppies in group three, the eclectic eaters, would immediately eat any kind of new food presented to them so long as it wasn't bitter, sour, or stale.

Zing-yang Kuo went on to conduct the same experiment with kittens and several species of birds, and the results of these experiments were identical to the one he had conducted with puppies: animals who were hardwired to consume a variety of foods became monovores when raised on an unvarying diet. As Kuo wrote, "Young animals grow up with a more or less fixed food habit, not because it is species-specific but because of the kinds of food they were fed in early development, whether by their own parents or by human beings."

Raised in a family of eclectic eaters, I could readily agree with Zing-yang Kuo. Everyone in our family ate widely, and so did our dogs, who were fed table scraps. Continuing in this tradition, I had given Merle as many different foods as he cared to consume in addition to his kibble, and having now read about the historic omnivory of dogs, I was determined to follow a similar course with Pukka. But would feeding him ten different kibbles give him a healthy diet? Even if I rotated his kibble, was corn really a good thing to feed a dog? Might he live longer on a diet of raw meat, bones, and vegetables?

To answer these questions I tried to find someone who could provide me with more perspective than I had heard in the polarized dog food debate, a veterinarian who wasn't shilling for a dog food company, whose credentials were impeccable and respected, and who brought some science to an issue where opinion and anecdote have reigned.

CHAPTER THIRTEEN

Should a Wolf Eat Corn?

THIS VETERINARIAN TURNED OUT to be Dr. Joseph Bartges, both a DVM and a PhD, and a professor of medicine and nutrition at the University of Tennessee Veterinary Medical Center in Knoxville. He was in green scrubs on the April day we met, his light brown hair parted in the middle, his quiet measured voice and wire-rimmed bifocal glasses giving him the air of a dispassionate scholar. And from the moment our discussion began he was evenhanded, repeating what the National Research Council, which publishes independent scientific reports for the National Academy of Sciences, wrote in its 2006 report on the nutritional requirements of dogs and cats: "There appears to be no requirement for digestible carbohydrate in dogs provided enough protein is given." However, Joe also wanted me to appreciate that dogs, and even cats, could eat grains "just fine, utilizing, digesting, and absorbing carbohydrates without problems."

"Which is better for them, though?" I asked.

Instead of answering my question, he told me a story. "When I grew up," he began, "we had dogs. They lived outside and they were fed the cheapest thing my father could buy—co-op dry food, nothing else, and occasionally they got hamburger or eggs. The Collie lived to twenty-one, the Dachshund to nineteen, and the Elkhound to eighteen. I had a cat who lived to be twenty-one and ate dry cat food since she was a kitten. And she didn't die of diabetes, renal failure, or thyroid issues. She died of lymphoma. If I had fed her a raw-food diet, would she have lived to twenty-four? I don't know." He shrugged.

"Here, we don't try to talk people out of a particular diet. We say, if you're going to feed that diet, what are the pros and cons of it and what are the ways to feed it safely? Going on the information we have—min-imal-maximal nutritional requirements for dogs—how can we meet those guidelines with what you're feeding and to the best of our knowl-edge right now? So we balance raw-food diets—beef, deer, duck—and the interesting thing, down the road, will be to see how raw-food diets compare to traditional diets beyond just anecdotes."

"By 'traditional' do you mean commercial kibble?"

He nodded. "There are many good commercially available diets, many of which give many animals very long and completely healthy lives. Do some of these diets cause death, disease, or anything else, di-rectly, in a one-to-one ratio? Probably not. Do they modify genetic po-tential? Possibly, just like smoking. Some people get lung cancer when they smoke and some don't."

It was important, he amplified, for people to experiment: to feed their dogs a variety of diets; to keep the ingredient labels from the packages for reference; and to carefully observe how the dog did on different foods.

"Do you mean rotate a dog's food?"

"Many animals do fine on one food," he answered. "Is there a scien-tific basis for rotating food? Not really. At least none that I'm aware of." He then explained how there were many advantages to rotating food, whether it was commercial, or raw, or mixing homemade diets with commercial ones. Rotating foods didn't lock a dog into a spe-cific texture, flavor, or type of food, so if you ran into some issue and you needed to change the food, anecdotally it was easier to modify the diet. There was, of course, the old argument that if a dog ate widely and developed a food allergy you wouldn't know what it was allergic to. But most of the time food allergies weren't true immune disease. They were an intolerance to an ingredient. "It's like if you eat Mexican food and get heartburn," he said. "That's not an allergy. And a lot of dogs and cats are food-intolerant in this way. That's where a rotation diet can help quite a bit. You can find things that work and those that don't."

He paused, then added, "It's also why you need to carefully observe how your dog is doing. Is their coat good? Are their stools loose or too firm? Do they have an odor? Are they active? Do they have good mus-cle tone? Are they overweight? Are they thin? Are they sleeping a lot?"

"Could a dog look really good," I asked Joe, "and internally not be that good?"

"Absolutely," he said. "Not only physiologically, but pathologically. We see patients that outwardly look good, but have a big intestinal tumor. That's where going in to your vet for evaluations and examinations is important. Sometimes it can be subtle things that your vet will notice. I've seen dogs that are hypothyroid with no clinical signs except that they're incontinent. And then we address their diet."

"So," I ventured, "given everything you've said – rotate foods, dogs do fine on carbs, but they can also do well on raw food – it sounds like there is still no hard, fast, scientific evidence about which diet is best for canine health and longevity."

A quiet man who chose his words with care, Joe Bartges now laughed out loud. "Give me a million dollars" – he smiled – "and twenty years and I'll have the answer for you."

Of course, what Joe was referring to is the lack of a study comparing genetically similar dogs who have been fed grain-based and grain-free diets for their entire lives. Despite this hole in the evidence, we can nonetheless draw inferences about the best way to feed dogs from the many studies that have examined other aspects of canine nutrition.

One of the most revelatory was done at the Nestlé Purina Research facility in St. Louis and involved pairing Labrador Retrievers from the same litter. On a daily basis, one member of each pair was fed 75 percent of what its sibling was given. The dogs were then followed for fourteen years, until all of them had died, and the results were remarkable. Those dogs who ate their fill each day had a median life span of 11.2 years, while the median life span of the dogs on the restricted diet was 13 years. In other words, those Labs who ate fewer calories lived almost two years longer.

Moreover, there were extraordinary differences in the frequency and onset of the chronic diseases that the two groups of Labs experienced. By the time the dogs were five years old, 52 percent of the dogs eating a full diet had osteoarthritis in their hips compared to 13 percent of the dogs on a calorically restricted diet. By the time the dogs were eight years old, 77 percent of the full-diet dogs had osteoarthritis in their shoulders and elbows, while only 10 percent of the diet-restricted dogs did. Strikingly, the insulin levels of the calorically restricted dogs were 32 percent lower on average than those of the dogs on a full diet, and although the two groups of dogs developed similar kinds of cancers, the diet-restricted dogs developed them two years later than their well-fed companions. And these dogs, it must be remembered, were genetically similar — they were siblings.

Calorically restricted diets in humans have been shown to have similarly protective effects. Individuals on such diets have low insulin and low blood-glucose levels, have a lower incidence of chronic diseases, and tend to live longer. These cross-species findings are persuasive. Whether you're a human or a dog, if you want to live longer, it's probably a good idea to reduce your glucose and insulin levels by eating less food, or changing the types of foods you eat, or both. For dogs, this would mean eating more meat and vegetables instead of corn and rice.

Corn and rice are rich in soluble carbohydrates, and they raise blood glucose levels quickly. In fact, when French researchers measured blood glucose levels in healthy adult Beagles, they found that the amount of starch in their diet was the major determinant in how much their blood sugar spiked after eating. By reducing the amount of starch in canine diets, wrote the authors, we could help manage the increasing problems of canine obesity and diabetes.

This is one of the central themes of the Australian veterinarian Dr. Ian Billinghurst, whose work has changed how many people feed their dogs. In his 1993 book *Give Your Dog a Bone,* Billinghurst recounts that he had been feeding his dogs raw meaty bones and table scraps, but decided to experiment and feed them commercial dog food. Within months, Billinghurst's previously healthy dogs began to exhibit the same maladies that he was seeing in his clients' dogs: skin problems, runny eyes, scruffy coats, sore ears, bad breath, and smelly stools. He switched his dogs back to raw meaty bones, vegetables, and table scraps, and their health problems disappeared.

Upon finishing his book, I wondered if he might expand on his now nearly twenty-year-old observation that dogs who eat a grain-based diet suffer from premature aging and degenerative diseases. Calling him at his office in Bathurst, New South Wales, I found him to be as friendly and informal on the phone as in his book, saying "no worries" when I thanked him for fielding my call between consults.

He began by telling me that during the last fifteen thousand years dogs had become less hunters and more scavengers. "Our Australian dingoes, for example, are very opportunistic. One year when insects are prevalent, that'll be their entire diet. Another year it might be rats and mice or bush turkeys. They're very omnivorous and in hard times, when little food is available, they'll eat the gut contents of any prey they kill or scavenge." He wanted me to understand that this vegetable matter in no way resembled the high-carbohydrate kibble that many dogs eat year after year and that resulted, as the French researchers discovered, in elevated levels of blood sugar, known as hyperglycemia.

"Corn is particularly bad in this regard," he said. "The hyperglycemia it causes creates high levels of insulin. In turn, high levels of insulin elevate the activity of an enzyme called delta 5 desaturase, and it's this enzyme that begins a chain reaction, culminating in the production of arachidonic acid." Herein lay the problem. Arachidonic acid caused inflammation and it was inflammation that, as he said, "aids in the initiation and progress of the degenerative diseases associated with aging: cancer, arthritis, inflammatory bowel disease, allergies, and autoimmune disease."

"So what's the solution?" I asked.

"Don't feed your dog high-carbohydrate kibble," he replied. "Give him raw meaty bones — chicken carcasses are still my favorite — along with ample green leafy vegetables. That way, you won't start the inflammatory chain reaction."

Green leafy vegetables, he went on to explain, provided age-delaying antioxidants and phytochemicals, which protect against cancer. This contention has been well documented by others. Researchers at Purdue University's School of Veterinary Medicine have found that Scottish Terriers who consume green leafy and yellow-orange vegetables at least three times per week reduced their risk of developing bladder cancer by between 70 and 90 percent. The human medical literature also mirrors this finding: people who eat vegetables and fruits that contain phytochemicals reduce their risk of cancer.

Feeding dogs a less starchy diet — lower in grains, higher in protein, and with a variety of vegetables — may also have two other important benefits. First, by dampening insulin spikes, a low-carb diet reduces the amount of bioavailable insulin-like growth factor-1. As we discussed in chapter 2, lower levels of IGF-1 have been associated with longer life spans, no matter the species.

Second, a low-carb diet enhances the physical fitness of dogs. Using sled dogs as subjects, researchers have shown that when dogs are switched from a high-carbohydrate diet to one containing high protein, they have more red blood cells, more hemoglobin, and a higher VO_2max — the measure of an individual's ability to transport and use oxygen and thus an indication of aerobic performance. The sled dogs also had higher levels of calcium, magnesium, and albumen, all of which enabled them to better endure exhaustive exercise. In short, they could race longer and faster. As an added benefit, these dogs had fewer soft-tissue injuries on the high-protein diet. Lastly, the high-protein diet eliminated the dogs' coprophagy — eating feces — a not uncommon behavior in dogs who are fed high-carb diets and who may eat feces as a way to consume nutrients that they aren't getting in their food.

Similar endurance tests have been done using Beagles running on treadmills. When the dogs were switched from a high-carb diet based on grains to one containing only pigs' lungs and whole chickens, the results were "profound," as the researchers stated. The Beagles' endurance was 31 percent better on the high-protein diet than it was on kibble containing grain.

Another study has been done comparing the performance of hunting dogs — English Pointers hunting quail in Georgia. Those Pointers who ate a high-protein diet found more birds per hour and more total birds per hunt than those on a high-carb diet. The high-protein dogs were also able to withstand heat stress better because they had lower core body temperatures. And still a fourth study flip-flopped the diet of sled dogs from 60 percent carbohydrate to 60 percent fat and found that the dogs on the high-fat diet were better able to mobilize their free fatty acids and improve their aerobic performance, even when they were untrained.

One caution about high-protein diets has to be noted: dogs who display territorial aggression may have their behavior exacerbated by eating too much protein, whether it's in kibble or raw food. Researchers have found that a low-protein diet can actually help these dogs, lessening their aggressive protection of their territories.

Pet food manufacturers have begun to pay attention to this evidence and have steadily added grain-free or low-grain offerings to their lines, advertising them as improving the performance of working and sporting dogs and aiding those dogs with skin allergies. In some of these kibbles, sweet potato has replaced corn, rice, or wheat as a carbohydrate source with enough starch to permit extrusion. Unlike white potatoes, sweet potatoes have a low glycemic load while being rich in both antioxidant and anti-inflammatory nutrients.

Even though such high-protein, low-carb kibbles have the potential to improve the health and performance of dogs, we shouldn't automatically reach for a bag of dog food that advertises itself as "grain-free" and assume that what's inside is healthy. Instead, we should follow Dr. Joe Bartges's recommendation to read the ingredient labels, paying particular attention to artificial colors and preservatives.

Both the UK Food Standards Agency and the US Food and Drug Administration have begun to look at the association between artificial food colors and hyperactivity in children, an association that may affect dogs as well. Since dogs don't care whether their kibble is red, blue, or yellow, why not put the whole issue of artificial food colors to rest and buy dog food without them?

Nor should we reach for kibble that's preserved with BHA, BHT, or ethoxyquin. The International Agency for Research on Cancer, an arm of the World Health Organization, has found that there is *sufficient evidence* (the italics are theirs) for the carcinogenicity of BHA, and *limited evidence* for that of BHT. Ethoxyquin — a pesticide developed as an antioxidant to retard spoilage and increase shelf life in pet foods — has not been completely tested for its carcinogenic potential, according to the US Environmental Protection Agency.

Such controversial preservatives are easily avoided, since scores of pet food manufacturers have been proactive and replaced them with benign natural ingredients that act as antioxidants — rosemary and sage, for instance, as well as vitamin E, which is often called "mixed tocopherols" on the ingredient labels of pet foods. If one can afford the difference in price between kibbles preserved with antioxidants whose safety is still debated and kibbles that are naturally preserved — an additional cost of about $40 per year for a thirty-five-pound dog — why not spend that $40, eleven cents a day, and have peace of mind?

Far more difficult to avoid are grains that have been sprayed with pesticides as well as having been genetically modified. In the United States, one-third of all agricultural pesticides are applied to corn, and over 90 percent of the soybeans and 85 percent of the corn grown have been genetically engineered. Such crops — known as GMOs for "genetically modified organisms" — aren't merely genetically reconfigured to be resistant to certain herbicides and insecticides; they also contain the residues of these toxic compounds because they are repeatedly sprayed with them.

In the 1990s, Monsanto became the innovator of this agricultural technology when it created seeds that were resistant to its own world-famous weed killer, Roundup. Crops grown from these seeds are called "Roundup Ready," meaning that they can be sprayed with Roundup, which contains the herbicide glyphosate, with no ill effects. However, the effects of GMO crops on human and animal health remain unknown. French scientists who fed rats Roundup Ready corn discovered toxic effect in the rats' kidneys, livers, hearts, adrenal glands, and spleens after only ninety days on the diet. These scientists cautioned that their three-month-long study would not show carcinogenic effects or disruption of the endocrine system and recommended that studies of up to two years in length be done.

We are all now part of this experiment—if we eat genetically modified foods—and our dogs are one of the experiment's primary subjects since millions of them eat corn every day. Until more is known about the safety of GMO foods, those concerned about their health risks can try to feed their dogs kibbles made from organic grain or kibbles that contain no grain at all.

One of the questions that most intrigued me about dog food—and one I wanted to answer before deciding what Pukka's diet would be—was whether the rendered products so many kibbles contain, like meal made from beef, chicken, lamb, fish, or bones, are in fact safe. Such meals inexpensively boost the protein content of kibble and are made from the organic protein leftovers from restaurants, supermarkets, and fast-food chains, as well as from the livestock and fish industries. They include carcasses, trimmings, and oils. Renderers grind, cook, and centrifuge these leftovers, separating the liquids from the solids so as to create the meals, fats, and oils that go into pet and livestock feeds. Many rendered products are also used to make soaps, candles, lubricants, tires, cosmetics, asphalt, fertilizer, and biodiesel fuels.

There would be no modern meat industry without rendering, since the leftovers of slaughterhouses would soon overwhelm landfills and create an enormous health hazard as billions of tons of organic waste rotted. Instead, rendering recycles these wastes into valuable products. However, critics of the pet food industry, starting in the 1990s, have claimed that rendered meals have their origins in a shady brew of disabled and diseased livestock, roadkill, dead zoo animals, garbage from restaurant and grocery stores, including plastic food wrappings, as well as dead dogs and cats picked up from animal shelters and veterinary practices. These criticisms have not gone away and, if true, would mean that Fido is eating Rover.

The latter charge was lent credence when the FDA's Center for Veterinary Medicine began to hear from veterinarians that sodium pentobarbital, the drug commonly used to euthanize dogs, cats, and other animals, seemed to be losing its effectiveness. The CVM, thinking that perhaps dogs were being exposed to sodium pentobarbital in their dog food as a consequence of eating their fellows, and were thus becoming less responsive to the drug, decided to investigate.

Dozens of pet foods, purchased in and around Laurel, Maryland, in 1998, were found to contain sodium pentobarbital. Surprisingly, DNA tests showed that no dog, cat, or horse DNA was present in the implicated pet foods (horses being the other animal typically euthanized with the drug). Mysteriously, the origins of the sodium pentobarbital have remained unidentified to this day, fueling ongoing suspicion about the quality of kibble.

Wanting to get to the bottom of the issue and discover what really goes into the rendered products that so many of our dogs eat, I began by calling the National Renderers Association, where a high-placed official told me that to his knowledge no plant in the United States currently rendered dogs and cats into pet food. Of the 205 plants that are members of the National Renderers Association, 103 now use Hazard Analysis and Critical Control Point (HACCP) monitoring, the same source-to-endpoint oversight used in many branches of the food industry to ensure quality and prevent the spread of food-borne illnesses and terrorist attacks on the food supply. These are the plants from which large pet food manufacturers are said by the National Renderers Association to buy their ingredients, and Hill's Pet Nutrition confirmed to me that it required signed affidavits from its suppliers, certifying that there was no roadkill or pets in its raw materials.

These assurances, I soon discovered, didn't mean that dogs and cats were no longer rendered. Doing a search of public records, I found two companies — one with plants in Reno, Nevada, and Sacramento, California, and the other in Los Angeles — that still accept dogs and cats from animal shelters and vets.

I called both factories. The owner of the first, which does business under a variety of names — Koefran Rendering, Sacramento Rendering, and Nevada By Products — told me unequivocally that his business did not render euthanized dogs and cats. Two days later, when I called the manager of the Sacramento City Animal Shelter, he confirmed that Koefran Rendering picked up dogs and cats twice a week, Tuesdays and Thursdays. Subsequent interviews with individuals who worked at one of Koefran's plants led me to believe that once the dogs and cats had gone through the rendering vats, their cooked remains were not turned into pet food but buried in local landfills.

The owner of the second plant, Western Rendering Company, would not speak with me. Saying that it was "an urban legend that's been around for years that dogs and cats have been used in pet foods" and that "I was probably from PETA and wanted to make some misleading video," he slammed the phone down.

I got a far different reception from another renderer, the CEO of West Coast Reduction in Vancouver, British Columbia. He told me that his plant did not accept dogs and cats, and he'd be happy to show me this personally, giving me a tour of his entire facility, which he considered a flagship of the industry.

And so I set off for the west coast of North America, stopping first in southern California, where Los Angeles County's Department of Animal Care and Control disposes of about one hundred thousand animal carcasses annually. About 70 percent of these carcasses are dogs and cats (the rest are a variety of road-killed wildlife, other pets, and horses), and the director of the agency, Marcia Mayeda, told me that rendering them was the department's only option for their disposal since the dozen local animal crematoria couldn't handle this quantity of dead animals. Furthermore, southern California's stringent air quality regulations wouldn't permit the building of a new crematorium capable of handling this many carcasses.

Mayeda also emphasized that even if such a facility could be made to comply with the region's air quality standards, her agency couldn't find the funds to build a state-of-the-art crematorium. And why bother? There was already a good system in place. For years, she explained, dogs and cats euthanized in the county's animal shelters had been taken to Western Rendering. I asked her if I could watch the pickup of the animals at one of the shelters to document that this was in fact being done, and what then happened to the bodies, and she said, "No." Undercover videos had been made, blowing the issue out of proportion, creating bad PR, and not giving both sides of the story. "And so why not set the record straight?" I replied. She hesitated. I cajoled. Finally, she agreed, with one condition: I couldn't bring my camera.

The low yellow buildings of the Downey animal shelter, which is just about in the center of the greater Los Angeles area, stands between a busy street — Garfield Avenue — and a line of railroad tracks, behind which is a sprawling vacant field and warehouses. On the day I was there, a flatbed truck drove to the rear of the shelter at 11:30 A.M., out of sight of the public entrance. It was about thirty feet long, its blue plywood sides shielding what was inside from view, and unmarked except for small white letters and numbers stenciled on the driver's door: D&D, INC. CA54799. The driver was a lean, lithe, dark man in sturdy gray work trousers and a beige shirt. He also wore a ball cap and big rubber gloves, and he expertly spun four barrels full of dead dogs and cats onto the hydraulically lowered tailgate of his truck. I asked if I might ride up with him, and he said I could.

When we came even with the bed of the truck, I saw twenty-nine more of the same red and blue barrels, which he had collected from the other LA shelters, beginning his rounds at dawn. They, too, were full of dogs and cats piled helter-skelter atop each other, every color and shape imaginable, except really big dogs. A few flies buzzed along the rims of the barrels, but there was no sense of carnage because the dogs and cats were all intact, not dismembered, wounded, or bloody. Many looked to be sleeping peacefully. Not a single one wore a collar. Nor did it seem like these dogs and cats had become refuse. There was not a shred of discarded packaging, kitchen waste, or garbage of any kind.

This was the driver's last stop, and he pushed the barrels onto the remaining few feet of space at the end of the truck's bed. Returning us to the ground, he raised the tailgate and bid the shelter workers goodbye. I asked him if I could follow him in my car to the rendering plant, to see what happened to the dogs and cats, and he said, "Sure."

So off we drove through the inner city and industrial parks of greater Los Angeles, coming at last to a low canyon of factories where we turned into the unmarked gate of Western Rendering, owned by the person who had slammed the phone down on me. Above its cinderblock walls rose large, dark cookers and giant vats, steam emanating from pipes and chimneys, the entire affair, occupying part of a large city block, strung together by catwalks and tentacles of exposed pipes.

A tall, brown, dilapidated building, its roof partially peeled away, stood in the center of the complex, looming over everything like the ghost of the Industrial Revolution.

The truck proceeded through the yard and backed toward a large pile of dead animals. From a distance, it was hard to see exactly what kind of animals they were; there seemed to be cattle in the pile. A great mound of them lay before a chute, where a conveyor belt took them up into the cavernous mouth of the tall building.

I parked alongside a row of trucks and cars and walked toward the pile of dead animals, but I didn't get far. A security guard stopped me and asked me what I was doing. I replied that I was an author who wrote about dogs, that I had been observing at the Downey Animal Care Center, and that the driver of the truck had let me follow him here to see how the dogs and cats were processed.

The guard told me that I needed to speak with the owner and escorted me to a long low trailer with a set of wooden steps leading up to a side door. He knocked and said a few words, and a moment later a slight man of medium height stepped out, almost limp in his posture. He wore a black PGA ball cap, rectangular metal-rim glasses, and a faded beachcomber shirt hanging outside of his black chino pants. He told me that he was Bill Gorman, the president of Western Rendering. I told him my name and reminded him that he had refused to speak with me on the phone. I was wondering—now that I was actually here—if he'd tell me about what the dogs and cats were turned into, and if I might see the operation of his plant.

"I've gotten burned so badly by the press before," he replied, his voice implying that he was disgusted with the whole sorry business. "How do I know who you really are?"

"If you wait a minute, I'll show you." I went to my car and got a copy of *Merle's Door*. Gorman had gone into his office, paneled with dark imitation wood on which many memos were pinned. He stood behind a cluttered metal desk with a computer, everything shabby and looking as if it hadn't been refurbished in years. I handed him the book, and he gazed into Merle's eyes for a few moments before reading the text on the back cover, his face growing thoughtful. Ruffling the pages, he saw the photo insert, and he studied the images for quite a while. Then, slowly and reluctantly, as if what he was about to do was against his better judgment, he sat down. Placing the book on his desk, he said, "Okay, what do you want to know?" He motioned to an old brown couch that sat opposite his desk.

"What you do here," I said, sitting down. "What happens to the dogs and cats. Your side of the story. Your chance to tell it like it is."

He considered this for a few moments, then said, "We're a large-tissue sterilization plant. That's the real purpose we serve. Incineration of animals is cost-prohibitive and constrained by air pollution regulations. You can't bury this much decomposing animal matter. The cookers take in four to five tons of material. Over four hours we bring that material to 265 degrees Fahrenheit and hold it there for thirty minutes. The material is then deemed sterile, free from animal pathogens, and goes through several more steps until the product looks like dry coffee grinds. This is called dry rendered tankage. It's very high in protein, 61 to 62 percent, and it also contains ash as well as phosphorous and calcium. This process completely dehydrates the original material, reducing its volume and mass."

Gorman went on to explain that during the last thirty years, dry rendered tankage had been exported to Pacific Rim countries for swine food. But over the last ten years, aquaculture — fish farms — had begun to take hold in the Philippines, Indonesia, Vietnam, and Thailand. "Whenever there's a need for a protein ingredient in the fish-feed formulations," he said, "we'll get an inquiry from an agricultural commodity broker, and we fill that order. Before the current focus on fish, dry rendered tankage was used in formulations to feed eels, which are considered a delicacy in Asia.

"This material, the dry rendered tankage," Gorman went on, "could be used in chicken feed. We also take in sheep, cattle, pigs, everything and anything, and it all gets mixed together in one run. Then it's loaded into overseas shipping containers, twenty-four tons per container, but it doesn't have an unlimited shelf life. We add ethoxyquin to it, similar to BHT. It gives it several months' shelf life. If there is no request, the tankage goes to a landfill, and we lose $42 per ton. If we sell it for fish food at $200 per ton, we break even. We are, of course, paid by the LA County Animal Shelter System to pick up animals."

"Can I see how it happens?" I asked him.

He stood and walked to the door, leading me through the yard toward the pile of dead animals and stopping fifty yards from it. "This is as far as I'll take you," he said.

I could now see that the long pile of dead animals—what looked to be cattle as well as the dogs and cats—had blue and black trash bags mixed among the carcasses. I mentioned this to him, and he said, "The bags are torn off by the conveyor screws and filtered by screens that also take out any other foreign objects. Once a week the conveyor screens are cleaned out." He pointed to them. "Our other main activity is the intake, refining, and sterilization of waste cooking oils from grease peddlers, who collect from restaurants and fast-food outlets like Dairy Queen and McDonald's. Revenue-wise, that's our largest activity. We refine and sterilize the waste cooking oils, half a million pounds per week. These products are then used in livestock feeds. It's 100 percent vegetable matter, sprayed on corn."

As he spoke, two workers on the conveyor belt rooted among the dead animals. They appeared to be separating the animals and clearing something from them.

"It is *very, very* important," Bill Gorman went on, emphasizing the two *very*s, "to realize that *none, none* of the grease from the animal rendering process goes into the vegetable oil grease. The various rendered end products are defined by their physical characteristics and titers—the temperature that they go from a liquid to a solid and vice versa. They're also defined by color. It is *impossible*"—again he emphasized the word—"to confuse dry rendered tankage with tallow that goes into pet food because of color and physical specifications. Tallow is white; dry rendered tankage is dark brown. Plus, pet food manufacturers check specs all the time. Any euthanized animal will carry the chemical marking of sodium pentobarbital, even though most of it is volatized off during the rendering process. Pet food buyers reject an entire load if they get a positive marker for sodium pentobarbital."

Like many people who are at first reluctant to talk, once I had given Bill Gorman the chance to explain what he was about, he kept on talking, especially because it was apparent that I was sincerely interested in what he was saying. He was fascinating; he was well versed; and he was taking the time to illuminate the fine points of an industry about which few of us have an understanding even though we use its products every day. When he seemed at last finished, I asked him if he'd like to add anything. Like many others who won't reveal what's most important to them unless prompted, Bill Gorman saved the best for last.

"My goal," he said warmly, "is to generate renewable energy from the animals that come in. The carcasses would have to undergo pre-drying down to 30 percent moisture instead of 90 percent, and undergo additional sizing. The material would then go through a plasma arc and be turned into synthetic gas, syngas, which would be just as useful as propane, methane, or natural gas. I could run my entire facility on part of the gas and sell the rest to an electric utility."

Instead of appearing tired and furtive, Bill Gorman now looked expansive and enthusiastic as he described his dream. If the high kill rates of the Los Angeles shelters continue, dogs and cats might someday light the homes of California.

I thanked him for his time. He nodded and then asked if I was going to see any other rendering plants besides his. I told him that I was going to fly up to Vancouver to visit West Coast Reduction.

"Oh," he said with undisguised admiration, "you'll be seeing the Taj Mahal of rendering."

And so it was.

At the sentry station guarding the secure area of the Port of Vancouver, I and my driver's license were photographed — very official, very routine — and once through the gate I drove amid freight trains and semis while in the distance red cranes lifted steel containers off of moored ships. I went through a chain-link fence and into the guest parking area of West Coast Reduction, where I was greeted by a uniformed guard. Above us rose catwalks, steel pipes, and a six-story-high vat, all of them gigantic in scale and gleaming as if they had just emerged from a car wash. And one could say that they had. It had showered the previous evening, and in the concrete loading yards men in hard-hats and high rubber boots hosed down the vast aprons of concrete.

I was shown to a modern waiting room with a smiling receptionist and green plants, and Barry Glotman, West Coast Reduction's president and CEO, came down a flight of stairs and affably shook hands with me. A very tall man with a large hawkish nose and a high forehead, he escorted me into an elegant boardroom with the requisite long polished table and ten high-backed padded chairs. In a corner stood a sample case of the company's products, stored in labeled bottles: top white tallow, technical tallow, biodiesel, mixed fish oil, bone meal, hydrolyzed feather meal, porcine meal, corn oil, canola oil — twenty-four bottles in all. Obviously, this place was no stranger to visitors.

We were joined by the director of technical and environmental services, as well as the director of sales and marketing, and the three men
proceeded to spend an hour talking with me while showing me a PowerPoint of how rendering worked, a schematic and animated version
of what Bill Gorman had told me.

"The industry has come a long way from what people thought a rendering plant was," said Glotman once the technical aspects had been
explained. "We're part of the food chain, and it's a very important part
from the standpoint of sustainability. We need to feed hogs and chickens and dogs and cats, and there's valuable protein that needs to be
recycled. We produce a value-added product. When you incinerate
something, you're not producing any value. At least we're producing
some value at the end of the day, and the carbon stays in the food chain
rather than in the atmosphere."

I was given a hard-hat and a lab coat, and out we went to the yard
for a tour, Glotman immediately pointing out how raw materials were
strictly separated. The fish arrived in fish trucks, the pork in pork
trucks, the poultry in poultry trucks. The trucks were weighed on
scales, the raw materials coded so they could be traced. This was part
of the HACCP protocol. No bovine material ever came into this plant
because of mad cow disease and the possibility of infecting other protein sources with prions. Cattle were processed in rendering plants on
the prairies, and those cattle that were deadstock — fallen cattle who
did not go through the slaughterhouse — were rendered separately as
specified risk material. This product never went into feed or fertilizer.
It was buried in a landfill.

On we walked, entering the left side of a huge warehouse bearing a
sign that read PORK ONLY. I looked down into a twenty-foot-deep bin
full of pork bones. On the right side of the warehouse, separated by a
wall, was another equally deep bin, this one full of chicken parts — carcasses, feet, and some feathers. Conveyors took the pork and poultry
off to another part of the building to be ground.

From there we walked across the yard, alongside railway tanker cars
filled with animal fats, and climbed steel stairs into an adjacent building where we could look down through a maze of pipes to cylindrical
vats in which the ground chicken and pork were being cooked. In a
nearby glassed-in control room, a man sat in front of three computer
screens that overlooked the vats.

"Weeks from now," Glotman said, "we can go back and see if there is an issue with any of the products we made. Some of our most diligent customers are pet food manufacturers, who do rigorous inspection tours, and one of the things they're looking for is to make sure that there aren't dogs and cats in the products they're buying."

I could certainly see that there was not a hint of a dog or a cat going into any of these products.

The rest of the process separated the cooked slurry into fats and proteins, using first a centrifuge and then a screw press that squeezed out the remaining fat. We then visited the fish bins, piled with hake and a few salmon, all filleted, only heads, tails, and spines left. Once again, Glotman emphasized that all these raw materials – poultry, pork, fish – were picked up fresh daily and that the air in the warehouses was scrubbed and filtered to remove odors. And indeed I could feel a current of air moving briskly through the giant room, and there was barely any fishy smell.

We saw the grinding rooms, and we took a turn through the laboratory, full of graduated beakers of fats and tallows and plastic bags containing a variety of meals, each of them labeled with its time and date of manufacture. These samples were refrigerated for two years so that if a customer called with an issue, the sample could be reexamined.

An hour and a half later, we were back to where we had started in the boardroom. There we said good-bye and made small talk, Rob Jones, the director of sales and marketing, sharing some stories with me of his Labrador Retriever, with whom he had hunted pheasants and ducks for many years. The dog had passed away at fourteen. Rob now had a Springer Spaniel, five years old, who had grown up on Costco lamb-and-rice formula, which contained bone meal, and the dog was, he told me, "as healthy as could be."

I had now seen two sides of the rendering industry, and I thought it would be instructive to observe how its various meals and fats are blended with other ingredients – grains, whole meats, vitamins, and vegetables – to make dog food itself, in other words to see how those little nuggets that pour so easily into our dogs' bowls are actually created. So I called a couple of dog food companies to ask if they would give me a tour.

The first one I asked was Purina, which, coincidentally, had approached me through its marketing agency to host its upcoming multisegment TV show about enhancing the lives of our pets. In return for my hosting about twenty of these shows, Purina would produce a coffee table version of *Merle's Door* that would be sold in specialty pet stores like Petco and PetSmart. Purina would also create and make an initial contribution to a charitable fund, named Merle's Fund, through which I could direct monetary support for animal charities. I'd be fiscally compensated for my TV work and provided with what was called "appropriate quantities of Pro Plan or Pro Plan Selects" for my current dog.

Naturally, I asked Purina if it wanted me to promote its dog food along the way, and the person with whom I had been corresponding, David Boyd, the creative director for Pro Plan, said that would be nice. I responded that I was writing a book about dog health and longevity, there would be chapters on nutrition, and I couldn't really be a spokesperson for any particular dog food and still maintain my objectivity. Boyd understood completely and said that if there was ever anything he could do to help with the new book, please let him know. I said there was — could I have a tour of Purina's dog food plant and ask its staff some questions about its dog food, particularly the pros and cons of feeding dogs grain? He ran my request up the flagpole and several days later replied that, unfortunately, I couldn't have a tour. What went on in Purina's plants was proprietary. So I asked if I could e-mail Purina's staff some questions, and he said of course and pointed me to the right person. As of this writing, I'm still waiting for an answer.

So I approached Hill's Pet Nutrition with the same request: could I tour its plant and talk with staff nutritionists and veterinarians. After a month of checking out my bona fides, Hill's gave me the go-ahead to visit its Topeka, Kansas, facility. But just a few days before I was to get on the plane, the company's associate communications director, Luce Rubio, called me and told me that higher-ups on the corporate ladder had rescinded my invitation. I asked if I might come to Topeka anyway and simply meet with Hill's nutritionists and veterinarians to discuss the many complex issues surrounding canine diets. No, said Rubio, there could be no face-to-face communication between me and any of Hill's personnel. They would be happy, however, to answer my questions by e-mail. So I submitted my questions, the most important being about the role of grains in canine diets. The answer I received was unsigned and not attributable to any one person. It said in its entirety:

Grains are good for dogs and help provide the right balance of nutrients. Dogs, like humans, are omnivores, not carnivores. An important myth to dispel is that dogs and cats in the wild do not eat grains. Selected grains provide great value to the nutrition of dogs and cats because they provide *carbohydrates as an energy source.*

Feeding excess protein as an energy source can cause an increase in nitrogenous wastes, which can place undue stress on the kidney. Millions of cats and dogs suffer from undetected kidney malfunction, because it cannot be diagnosed until 75% of the kidney function is lost. Our nutritional goal at Hill's is to provide nutrition that avoids undue kidney stress by avoiding excess nitrogenous wastes.

Selected grains also enable a nutritionist to formulate a food that *avoids excess fat.* Excess dietary fat increases body fat, which has been linked to diabetes, cardiovascular disease and arthritis.

This answer from Hill's puzzled me on several counts. To begin with, no wildlife biologist I had ever read had observed wild dogs or cats eating grain. Nor can we find any mention of this habit in legend, literature, or anecdote.

As for the point Hill's made that excess protein causes kidney disease, I could find no corroboration for their take on the problem in *Small Animal Internal Medicine,* a standard veterinary text published by Elsevier, an independent scientific publishing house that also produces such reference books as *Gray's Anatomy* and the journal *The Lancet.* The author of the section on renal failure is Dr. Gregory Grauer, Professor and Jarvis Chair of Small Animal Internal Medicine at Kansas State University's College of Veterinary Medicine, and he makes it clear that it is *decreased* dietary protein — in other words, too many carbohydrates, as are found in many kibbles — that magnify the risk for acute renal failure, the exact opposite of what Hill's maintained. Furthermore, dogs with renal failure should be fed, as Dr. Grauer writes, "the maximum amount of high biological value, highly digestible protein that the animal can tolerate at his/her level of renal function."

I also had to wonder why Hill's would assert that dietary fat increases body fat. The peer-reviewed literature on performance in dogs demonstrates that aerobic performance improves when dogs eat fat, even when they are untrained. If they became more obese by eating more fat, they would hardly be improving their aerobic performance.

Feeling that Hill's answers were somewhat misleading, I contacted a well-known veterinary researcher with whom I had struck up a correspondence on canine health, asking him for some perspective on Hill's response. A few months before, he had mentioned to me that he and his colleagues were encouraging the Morris Animal Foundation to do a large, lifetime, prospective cohort study of dogs so as to identify the genetic, dietary, and environmental causes of cancer. In early 2010, MAF was at last going to vote on funding the study, with a generous budget of about $20 million.

He now told me that he and his colleagues had withdrawn from the Morris Animal Foundation's cancer study because of ethical concerns about how it was being conducted. The MAF study was going to be done "in house" — in other words, at the foundation. He believed that such a study should instead be located at an academic institution with no vested interest in the results.

As for how I was being held at arm's length by Purina and Hill's, this researcher, who asked that I not use his name, wrote me: "You are now finding out what I have learned over the past thirty years. That is, pet food nutrition is approximately 10% science, 50% spin, and 40% influence. Most pet food research of practical importance to pets and owners is funded either directly through industry (either pet foods or pharmaceutical) or indirectly through private groups like the Morris Animal Foundation."

This researcher went on to write that Bette Morris — the spouse of Dr. Mark Morris Jr. (the son of the founder of Hill's Pet Nutrition) — had donated $12 million to the Morris Animal Foundation to support the National Canine Cohort Cancer Study, from which he and his colleagues had withdrawn their support. In addition to Bette Morris being an influential MAF board member, so was her son David.

"Do you think," this scientist asked me, "that they would support any cancer research or subsequent publication of findings that might cast aspersions on the quality of commercial pet foods, particularly the Hill's brand?"

Wondering how much truth there might be to these assertions, I wrote to David Haworth, the president and CEO of the Morris Animal Foundation, describing what this scientist had told me. Haworth responded that the study to which this scientist had referred was now called the Canine Lifetime Health Project, the first phase and core of which was now called the Golden Retriever Lifetime Study. It would enroll three thousand US Golden Retrievers between the ages of six months and two years and follow them for ten years. As I had been told, the study was trying to identify the genetic, nutritional, and environmental risk factors for the development of canine cancer and would look at what and how much the dogs consumed, the kind of water they drank, and how much they exercised.

The ethical concerns of the scientist with whom I had corresponded were valid, and therefore MAF had decided that the collection of data would be done by the private sector while the analysis of it would be done by university-based researchers, specifically by expert panels in genetics, nutrition, and environmental exposures. The study would be funded by a combination of private donations and contributions of lab space and server time from five corporate partners: the laboratory VCA-Antech, Pfizer Animal Health, the dog food manufacturer Blue Buffalo, Petco, and Hill's Pet Nutrition. As for worries about the undue influence of the Morris family on the study, it was true that Bette Morris had pledged a substantial sum of the family's money to the project, $10 million, but he assured me that today the Morris Animal Foundation was "unaffiliated with any company or interest outside what is best for companion animals and wildlife."

He had sent me a PowerPoint on the project, and nowhere in it could I find any mention of the study's evaluating the influence of grain-free diets on canine health and longevity. This seemed like an omission. Current research, as I had learned, shows an association between high-carbohydrate diets, the insulin spikes they produce, and an increased risk for cancer and diabetes. There is also a considerable body of historical evidence – dozens of reports and studies in the anthropological and medical literature – demonstrating what happens to indigenous peoples when they switch from their traditional diets to ones introduced by modernity. Within a matter of decades, they are suffering from the very same chronic diseases as the people who colonize them – diabetes, high blood pressure, heart disease, and cancer. We could make the same observation about dogs: they no longer eat their ancestral diet, and millions of them die of cancer. Shouldn't the MAF study try to recruit enough dogs eating a historic diet, one not containing grain, so as to give us an answer about the association between carbohydrates and canine cancer?

Unfortunately, Haworth replied, the study hadn't been balanced for diet, though it was for gender, hormonal status (neutered or intact), geographic region, and the jobs the dogs performed – hunting, showing, service, or companions. If there were enough owners feeding a grain-free diet of whatever type, the study might be able to come up with some conclusions, but he wasn't sure that the initial Golden Retriever study would be able to give us any data about the best ways to feed dogs. "What you're proposing," he concluded, "is a terrific ancillary study to be run once the data is flowing into the Golden Retriever Lifetime Study."

I asked him why such a study couldn't be done right now. It would address what was arguably the single most important question about canine nutrition that remained unanswered: should dogs eat grain as the primary ingredient in their diet? There was tremendous public interest in finding an answer to this question, and the study wouldn't be that difficult to design or expensive to complete. Dr. Joe Bartges had said he could do it for $1 million.

When Haworth pointed out that the study would in all likelihood cost $10 million, I responded that this was chicken feed — to mix metaphors — for a dog food industry that makes $15 billion annually.

"I don't think the fifteen-billion-dollar industry should be obligated to look at that question," he answered, "but others, particularly the academic researchers, should be asking the questions and finding funding sources to get them addressed." He immediately acknowledged how challenging that funding environment was. "But," as he said, "blaming the lack of a study on an industry that has no incentive to run it seems misplaced."

And therein lies the crunch in which we find ourselves. The pet food industry has zero incentive to run a study whose results might show that many of the kibbles it produces aren't ideal foods for dogs. Who then will give the Morris Animal Foundation, or another research organization, $10 million to address the question so many of us want answered: is what we're feeding our dogs really good for them?

CHAPTER FOURTEEN

Real Food, Many Forms

TWO YEARS AFTER beginning my investigation of dog food, I was still unable to state that dogs would lead healthier, longer lives if they ate one particular diet. However, the accumulation of scientific evidence—a low-carbohydrate diet reduces insulin spikes, protein improves performance, and vegetables are cancer-protective—led me to believe that my new dog would benefit from a grain-free diet in its original form. As a result, I fed Pukka wild game, bones, and vegetables, along with commercially prepared raw-food diets, both frozen and dehydrated, from the moment he arrived in Kelly.

These diets contain whole domestic meats, including organs like hearts, livers, and spleens, as well as ground bones and a variety of vegetables and fruits. There are no preservatives or colorings, and the diets are certified by AAFCO, the Association of American Feed Control Officials, to give dogs of all life stages adequate nutrition. This certification is the minimum standard that any dog food—kibble, canned, or raw—should meet, and you can find this guarantee somewhere near the ingredient label, if the dog food has passed the AAFCO test.

Pukka's frozen diet comes packaged in eight-pound plastic bags—chicken, lamb, duck, venison, turkey, and sardines—and one of the most exciting canine events on our road has become the arrival of the semi that delivers these food bags, nestled in insulated cardboard boxes, along with crates of frozen bison bones and turkey necks. After the driver offloads them onto the driveway, I carry them to the porch, where I sort the bags into piles for several friends with whom I buy dog food in bulk. In the meantime, the dogs themselves—almost a dozen from up and down the road — come at a run to supervise my division, smelling each box with wagging tails.

Once done with my sorting, I put Pukka's share on a dolly and wheel it into the house, breaking into song and changing the words of the well-known hymn to fit the occasion:

> Bringing in the bones,
> Oh bringing in the bones,
> We shall come rejoicing,
> Bringing in the bones!

High-stepping to the tune, the privileged five — Pukka, A.J., Burley, Goo, and Buck — follow me into the laundry room, where we have a freezer, its upper shelves laden with white packages of elk, grouse, and pheasant, bags of elk organs, and rib bones and leg bones, its empty lower shelves waiting to be replenished with this bimonthly bounty. Standing shoulder to shoulder behind me, the five of them watch the transfer of the bags into the freezer with contented gazes, their expressions as self-satisfied as those of Swiss burghers overseeing a Zurich banker locking their gold into his vault.

Although their smugness is understandable — they get more bones than any of the other Kelly dogs — only Pukka has any real grounds for complacency. He alone has actually earned part of his weekly meat, helping me to fill the freezer during the fall hunting season. This partnership did not happen overnight.

Initially, and like many modern people, he had no firsthand experience to show him that meat in fact comes from animals. Running down a cottontail rabbit when he was seven months old, he caught it in midleap and dashed back to me, laying it at my feet and bursting with pride.

"Well done!" I praised him, stroking his back. "And now that you've caught it, you can eat it."

He looked at me with perplexity: "Eat it? But it's not in patty form."

No amount of cajoling would get him to eat the rabbit on the spot, as Merle had done with ground squirrels when he caught them, and so I put the rabbit in my pack and took it home, where I placed it in his bowl. Even having the rabbit in the very bowl out of which his raw-food breakfasts and dinners came did not give Pukka the notion that the rabbit was food. He removed it and played with it as if it were a stuffed animal.

His naïveté when it came to knowing that there was meat inside the fur was not unusual, and not just because he was a domestic dog. Wolf puppies do not initially eat whole prey. They eat the predigested meat that their parents regurgitate for them — canid baby food — and then they watch their parents and older siblings catch and open up larger prey. How Merle became such a highly accomplished ground squirrel hunter — gobbling them down a moment after he caught them — I can't say. I wasn't on hand to see whether he watched a coyote or another domestic dog hunting rodents, or whether hunger and trial and error had been his primer.

Taking the rabbit from Pukka, I told him, "Little Sir, this is not a toy. It's a real rabbit. You killed it, and now you have to eat it. That's the deal."

I put it back in his bowl. He lay down about ten feet from it, glancing at the rabbit, glancing at me, and glancing at the holy freezer, out of which came his daily supply of elk or commercial raw-food patties. We had been hiking all day, and his expression said, "I could really use some dinner."

"You have dinner," I replied, gesturing to the bowl.

He put his head between his paws and regarded me despondently.

"Okay," I relented. Had he been a wolf puppy, he would have had proper role models who would have taught him what to do. So I took the rabbit to the kitchen counter and acting as his wolf parent, I skinned it, leaving patches of fur on it here and there. Cutting the rabbit into pieces, I put it back into his bowl along with its entrails.

Pukka had watched the process with increasing interest. He now took a sniff and comprehension lit his eyes: "Ah-ha! I get it! Cut up nicely, this rabbit smells and looks like dinner." He proceeded to eat the entire rabbit, paws and all, saving the head for last, his eyes closed in rapturous delight as he steadily crunched and swallowed it. At that moment — the rabbit's ears sticking from his lips — he certainly appeared to be 98 percent carnivore, an impression that vanished a few minutes later when I made myself a salad for dinner.

Sitting by my side, he gazed up at the cutting board on which I was chopping vegetables. Occasionally I handed him a piece, which he took gently from my fingers and chewed diligently. Since he had now been trained to leave the kitchen or the table when asked, I was no longer worried that he'd become a begging dog, and I would give him all sorts of foods so as to see what he wanted to eat. So far, broccoli, cauliflower, and carrots were his favorites, along with red peppers, tomatoes, zucchini, apples, pears, mangoes, bananas, kiwi fruit, and cantaloupe, whereas spinach, kale, and lettuce were spurned. That's putting it mildly.

The first time he sampled these greens, he opened his mouth in disbelief, let them drop to the floor, and gave me a look that said, "You have *got* to be kidding me." Merle's reaction to greens had been much the same. But if I chopped greens finely and mixed them into Pukka's elk meat, he would eat them, no questions asked.

Like Merle, Pukka would also eat every kind of berry except blueberries, consistently refusing them, as Merle had done, an interesting similarity for which I have no answer. Then, at twenty-two months old, Pukka began to eat blueberries, reminding me that dogs, like people, have tastes that mature and change.

I was adding this large variety of vegetables and fruit to Pukka's diet not only because they contain phytochemicals that protect against cancer, but also because they provide fiber. In the wild a dog would have to eat through hide and fur to get to the meat and bones beneath, and that hide and fur help in its digestion and elimination. As Melinda Miller, the president of the North American Raw Pet Food Association, told me, "Fruit and vegetables help to keep things moving."

This, then, became Pukka's diverse diet — raw meat, raw bones, raw vegetables, and a bit of fruit — his meals, whether commercially prepared or assembled by me, often accompanied by the ditty that I had made up to accompany one of his favorite entrées, raw chicken: *"Le poulet, le poulet, ton favori est arrivé!"*

Wag-wag-wag went his tail — "Chicken or *poulet,* I'll take it either way" — and he'd lick his bowl clean. Indeed, until he was about ten months old, he'd turn his bowl over when he was done and lick the outside clean as well.

What's been fascinating to observe during this time is how Pukka has turned into a living example of what the performance studies have shown. On a high-protein, high-fat diet, he has great endurance — twenty-mile hikes and breaking trail through deep snow all day hardly tiring him out — but many young dogs have such endurance. What has separated Pukka from his peers is his surprisingly efficient thermoregulation. On a hot summer day when other dogs are panting, Pukka has his mouth closed. He will take a four-hour-long mountain bike ride in July, when the temperature is in the eighties, and drink no more than a liter of water along the way and none when we're done. By comparison, Merle, at Pukka's age, would drink several liters of water on such a ride. Nor does Pukka eat anywhere near the amount of snow when we ski as Merle did.

When we're home, A.J., Burley, Goo, and Buck – all of whom eat mostly kibble, not raw food – will come through the dog door on a hot summer day and empty Pukka's water bowl several times, whereas Pukka will drink about 70 percent less than what they consume from dawn to dusk. The difference in water consumption between the dogs has two causes: compared to kibble – either grain-based or grain-free – there's a considerable amount of starting moisture in raw meat, bones, and vegetables, and once a dog has metabolized its food, nearly twice as much water is produced from fat as from carbohydrates. In this regard, raw food may have an advantage over a baked product like kibble, as it provides moisture in the original form that dogs consumed when they were eating prey or scavenging in village refuse piles.

Pukka eats no poop, whereas Merle found it a delicacy. Pukka has no gas; Merle did on occasion. Notably, Pukka does have gas if he eats kibble. His breath is consistently sweet while Merle's could make me recoil. In addition, Pukka hardly sheds and rarely needs brushing, and his turds are tiny compared to those of dogs who are his size and who eat kibble. Besides being small, the turds also have very little odor, both of these attributes being of considerable benefit when we're walking in populated areas and I have to bag his poop and carry it in my fanny pack until I find a proper receptacle.

Were it legally possible, I would feed Pukka solely on the meat, bones, and organs of wild game, supplemented with vegetables and fruit, since wild game is free-ranging, contains no antibiotics or hormones, and lives in a relatively pesticide-free environment. However, it remains legally impossible to hunt enough big animals in one season to feed a large active dog like Pukka. Consider that when he was between fifteen and twenty months old – the equivalent of a rapidly growing teenager – he would eat between five and seven pounds of meat, bones, and vegetables in a day (depending on how long we hiked), or 9 to 13 percent of his body weight. This would be like a 150-pound boy eating fourteen to twenty pounds of food every twenty-four hours. Yet, like many athletic teenagers, Pukka remained as lean as a rail no matter how much he ate. Now, as an adult dog of seventy pounds, Pukka is still lean as a rail and eats about thirteen hundred pounds of meat and

bones in a year. In terms of animals on the hoof, this is the equivalent
of nine elk, or thirty antelope, or twenty good-sized deer. Ten thousand
years ago, this was the reason Chinese farmers turned wolves into rice-
eaters.

It is still the reason — along with the time required to prepare homemade raw meals and a lack of freezer space to store a substantial quantity of commercial raw food — that most dogs don't eat the way Pukka
does and kibble remains so very popular. Wouldn't it be wonderful,
though, if a company produced kibble that was convenient to use, easy
to store, and made from all these wholesome raw ingredients?

An ever-increasing number of pet food manufacturers have done
just that, and one of them, Natura Pet Products, finally allowed me to
see the day-to-day operation of its plant. Commissioned in 2003, its
Fremont, Nebraska, plant turns out 100,000 tons of kibble annually
from a complex of sprawling buildings topped by a 128-foot-tall tower
that rises incongruously from the plains.

After donning a hard-hat, lab coat, and safety glasses, I was led
through the plant by Sean Gilpin, Natura's director of training and
event planning. The noise of machinery was loud; giant vats and tanks
were at every turn; and a meaty smell hung in the air. Yet everything
was so clean and polished that the entire facility reminded me of a
cross between a laboratory and an industrialized kitchen.

EVO Large Bite Chicken and Turkey was the run of the day, and
Sean, a beaming red-cheeked man with a rim of white hair, explained
that Natura's innovative kibble was grain-free — containing no corn,
wheat, soy, colorings, or by-products — and relied on an enhanced extrusion process that allowed higher concentrations of meat to be included in the dough. In addition to whole meat, Natura's kibble contained turkey and chicken meal.

We stopped at the truck bays, where semis waited to be unloaded.
No material could be brought into the plant before samples were
tested for quality, two of the criteria being that all ingredients had to
be human-grade and of US origins. If they met Natura's specifications,
the materials were then bar-coded so they could be traced throughout
the entire production process.

We passed the glassed-in laboratory where the tests were conducted
and marched down cavernous halls to a two-story-high mixing area,
where conveyor belts brought in apples, potatoes, and carrots to be
ground with turkeys, chickens, and vitamins. This slurry was then

heated. Sean led me to the extruder room, full of chutes, pipes, and tanks, where we saw the cooked mixture being forced through the extruder plate, a die the size of a manhole cover, its small openings shaping the spongy dough into kibble.

Reaching out, I let the warm soft bits fall into my palm and had a taste. My first impression was of sawdust moistened with chicken and turkey flavoring, underlain by a hint of vegetables. Sean, seeing my unimpressed look, said, "I could make a dog eat a rock by putting the right flavoring on it."

He then asked me to remember that I was sampling the half-finished product: within minutes, tasty fats and oils would be sprayed on the kernels so as to make the "rocks" palatable for the canine consumer. The difference between the kernels I had just tasted and the ones that came out of a conventional extruder was that Natura's state-of-the-art equipment had eliminated the need to use starchy grains, allowing its kibble to contain more vegetables, fruits, and whole meats.

We climbed several stories of stairs and entered a tower of screens and filters where the extruded kibble was being dried before being conveyed to a room of vibrating beds that shook out the fines. From there, the kibble was sprayed with the fats and oils that Sean had mentioned, as well as with probiotics, and then it was vibrated once again before being conveyed back down several stories, where the finished product was bagged, sealed, and laser-imprinted with time, date, and batch stamps in a room as big as a football field. Each bag was then placed on a pallet by a robot, whose giant metal claw handled the bags as carefully as if they were newborn infants. Men on forklifts immediately whisked the pallets into a gigantic storage area, where semis were loaded before driving off to pet and grocery stores across the land.

Start to finish, it had taken fifty-five minutes for the fruit, vegetables, turkeys, and chickens to become kibble. We walked back to the bagging area and found a technician in a white lab coat — everyone was dressed in white lab coats and white hard-hats — randomly pulling bags of newly finished kibble off the assembly line, opening them, and scooping out samples for testing.

I asked if I could taste some, and he handed me one of the small plastic bags that he was making up. I poured a handful of the brown kernels into my palm, popped them into my mouth, and chewed. The kibble was crunchier than before and now tasted more strongly of chicken and turkey. It seemed amazing to me that all the delicious-

smelling raw ingredients that I had just seen come into the factory had
been transformed into this rather bland stuff. The human equivalent
that came to mind was energy bars. Though I have been thankful for
their calories and convenience while backpacking, skiing, or riding a
bike, I've never found them as satisfying as a real meal.

Perhaps our dogs feel the same. Certainly the five dogs whom I
know best seem to feel that way even when it comes to very good kibble like EVO. They are never as excited about it, or any other kibble for
that matter, as they are about raw meat. To be fair, they'll scarf down a
bowl of kibble in under fifteen seconds, but when they smell raw meat
going into their bowls their entire body language undergoes a transformation. Their tails begin to turn like windmills, and they stand on
their hind legs to peer over the counter while saliva drools from their
mouths. They never act this way over kibble.

Pukka, who eats a more varied diet than any of his four friends,
makes even finer discriminations among foods. He becomes orders
of magnitude more excited over a homemade raw meal than over a
commercial one. Watching me mix the ingredients, he groans in anticipation. Given his reaction, I initially thought that he'd gobble his
made-from-scratch meals in a few seconds, but I was mistaken. He
lingers over them, eating them in the prescribed manner of a wolf. He
first removes the elk rib that I've laid atop his bowl and sets it aside.
He then eats the organs, picking out the chunks of liver, heart, and
lungs, even if they're buried, and virtually always in that order. Next
he will methodically chew his meat and vegetables, sometimes bound
together by a raw egg, shell included, and finally, he carries the rib to
his bed, where he chews it, eyes half closed, as if it were dessert.

As time has gone on, I've also seen another side to Pukka's discriminating palate. He will occasionally reject the food I set before him. The
very first time he did this, turning his nose up at commercially prepared raw lamb patties, I couldn't tell if he was ill or being choosy. Trying to determine which, I offered him raw elk. He sniffed at the meat
and walked away. Since he had just been outside, roughhousing with
Burley in the snow, I didn't think he was very ill. I might never have
discovered the fine shades of his palate had chance not intervened.

Needing to start a fire in the woodstove, I saw that I was out of ker-
osene-impregnated sticks. I went to the pantry, and Pukka followed
me, slipping between my legs and sniffing at the bag of commercially

dried elk chips that sat on the floor. Looking up at me, he gave his tail a hopeful wag.

I opened the bag and offered him a few chips. He vacuumed them off my palm. I filled his bowl and he inhaled them, now wagging his tail with hearty enthusiasm: "That's exactly what I wanted for breakfast—*dried elk.*"

Obviously, on this particular morning he did not want lamb or raw elk, he wanted dried elk. Over the ensuing months, and with no discernible pattern, he would continue to make his changing preferences known: "Today I do not want sardines, I want chicken. Yes, I do love my chicken, but this morning I'd rather have raw elk. I know I love raw elk, but this evening I prefer dried elk." And what is wrong with a dog acting this way? How many of us linger over a restaurant menu, discuss it with our dining partners, and change our minds several times before ordering? Dogs really do have gustatory preferences. It's just hard to notice them when they eat the same meal their entire lives.

Unfortunately, if you decide to vary your dog's kibble diet with raw food, you won't get much support from the professional veterinary associations of the United States and Canada. On their websites, both the American and Canadian Veterinary Medical Associations warn about the risk of contracting *Salmonella* from raw dog food, the CVMA going so far as to categorically denounce raw food as a dangerous fad. At least the AVMA, after suggesting that people avoid raw-food diets for their pets, points out some commonsense procedures to minimize the chance of infection from bacteria: wash your hands thoroughly after handling pet food; don't allow children to handle pet food or make sure that they also wash their hands if they do; don't let immunocompromised individuals touch pet food; and use the same care in washing off the pet's utensils and containers as you do your own.

To its credit, the AVMA evenhandedly uses the words "pet food" instead of "raw pet foods" in these safety precautions. It does so because it's not only raw foods that are liable to become contaminated with *Salmonella* or other pathogens. Between 2010 and 2012, dozens of popular varieties of kibble were recalled because of potential or actual contamination with *Salmonella* or aflatoxin, the latter caused by a mold. Wondering whether Pukka's food might be similarly contaminated with *Salmonella,* I sent off some of his commercially prepared lamb, chicken, and venison patties for pathogen testing by the Wyoming Department of Agriculture Analytical Services, and the results showed that none of the samples were infected. Does this single test mean that his raw foods will always be free of *Salmonella?* Of course not.

What determines whether a pet food – kibble or raw – will be contaminated by pathogens are the actual conditions in the factory at the time a food is being manufactured, as well as the origins of the factory's raw materials. As was demonstrated by the pet food disaster of 2007 – when hundreds of dogs and cats died after their foods were poisoned by melamine-adulterated wheat gluten that originated in China – the conditions in pet food plants, and the reliability of their suppliers, vary widely. Indeed, the myriad of international suppliers from which large pet food companies draw and the multitude of ingredients that go into many kibbles increase the chances that one of these ingredients may be of poor quality or toxic.

This is why I've felt safer feeding Pukka a commercially prepared, AAFCO-certified, raw-food diet than a mass-produced kibble. His raw-food diets contain free-range meats and organic fruits and vegetables, and on their labels the names of the ingredients are listed in plain English: lamb, chicken, kale, blueberries. With little time and effort, I was also able to verify their individual producers in the United States and New Zealand. By contrast, the labels on some kibble bags display a list of tongue-twisting ingredients. These many additives, often bought through a long chain of second- and third-party suppliers, are put into the dough or sprayed on the kernels so as to restore the nutrients that have been cooked off in the extrusion process.

Even after taking all these precautions, I was still left with one concern about raw-food diets, which the veterinarian Richard Pitcairn describes in his book *Dr. Pitcairn's Complete Guide to Natural Health for Dogs and Cats.* He believes that heavy metals such as lead, mercury, and arsenic are ubiquitous in meat-based diets. He therefore advises that dogs be fed home-cooked grains and a very small amount of meat, if any at all.

Pitcairn published these recommendations in 2006, and I wondered if he had any new thoughts on the subject, so I called him and asked if he was still backing what was virtually a vegetarian diet for dogs. He said that he was, for the same reasons as before: heavy metals ending up in bones. "If you're feeding meat and bone," he told me, "you're feeding more heavy metals, even if you're feeding organic."

His contention is substantiated in the scientific literature, at least for lead, which is preferentially sequestered in the bones of mammals rather than in their muscles. But after further research, I discovered that one can't simply divide the world into plants and animals and categorically state that one or the other contains more heavy metals.

Plants may actually contain more heavy metals than meat or bone because these substances, particularly lead, have low mobility and are concentrated in the top one inch of soil. Shallowly rooted plants, like grains, then accumulate them. Surveys done by the Global Environmental Monitoring System/Food Network across thirty nations have found that cereals actually have about ten more micrograms of lead per kilogram than do vegetables, fruit, and meat, and the EPA discovered that the concentrations of lead in meat and grain are almost identical.

Since neither agency looked at pet foods, and I couldn't find anyone else who had, I decided to conduct my own study. I took three commercial kibbles, five commercial frozen raw-food diets, two dried ones, and some burger from my 2008 elk, as well as some organic rice and some organic oats for comparison's sake, and shipped them off to a nationally certified laboratory, Doctor's Data, which conducts food and water testing. The results were instructive.

Only three foods out of the thirteen had no detectable levels of lead, a testament to how airborne lead-containing pollutants from industry and the historic use of leaded gasoline have contaminated most of our food with a toxic substance. The three lead-free foods were my 2008 elk, a dried salmon dog treat, and the organic oats. In fact, the elk I had shot in the Gros Ventre Mountains east of Jackson Hole, far from highways and factories, had the fewest heavy metals of any of the thirteen foods I tested. It contained some trace amounts of aluminum, antimony, cadmium, and copper. People from John Muir to Aldo Leopold have called wilderness "pristine," and this was a numerical confirmation of that aesthetic premise. The only other sample nearly as clean as the elk was the organic oats, which contained the same four heavy metals as the elk plus nickel and tin.

On the other hand, the organic rice — an ingredient in many vegetarian-based dog foods — contained seven heavy metals and two to three times as much lead as two of the raw dog foods made from the meat, innards, and bones of lamb and chicken, the opposite of what Dr. Pitcairn had predicted. The rice also contained 220 parts per billion of arsenic, whose level in drinking water is set at zero by the EPA so as to avoid adverse health effects. The three commercial kibbles, each containing several rendered animal meals, were the most contaminated with heavy metals of all the samples, one of them containing fourteen out of the sixteen heavy metals for which the lab tested.

Although my little test was a one-off view of thirteen dog and human foods and has no statistical relevance, it does offer some insight for those concerned about heavy metals in foods, dog or human, especially when coupled with the more extensive studies done by the Global Environmental Monitoring System/Food Network and the EPA. The crucial factor that determines the heavy metal content of a food is not whether it's animal or vegetable, organic or conventional, but rather the heavy metal content of the soil in which plants are grown and which plants an animal then consumes.

These findings also reinforce the wisdom of what Dr. Joe Bartges told me: it pays to rotate your dog's food. Rotating your dog through a varied menu minimizes the risk of feeding it the same heavy metals year after year, whether the dog is a carnivore or a vegetarian. After all, there's no telling that just because one batch of lamb, or one source of rice, is low in heavy metals, the next one will be, too.

After my test, I chose those samples that had the least amount of heavy metals and rotated Pukka through them, adding new kinds of raw foods as they come onto the market. In addition to letting Pukka eat widely, I also give him DHA (docosahexaenoic acid), an omega-3 fatty acid that has been found to have anticarcinogenic properties. He and I take our DHA together, 1,000 milligrams a day, with our breakfasts.

As for rawhide chews, pigs' ears, and treats, Pukka doesn't get them — nor do A.J., Burley, Goo, and Buck when they're at my house — unless I can substantiate what goes into the treats. Often, this is impossible. Many of these treats have no ingredient labels, and a large number of them come from China, where the pet food industry is rife with mislabeling and corruption. Nonetheless, Pukka and his friends don't seem to mind their absence. On many a day they get a footlong turkey neck, as big around as my wrist, and on other days an elk or bison bone. I've yet to hear any complaints.

There are some foods that dogs shouldn't consume even if you can verify their origins and lack of contaminants. Raw fish isn't a problem except for members of the salmon family: salmon, trout, char, freshwater whitefish, and grayling. Their flesh can be infected with a bacteria that can give dogs salmon poisoning. Ninety percent of dogs with salmon poisoning die within two weeks — vomiting, feverish, and weak — unless treated. Fortunately, treatment is simple — an antibiotic and a wormer — and prevention even simpler: don't feed raw fish from the salmon family to dogs. Cats are not affected by the microorganism.

Dogs should also not have chocolate. It contains theobromine, a naturally occurring alkaloid molecule similar to caffeine, and with some of caffeine's stimulating effects. In dogs it can cause hyperactivity, cardiac arrhythmia, and seizures. For the same reason, dogs should not be given coffee, tea, Coke, or Red Bull. However, if snagging the occasional bit of chocolate were fatal to dogs, there'd be a lot more dead ones each year. Dose — how much the dog eats as a function of its weight — matters. For milk chocolate, the toxic dose is about one ounce per pound of dog (sixty grams per kilogram), and this is why Merle, who loved chocolate, never keeled over after vacuuming up a few squares of a Hershey's bar when they fell to the floor. As a seventy-pound dog, he would have had to eat a little over four and a quarter pounds of chocolate in one go to be poisoned. By contrast, if a four-pound Chihuahua eats a small chocolate bar, it could have a fatal seizure.

The same dose-dependent rule holds true for raisins and grapes: these fruits are toxic to dogs and can cause acute renal failure, but a seventy-pound dog would have to eat twelve ounces of raisins to consume a toxic dose. On the other hand, a four-pound dog can get a potentially lethal dose after eating no more than a small handful.

Macadamia nuts — one nut per kilogram of dog — can cause muscle weakness. Garlic and onions eaten in large quantities can cause hemolysis, the destruction of red blood cells; eaten regularly in smaller quantities, they may cause depression and anemia. Xylitol, which sweetens gum, candy, breath mints, and toothpaste, can cause hypoglycemia and collapse in dogs. Although it's doubtful that anyone would feed raw dough to a dog, be careful about leaving bread to rise unattended on a countertop. A dog I knew nailed a dozen waiting-to-be-baked dinner rolls and the carbon dioxide given off by the yeast would have ruptured her stomach and killed her had her vet not pumped out her gut.

Beyond these basic recommendations, it's hard to give advice. For instance, the website of the American Society for the Prevention of

Cruelty to Animals cautions against feeding dogs avocados because they can cause vomiting and diarrhea, yet I've watched my dogs eat avocado quarters with no ill effects. As is the case with many fruits, the most serious danger can lie in the pit, which can lodge in a dog's throat and choke it. If you're going to feed fruit, remove the pits.

Certainly, the greatest challenge any of us faces when trying to decide what to feed our dogs is that of accurately translating what they themselves are telling us about their diets, especially when it comes to subtleties. They can't say, "This food tastes great, but leaves me a little bloated. I have terrific energy on this food, but not so much on that one." These ambiguities may disappear as the science of nutrigenomics matures.

Measuring how nutrients interact at the level of the genome, nutrigenomics uses genetic tests — much like the ones that identify genes that predispose an individual to disease — to identify the molecular dietary signature of a dog or a human. In this way the technique can predict with great accuracy whether an individual should eat corn or beef, rice or chicken, or soy or lamb. In 2011 the veterinarian Jean Dodds brought us closer to this goal by launching a saliva-testing technique called "Nutriscan." Far more accurate than blood tests for so-called food allergies, which are rare, this technique may reveal common food sensitivities before they manifest themselves as clinical disease.

The other challenge faced by some of us who want to feed our dogs a diet of commercially prepared raw food is its cost. At the recommended feeding levels for a seventy-pound dog, it costs me $2,500 a year to feed Pukka a commercially prepared, AAFCO-certified raw-food diet, almost all of whose ingredients are free-range and organic. By contrast, if I fed Pukka a popular kibble from a big-box store, certified by AAFCO, whose first ingredient is corn and which also contains wheat middlings, soybean meal, brewer's rice, and animal fat preserved with BHA, along with the artificial colors yellow #5, yellow #6, red #40, and blue #2, it would cost me $150 annually.

There are many gradations in between these two extremes from which to choose. For instance, convenient, grain-free kibbles that contain human-grade meat and are preserved with herbs and vitamin E, so they have a reasonable shelf life, cost about $500 a year to feed a seventy-pound dog. That's still more than twice as much as the $229 per year — 67 cents per day — that surveys by the American Pet Products Association show the average American spends on dog food.

Pukka's diet has an additional cost, a hidden one that's not often mentioned when dog foods are discussed. But virtually all of us who live with dogs impose it. It's the annual cull of tens of millions of animals who are raised in factory farms, under appalling conditions, before being slaughtered, in part, to feed our dogs and cats.

When Merle was alive, I chose not to think about my participation in this factory-farming system, turning a somewhat blind eye to the fact that one of Merle's kibbles contained mass-produced chicken. After all, he was my dog, he needed to survive, and I myself was not eating those chickens, each of them living on less than a square foot of space with their beaks cut off so they wouldn't peck their fellows to death. I was eating grouse and mallards and elk, who lived wild and free until the moment I shot them. But with Pukka — who was now consuming over one thousand pounds of chicken, turkey, lamb, and farmed elk each year, in addition to the wild elk and birds we hunted — it became impossible not to address the question of where on the food chain my little wolf should eat.

CHAPTER FIFTEEN

Whom Shall We Eat?

OVER OUR FIRST year and a half together — as Pukka went from a fourteen-pound puppy to a seventy-pound dog — we became a food-making team, the evolution of our partnership beginning in the very same way that wolf parents teach the basic skills of hunting to their new pups. When these happy-go-lucky, carefree youngsters are about four months old, the alpha male and female lead them away from the den to begin the discipline of catching their own food.

In just this way, I took Pukka away from the village one morning just before his four-month birthday, driving us five miles north of the house to the Coyote Rock trail, which climbs through a steep evergreen forest and ends on a spectacular ridge overlooking Jackson Hole. I knew that along the way we would pass through a variety of habitats — conifer, meadow, and aspen — where many different species of wildlife live. I hoped that Pukka would meet some of these animals face to face and be pleasantly introduced to how much fun smelling, seeing, and following them might be. In this I was not mistaken.

Not five minutes from the car, at the first bend in the trail, a red squirrel came down the trunk of its tree and began to chatter at him.

Pukka stopped in his tracks and looked bewildered. For over a month he had been chasing butterflies, houseflies, and grasshoppers, and the large, noisy, and aggressive squirrel seemed to intimidate him.

Turning to me, he asked his usual question with an inquiring look of his eyes: "What animal is that?"

"That's a squirrel," I told him. "Red squirrel."

The brave squirrel stomped its front paws, its bushy tail whipping

angrily as it chided Pukka in no uncertain terms, telling him to get off
its trail.

"Squirrel," I repeated. "He's telling us to go, and maybe we should."

On we went, leaving the evergreens behind and entering a stand of
aspen filled with brightly colored wildflowers. At its edge, in a meadow
of knee-high grass, we got lucky: a young grouse burst from under
Pukka's nose and flew off into the deep blue sky. Pukka looked surprised: "Did I do that?"

"Grouse," I told him. "Grouse." And I gave him a tiny salmon treat,
reinforcing his having flushed the grouse, accidental though it had
been, for I wanted him to make the connection that it was good to
boost grouse into the air, as they are one of the sweetest-tasting birds
in the land and I hunted them often.

A moment later, two more grouse burst into the sky, only feet
from us. They were also young — they must have been from the same
clutch — and Pukka stared at their departing flight with furrowed
brows: "Hmm, to be noted, birds who whir."

At the end of the meadow the trail entered another stand of aspen, this one much larger, a veritable cathedral of old growth — cool,
sun-dappled, and lusciously green. We climbed through the trees for
almost a mile, gaining altitude, before the trail leveled off in another
meadow at the crest of the ridge. And who should come walking across
the meadow, heading directly toward us, but a band of twenty cow elk,
aglow in the morning light, their summer coats auburn, some of the
late-born calves, perhaps only five weeks old, still bearing white spots.

In the lead was a very tall and regal elk, her head held high, her
black nose glistening. She was probably one of the oldest cows in the
band, and perhaps the most learned of her extended family, her calf
directly behind her. Behind the two of them walked the lead cow's
sisters and daughters, followed by their own young calves, the line of
them strolling in a stately procession, their faces full of July's serenity.
Midsummer was a very safe time for these elk: all the calves were now
old enough to outrun wolves and grizzly bears; the adults were well
fed and not weakened by deep winter snows; and the season in which
humans hunted elk was long gone and still far in the future. The elk
could not have been more placid and serene.

I stood very still. Pukka did not see them.

"Elk," I said in a stage whisper and pointed.

He followed my finger and saw them immediately: the tall, noble deer, as large as horses, no more than thirty yards off. Leaning forward, he became still, taut, and alert, his eyes transfixed upon them.

On they came. There was not a bit of wind to reveal us.

A moment later, the lead elk suddenly caught sight of Pukka and me, stopped, did a double take, and then stiffened in recognition: human and dog. She blew out two explosive puffs — "*Poo! Poo!*" — the sound of her breath shattering the cool morning air.

Only part of her call was a warning to her herdmates. The rest was incredulity: "How did you get there? I didn't smell, hear, or see you until you were far too close!" The disbelief in her eyes was palpable, as was her critical self-regard: "Did I ever screw up. *Moi!* Such a wise old elk."

And with that she wheeled, nose angled toward the sky in the classic alarm pose of elk. Behind her, all the elk simultaneously wheeled and fled, trotting across the meadow in a tightly bunched band.

Pukka had not known what to do with the squirrel or grouse, but the fleeing elk tripped something ancient, waiting, and ready in his brain, the very same genetic inheritance that makes chasing elk so much fun for wolves and running after soccer balls so much fun for people. A golden streak, he sprinted after them.

"Pukka!" I called. "Leave it!" He stopped, looking back at me. I raised a hand, meaning "wait." Longingly, he turned to gaze at the elk. But he didn't move.

My heart soared. Twenty running elk, and he stayed put.

"Well done, Pukka!" I cried loudly. "Excellent!"

At the sound of my voice, the elk stopped, turned, and stared at us. Neither Pukka nor I moved a muscle, nor did the elk, for a long few seconds. But they were taking no chances. Once again they wheeled as one animal and disappeared down the other side of the grassy ridge.

"Let's go," I called and ran forward. Pukka dashed ahead of me, coursing through the yellow flowers, nose down and drinking in the elk's wild musky scent, which hung in the air, obvious as a barnyard.

On the other side of the ridge I stopped, and Pukka gave me an inquisitive look: "Aren't we going to follow them?" Squirrels and grouse may not have gotten his attention, but the elk most certainly had.

"They're too far away," I told him. "This fall I hope we'll get an elk."

He pressed against my legs, and I petted him lavishly, praising him. He wagged his tail in delight: "That was so exciting!"

We turned to the west and ascended Coyote Rock, coming over the crest of the ridge to see the valley of Jackson Hole spread before us, immense, sprawling, and verdant, and capped by the snowy Tetons. Coming to a halt, Pukka gazed at the mountains soaring skyward across the valley, letting his eyes roam from the distant town of Jackson to the foothills of Yellowstone. Wheeling suddenly, he stood and put his front paws on my belly, his tail beating madly. Turning, he stared back to the Tetons, wagging his tail harder and harder, as if to say, "Wow, Ted, that is quite the view!"

"It is, Pukka!" I agreed. "One of the best."

His actions — as understandable as those of a person who had come upon this grand landscape for the very first time — reinforced my long-held belief that dogs have an aesthetic sense. I had seen Merle and Brower gaze at grand vistas with similar delight, enthusiastically wagging their tails when they reached high prospects and then settling down to gaze at them intently. I had also watched wolves and elk, bears and lions, mountain sheep and deer gaze at the majestic country beneath them with equal intent and seeming affection. Watching such behavior over many years, I've had to conclude that an aesthetic appreciation of panorama isn't limited to ourselves and our dogs. When I've also taken into account that many of these animals play joyfully, fall in love, and mourn their dead, it has made killing some of them for food a conflicted business indeed.

If their lives are as bright, bold, and emotion-filled as ours, I've asked myself, do I have the right to take their lives, especially if there are alternative foods for me and my dog to eat? Corn, for instance. Nor was I willing to be parsimonious and leave out cattle, chickens, turkeys, pigs, and sheep from this question simply because most of these animals spend their lives confined.

A big question . . . and not one that I cared to answer right then and there, high above Jackson Hole, on a silken golden morning, with the Tetons spread before us and breakfast done and lunch still far away.

So we took in the view a while longer before turning downhill and heading home. Along the way we saw a deer and the same chattering squirrel, and Pukka ignored both of them. He also found another grouse, whom he actually nosed into the air, a look of dawning realization crossing his young face, one brow going up, the other down: "That delicious feathery smell goes with that bird whose wings say *whirrrrr.*"

Then we saw a bison, a big male, massive and chocolate-brown in the sun, a magpie on its back.

"What a wildlife extravaganza, Pukka!" I exclaimed to him. "You are one lucky dog. Look, bison." I pointed to the animal.

He turned and declined his nose at me, giving me a mildly disappointed stare: "I know that's a bison. I've seen plenty of them." Despite his wide familiarity with bison, he turned back to this one and watched it graze with considerable attention and also a kind of gauging of its size, which I had not seen him do before. Before, he had looked at bison and shrunk back within himself. Now, after our morning chase of the elk, he gazed at this very large animal with the air of someone who is calculating whether there is a chance, a remote possibility, that he might catch one.

"I don't think so," I told him.

He glanced back at me: "Maybe not now . . . but who knows."

Time proved that he was not joking about this. He eventually chased and cornered a bison, fortunately without any injury. The bison lowered his horns and charged, and Pukka, like Merle before him, skittered away with a look that said, "Okay, I don't think I'm going to chase bison." Long before that day came, however, he decided to apply himself to grouse — more than apply himself. He fell in love with them, finding and flushing these swift noisy birds wherever we went, the unfolding of his birdy genes nudged along by me. I would toss rubber grouse into the air, fire a shotgun, and let him retrieve them. Just as he had no fear of thunder and fireworks, he had no fear of guns. In fact, unlike Merle — who detested shotguns being fired over his head and only tolerated rifles because they produced elk meat — Pukka loved all firearms beyond measure, a result of his having heard their actions opening and closing in Doug's shop while he nursed alongside his brothers and sisters.

If he so much as heard the action of a firearm opening someplace in the house, he would come running. Seeing me holding a shotgun or a rifle, he would leap into the air, kissing the gun and then me.

"Let's go! Let's go! Let's go!" his tail would lash. Any delay on my part — finding my hat, locating his whistle, searching for my sunglasses — caused him to chafe with impatience, and on one of our very first grouse-hunting trips, when I had gone back to my office to answer a phone call, he seized the cased shotgun in his mouth and tried to carry it to the car.

He was only six months old at the time, and it was all he could do to carry the weapon, yet he made a commendable effort to get it through his dog door, pushing hard, backing up, and pushing again, while the cased shotgun, far longer than the dog door was wide, barred his exit.

After trying to go through one more time, he backed up and glanced over his shoulder at me. I stood very still, giving him no encouragement, for I wanted to see what he would do on his own. Dropping the shotgun to the floor, he gazed down at it. Then he looked up and studied the dog door. Had he been a carpenter, his look could not have been clearer: either the dog door needs to be made wider, the shotgun shorter, or I need to try something else. He stood very still, looking from the dog door to the four-foot-long shotgun case, and back. Then he moved.

Picking up the end of the cased shotgun in his mouth, so that its length lay along his flank, he stepped through the dog door, pulling the shotgun behind him.

"Brilliant, Pukka!" I cried.

He only got halfway through the door before he and the cased shotgun became wedged in the narrow opening. He couldn't go back; he couldn't go forward; he was stuck like a cork in a bottle. Gently I pushed him through, into the mudroom, and opened the outer front door. Still holding the shotgun case by its end — it was too long to go through the human door sideways — he dragged it outside, and now having no constraints on space, he immediately dropped it, grabbed it by its midsection, and pranced to the car as if he had discovered the theory of relativity. And in his six-month-old universe he had.

After that, grouse and the other upland birds we hunted — pheasants and chukars — became his passion. Even in the winter, spring, and summer, when I was carrying no shotgun and he knew that it wasn't hunting season, he would course the ridgetops as we skied or hiked, going far, far out of his way to find grouse and boost them into the air, gazing at their departure with the soft rosy smiles that art lovers wear in the presence of a masterpiece. Looking over his shoulder at me, he would grin expansively: "Ah, Ted, did you see that! A grouse! The apex of my wildlife pyramid."

If we were lucky and got some birds, he'd carefully watch me prepare them for the freezer as I cleaned them on the outside picnic table. Periodically, I'd hand him a wing, a head, a clawed foot, or some entrails, all of which he'd munch like candy. Once I was certain that a bird contained no pellets, I would give him its carcass, and he would lie on the grass with it, chewing his dinner methodically, taking twenty-five minutes to eat the entire bird, an illustration of why dogs who have to chew raw prey, as opposed to inhaling kibble, have clean teeth.

When done with his meal, he would watch me wrap the rest of the birds — now cleaned and resembling grocery-store chickens — in white freezer paper. Like a scrupulous quality-control inspector, he would follow me to the freezer and watch as I placed the birds on the shelves, their reemergence, unlike the daily appearance of his dog food, random, and therefore one of the great mysteries of his life. Nonetheless, my removing them from the freezer was always cause for high excitement and periodic returns from his forays outside to cast a discriminating eye over the birds thawing on the counter.

Somehow he would always manage to be at my side when I prepared them for the grill, watching with unwavering attention as I squeezed lemons into a bowl, added olive oil, shoyu, and a bit of maple syrup, shook in dill, ginger, garlic, and cayenne, basted the birds, and then left them on the counter to marinate — a lengthy and unnecessary step in his opinion — before carrying them to the porch, where I laid them, flaming and steaming on the hot grill, he sitting as close as possible to their tantalizing aroma without actually singeing his whiskers.

"Oh, he's a grill dog. I can see that now," I would tell him as I closed the lid.

A slight wag of his tail: "No need to grill them, Ted, as I've made clear to you. I'll eat them raw."

"Patience, monsieur, patience," I'd counsel.

He'd follow me inside and lie down between the kitchen and the front door, covering any move I could make toward the cooking birds.

Shortly, when I brought them to the table, he'd sit a diplomatic few feet away while I carved, tilting his head significantly toward me, a gesture that in a human would have been equivalent to a polite clearing of the throat: "Excuse me. I believe it was I who scented that pheasant, flushed him, and then found him in the underbrush, bringing him to you and placing him in your hand, and so. . . ." And of course, I would give him his allotted share.

The only other animal who managed to fix itself so firmly in Pukka's wildlife pantheon was no bird at all but the animal whom he had seen, smelled, and eaten since we had driven from Minnesota to Wyoming when he was a puppy, and whom we had chased across the summit of Coyote Rock: elk. In fact, all his earliest training was conducted with elk jerky as a reward.

The only problem that Pukka faced with learning to hunt elk, in addition to birds, was the same epistemological dilemma facing all dogs who live with humans. They must deal with our annoying habit of splitting the world into distinct classes of objects. Dogs, on the other hand, want to lump objects into as few categories as possible, at least when lumping facilitates their getting something they want. The food on your table is like the food in my bowl, and so it's fair game; your human bed is like my dog bed, so I should sleep on it; if I flush grouse and pheasants and they fall from the sky after you shoot, and they feel so good in my mouth when I retrieve them, why can't I flush elk in the very same way?

His conflation of bird hunting and elk hunting was precisely what happened the first time Pukka and I went out after elk. Instead of waiting patiently by my side when we spied the elk grazing two hundred yards ahead of us, and then crawling alongside me in a slow and careful approach, he rushed the elk, apparently trying to flush them, since he did not chase them as they fled. Instead, he dashed back to me with a look of puzzlement and deep disappointment on his young face. "Are you not carrying a gun?" said his quizzical look. "Are we not obviously hunting? Have I not flushed numerous grouse and pheasants and chukars in precisely this way, and have I not retrieved them when they fell from the sky after you shot them? What is going on? I held up my end of the bargain, but you failed yours miserably."

"Sir," I sighed, "this is not bird hunting. You don't flush elk. They were too far away to begin with. We look for them, we smell them. You can help me a lot in smelling them when they're still far away and then letting me know where they are, *but without chasing them*"—I emphasized these words—"and when we at last find them, you have to walk alongside me until we're very close . . . very, very close so there's no chance of my missing . . . and only then will I shoot. Then we'll have lots of elk meat to eat."

He considered all this as he sat before me in the cold October dawn, listening to every one of my words with a great deal of concentration: bird, flush, elk, look, smell, wait, close, eat. He knew a lot of these words, but of course not strung together in complex sentences. And so, naturally, my explanation did little good the next time we found elk.

Pukka did the very same thing: he chased the elk . . . or he tried to. This time I had put him on a leash. However, did he crawl alongside me as we had practiced — belly-crawling through the sage as I whispered, "Oh, yes, Pukka, this is the way we'll get an elk . . . so very quiet . . . just like two wolves . . . yes, wolves"? No, he did not.

The very next time he smelled and then saw elk in the distance, he lunged against his leash, whining, moaning, and jumping frantically into the air and actually barking at me sharply, "The elk are right there, Ted! Are you blind? Can't you see them? Shoot! Shoot! And I'll fetch the elk!"

It took many times out, over the course of many months, as well as an initial elk season during which he watched both me and then our friend Scott Landale shoot elk — shoot them while he was on his leash, held by one of us a hundred feet to the rear — to impress upon him that elk hunting is different from bird hunting. In elk hunting, quiet was our friend, patience our method, and stealth the only way to achieve the success he wanted: elk meat in his bowl. In fact, it took a year and a half, but there came a morning, when he was eighteen months old, when it all fell together for him and made sense at last.

We were walking into the wind, the November snow almost knee-deep, Pukka drafting off my left leg and slightly behind me, as we meandered through an open conifer forest, fallen trees here and there blocking our way. Jackson Hole lay far below us, to our right, and the upsweep of the Gros Ventre Mountains rose to our left. He and I had worked on his position — slightly behind my left leg — using a clicker and treats and a leash called a Gentle Leader, which fits over a dog's muzzle. If the dog pulls against the Gentle Leader, it exerts downward pressure that most dogs don't like. I had also changed our word from *heel* to *behind, behind* more accurately describing where I wanted him on a narrow trail. I had also spent a great deal of time reinforcing his hand signals, for I didn't want to speak with him, even in a whisper, while hunting elk, as their hearing is legendary.

Having practiced these skills for well over a year, we slipped smoothly through the woods, listening to the wind and smelling what it brought us. For as far into the distance as we could see, the snow was pockmarked with elk prints and elk poop and elk urine, hundreds of elk having come down through the forest the night before, pushed from the high country by the deep and early November snows. Suddenly, Pukka quickened his pace, stepping in front of me, his nose raised into the wind, his mouth partially open, his nostrils twitching. He raised his right paw, in the classic position of a pointing dog, and ever so slowly turned his head to look at me, holding my eye with unmistakable meaning: "I smell elk."

He had come a long way from the puppy who had bounded ahead of me the previous hunting season, trying to flush elk as if they were pheasants.

I nodded, not uttering a sound.

We began to move forward slowly, both of us sweeping our eyes over the forest, and within another hundred yards I smelled the elk myself: musky, slightly sweet, a bit pungent.

Raising my eyebrows, I looked at Pukka. Keeping my elbow by my side, I pointed into the wind and mouthed, "Elk."

He gave me a look that said, "I told you so."

A few moments later, we saw two elk drifting uphill through the forest about two hundred yards ahead of us — too far away for a certain shot in this mix of spruce and firs. Pukka turned and gazed at me pointedly: "You do see them, don't you?"

I nodded.

We waited for the elk to disappear, then moved on, the scent becoming stronger, and Pukka, now excited, began to edge ahead of me — five feet, ten feet, fifteen feet — forgetting that this was a joint effort and if he got too far ahead he might spook the elk.

He was looking into the wind, away from me, and I made a tiny noise with my tongue against the roof of my mouth: "Tsk." He turned, and I pointed to the snow next to me. He returned, and we walked on side by side.

A gully fell below us, thick with subalpine firs, the head of the gully rising into the steep forested hillside to our left.

In the trees above the gully, someone moved.

The movement turned into a reddish-brown blur, and the blur into an elk, with its head down, walking slowly, grazing, and pushing its nose deep into the snow for the grass beneath.

Pukka stopped; I stopped; and we watched. The elk was only sixty yards off, but because its head was down and facing slightly away from us, I couldn't tell if it was a cow or a bull elk, and only cows were now legal to shoot.

A minute went by, then another, and finally the elk raised its head – no antlers. Pukka had planted his butt in the snow and was watching the elk with attention and composure. He, like Merle, now understood what we were about – waiting, not chasing, was the only way he was going to eat elk.

The smell of the other elk flowed strongly from the gully before us, and I weighed whether to wait for one of them to appear and perhaps give me a closer and clearer shot or to shoot the elk who was moving slowly through the forest, only sixty yards off, but who had not yet offered a perfect broadside shot. So many things could go wrong if I waited. The wind could shift, taking our scent to the herd, or simply our presence – our intent, our focus – might be communicated to them. Better to try for the elk we could see. There was one small opening, between two trees, into which it appeared the grazing elk would step, and at that moment I would have a clear shot behind her shoulder, an eighteen-inch circle in which her vital organs lay. Slowly, she grazed on, and I sent the thoughts from my mind to hers: "Please stop. Please give us your gift of food." And in that small opening, she suddenly stopped.

I had seen this happen so many times before, a circumstance that the old hunting peoples believed was not chance. They maintained that animals give themselves to you, but you have to ask for their lives, and you have to ask politely. Such old wisdom has lost its power in a world where food comes easy, but Pukka and I were now far gone from that world, high above the valley floor and connected only to the wind, the elk, the snow, and the smells they brought us.

If I made the shot – and I knew I would or else I wouldn't be taking it – I would then have to skin the elk, quarter her, fillet her rib and neck meat from the bone, put all the quarters and boned-out meat in muslin bags, and drag them away from the carcass so as to keep them from wolves, coyotes, bears, ravens, magpies, and eagles – who would be attracted by the skeleton and the gut pile – then remove the heart, liver, and lungs, sawing out the ribs as well (all of these delicacies for Pukka), and when these several hours of work had been accomplished (often while it was snowing, or below zero, or at night by headlamp, the elk having been shot in the last few minutes of the dusk), I'd wash my hands with snow or wipe them on leaves, and then I'd hike back to the roadhead for a sled, a big backpack, or horses and immediately turn around to return to where the elk had been cached so as to carry her down to our world (sometimes requiring several trips if I was the horse), where at last she'd be turned into all the cuts that miraculously appear in the grocery store: burger, steaks, chops, stew meat, salami, sausage, jerky. For me, this hard work remains hunting's most power-ful lesson, for it demands hands-on intimacy, first with the land and then with the animals who give their gift of food.

If the giver of this year's gift had any overt notion we were there, she didn't show it, and that was always my hope, as frightened animals pumped full of adrenaline don't make for tender or tasty eating. She continued to graze, her flank visible between the two trees. I raised the rifle and paused — as I have always paused at this avoidable yet ineluc-table moment, the etymology of the word *ineluctable* quite fitting for the dilemma faced by all of us who reflect upon the origins of our food. In Latin, *ineluctabilis* means that "from which one cannot extricate one's self."

Caught once again, I ran all the unsettling questions through my mind, the very same questions that I had thought of as Pukka and I stood upon Coyote Rock after seeing the peaceful summertime herd of elk, one of whom might be the very elk before us now: Why take this elk's life and not someone else's? Why cause this pain, if there are alternatives? Why not tofu, rice, and corn?

Once, in an attempt to avoid inflicting such pain, I became a vegetar-ian and spent three years not eating meat. But the practice never sat easy with me. Physiologically, I did not feel well, oats and tofu leaving my stomach riled. Ethically, I was also troubled by my vegetarianism, since eating vegetables has its costs as does eating meat: the many small animals — rodents, snakes, and ground-nesting birds who are killed as vegetables, beans, and grains are harvested by machinery, not to mention the animals poisoned by pesticides. One can, of course, eat organic vegetables, but unless one is growing the crops oneself or buy-ing them locally from people who are not using large farm machinery, some of the costs of conventional farming are also tied up in the pro-duction of organic crops: real animal lives lost. And such costs — "ex-ternalities," "collateral damage," call them what you will — make our attempts to reduce the suffering we cause by our eating, and our dogs' eating, full of unforeseen ramifications.

For example, industrial-size organic farms use compost to maintain the soil's fertility, trucking it in from long distances and using consid-erable amounts of fossil fuel to do so. The compost is also sometimes augmented with fish emulsion and pelleted chicken manure, which equates to animal lives going into our organic vegetables. Depending on the organic farm, it can also burn more diesel fuel than its conventional cousins because of the intensive weeding that goes on in a pesticide-free environment. And using more diesel fuel to weed and to irrigate equals more animal lives lost. Think of the *Exxon Valdez* and Gulf oil spills, which were just the big ones that attracted everyone's notice. Before the Gulf oil spill in 2010, about two hundred other major spills around the world had occurred between 2000 and 2009 — "major" being defined as greater than seven tons or a little over two thousand gallons. Two thousand gallons can kill a lot of shrimp, fish, and marine birds.

And then there are the deer — about 30 million of them in the United States alone. No one — not agribusiness, not industrial-size organic farms, not small-scale farmers, not even backyard gardeners — can grow vegetables where deer live without someone controlling their numbers or putting up a great deal of fencing. This is because deer love to eat some of the very same foods we do: salad greens, peas, chard, squash, fruits, grains, and soybeans. In the Midwest, 40 to 60 percent of a deer's diet is cultivated plants, not wild ones. In Iowa, corn, soybeans, and alfalfa make up 80 percent of the food eaten by deer. A farmer can put up a fence to protect such crops, but that simply redirects the deer to unfenced farms, and few people will fence large farms; it's too expensive, since it takes an eight-foot-high fence to keep deer out.

Controlling deer numbers thus falls to the lot of public hunters, who kill deer each fall and welcome the job since they like eating deer and so do their dogs. The hunters have taken the place of historic predators like wolves, and we could of course reintroduce wolves to control the deer, as they once did before we turned a good part of the temperate world into cities and farms. But most people do not like living near wolves, since some of them will kill livestock in addition to deer. Wolves will also kill domestic dogs, whom they consider interlopers on their territory, and even those of us who love wolves dearly would rather not have our dogs killed by them.

We might, as some suggest, put all deer on birth control, but such a project would be so massive and expensive that no one seriously entertains the notion except with respect to small local herds. After all, public hunters *pay* for the chance to shoot deer, and the money generated by their hunting licenses funds the management of both hunted and nonhunted wildlife. Consequently, there are deer lives embedded in much of our vegetarian fare — especially tofu, soy milk, soy burgers, and soy ink — as well as in the corn and soy that go into countless bags of dog food.

Considering all these factors, I naturally had to ask this question: might it not be better for me and my dog to simply eat the deer — especially if the deer (in our case elk) live within sight of our house — rather than import tofu or corn- and soy-based kibble thousands of miles from where they are manufactured? After all, the tofu and kibble have deer lives bound within them from the start. What sort of diet, I asked myself, actually causes the least amount of harm to feed me and my dog?

To get a better handle on this question, I asked Dr. David Pimentel of Cornell University's College of Agriculture and Life Sciences to help me calculate how much energy it takes to produce three different basic foods that I eat: elk, potatoes grown on the west side of the Tetons in Idaho, and rice and canned pinto beans from California. We took 150 pounds of elk meat — the amount I often get from a big cow elk — and set that as our baseline, converting the potatoes and the rice and beans into calorically equivalent amounts of elk meat.

We then figured every imaginable facet of production: my driving to and from the trailhead to hunt; the energy it takes to produce my automobile and rifle and cartridges; the cost to run my freezer; the cost of running tractors in Idaho and California; the cost of fertilizer and irrigation; the cost of canning the beans; and the cost of shipping the potatoes about fifty miles from Idaho, and the rice and beans nine hundred miles from California, to the grocery store in Jackson Hole.

When we were done, the results vividly demonstrated the value of eating locally: My yearly elk cost planet Earth 79,000 kilocalories of fossil fuel energy for me to hunt and store. The Idaho potatoes cost Earth 151,000 kilocalories of fossil fuel energy, and the rice and canned pinto beans cost the planet 477,000 kilocalories. By way of comparison, it costs planet Earth 3,900,000 kilocalories of fossil fuel to grow 150 pounds of corn-fed beef.

Obviously, if one lives close to farms in California, it might be wise to eat rice and beans and avocados and everything else a warm sunny climate produces. If one lives next to the ocean, fish would be a good idea. And if one lives in the cold snowy mountains where elk make their home, as I do, and the mountains grow these elk without pesticides, antibiotics, hormones, or heavy metals, and with a low input of fossil fuels, perhaps the ecologically appropriate thing to do is to eat elk, as I have done and my dogs have done. The same holds true for anyone who lives where big mammals live — deer, elk, moose — and this includes all suburban people, who can still hunt deer very close to their homes, using quiet bow and arrows, just as the hunter-gatherers who lived on these very same lands did but a few centuries ago.

What should be clear is that corn-fed beef is an ecologically costly food to eat. It takes nearly fifty times the amount of fossil fuel to grow a pound of corn-fed beef than it does to grow a pound of elk, and that calculation doesn't include the staggering amounts of water, pesticides, and antibiotics that go into producing factory-farmed beef as well as the erosion of rangelands and the pollution of waterways from feedlots. Nor does it include the substantial addition to the world's greenhouse gases from the combustion of fossil fuels in the combines used to harvest corn, in the semis used to transport cattle, and in the generation of nitrous oxide from manure and the release of methane in the form of cattle farts.

For all these reasons I don't eat beef and don't feed it to Pukka. Moreover, beef isn't as healthy as elk meat or the meat of other wild grazing animals. The meat of these wild grazers is full of omega-3 fatty acids (good for one's heart and memory) and conjugated linoleic acid (found to be anticarcinogenic). In fact, the meat of elk and other grazing wildlife contains four times the amount of omega-3 fatty acids as the meat of a corn-fed steer and three times the amount of a grass-fed one. Elk meat also happens to be very tasty — the cows more so than the bulls — and their tanned hides make lovely clothes and blankets.

Enough, though, for hunting locally. Consider its downsides, foremost being that the elk is a beautiful and noble animal and is clearly aware of the charm and beauty of its own life. Wouldn't it be better to spare this charismatic being and eat vegetables instead? But if we do, how do we then account for all the small animals who are inadvertently killed by the machinery of farming?

The double bind is not an easy one to escape. Some of us slip from its clutches by calculating the fossil fuel costs of different diets, as I've done, and then deciding that hunting locally harms fewer individuals, at least when one hunts big mammals. This view is an offshoot of

Buddhist doctrine, which believes that all animals are equal and thus a person accrues less bad karma by eating one big animal — one consciousness (an elk, a yak) — than by eating many small animals, many consciousnesses (a hundred chickens, ten thousand shrimp).

Others escape this double bind by buying humanely raised, grass-fed, free-range livestock instead of factory-farmed meat. Still others escape through denial: they simply don't think about the lives lost through factory farming, since it's unsettling to do so. And an increasing number of people become vegetarians and sometimes turn their dogs into vegetarians as well.

Given that billions of sentient beings are killed to feed us and our dogs, this isn't an unreasonable position to take — if one exercises a great deal of care in making sure that such vegetarian dogs, and especially vegetarian cats, who are obligate carnivores, get all the nutrients they need. Even Dr. Ian Billinghurst, who doesn't promote canine vegetarianism, states that "dogs will thrive on a properly constructed vegetarian diet," his operative words being "properly constructed." If you decide to turn your dog or cat into a vegetarian, neither of whom would choose such a lifestyle on its own, you owe it to them to buy commercially prepared vegetarian pet food that is AAFCO-certified as being nutritionally complete, or you need to consult a skilled veterinary nutritionist who can help you create such a diet at home.

Ian Billinghurst also asks people who are determined to turn their dogs into vegetarians to recall that omnivorous dogs are still very much carnivores and that tearing at bones and big lumps of meat prepares a dog's digestive system for the food that is to come. A stew of rice and vegetables, which the dog hardly chews, does nothing for a dog's teeth and gets to the stomach before the parasympathetic nervous system is aroused from the act of chewing and sends a message to the stomach to begin its secretion of digestive juices. Billinghurst also asserts that ripping and tearing bones and meat is emotionally very satisfying for a dog and positively stimulates its immune system, a benefit that vegetarian dogs no longer enjoy. Anyone who has watched dogs eating bones might agree.

Dr. Karen Becker, the resident veterinarian at Mercola Healthy Pets and a vegetarian herself, takes Billinghurst's cautions one step further. She never recommends that dogs and cats be turned into vegetarians because she sees far too many of these animals becoming malnourished. For those of her clients who remain troubled by the carnivorous nature of their dogs and cats, she advises, "If you really want a vegetarian companion animal, get a bunny."

One final point about vegetarian dogs is worth considering: they are not removed from the animal food chain. The chicken, cow, or lamb won't be in the bowl of a vegetarian dog, but some combination of other lives — mouse, warbler, snake, deer, the possibilities are many — will be. That's not to say one shouldn't make dogs into vegetarians or adopt a vegetarian lifestyle oneself as a way to reduce the suffering of animals. It is to say that the ineluctable costs of eating are difficult to avoid.

Perhaps, on a personal level, the best each of us can do is to look at all the costs of our own and our dogs' diets and try to reduce the gratuitous harm we cause. For me that has meant finding humanely raised, free-range livestock to feed Pukka. I'm aware that these animals are not as free as the elk behind whose shoulder I was now sighting my rifle, but eating such free-range livestock was a compromise that I have been willing to make so as to feed Pukka — and occasionally myself when the elk meat runs out. The only reason most dog foods don't contain such sustainably grown, humanely raised, free-range animals — which would markedly reduce both animal suffering and environmental damage — is that not enough of us have asked for such products.

In that asking lies the future. In the present, no matter where we eat on the food chain, we can offer our thanks — our very heartfelt thanks — to all those beings who, near and far, directly or indirectly, fill our bellies and the bellies of our dogs, giving us our lives each and every day.

Which is what I now said to the elk: That I wished I knew of another way to feed myself and my dog that didn't entail taking someone's life, somewhere. That I was sorry that it was she whom we had met on this snowy November morning. That I was grateful — grateful to my core — for the food, for the life, she was about to give us, and I hoped that someday my bones, and Pukka's bones, would help to grow her children's bones, just as Merle's bones were now making grass for the children of the elk who had fed him through his years.

It was not a long grace — she had begun to move — and if Pukka and I were going to eat her, the time had come. And although I had remorse — how could I not have remorse in taking such a life? — I didn't hesitate any longer. So many of these questions, so many of my doubts, had finally dissolved when I was willing to stand in the circle that fed me, nourished by those ahead of me, food for those to come.

The shot, as always, was muffled by the forest. The elk fell where she stood, and a moment later fifteen elk — five great antlered bulls and ten cows — trotted out of the gully and looked around, their faces a study in attention, curiosity, and wariness: Did you hear a shot? I thought I heard a shot.

Crouching, I put a hand on Pukka's shoulder as he sat by my side. It was unnecessary. Though he was trembling with excitement, he sat perfectly still, watching the elk but twenty feet away. The wind was blowing from them to us, and we had settled deep in the snow behind a log. We might as well have been invisible. Seeing nothing amiss, the elk slowly began to wander uphill, passing within forty yards of their fallen herdmate and not noticing her, as she, too, was blocked from their sight by fallen trees.

I kept my hand on Pukka's shoulder, but he continued to sit quietly, entranced by the elk moving upward through the steep trees, into the mist, into the deep and silent snow. The last elk disappeared, and still we didn't move. I had no worries about losing the elk who had fallen. I had seen her kick twice and lie still. We had done what we had come to do, she was not going anywhere, and there was no need to move about and send her herd into flight.

A couple of minutes later, several barking calls floated down through the snowy trees: "Where are you? Where have you gone? Come to us. We're missing you." Her herd had finally noticed that she was not among them. And if those calls didn't tell me the cost of making food — whether it was shooting an elk, or cutting a chicken's throat, or sweeping up a mouse in a combine — nothing ever would: most of us belong to a family and are missed when we fall.

At last, when we could no longer hear their calls, Pukka and I contoured around the head of the gully and found the elk lying upon her side as if sleeping: a great reddish-brown deer, five hundred pounds, and astonishingly large now that we were close upon her and had some perspective — from her hooves to her ears, she was six feet tall.

Pukka smelled her tan rump, her brownish flanks, and her darker head, his sucking intakes of breath loud in the silent forest. An instant later, he whirled around and began to dance before me, leaping high into the air and kissing me on the mouth. Landing in the snow, he sprang up and planted another smooch on my lips. Then he ran around in circles, grinning madly. Hurling himself against my chest, he panted in triumph, "Ha! Ha! We did it! We did it! Ha! We got an elk!"

No angst there. After all, he was mostly wolf.

"What an elk dog!" I cried, gripping him by the shoulders. "What a champion! You were as quiet as could be!"

He lifted his head in joy, arching his back under my pets, his tail pummeling my chest.

When I was done congratulating him, I knelt by the elk's neck, put a hand on her shoulder, and said my thanks to her once again, as well as another apology for having taken her life. Placing my nose between her ears, I smelled her forehead, which smelled sweetly of musk and pine. Like all elk, she rubbed her head against the evergreens. In a place where words were still visitors, these mingled scents — elk, pine, snow, wind — attached me most to home. I looked at her great brown eyes, her long regal snout, memorizing the perfection of her form. If I was going to eat meat, and if my dog was going to eat meat, I needed a face on my plate to which — to whom — I could say my grace. This year it was hers.

Pukka sat quietly and watched me. I put an arm around his shoulders and said, "Smell there," touching my finger between her ears.

He leaned forward, put his nose into her hair, and breathed.

"Mmm-mmm-mmm," I said. "Elk, they're the best."

He swished his tail in agreement.

"And so are you," I added, giving him a kiss on the cheek.

CHAPTER SIXTEEN

The Worst Word in the World

ALTHOUGH PUKKA WAS a constant dreamer, I was not. As far as I know no one has ever accused me of yipping, yowling, whining, and growling in my sleep, accompanied by shaking, shivering, and running in place while wagging my tail. Being a rather light sleeper — many years in wild places cemented the habit — I banished him to the corner of our bedroom. At first light, fresh and well-rested despite the miles he had run in his dreams, he would stretch himself in a doggy bow and pad softly to my bedside. There he'd sit in absolute silence, gauging whether I was awake. Seeing or hearing no movement from me, he would begin to hum, barely audible but incessant, all the while sending me a penetrating telepathic gaze, "Oh, Ted, are you awake yet?"

"How could I not be?" I'd say quietly. If it was still dark outside, I'd add, "Too early." For some reason, this was the command he responded to most promptly. Without a second's hesitation, he'd pad back to his bed for another hour's sleep. But if I said the longed-for two words, "Okay up," he'd leap upon me, rubbing his head over my face as the happy lashing of his tail exclaimed, "What a long night! How I missed you!" By his exuberant greeting, you would have thought that we had spent the last six hours separated by the breadth of a continent rather than by twelve feet.

"Good morning, Sir," I'd say. "How did you sleep between your dreams?" He'd throw himself against me, flank to flank — "Ah, touch, yes, that's better!" — and rolling onto his back, he'd fling his legs wide for his accustomed dawn belly rub.

I'd stroke from his chin to his neck, to his chest, to his belly, and there, on one July morning when he was a little over four months old, my hand stopped. I lifted my hand to verify — with sight — what touch had revealed. On his abdomen, just to the right of his penis, lay a round pink lump the size of a raspberry. It had not been there the day before — at least I didn't think it had been there the day before. But it must have been, given its size. Gently, I touched the growth with the tip of my index finger. Firm. Quite firm. Pukka didn't flinch. Staring at the nodule, my thoughts raced down that long ugly road toward a word I wouldn't say. But no matter how much I stared at the lump, it didn't go away.

Not changing my happy tone, I said, "How about our morning walk?" Getting out of bed, I dressed, and off we went on our river loop, he jigging before me — loose-jointed, big-pawed, clumsily graceful — his tail flagging as he leapt at the small white butterflies who wafted above the sage bushes. Suddenly, he made an arcing leap after one, and the butterfly, feeling his approach, jigged sideways — unsuccessfully. With a snatch of his jaws, Pukka plucked the butterfly from the air, landed lightly, and swallowed it, cocking his head as he appraised what he had eaten. Making a disgusted face, he flicked his tongue in and out, trying to rid himself of what was obviously an awful taste.

"See," I told him, reflecting upon my own recent flights after a certain butterfly, "beauty sometimes hides a bitter pill."

Declining his nose, Pukka gazed at me from the tops of his eyes: "Why didn't you tell me they tasted so bad?"

"I've never tasted one," I replied, laughing, and as I did I realized that for the space of several minutes I had forgotten about the lump on his belly.

We made our way to the beaver ponds, he retrieved a stick that I threw, and we headed upriver, coming to the long wide pool below the small bridge. On the opposite bank, two figures, gilded by the rising sun, moved among the cottonwoods: a woman and her dog. As the angle between us changed, the two figures became recognizable: Marybeth Minter and her Border Collie, Lacey.

Pukka and I crossed the bridge; he and Lacey greeted each other while Marybeth and I did the same. As Lacey playfully attacked Pukka, I said, "I was going to call you today. I found a lump on Pukka's belly, and if you had an opening this afternoon, maybe I could bring him into town and you could look at it." She said, "Why don't I look at it right now?"

There is something very comforting about meeting your vet on your morning walk, especially on the morning you've discovered a lump on your dog's belly. So I told Pukka to lie down, and as he did, and Marybeth bent over him, I thought, "If we have to get a bad diagnosis, what better place to get it than here?" Far better to hear the worst along the hush of a river, beneath the spreading cottonwoods, with the meadowlarks singing and my puppy lying on his back in the morning's warm sunshine.

"It's a grass awn," said Marybeth, standing up. "A grass seed got under his skin and is now inflamed and encapsulated. It'll break in a couple days. It's nothing to worry about."

I stood up and looked at the blue Wyoming sky—the river flecked with sun, the birds still singing—and felt foolish, overprotective, hypochondriacal, and vastly relieved.

Sensing my embarrassment, Marybeth said, "It pays to check these things. Because you never know. And it doesn't matter that he's only a puppy. I see lots of young dogs with cancer."

This was precisely Marty Goldstein's point as he held up a color photograph of a three-month-old Labrador Retriever puppy with a very red and ugly-looking rear paw. It was midmorning, Marty was between patients, and we were seated in his small book- and file-lined office. The author of *The Nature of Animal Healing* and the host of an animal-health radio show, Marty is also a veterinarian with a large and wide-flung client base, his average patient traveling many miles to visit him at his clinic in South Salem, New York. It's a part of the United States whose spreading oak trees, winding roads, stone walls, and old gabled homes have always made me think that Ichabod Crane or George Washington might come riding round the next bend, and in fact Marty did remind me of Ichabod Crane—lean, tall, and eagle-nosed, with piercing hazel-green eyes and a grizzled, neatly trimmed beard. Not a shirt-and-tie kind of vet, he was dressed in jeans, running shoes, and a white zippered T-neck sweater with a sheriff's badge pinned to his chest. The badge had a dog's face on it, and the message was apparent for anyone who cared to observe it: around here the dogs ruled.

Still holding up the photo of the Lab puppy, he said, "When I graduated from Cornell vet school in 1973, cancer was a disease of the old, and it seemed like its incidence was in the low teens—maybe 11, 12 percent—and maybe one out of ten dogs we saw died of cancer. Look at the Morris Animal Foundation cancer survey published in 1998, which asked, "What did your dog die of?" Forty-seven percent of the survey's respondents said, 'Cancer.' There's no doubt that cancer has increased, and the age at which it occurs has gotten younger and younger. You never saw a three-month-old dog with cancer in the 1970s and 1980s. You just didn't see it. It didn't exist. Now it's a commonplace thing." He held the photo higher, offering the evidence.

I remarked that many vets would say that we're now finding more cancer in dogs because the dog population as a whole is aging — better veterinary medicine has extended their lives — and our diagnostic techniques have grown more sophisticated, so we can discover cancers that went unnoticed before.

"Bullshit!" said Marty flatly. "Pictures speak louder than words." He pointed to the photo. "Three months old. Look at the inflamed red patch on the dog's pad. How diagnostically advanced do you have to be to say that this is a tumor? It's eaten 75 percent of the paw, and it spread to the lymph node, confirmed by Colorado State University Veterinary College as a mast cell cancer. Prognosis for survival was probably about five months."

He took out another photo from the looseleaf notebook on his desk, his case studies, his crusade. "Boxer with lymph cancer of the chest and the abdomen. You can see it with your naked eye. You don't need a CAT scan. It's eroding out of both cavities. This dog is eight and a half months old in this picture. He died three months later. We never got a chance to work on him."

He held up another photo — a four-year-old cat, oral cancer — and still another — a thirteen-month-old Tibetan Terrier, five surgeries for throat cancer — and yet a third, saying, "Nineteen-month-old Golden from New Jersey. This is a fibrosarcoma. It's already eaten 50 percent of the head. Do you know how many young Goldens we see here with cancer? Young! Two years old — lymphoma. It's insane."

The phone rang. It was the actress Kelly Preston calling for a consult. Marty excused himself and took the call while I wandered down the hall, looking at the signed photographs, lining the walls, of famous people whose dogs' lives Marty had improved or saved: Oprah Winfrey, Martha Stewart, John Travolta, Cesar Millan. Of Millan's dog, a Pit Bull named Spotty, Marty had told me, "Squamous cell carcinoma on the abdomen. Cesar flew him here — we did cryosurgery — saved his life for a while longer."

After the phone call, Marty saw a mix of clients — a physical therapist from Brooklyn with a Chihuahua named Kareena; a businessman from New Canaan, with a Golden Retriever named Grandpa; and the actors Keith Carradine and Hayley DuMond, from LA and New York, and their eleven-year-old cat Mr. Toodles, Marty using each consult not only to get at what was going on with the particular dog or cat (two cancers and an inflamed eye), but also to give a tutorial: inbreeding, overvaccination, and poor diet — grain-based kibbles in particular — had greatly contributed, according to him, to this epidemic of cancer. He talked about how radiation and chemotherapy — standard cancer therapies — could win the battle and lose the war, weakening the patient with the aim of completely eradicating the tumor, a goal that wasn't always necessary; rather, what was necessary was to improve the patient's quality of life and try to extend it, whether or not the tumor remained in place. He talked about the many successes that he had had with cryosurgery, the body replacing the frozen cancerous growth with healthy tissue. A powerful and animated speaker, he was teasingly funny with the people, trying to bolster their spirits and fight their hopelessness; he was intimate and gentle with the dogs and cats, talking to them as if they were people themselves; and for everyone — people and animals alike — he had a story about a dog or cat who had been saved at death's door.

At the end of the day, Marty once again held up the photo of the puppy with 75 percent of its paw eaten away by the mast cell tumor. "The breeder's vet wanted to amputate the paw," he explained, "and the breeder said, 'No way am I going to amputate the paw of a three-month-old puppy.' Instead, he saw two board-certified oncologists. They wanted to give this three-month-old puppy twenty-five radiation treatments, five days a week under general anesthesia, followed by chemotherapy, and even with that they were only willing to give the dog about five months to live, maybe a bit more if he was lucky. The breeder brought him here; we froze the tumor, a twenty-nine-minute procedure — *twenty-nine minutes* — and cryosurgery isn't even holistic medicine. It's a conventional procedure, but unlike any other form of surgery, it has immune-stimulating effects, and it bought us time for our adjunctive therapies, like nutraceuticals, to work and reestablish the health and integrity of that pup's immune system. Notice the date." Switching photos, he showed me an image of the cryosurgery. It was from January 2005.

"Four years later," Marty continued, "that dog is still alive and so strong that he ripped the breeder's rotator cuff off."

He laid down the photos and looked me in the eye. "But the real question is: what is a three-month-old dog doing with terminal cancer? You just didn't see cancer in young dogs thirty and forty years ago. Why is this happening? Bad luck? I don't think so." He shook his head. "As a populace, as a society, what have we manifested? Disease. And we're not just dealing with cancer. We've just gotten sicker and sicker."

"Do you have some data proving that there's more cancer in dogs now?" I asked. "Statistics at the various canine oncology centers that might show such an increase?"

Never having been at a loss for words during the entire day, Marty Goldstein now slowly shook his head and said one word: "No."

Marty Goldstein wasn't the only veterinarian with whom I spoke who believed that the incidence of cancer in dogs had increased during the last five decades. Richard Pitcairn, the author of *Dr. Pitcairn's Complete Guide to Natural Health for Dogs and Cats,* told me, "I graduated UC Davis in 1962, and I don't remember seeing cancer in younger animals when I began to practice. Most of the cancers that occur in animals are quite obvious—they develop bone cancer or they have visible tumors. It doesn't take sophisticated diagnoses to see them. I don't think there's any question that cancer is increasing in dogs." Ron Schultz, one of the veterinary world's leading immunologists, also told me during our visit that in certain breeds cancer was "absolutely" increasing and that he was seeing more of it in younger dogs. Kim Henneman of Animal Health Options in Park City, Utah, a veterinarian with many performance and sled dogs in her practice, pointed out that she, too, had seen a rise in the number of cancers she was treating, and she could verify this upward trend from her case records covering the years between 2002 and 2011. She had not introduced new diagnostic techniques during this period, she added, nor had her patient base gotten older; however, she couldn't discount the possibility that she was getting more referrals as her success in treating cancer had become known and her reputation had spread. Capturing the sentiment of many of these veterinarians, Allen Schoen, the veterinarian-author of *Kindred Spirits,* told me, "From my observation, it appears that there's a growing incidence of cancer in dogs, just as in people, and it seems to have multifactorial causes: an interaction of genetic predispositions, poor-quality food with possible carcinogens, excessive vaccinations that impact the immune system, and environmental toxins."

The perception that cancer has been increasing in dogs isn't limited to the United States. Roberta Benini of Italy's National Veterinary Council pointed out to me that "twenty years ago all the vet students would want to see a cancer because it was unusual. Now it is quite common." And Frantz Cappé, from the Clinique Veterinaire in Paris, had a "first impression that cancer was increasing," in puppies as well as in older dogs, though he qualified his statement by adding, "I don't know if cancer is being diagnosed more and if treatments are better."

Many other veterinarians made this same qualification, saying that, yes, they were seeing more cancer, but that it didn't necessarily mean that the incidence of cancer was increasing in the dog population. Bruce Fogle, meeting with me in his London office, best summarized this widely held position. "Am I seeing more cancer today?" he said reflectively. "I think I probably am, but that's because I'm seeing so many older dogs and cats, when in years past they were being killed off by infections or road traffic accidents at much earlier ages. Not only am I seeing many more older dogs than I used to, but I can also diagnose things that I previously couldn't diagnose, so it's easier to find cancers. MRIs are the classic example. I used to think brain tumors were rare in dogs, but once MRI came along, we learned that brain tumors do occur, and they're twice as common in dogs as in humans."

Lisa Barber, head of the oncology service at the Cummings School of Veterinary Medicine at Tufts University outside of Boston, expanded on Bruce Fogle's observation by telling me a story. During her first week in practice — she graduated vet school in 1992 — she palpated a mass in the abdomen of a cat and began to work it up — in other words, to run it through some tests to diagnose what the mass was. She was pulled from the examination room by the veterinarian who owned the practice. "What are you doing?" he asked her. She replied that she was trying to diagnose and then treat the cat. Her boss said, "We don't do that here. The cat clearly has cancer. Why are you wasting the client's money?"

Lisa told me this story to illustrate how times had changed. Today she and her fellow oncologists diagnosed and treated dozens of such cats and dogs every week, and their people were willing to spend considerable amounts of money to save their lives. These animals had now become cancer statistics in the Tufts veterinary medical database. By comparison, Lisa's first employer believed that it was a service to his clients to euthanize an animal with obvious cancer or to let it live until it became too ill, at which point it was put down. All these animals had not been captured as cancer statistics, Lisa explained. Now they were, and this gave the impression that cancer was increasing.

Traveling from one veterinary practice to another, I repeatedly heard this split in opinion: we're seeing more cancer; no, we're not — it's an artifact of more sophisticated diagnostic techniques and better record-keeping. In an attempt to break the tie, I decided to review the records stored in the Veterinary Medical Data Base, at Banfield Pet Hospital, with its many locations across the United States, and at various veterinary cancer registries in Europe. I enlisted the help of oncologists, statisticians, and a researcher, but after several months of looking, we only reaffirmed what others had already noted: there were too many holes in the veterinary databases to show any valid trends, one of the most notable being the lack of any nationwide dog censuses. Were there 60 million dogs in the United States in 2012, or were there 80 million? How many dogs were alive in 1964 when the VMDB began? What was the dog population of Europe then, and what is it now? No one knows for sure. Nor are death certificates required for dogs, and many dogs are euthanized without a biopsy or a definitive diagnosis. Given that we don't know what millions upon millions of dogs die from, and we don't know their total population, we can't measure morbidity or mortality rates as accurately as we do for people.

Having failed to answer the question of whether more dogs are dying of cancer today than used to be the case, I decided to set it aside for a moment and address what seemed to be two more pressing issues: Is there anything we can do to prevent canine cancer? And if our dogs do develop the disease, what can be done to cure them or to improve the quality of their lives in the time remaining to them? With these questions in mind, I began a tour of canine oncology centers, starting in the West and moving east.

The Angel Care Cancer Center sits on the coastal hills near Carlsbad, California, about three miles from the Pacific Ocean. A pleasant building of tan concrete, with big panes of glass, it was founded in 2004 by a team of veterinary specialists led by Dr. Gregory Ogilvie, a former professor at Colorado State University's Animal Cancer Center and the director of its Medical Oncology Research Laboratory. Greg has also taught in Europe, Latin America, and Asia, has co-authored more than two hundred scientific articles, and has used his considerable academic, clinical, and research experience to help create one of the world's most advanced animal oncology centers, a facility that not only treats patients but also explores new therapies to prevent and battle cancer, many of them based on naturally occurring compounds.

There were glassed-in operating theaters, an extensive laboratory, CT and ultrasound rooms, a hyperbaric chamber for victims of stroke, brain damage, and burns, as well as radiation theaters housing a linear accelerator and a CyberKnife Robotic Radiosurgery unit. One of the theaters was large enough to accommodate horses and dolphins, the latter increasingly affected by squamous cell carcinomas on their tongues, a result of their frequent exposure to ultraviolet light when they perform, mouths open, for audiences at Sea World.

As in every oncology center I visited, the day began with grand rounds—the oncologists, radiologists, surgeons, and vet technicians walking past the kennels while describing the progress of their patients: "Misty is a ten-year-old Golden Retriever with osteosarcoma. A gastrostomy was performed. A seven-centimeter-diameter cystic mass was removed. Multiple biopsies were obtained.... Kelly is a seven-and-a-half-year-old.... Hank is a...."

On we went, Greg—a slim man with the build of a long-distance runner—striding out in a blue dress shirt, a yellow tie imprinted with cats and dogs, and stone-white khakis and brown oxford shoes. A stethoscope was draped around his neck; his gray hair and mustache were neatly trimmed; his narrow face beamed; and his blue eyes were eager. He seemed totally in love with his work.

Rounds done, we headed off to see his first patient, accompanied by a young veterinarian from Venice, Italy, Clizia Mascotto, who was studying at Angel Care for a couple of months. The meeting that was about to take place was representative of virtually all the meetings I would see between an oncologist and a new client and patient at the facilities I visited: the Colorado State University Veterinary Teaching Hospital in Fort Collins; the University of Missouri Veterinary Medical Teaching Hospital in Columbia; and the Cummings School of Veterinary Medicine in Westborough, Massachusetts. These meetings were representative of what people whose dogs have cancer can expect from an advanced animal oncology center in terms of taking a history, discussing diagnostic tools and treatments, and giving an estimate of costs.

Trailed by Clizia and me, Greg entered one of the consultation rooms, where we found a petite blond woman in her forties named Magda. She was seated in one of two upholstered armchairs, and by her side sat Gwen, her trim seven-year-old Boxer, her muzzle, chest, and paws sparkling white. Magda wore a gray shawl cardigan and had sunglasses perched atop her head. With a worried expression, she was reading the folder that the front desk gave each new client. Having read it myself, I knew why she appeared troubled.

"The word cancer is as dark and empty as the disease it defines," the handout began. "A diagnosis of cancer often brings with it feelings of overwhelming fear, a spiraling sense of loss of control, and most dev-astating of all, the loss of hope." The rest of the folder was filled with information about the clinic and its treatment protocols — both medical and nutritional — the entire package designed, as it said, to "dispel the myths of the disease as well as its treatment . . . so that we may chip away at the fears about cancer that are encased within us all and begin to replace them with truths."

Greg shook hands with Magda and introduced us. Kneeling beside Gwen, Greg held her shoulders and talked to her softly while running his hands over her and examining the nasty-looking growth on her lower left rear leg. Still kneeling, he looked up at Magda and asked her what she could tell him about Gwen.

Magda recounted how she had taken Gwen to their vet when she noticed the lump, and he had said, "If it doesn't change color, I'm not going to do anything with it."

"Then all of a sudden in the last couple of weeks," Magda exclaimed, sounding aggrieved, "it's gone *boing!*" She took Gwen back to their vet, and he diagnosed the lump as a mast cell tumor.

Greg gave the smallest of sighs before saying, "Mast cell tumors are really common in Boxers, and in all other dogs as well. The big question, though, is whether we're just dealing with the tumor on Gwen's leg or do we have to worry about it having gone elsewhere." Mast cell tumors, he continued, like to metastasize to the liver, spleen, and lymph nodes, but before we determined if that had happened, he wanted to call in Dr. Sarit Dhupa, the director of surgery at the clinic, to look at Gwen's leg.

Dr. Dhupa was summoned, and a few moments later he came into the room, a dark-haired, round-faced man, wearing blue scrubs and a warmhearted smile. After examining Gwen's leg, Dr. Dhupa knelt by the other chair, following the lead of Greg, who had continued to sit on the floor with Gwen. "If we assume that this is the only affected area," he began, "from a surgical perspective, we have two options." The first was to debulk the tumor locally, which would be difficult, since it was located on the narrow part of Gwen's lower leg. If the disease hadn't spread, the other option — he paused — was an amputation.

Magda sucked in her breath, then let it out with a pensive hum. She held her hands in her lap and looked at them for several long seconds; then she looked at Gwen, who was gazing at her with a worried expression: "Are you all right? Why did you make that sound?"

"Nobody wants to take off Gwen's leg," Greg began, "but what we do depends on your goals. Fundamentally, it comes down to this: do you want to help a little bit, do you want to help a moderate amount, or do you want to help a lot? There are different strategies that we can put together to meet your goals."

Dr. Dhupa excused himself to go to his next surgery, and then Greg gave Magda a mini-tutorial on mast cell tumors. Drawing on his clipboard, he showed her how these sorts of tumors had tentacles that extend far beyond the tumor that one could feel. They also release chemicals that cause bruising, bleeding, swelling, and stomach ulcers, and that was why he encouraged her to go to her pharmacy or grocery store right away and get some Pepcid or Prilosec for Gwen. He also wanted Gwen to have another supportive therapy, a natural fatty acid called DHA, docosahexaenoic acid, 1,000 milligrams a day, which Magda could get at CVS Pharmacy, Wal-Mart, or Target. "It has anticancer effects," he said.

Gwen sat patiently and looked from Greg to Magda with a bit of concern. We all looked at Gwen, who licked her lips, and Clizia began to pet her.

Turning back to Magda, Greg said, "The first question that I have for you is, has this spread?" He then walked Magda through the tests that would determine whether the tumor had metastasized — an ultrasound of Gwen's internal organs and aspirates from her liver, spleen, and lymph nodes as well as a bone marrow sample. Once this information was known, Magda could set her goals for Gwen's treatment.

"Some people," Greg said, "who are on one end of the spectrum, will say, 'You know, I'd just like to provide comfort.' Then giving DHA and

Pepcid or Prilosec, plus a drug called prednisone, which reduces inflammation, can be very helpful. Other people will want to provide comfort, but will also try to control the disease." Greg then summarized this more extensive treatment: he would use a drug called vinblastine, derived from the periwinkle plant, which would be given intravenously. Although vinblastine had the longest track record in reducing the size of mast cell tumors and controlling them, it didn't cure all of them. There was a new drug called Palladia, approved by the FDA specifically for dogs and mast cell tumors. If Magda wanted to enroll Gwen in a clinical trial, she could get the drug free.

Magda's face took on a hopeful look, and Greg struck a cautionary note. These drugs would control the mast cell tumor; they wouldn't necessarily cure it. For a cure, both chemotherapy and an amputation might be necessary. Stoically, Magda gave a small nod, and then Greg reviewed everything he had written on the clipboard with her, asking if she had questions and answering the ones she had about the side effects of the drugs, which were minimal.

In the days to come, I would repeatedly see Greg go to great lengths to explain to clients what was going on with their dogs. He would actually turn the computer monitor — showing a dog's CT scan and an obvious tumor — toward clients who had averted their eyes, gently asking them to please look at it. About his methods — not merely treating dogs with cancer, but also educating their people about the disease — he would say, "By seeing it, then you own it, then you control it."

When Magda had no more questions, Greg told her that he would get her a quick estimate and be right back. Turning to Gwen, he added, in the high-pitched voice that we reserve for dogs and children, "We'll be right back, Gwen."

As we walked down the hall toward the procedure area, I asked Greg if it might have been wise for Gwen's vet to aspirate or biopsy the lump on her leg the first time he saw her, when it was still small, rather than waiting so long. Stopping in midstride, he turned to me and said forcefully, "With early detection and diagnosis, that great big mast cell tumor we just saw could have been a little tiny surgery instead of the amputation we now have to do. When I give lectures, I show veterinarians cases just like this one and make them promise me that they will never tell a client, 'Let's just watch this and see if it grows.'" The irony in all this, he added as we resumed walking, was that what would have been an inexpensive aspiration and excision was now going to cost Magda thousands of dollars and Gwen her leg.

Over the next few months, I would hear versions of this story many times from the fifty or so people who obligingly allowed me to be in the room while their dogs were examined, tested, and treated: "My vet said, 'Let's watch this,' and now I'm here, and my dog has cancer." Significantly, every single oncologist with whom I spent time repeated what Greg had told me. Kim Selting, associate teaching professor of oncology at the University of Missouri's Veterinary Medical Training Hospital, said, "Ideally, any lump or bump has a needle stuck in it at least one time." Lisa Barber, the head of the oncology department at the Tufts University Cummings School of Veterinary Medicine, said, "We have animals that come in and have twenty-four lumps on them, and we aspirate all of them. It takes three seconds to do an aspirate." Susan Lana, associate professor of oncology at Colorado State University's College of Veterinary Medicine and Biomedical Sciences, told me, "We have a little saying around here, 'You know the four most dangerous words in the English language? Let's just watch it.'"

"Why, then," I asked her, "do so many vets in general practice say, 'Let's just watch it'?"

"Not every vet school," she replied, "has the same amount of oncology training — either didactic or clinical — in its curriculum. We have a big center, and we have a very active oncology curriculum, but not every vet school does."

Some veterinarians' lack of oncological training of course brings up the question of what to do if your dog develops a lump and your vet says, "Let's just watch it." You can insist that your vet aspirate the growth and diagnose the sample or that it be sent to a qualified pathologist. You can go to another vet. Or you can ask your vet for a referral to the canine oncologist with whom your vet almost certainly works. You can also do an Internet search for a board-certified canine oncologist. Instructions for how to do this can be found in the notes.

Magda signed off on the estimate for the workup, and Gwen was brought into the large procedure hall, where her belly was shaved in preparation for her ultrasound. Also leashed to various kennel doors and stainless steel examination tables were Hank, a six-year-old Pit Bull, in remission from lymphoma; Molly, a thirteen-year-old Springer

Spaniel, in remission from a rare form of leukemia; and Buster, a six-year-old mixed-breed, getting his doxorubicin chemotherapy from a vet tech dressed in a blue gown, rubber gloves, and goggles. Obviously, the chemical going into Buster was toxic, as the large red poison warnings on the nearby fridge — where the chemo drugs were stored — made clear. Buster, too, was in remission from lymphoma, and when I remarked that chemotherapy certainly seemed to be working for these dogs, the vet tech said that, yes, it was, but in most cases chemo didn't cure the disease, only put it into remission.

Greg, just finishing with taking a blood sample from one of the dogs, added that dogs whose cancer recurred could be put back in remission several times, occasionally over a period of years. At Angel Care, the oncologists treated lymphoma with a cocktail of chemotherapeutic drugs — vincristine, asparaginase, prednisone, Cytoxan, and Adriamycin (the last being the brand name for doxorubicin) — which, when used in conjunction, were called the Wisconsin Protocol. They were administered over a twenty-five-week period, the drugs changing week by week. At some of the other oncology centers, similar drugs were used but were administered over a fifteen-week period.

About these differences in treatment protocols, Tufts's Lisa Barber, a tall blond woman with a ready sense of humor, told me with a laugh, "There was a time when we were naive and idealistic enough to believe that if we just knew exactly how to schedule and dose the drugs, we would make a significant difference in treating lymphoma. We haven't done that."

Despite tweaking the timing and dosage of these drugs, she explained, and adding new ones in clinical trials, veterinary oncologists hadn't been able to markedly improve median survival times for dogs with lymphoma. Survival time remained at about one year, depending on the stage of the disease when treatment was initiated and the type of lymphoma the dog had. Dogs with B-cell lymphoma survived nine to twelve months, whereas those with T-cell lymphoma averaged only half a year. Important to keep in mind was the fact that most dogs did remarkably well on these drug cocktails and didn't suffer the side effects that people experience when undergoing chemotherapy: loss of hair, appetite, and weight. Moreover, most dogs felt well enough to continue their normal activity while getting their treatment.

Since dogs with lymphoma did so well on chemotherapy, why then, I asked, weren't more of them being cured of their disease? Lisa Barber best summarized the many similar answers I received to this question by pointing out that dogs are not able to consent to their care. Therefore, the veterinary profession has made the decision not to put dogs through the same aggressive chemotherapy that people undergo. The object in veterinary medicine is to improve a dog's quality of life and extend it, not necessarily to cure its disease. She went on to say that if one compared the survival rates for people and dogs with non-Hodgkin's lymphoma, the survival rate in people also left much to be desired: the five-year survival rate for people with non-Hodgkin's lymphoma was 69 percent.

Yet, as Dr. Steven Suter, assistant professor of oncology at the College of Veterinary Medicine at North Carolina State University, told me, "The 70 percent of people who make it past five years are essentially cured of their disease. They do not relapse and die." Not so with dogs who, on average, do not survive beyond a year once they have lymphoma.

To improve their survival rate, Steve treats the disease much more aggressively than has been the rule in the past. Starting in 2008, he and his colleagues began to offer bone marrow transplants for dogs who have already received chemotherapy and are in clinical remission. The technology is the very same one that was originally tested on dogs so as to be used with humans. No bone marrow is actually harvested during the treatment. Instead, the dogs are treated for five days with a drug that drives healthy stem cells from their bone marrow into their bloodstream, and from there these cells are harvested using leukapheresis machines. The stem cells are screened to make sure they're cancer-free, and then the dogs are given chemotherapy and radiation to kill any remaining cancer cells before their healthy stem cells are reintroduced. Having helped to develop lymphoma treatment for people, dogs can now be given the standard of care available to humans with the disease.

Because the relapse rate in Steve's patients is still about 60 percent, he has theorized that some cancer cells escape the initial rounds of chemo and radiation and remain lurking in the lymph nodes. He is now increasing the dosages of both the chemotherapy and radiation in an attempt to kill these lingering cancer cells before a dog's harvested healthy stem cells are reintroduced.

The cure rate for dogs who have received bone marrow transplants at North Carolina State is about 30 percent—defined as surviving more than two years – and this represents a tremendous improvement over survival rates with chemotherapy alone. Unfortunately, a bone marrow transplant is not cheap. Although it's approximately one-fifth the price of the very same procedure in human medicine, it still costs about $15,500, a fee that comes on top of several thousand dollars for consultations, diagnostic tests, and the first round of chemotherapy to put the disease into remission, which alone averages about $3,000. In fact, radiation and chemotherapy for a dog with lymphoma can easily cost $10,000 before a bone marrow transplant. Even with pet insurance, these fees quickly exceed the maximum policy term benefit – $14,000 per year for America's largest pet insurer, Veterinary Pet Insurance – putting the extensive treatment of canine cancer out of the reach of many people.

Sometimes money isn't the only factor influencing a dog's survival. Where people seek care for their dogs plays a role in how well their dogs fare. For instance, oncologists at Colorado State University do not use the canine melanoma vaccine to treat dogs with melanoma, claiming that the data for its efficacy is insufficient. Every other facility I visited uses the vaccine, claiming that it is effective for dogs with the disease. If your dog has melanoma and you want it to receive the vaccine, you'll have to go someplace besides CSU.

On the other hand, CSU uses limb-sparing surgery instead of amputation for some dogs with osteosarcoma, removing the tumor and replacing it with a bone graft or metal implant. Oncologists at CSU believe the procedure to be very successful. Yet oncologists at Tufts are not enamored of limb-sparing surgery and suggest that amputation gives a better result: fewer infections and more mobility, as a countless number of spry three-legged dogs can attest. If you think that your dog is better served with four legs than three, you may have to travel to find a surgeon who will do a limb-sparing procedure, keeping in mind that it is not known at this point if limb-sparing surgery ultimately increases life span.

You will also have to travel to a specialized oncology center if your dog needs radiation therapy from a linear accelerator, a giant machine that delivers high-energy X-rays precisely to a tumor and costs between three and four million dollars. Refurbished linear accelerators can be had for $100,000, putting them within reach of some private veterinary practices. However, most of these units are found at veterinary training centers.

Chemotherapy, on the other hand, is offered in some small private practices and could be offered in far more if veterinarians were willing to learn how to administer the different drugs and handle the minimal side effects that occur in dogs. Kim Selting of the University of Missouri, a slim, dark woman with a quiet air of proficiency, encourages vets to acquire these skills, which not only would save their clients travel time but would also save the lives of dogs who might otherwise not be treated. In addition, vets who offer chemotherapy would acquire a new source of revenue.

To aid general practitioners, as well as the public, in the treatment of dogs and cats with cancer, Kim has developed a website called Vet Cancer Trials, which has a search engine that allows users to find a clinical trial that might be of benefit to their particular dog or cat at one of eighteen cancer treatment centers around North America. Her website lists dozens of such trials, which tweak dosages, add new drugs, and try them for varying lengths of time. Most of these trials play on similar chemotherapeutic themes, all of the oncology centers that I visited using the same basic protocols in the treatment of lymphoma, mast cell tumors, and osteosarcoma.

Much as I searched, however, I couldn't find a single clinical trial that studied the relationship of diet to cancer treatment or prevention, and when I asked oncologists whether they included nutrition as part of their cancer treatment, I found opinion divided. Greg Ogilvie recommended high-fat, low-carbohydrate diets for his patients since the majority of cancer cells do not metabolize fats as well as they do carbohydrates. Greg also believed that there was enough evidence associating high-carbohydrate diets with increased risk for cancer to put dogs on low-carb diets as a preventative measure. He also recommended DHA supplementation for his cancer patients, as well as for healthy dogs and people, because of its cancer-preventative effects, and he pointed to a long list of scientific papers to support his suggestion. Kim Selting was also an advocate of DHA supplementation, saying that it had "the best track record for having anticancer properties."

But she and Lisa Barber both disagreed with Greg with respect to putting dogs on low-carbohydrate diets to prevent cancer. Kim said that she used such diets only with cancer patients who were experiencing weight loss, and Lisa remained "unconvinced" of their efficacy. Lisa also recommended that her cancer patients take an omega-3 fatty acid, but EPA (eicosapentaenoic acid) was her first choice, not DHA.

As for Sue Lana, she remained on the fence about the role of diet in cancer prevention and treatment.

When it came to recommending one of the many alternative cancer therapies advertised on the Internet — ozone, shark cartilage, and green tea are but a few — Kim advised people to be thorough in their homework, investigating the evidence for any alternative treatment's efficacy. For example, EGCG, epigallocatechin gallate, an element in green tea, has been found to inhibit the growth of cancer cells in vitro, but, she asked, how much green tea should you use on your dog, especially given that it contains caffeine? Might it interfere with another therapy being given? Which cancers might it work for? "My recommendation," she concluded, "would be to find a veterinarian who has researched alternative therapies and has long experience working with them." This is easier said than done. There is a search engine on the website of the American Holistic Veterinary Medical Association, but it's hardly complete and omits many veterinarians experienced with alternative therapies.

For Kim, "the holy grail of cancer therapy" was immunotherapy, our attempt, she explained, to teach the immune system to do something that it had failed to do in the first place: recognize the invading cancer as different from healthy tissue and kill it. Kim readily admitted that immunotherapies had proved ineffective many times during the past forty years, yet she was also aware of miracles happening when the immune system did kick in. She had seen reports of dogs with stage 4 melanoma who had complete remission of their tumors once they had taken the melanoma vaccine.

As of this writing, several naturally occurring compounds have proved to be promising immunotherapeutic agents for humans with cancer and also might help dogs. One such compound is PSK, polysaccharide K, found in the mushroom *Coriolus versicolor*. It's commonly used in Japan as an adjunct in human cancer treatment along with surgery, chemotherapy, and radiation. Another one of these compounds is Lentinan, found in shiitake mushrooms, and a third is a fermented wheat germ extract called Avemar, which has proved beneficial to some human cancer patients when added to their conventional treatments. All three compounds can be bought online. However, the correct dosage to give a dog is unknown. Those who want to use these compounds for treating their dogs have to read the human medical literature, consult with their veterinarians, and then make an educated guess. The same goes for those who want to use these compounds for treating their own cancer – it would be wise to consult with an oncologist first.

It is unlikely that in the foreseeable future researchers will find a single silver bullet – a single immunotherapeutic compound – that will fight or prevent all cancer. Instead, new cocktails of drugs and natural substances will be used to stimulate the immune system to fight cancer invaders by turning off damaged "driver genes," the ones that allow cancer cells to grow, or switching on "tumor suppressor genes," which, as their name implies, repress cell division. It is in managing the microenvironments of these particular genes that the future of cancer therapy, and perhaps prevention, lies.

Once Gwen's tummy had been shaved, she was given an ultrasound, and no sign of internal tumors could be seen. Nonetheless, the radiologist took aspirates from Gwen's liver and spleen, using long thin needles. Back in the examination hall, Gwen was lightly sedated, and Greg removed a tiny bone marrow sample from her shoulder. Staining the slide, he ran it over to the microscope bench, peered into the viewfinder, and said, "Crap."

Stepping back, he let Clizia and me look at the slide. "It's beautiful to look at, but...." He trailed off. In the microscope, I could see a field of round, blobby, purple mast cells. Gwen's tumor had metastasized to her bones.

Feeling low, we walked back to the consulting room, and Greg gave Magda the good news first – a perfect ultrasound and no visible tumors. Then he told her the bad news. Magda took a very long breath, held it, then exhaled slowly while staring at her hands clasped in her lap. After a while, she looked up. Eyes brimming, she asked Greg to amputate Gwen's leg, begin chemotherapy, and save her dog's life.

Over the next few weeks, Gwen responded well to chemo and was soon running around on three legs, but her limb and many thousands of dollars could have been saved had she been diagnosed and treated earlier. This lesson was borne home the very next day when Greg, Clizia, and I met Ziva, a sleek two-year-old Boxer whose people had taken her to the vet the moment they had discovered her lumps. Fortunately, their vet didn't say, "Let's just watch this." He aspirated the lumps, diagnosed them as mast cell tumors, and referred Ziva to Angel Care, where the tumors were removed before they had a chance to metastasize.

Several years later, Ziva still runs her nightly three miles, wearing her bright pink collar, proof that doing a weekly, nose-to-tail, hands-on examination of your dog can help it to live a longer life. Ziva is also the poster child for what I heard some oncologists repeatedly tell clients: "Cancer is the most curable of all chronic diseases," a maxim that for some cancers is absolutely true — if the cancer is caught early, and if people don't project their own fears of cancer upon their dogs, preventing them from getting the treatment they deserve.

The best example I saw of such projection was the man whose seven-year-old Golden Retriever had developed a mast cell tumor at the base of his tail. The dog's name was Charlie, and his cancer had not yet metastasized to his bones, internal organs, or lymph nodes. Greg gave Charlie an excellent chance of being completely cured — if his tail was amputated. However, Charlie's person — a tall, handsome, and athletic man named Doug, a successful entrepreneur, husband, and father — did not think that Charlie would want to lose his glorious feathery tail. After all, as Doug told me in a private moment outside the examination room, he himself couldn't bear the thought of losing one of his own legs to cancer, adding with impressive honesty, "Perhaps I'm too vain."

What would I do? he asked me.

I mentioned that Charlie had the potential to live another seven or eight years, and that he'd certainly learn to live without his tail. Merle hadn't actually lost his tail, but he had broken it badly and couldn't hold it erect, flagging his status to other dogs. Yet he compensated by holding his head higher.

"I don't know," Doug muttered. "I just don't know."

"Why don't you ask Charlie?" I said gently. "He'll tell you."

After a week of soul-searching, Doug overcame his preconceptions about self-image and allowed Charlie's tail to be amputated at its base. Today he and Charlie are still hiking over California's coastal hills.

In other cases that I saw, the life of a dog with cancer was saved because their person was willing to put the dog through some pain. Callie, a small, black, shy, nervous eleven-year-old Cocker Spaniel seemed the least likely candidate to endure discomfort, but her person, Mita, an abundantly optimistic woman, decided to put Callie through nineteen radiation treatments over the course of three weeks to eradicate her soft-tissue sarcomas. Callie was on pain meds during this time and needed to be anesthetized to have her burnt and slough-ing skin cleaned. But a year later, Callie still had her life — her cancer gone — and Mita still had her dog.

In still other instances, people saved their dog's life by going against the sound professional advice they had received from veterinarians who maintained that a dog's prognosis was hopeless and euthanasia was the only kind alternative. Such veterinary opinion is particularly common when a dog is of an age that veterinary medicine considers beyond the normal life span for the breed, rendering the dog unsuit-able for treatments that might be given to younger dogs.

This was the advice that Russell and Valerie received when their thirteen-year-old Golden Retriever, Barnaby, broke his leg while get-ting off his sofa. An X-ray revealed bone cancer, and after splinting Barnaby's leg, their vet advised them not to do anything about the cancer since Barnaby probably had only a few weeks left to live, a di-agnosis that a canine oncologist confirmed. To make matters worse, Barnaby had laryngeal paralysis and diabetes, the diabetes making him pant and the laryngeal paralysis making him aspirate his saliva, so he got pneumonia on top of his cancer.

Russell and Valerie — heavy, jovial people who radiated good cheer — were not yet inclined to give up on Barnaby, whom they had gotten as a nine-week-old puppy. They brought him to Greg Ogilvie for a sec-ond opinion, and Greg said, "Yeah, he's in trouble, but there are some things we can do, depending on how complicated you want to get and how much money you want to spend."

At the time, Russell was laid off and money was tight, but as he told me, "We had to treat Barnaby no matter what. He didn't want to die."

We were in one of the examination rooms of Angel Care's satellite clinic in Murrieta, California, as Russell related his story to me, and Barnaby was lying at his feet, following his words with a huge grin on his white face, the rest of his large, muscular body still coppery red. He thwacked his tail on the ground in agreement: "No, I didn't want to die. Not at all. I was not ready."

And indeed he wasn't. He had his leg amputated; he had four rounds of chemotherapy; his bone cancer went into remission.

Six months after my first visit to Angel Care, I returned to southern California to visit the dogs whom I had met, and I found Barnaby, now fourteen and a half years old, pulling himself around in a new wheel-chair and swimming twice a week to improve his strength, while on a low-carbohydrate diet of raw meat and ground vegetables. He was still grinning, lying on the grass outside the Murrieta clinic, his face radiant as he gazed up at Russell and Valerie.

I asked them how much Barnaby's care had cost, and Valerie said that she had lost track, but it had been between ten and fifteen thousand dollars. It had been a struggle to find the money – they had made many sacrifices – she immediately shook her head, lest I think she was complaining. Gazing down at Barnaby, she said, "I was ecstatic when he made it to his fourteenth birthday. Now, whatever amount of time we have left with him, I feel it's a blessing."

Almost a year later, Barnaby developed a mass in his liver that began to bleed. His kidneys were no longer working at their normal capacity, and he had a fever. "We were faced with the choice of putting him through another serious surgery and recovery," Russell told me, "or letting him go while he was in no pain and very little discomfort." They let him go. Barnaby was nearly fifteen and a half years old. He had lived two years beyond the discovery of his bone cancer. Given his size and breed, his survival was akin to that of a person in his late eighties who, given a mortal diagnosis, lives to be a hundred.

Barnaby, of course, was the very sort of dog, a Golden Retriever, whom we would expect to get cancer: an aging member of a breed that's very predisposed to the disease. But what about Aiko, a mixed-breed from the San Bernardino shelter who was the size of a coyote and whose coat looked like a cross between a German Shepherd and a red fox? He was one and a half years old when he came down with leukemia. Waiting for his first chemotherapy, he lay in my lap and looked up at me with his thoughtful reddish-brown eyes as I stroked him. His chemotherapy worked – for about a month – and then Aiko, which means "little loved one" in Japanese, rapidly declined, dying at home among his people. Why, to borrow Marty Goldstein's words, did a dog like Aiko – genetically diverse and as mixed-breed as they come – get cancer at such an early age?

A few months after returning from southern California, I found what might be an answer to this question, one of the two questions that inspired this book. I was reading the report of the President's Cancer Panel, *Reducing Environmental Cancer Risk*, and came to a section entitled "The Special Vulnerabilities of Children," in which the authors wrote that even though mortality from childhood cancers had declined from 1975 to 2006, owing to improved treatments, the incidence of cancer in US children under twenty years of age had strangely increased.

The causes of the increase, the authors went on, weren't known, but they had been too rapid to be of genetic origin. Nor could the increases in childhood cancers be explained by the introduction of better diagnostic techniques, such as CT and MRI, since an increased incidence due to more sophisticated technology might be expected to cause a onetime spike in rates, not the steady increases that have occurred in these childhood cancers over three decades. Cautiously, the authors concluded, "The extent to which environmental exposures are responsible for this trend remains to be determined."

Of course, it was hard for me not to replace the word *children* with *dogs*. As I've mentioned, dogs, like children, receive a larger dose of environmental contaminants per unit of body weight than do adults. Dogs are also more inbred than they were fifty years ago, as well as more sterilized and more vaccinated, and they eat a less varied diet. They are fatter. Perhaps all the veterinarians who claim that cancer in dogs is increasing are correct, and just as the incidence of cancer has increased in children during the last few decades so, too, has it become more common in dogs.

CHAPTER SEVENTEEN

Dog Speed

MY DOGS WERE OFTEN in my dreams, sometimes Pukka, sometimes Merle, sometimes both dogs together, the three of us falling into the ocean from dry land that crumbled beneath our feet, or from ice floes that cracked and opened around us, casting us into the surging sea. Perhaps I should have expected my worried subconscious to manufacture something like this: the dogs went out their dog door — out of my control — and my dreams of losing them came back through the dog door and roiled my sleep.

Not so in my waking life. I had hardly worried about Merle being injured when he was on his own, for he possessed commando-like survival skills and had quickly learned to leave cattle and wildlife alone, a good habit to have in country where ranchers and game wardens shoot dogs who chase livestock or wildlife and the wildlife can maim or kill a dog in a heartbeat.

Pukka, too, had quickly learned not to chase the big animals who lived around our home and in fact had been a model pupil after his incident with the otters, halting to my "leave it," returning to two blasts of the silent whistle, and standing at my side to gaze at elk, deer, and moose with a wagging tail that said, "I see you, but I'm a good dog and would never think of chasing you." He had obviously assimilated all of our positive-reinforcement training — done in and around the house, during hikes like the one up to Coyote Rock, and rewarded with elk and salmon jerky — and he could now roam on his own without my worrying about his safety.

Then, when he became a year old, an important part of what he had learned vanished. Seeing deer or moose, and sometimes even several bison, he'd launch himself at them like a missile, sending them into long flight, all the while ignoring my calls of "leave it," ignoring the double blast of the silent whistle, meaning "come now," and only returning after he had run the animals two or three hundred yards, his annoyed look at me saying, "I came! Why are you so upset?"

Pukka, in short, had become a teenager, and like many teenagers, he wanted to renegotiate the terms of his puppyhood agreements with me, changing "I shall not chase wildlife" to "I'll give them a brisk run and then come back to you." However, unlike allowing him to rumble instead of bark, I wasn't about to weaken my no-chasing rule. Such behavior would eventually get him injured or killed by a deer, moose, or bison, or he'd be shot by a game warden for breaking the law.

So we went back to reviewing his lessons from scratch — reviewing them in the house and on the lawn without any distractions — his "leave its," "stays," and "comes" picture-perfect. But did his picture-perfect behavior have much transference to those times when he was roaming freely before me? It did — so long as he was within twenty feet of me. Beyond that distance, my influence over him waned exponentially as the distance between us increased. If he spied a deer — his favorite animal to chase — when he was twenty-five feet from me, he'd edge away from me, breaking into a light-footed trot, his speed increasing, and my shouts — "Leave it, Pukka, leave it!" — left behind as he kicked in his afterburners.

My impression, as Pukka hurtled after these animals, was that he wanted to kill and eat them. There seemed to be no difference between his behavior and that of wolves running down their prey. The wolves were grizzled, and Pukka was reddish-yellow, but they both chased with equal fervor, mouths open in glee.

Then came the day when Pukka actually caught a deer and I had to reconsider what he was about.

The deer, a recently born mule deer fawn, sprang out of the tall grass in front of Pukka's nose and leapt into the Gros Ventre River. Three feet long and weighing about fifteen pounds, the terrified little fawn began to thrash away in the swift current, and Pukka jumped in directly after it. Swimming rapidly, he overtook the fawn, grabbed it by the neck, turned around, and swam back to shore. Landing on the bank, he laid the fawn gently down on the grass and stood over it, his inquiring look saying, "I did well, didn't I? You want me to retrieve, don't you? And I just did."

There was no time to answer. Teaching Pukka to have a soft mouth had worked wonders for the fawn. Uninjured, it sprang to its feet and dashed off to its mother, who was waiting at the edge of the forest. This time a "leave it" kept Pukka where he stood, watching his prize depart.

This incident made me ask myself: did Pukka really entertain the notion that he was going to retrieve a two-thousand-pound bison for me? Whatever his thoughts on the matter, I wasn't going to allow him to chase. It was one thing to shoot a big animal for food, and quite another to run it for sport.

Naturally, it would have been far simpler to leash Pukka while we were walking, and confine him to the house when we weren't, rather than go through the effort to change his mind about chasing wildlife. It's the solution that millions of people adopt out of necessity (cars being far more dangerous to dogs than wildlife), or because they're afraid their dogs will run off and never return, or because they don't have enough time to train their dogs not to run after cars, livestock, and big wild animals. But I have never found walking a dog on a leash much fun, either for myself or for the dog — especially in the wide-open spaces of Wyoming — and so I was determined to find a way to give Pukka freedom while impressing upon him the no-chasing rule.

With Merle, I had managed to do this by using a choke collar and a long length of climbing rope, jerking him to a stop when he chased cattle. After being halted in this way a few times, he decided not to chase them. He was a smart dog, and he also had a highly refined sense of manners. This method was harsh, to be sure, but it had been recommended to me by a veterinarian in 1991. I wasn't about to repeat it in 2010. I was older, and I hoped wiser, and far less willing to cause my dog pain.

With this in mind, I consulted Barbara Larkin, the Jackson Hole positive-reinforcement trainer whose puppy socialization classes Pukka had attended, and at her suggestion I bought him a Gentle Leader Easy Walk Harness. Unlike the one that I had used to teach him to walk by my side, which fit around his muzzle, this model went around his sternum and shoulders, just like a standard chest harness. But instead of having the leash's attachment point being between the dog's shoulders, which would give him something to pull against, the Gentle Leader's leash clip was at the chest. When Pukka pulled, the harness steered him to the side and directed his attention back to me instead of allowing him to stay focused on what was ahead — in this case, deer.

Once I had Pukka harnessed, Barb explained, I could take him to where he would see lots of deer and tell him, "Leave it." If he didn't chase, I could praise him and reward him with his favorite treat, elk jerky. If he sprinted after the deer, stopping him with the Gentle Leader would discourage him gently, turning his attention back to me, and in this way he would quickly learn not to chase wildlife.

The confounding variable proved to be that Pukka was perfectly behaved while on a standard-length leash, walking by my side like a show dog at Westminster. He'd see deer a ways off and say, "Oh, there are some deer. I know I'm not supposed to chase them," and he wouldn't. There was no training effect whatsoever for those situations during which he was off-leash and at a distance from me.

So I took one of the thirty-foot lunge lines that I used on horses and attached this to his Gentle Leader, this arrangement allowing Pukka to walk ahead of me at his trigger distance of just over twenty feet. The first time he saw a deer when he was at this distance from me, and I said, "Leave it," he ignored me and broke into a run. It happened so fast that I reacted instinctively. I grabbed the lunge line as Pukka ran it out, and I burned two livid welts in my palms before he came to a stop. That's when I started wearing leather gloves.

It didn't take long before Pukka had regained his puppyhood manners and was retrained not to chase deer — at least when he was no more than the length of the lunge line from me, thirty feet. But take him off the lunge line and let him get out to forty feet and everything changed, my calls of "leave it," and the peals of the silent whistle, vanishing into the air, as did Pukka, chasing deer and moose and bison toward the horizon.

Was he abashed at his bad behavior when he returned to my side? Of course not. He had only done what I had trained him to do: not to chase wildlife when he was thirty feet from me. This is a very important point to remember. Dogs, though willing to generalize, are also masters of detail: they observe the cues we give them and repeat the behavior we mark at precisely the moment we mark it by either saying "yes" or "good boy" or clicking a clicker. The latter was developed in the Harvard laboratory of the behaviorist B. F. Skinner in the 1950s and was then popularized by the psychologist and animal trainer Karen Pryor starting in the 1980s. It's a far more precise way than the ever-changing human voice to indicate to a dog when it has executed the exact behavior you want it to perform. In Pukka's mind, I had used the thirty-foot lunge line and clicker to impress upon him that he could not chase deer when he was precisely thirty feet from me: "Leave it, *click,* well done." I had not impressed upon him that he could not chase deer when he was forty feet from me, and so he did. Obviously, I had to find a way to teach him that "leave it" worked at all distances and no matter the temptation.

I could, of course, have tried to teach him another behavior to substitute for chasing wildlife. Barb Larkin, for instance, had taught Samantha, her Lab-Springer mix, to sit whenever she saw deer, elk, or moose. This lesson nearly had tragic consequences. When Samantha was faced with a herd of stampeding cattle, she sat in front of them, bringing up a fascinating question about her visual limitations or the principles of her reasoning. Was her eyesight so poor that she could not distinguish that the cattle weren't wildlife, or did she make the decision to take no chances about what she had been taught: four legs, big animals, sit down?

Jostling and bellowing, the herd enveloped her, and when the dust cleared, there was Samantha, the good soldier, still sitting where she had planted her butt, looking alarmed, but fortunately unscathed. Miraculously, the herd had parted around her.

Pukka's eyesight, like that of many retrieving and herding dogs, is keen, but might he use Samantha's reasoning with another herd of cattle or a herd of bison? Bison occasionally ran around the house in large groups, and they might not be so forgiving as cattle. And might Pukka sit in front of a charging moose whom we had inadvertently surprised on a ski trail?

Teaching Pukka to sit at the sight of large quadrupeds did not seem like a good idea, so I lengthened the lunge line, splicing two of them together to give me sixty feet of working room. However, Pukka — now forty to fifty feet from me as he began to chase deer and no longer a frolicsome puppy but an intact teenage dog, weighing nearly seventy pounds, all muscle, and jacked up on testosterone and adrenaline — would be moving so fast that it was like trying to stop a bluefin tuna with nothing more than my hands on the fishing line. He burned up a pair of leather work gloves, and he broke the chrome-plated snap swivel of his lunge line; that's how powerful his chasing drive was. Once, when I momentarily attached his lunge line to the trailer hitch on the Subaru and searched my pockets for his silent whistle, he scented a covey of chukars and dashed after them, ignoring my "leave it!" The lunge line caught me across the ankles and flipped me in the air. When I struck the ground, I broke two ribs. Lying there, my chest stabbing with pain at every breath and seeing him sprawled on the ground sixty feet from me, I wondered, "How is this positive reinforcement?"

It was then that I reconsidered a shock collar, one of which I had used to dissuade Merle from going to the house of a neighbor, Lucille Garretson, where she fed him Milk Bones, chicken breasts, and filet mignon stuffed with Roquefort cheese until he was as roly-poly as a sausage. Since Lucille, a sweet old woman, would not stop feeding him ("He looks so irresistible," she had said), and Merle had no intention of not going to her home, I felt that I had to do something. I could have closed off his dog door and confined Merle to the house but I didn't want to end his mayoralty so as to keep his weight down. He would sorely miss his visits to his other Kelly constituents, whom I had convinced not to feed him.

The shock collar proved to be the solution. It stopped Merle from going to Lucille's in pretty short order, but people in the positive-reinforcement dog-training world who read the story of Merle's experience with the shock collar gave me no end of grief for using it: I was a moron; I was cruel; they used some other names as well.

What this group of folks didn't seem to appreciate was that positive reinforcement doesn't always work when you're trying to influence a dog who's doing its thing — and often doing its thing at dog speed — far beyond the distance at which it normally responds to its commands and a clicker can be heard. Moreover, there are rewards that a person cannot trump with a treat, such as fleeing deer or filet mignon stuffed with Roquefort cheese.

As Pukka's case also demonstrates, one can have a dog who is trained from puppyhood to obey commands, but who forgets what he's been trained to do when the temptation gets big. Pukka is not alone in this regard. Very fit, very athletic dogs with a high prey drive can quickly get far from their people, entering a zone where nothing else in the world exists except what they're chasing. At that point, all their training in the house, in the yard, and in obedience school can go out the window. If you doubt this contention, go to any large dog park where dogs play with other dogs more than a hundred yards from their people, and then count how many of these dogs return to their people, first time, every time, when their person calls, "Come." First time, every time.

Once again, some in the positive-reinforcement camp say that this is to be expected, even with well-trained dogs, and that the solution to our dogs' ignoring commands at a distance is a good leash. As one person on a forum discussing this issue wrote, "I happen to see no problem in keeping my dog on a leash or long line for his safety (even though some may say *that* is inhumane), or to limiting his off-leash time to a limited set of safe areas rather than letting him off anywhere and everywhere." That's one way to keep dogs safe. But for dogs like Pukka and Merle — and for millions of dogs like them who love to run at dog speed, a speed that cannot be attained in a small fenced dog run — being restrained by a leash or a fence is not tantamount to being in jail — it *is* being in jail. And being in jail can have long-term health consequences, for both people and dogs.

Having been unwilling to keep Merle in jail, and now being unwilling to keep Pukka in jail, I revisited the shock collar, only to discover that, fifteen years after I had used one on Merle, it was no longer called a shock collar. It had been rebranded an "e-collar," or an "e-stim collar," partly out of political correctness and partly because the newer terminology more accurately reflects the increased sophistication of these devices. Whereas the shock collar I used on Merle had five crude settings, which I changed by installing different color-coded prongs, e-stim collars have twenty to thirty gradations, set with a dial, and can be programmed to give their stimulation for no more than one-tenth of one second, reducing people's tendency to express their anger at disobedient dogs by zapping them long and hard.

This was the type of collar I bought, first trying it on myself, and not merely holding it in my hand, but strapping it around my neck, exactly where Pukka would wear it, the two prongs on each side of my Adam's apple. I began at the lowest of the twenty-four settings that this particular collar offered, then worked my way up through the settings, and then back down, before deciding on an electric prick that made me jump — "Hello! I felt that!" — but didn't make me cringe. It felt akin to the bite of a very determined mosquito.

First, I let Pukka wear the collar for a week of fun outings without stinging him — walks, hikes, swims, and mountain bikes — as I was advised to do by the instructions that came with the e-collar and also by two dog trainers who had used such collars to train hundreds of field-trial dogs. Finally, on a cold, cloudy, late October afternoon, Pukka and I took a walk around the river loop, accompanied by A.J., Burley, and

Goo. Along the way I tested Pukka, not with the e-collar but with the silent whistle, blowing it when he was running full tilt with his pals two hundred yards ahead of me. Instantly, he'd race back with a happily wagging tail: "You whistled, Ted! Here I am, Mister Perfect Manners, Obedience Incarnate."

"Well done, Pukka!" I'd tell him.

"Huh-huh-huh," he'd pant. "You bet!" And off he'd run, rejoining his three pals.

On the far side of the loop, where the road comes down from the crest of the ridge, and we could see low yellow hills rising into forested mountains, Pukka suddenly peeled away from the other dogs. Halting on the shoulder of the dirt road, he gazed up to a distant stand of aspen trees, his body alert, his head raised, his mouth slightly parted, his eyes bright, and I knew he smelled deer.

He was gone before I could raise the whistle to my mouth, and he didn't stop when I called, "Leave it!" He was a hundred yards off when I blew the whistle twice, and a hundred fifty yards away when I blew it again, demonstrating nicely that a well-trained dog, given enough temptation, can be completely oblivious to the very commands that he obeyed perfectly only twenty minutes before and at an even greater distance. At nearly two hundred yards from me, he was running like a golden streak, nose and tail extended, straight up the hill toward the mule deer, who had turned and fled. I pressed the one-tenth-of-one-second button on the transmitter to give him what e-collar trainers call a "nick."

It was as if the hand of God came down from heaven. Pukka skidded to a stop and stared at the deer with a surprised look that said, "How did you do that?"

A moment later, without my blowing the whistle or calling a single command to him, he turned and sprinted back to me, coming to my side and sitting in place.

"Well done, Pukka!" I complimented him, stroking his ruff.

He gave the deer a long hard stare, and then he gazed at me, his face wearing a puzzled expression that said, "The weirdest thing happened, Ted. I was chasing those deer and I suddenly got this annoying sting on my neck."

"Really?" I said. "How odd. Maybe you shouldn't chase deer."

He gave me a sober look.

"Let's go," I said gently. "The boys are waiting."

And down the road we followed them.

Over the next two weeks, I had to give Pukka eight more nicks — calling "leave it" and then nicking him — eight more reminders that deer, moose, and bison were off limits. After that he did not chase them again for months, and when he resumed, he needed but a four-nick refresher course.

And that was that: amazingly, remarkably, wondrously. He did not chase big animals again, and it all happened without our doing any more training around the house; without my endlessly blowing the whistle; without my having to raise my voice when he was two hundred yards from me; without my offering him treats; and without my snubbing him with the Gentle Leader and both of us being jerked off our feet. A total of 1.3 seconds of electronic stings, reminding him not to chase, and he learned not to do it. Furthermore, he learned it at distances that mattered: hundreds of yards away from me, where my voice and whistle no longer had any power to influence him, yet the e-collar did.

Granted, Pukka had been given a great deal of positive-reinforcement training as a puppy. In fact, for the first seven months of his life, we went through "leave it" and "come" and "wait" nearly every single day for at least ten minutes, often longer, and once he had decided that he no longer wanted to pay attention to these lessons, we spent many days with the Gentle Leader and the lunge line, trying to reinforce the importance of not chasing wildlife. In other words, Pukka had a substantial amount of positive-reinforcement training under his belt before I ever put an e-collar around his neck. Perhaps if he had been a different dog — less committed to chasing and retrieving — that initial positive-reinforcement training would have been enough. In his case, it wasn't.

Was it cruel to give him those stings — 1.3 seconds in total — each of them feeling somewhat like a mega mosquito bite? It depends on your beliefs about the value of negative conditioning, which of late has gotten a bad rap. As the Harvard University child psychologist Dan Kindlon has written, we now live in a culture in which many of us "think we're psychically scarring our kids if we cause them the least bit of pain or suffering." Previous generations of mothers and fathers would have seen this as namby-pamby parenting. We think of it as positive reinforcement and shrink from inflicting the least bit of negative reinforcement upon our children, not only to spare them pain and suffering but also because we're afraid of being called abusive.

Don't misunderstand me: I'm not advocating that we harm children or dogs, not in the least. But the opposite, overprotective parenting, has clearly infiltrated the relationships that many of us have with our dogs. For example, millions of people now call their dogs "kids" and refer to themselves as their dogs' "mommies" and "daddies," which is to be expected when dogs are puppies but loses its charm when dogs turn into adults. Of course, there's a natural side to maintaining this relationship: everyone who has raised and loved a child knows that your child stays your child no matter how old *you* become. However, this doesn't mean that we continue to treat children like toddlers when they grow into teenagers and adults. Anyone who does so is seen as having missed one of the key responsibilities and ultimate joys of parenting: witnessing one's guardianship help to transform helpless beings into self-sufficient and self-actualized adults.

The revulsion in which e-collars are held by some positive-reinforcement dog trainers is a subset of this widespread infantilization of dogs and our unwillingness to inflict the slightest sting upon these surrogate children. The disdain for e-collars by some positive-reinforcement trainers is also a reaction to so many dogs having been dominated and abused for so long. The result has been dogma — negative conditioning is universally bad — and as a result, some people are reluctant to give their dogs any boundaries. Consequently, these dogs don't mature into adults. They stay children their entire lives and never become their person's partner and friend.

Obviously, some of us find subconscious benefits in this strategy: our children will eventually leave us — and sometimes our partners and friends abandon us as well — but dogs are loyal to the end by definition, and we can markedly enhance the appearance of that loyalty by reinforcing their dependence upon us. Then, when such perpetual puppies act out and can't be trained with love and positive reinforcement to behave at a distance, we reach for a leash and constrain them, eliminating their freedom and preserving their childhood status. If we have any second thoughts about keeping what appears to be a pretty smart being frequently tethered, we tell ourselves that they're "just dogs," highly domesticated creatures with little use for freedom as their aim in life is to be by our sides. This notion deserves serious reappraisal.

• • •

First, consider that a leash is not just a length of webbing, leather, or rope. It's a living nerve, transmitting the emotions of the person who holds one end – trust and cheerfulness as well as fear and insecurity – to the dog at its terminus. Because a leash is like an emotional telegraph, dogs who are scrappy when on their leashes often get along convivially when their leashes are taken off. They're no longer worrying about protecting the anxious people who are trying to restrain them.

One of the most poignant illustrations I ever saw of this phenomenon took place in Boulder, Colorado, on the Mesa Trail, which snakes along the open foothills west of the city. I was walking with my friend Arrow, a Border Collie, who was off-leash. Coming down the trail was a woman with a young, large Saint Bernard puppy, perhaps ten months old and still floppy and loose-jointed. Seeing Arrow, the much larger dog began to grin and wriggle all over: "Oh, boy! A dog to play with!"

Instantly, the woman tightened his leash, and I saw her body stiffen. It wasn't much, but it was apparent to anyone who watches the body language of people with dogs. She was anxious. And just as instantly, her dog stiffened. A moment later, Arrow, who had been wagging his tail – "Oh, a friendly dog up there" – also stiffened and began to growl.

We continued up the trail, and the woman stepped aside, pulling her dog toward her as we passed, the two dogs now growling at each other.

"He's afraid of other dogs," she said, grabbing his leash with both hands.

"I bet if you took him off his leash," I said, "he'd be just fine."

Her face became stricken. "He's gotten into fights," she replied.

"On the leash?" I asked.

"I can't trust him off it," she said, tightening the leash even more and dragging him backwards.

Arrow and I continued up the trail, leaving what was more than likely a perfectly happy, well-behaved Saint Bernard to his fate: becoming an increasingly reactive, paranoid, and unreliable dog because of his person and her unwillingness to see that her fears were not her dog's.

The second reason a leash isn't a benign training tool is that it doesn't give a dog the opportunity to make a wide range of decisions on its own, even if its person uses a retractable lead that allows a dog to roam at a distance of about thirty feet. If you happen to think that a thirty-foot lead gives a dog plenty of room to explore, imagine changing places with your dog. Put the collar around your neck and the end of the lead in your dog's mouth as you stroll through a mall. Every time you make a move toward a sporting goods store or a lingerie shop that's forty feet away, your dog brings you up short. The message is soon driven home: what's beyond the end of your leash doesn't matter.

The effects of constraining a dog's experience in this way have been explored by researchers at Loránd Eötvös University in Budapest, where some of the world's more interesting investigations of the cognitive abilities of dogs have been done. In looking at the relationship between a dog's dependency on its human and its ability to solve problems, these researchers discovered that dogs who were strongly dependent on their humans, fulfilling the role of a child substitute, were not as good at solving problems as dogs who were less dependent.

At the University of Illinois other researchers have shown that mice who exercise on a running wheel are smarter — have more neurons in their brains and perform better on cognitive tests — than mice who have many toys to play with but don't exercise. In addition, aerobic exercise has been found to delay the cognitive impairment of aged mice, increasing their mental acuity. A dog strolling at the end of its leash, even a thirty-foot-long leash, doesn't receive any of these benefits.

"So what!" you might say, as one person told me, only partially joking. "My kids are too smart for their own good. I need Einstein in a dog?"

Fair enough. But constantly keeping dogs on-leash may do more than stifle their mental development. It may also compromise their health, and not only because they get less aerobic exercise.

Numerous biologists, sociologists, and anthropologists have now demonstrated that the inability to make one's own decisions — whether one is a baboon, a zebra, a wolf, or a human being employed at rote and unsatisfying work — can lead to increased incidences of disease and premature aging. The overriding conclusion that has emerged from such research is that autonomy and health go hand in hand: the lower your station in your particular group's hierarchical or socioeconomic ranking, the more chronic stress you endure, accumulating stress hormones like adrenaline and glucocorticoids. Their effects — fight or flight — are supposed to be short-lived, but when constantly secreted, stress hormones can lead to a compromised endocrine and immune system.

Since the majority of us now live in cities and suburbs—places where the freedom of dogs is highly circumscribed—it's difficult for us to imagine that dogs might find being constantly controlled stressful. However, research done at the Konrad Lorenz Institute for Evolution and Cognition in Vienna has shown that dogs do get stressed when they perceive that they are being treated unfairly—for example, when they're on a leash and other dogs are walking freely or when their friends are given food and they are not. This last circumstance was the subject of the Austrian study. Pairs of dogs were asked to give their paws and were rewarded with food for complying. Soon one member of the duo was rewarded for giving its paw when asked while the other dog was given no reward for the same request. Not only did the unrewarded dog soon stop giving its paw, but it would also begin to show the classic signs of a stressed dog: scratching, yawning, licking its mouth, and avoiding the gaze of the dog who had gotten the food.

Human studies have shown that experiencing this sort of inequality—in other words, being a have-not—can actually lead to a shortened life span. Scientists at the Twin Research and Genetic Epidemiology Unit at St. Thomas' Hospital in London looked at over fifteen hundred female twins and found that twins of lower socioeconomic status had shorter telomeres than their better-off siblings, even after correcting for smoking, obesity, and physical activity. Telomeres are the caps at the end of our chromosomes. They protect them from fusing as they divide, and they also prevent the main body of the chromosome from losing essential genes. However, telomeres are not immune to wear. As our cells divide, the telomeres at their ends grow ever shorter, like the tread of a tire wearing down and eventually exposing the core. Since telomeres shorten over time, they can serve as a biomarker of a cell's biological age. Thus, the economically poorer twins with shorter telomeres were biologically older than their more-advantaged twins, even though they were the same chronological age.

In some cases we become stressed regardless of our economic well-being, and this sort of stress can also contribute to a shorter life. One US study compared mothers with healthy children to those with chronically ill ones. The longer a mother cared for her chronically ill child, the higher her levels of stress as measured by oxidative damage to her DNA. In addition, the telomeres of the stressed mothers were significantly shorter than the telomeres of mothers who had healthy children, making them biologically nine to seventeen years older, depending on how long their stress had been going on.

Although exercise is not a cure-all for such chronic stress, being physically active can help to buffer its damage, as a sequel to the twin research showed. The physically more active twin in this study was biologically ten years younger than his or her chronological age.

These findings are worth considering when it comes to deciding how much off-leash time a dog needs, especially when we consider that status and autonomy play an important role in how much stress wolves experience. In captive wolf packs, the subordinate individuals—wolves whose actions are constantly restrained by more dominant members of the pack—have higher levels of stress-related hormones than the alpha wolves. However, the same relationship—low social status equating with high stress—has not been found in wolf packs living in the wild.

In the wild, alpha males and females share the leadership of their packs and then devolve that leadership to their maturing teenage pups, who are permitted to make key decisions about where to hunt, whom to hunt, and when to move the pack. These teenage wolves, commonly thought of as subordinate individuals, soon undertake long exploratory journeys on their own during which they enjoy unlimited personal freedom, going far off-leash, so to speak, as they find their own way through wild country, hunt their own food, and learn about the world without the influence of their parents.

Moreover, it has been discovered that when these young wolves return to their packs, it is they who do most of the pack's hunting, since the peak physical abilities of a wolf begin to decline at about three years of age. Contrary to popular belief, it's these young wolves who often get to eat first, their parents, the alpha wolves, waiting for them to have first dibs. Eventually, some of these young wolves disperse and become the leaders of their own packs, just as human children go off to lead their own lives and found their own families.

The freedom and autonomy that these young wolves experience has a noticeable physiological effect. They have lower levels of stress hormones than do the alpha wolves of their pack—the opposite of what has been found in captive wolves. The stress of guarding infant pups and defending the pack's territory against other wolf packs has been theorized to place a strain on the alpha pair, whereas their teenagers enjoy a rather carefree life, roaming, hunting, and playing.

This is the important point for all of us who hope to give our dogs longer lives: if a dog is always kept on a leash, if it can't roam about on its own, exploring and making its own decisions — at a minimum, having off-leash time in a good-sized dog park — its stress levels may be higher than those of dogs who enjoy off-leash time, gaining both aerobic exercise and autonomy. This is especially true for those dogs — leashed or unleashed — who have humans who are always telling them what to do. These dogs may then become like subordinate wolves in zoos: picked upon by their superiors, unable to change their situation, stressed, and unhappy.

For all these reasons, I felt it crucial that Pukka have freedom to roam and make some of his own choices — something he could not do if he continued to chase wildlife. I was willing to sting him with the e-collar so he could have his freedom and the possibility of a healthier life.

No scientist has yet done a controlled study showing that dogs who have jobs — herding, hunting, guiding, therapy, search and rescue — or who get to play, explore, and make decisions on their own while off-leash live longer lives than those who don't. But the worldwide evidence from animal and human studies that inequality leads to stress — which, in turn, can lead to shorter life spans — might persuade thoughtful people to give their dogs more off-leash time.

Living in the village of Kelly — surrounded by millions of acres of wilderness — this was an easy practice to follow, first with Merle, who came to me with his roaming ways well formed, and then with Pukka, who had inherited Merle's door. I had been curious to see what Merle did with his free time, and now I was equally curious to see what Pukka did with his.

With Merle, I had tried to learn his whereabouts by surreptitiously following him, but I wasn't always successful. If he spotted me, skulking from house to house and hiding behind trees, he'd do an about-face, trot over to me, wag his tail, and say, "Fancy meeting you here, Ted," and then refuse to go on by himself. "After you, Merle," I'd say, extending a hand down the road.

"Ha-ha-ha," he'd pant and sit down. "You lead, please."

Pukka, too, was reluctant to reveal where he went and would have none of my tailing him. Lifting his head and sniffing, "Oh, Ted's nearby," he'd come running. "Ha!" he'd exclaim, finding me flattened behind a tree. "What are you doing hiding behind that tree?" He'd smell the ground around me to discover if he had missed something important. Finding nothing, he'd give me his accustomed affectionate shoulder rub, by which he'd say, "Looks as if you're going for a walk! Great. Let's go together!" Then, just as Merle had done, he'd wait to see what I had in mind.

Doubting that I could become a better spy—his nose was too good—I bought a GPS collar. With the sending unit around his neck and the receiving unit on my desk, I was able to watch a small schematic dog on the receiver's screen traveling around Kelly and leaving a red track as Pukka visited the locations whose latitudes and longitudes I had programmed into the device: A.J., Burley, and Goo's house, the creek, the Gros Ventre Bridge, the swimming hole, Buck's house, the post office, the café.

Soon I knew exactly where Pukka went and hung out and how he used our house like a hub, coming and going so often along the same routes that he wore trails through the grass. I also learned that he traveled at an average speed of 3.4 miles per hour, achieving a maximum speed of 16.4 miles per hour, and covered an average of 3.2 miles per day over a period of fourteen days while wandering around the village, that daily distance being in addition to our afternoon hike or mountain bike ride, which often amounted to another five to ten miles. He also accumulated another mile or so of high-speed sprints as I threw him a ball, a Frisbee, or a rubber bird dummy.

I was particularly impressed at how fast Pukka traveled when he was doing no more than coming and going from the house. I would watch him schematically on the GPS screen and then frequently go to the upper deck to gaze at him moving briskly across the fields, trotting effortlessly at about three times my walking pace, his mouth parted in a soft grin, his golden legs prancing, his tail erect and wagging gently, saying, "I am a dog in my kingdom, and all is well . . . all is well."

"My lightfoot lad," I would think, seeing him in his prime.

As for what he was doing on these walkabouts, the GPS led me to an answer. I could walk or mountain-bike over to where he had parked himself and watch him encouraging Christie and Hermann, an older, athletic, dog-loving couple, to play a game of fetch, or fraternizing with the tourists at the Kelly Café, or swimming in the creek.

The GPS collar also revealed Pukka's understanding of geometry. Having explored the topography of Kelly on his own, and having found the shortest way between destinations—the dog's way—he would cut the hypotenuse between two points instead of taking the way we usually drove or walked. "Huh-huh-huh," he'd exclaim to me, if I suggested taking the longer way when we were on a walk. "Follow me. It's much quicker!"

He then applied his geometrical insight to mountain biking. The first time we descended the many switchbacks of Phillips Ridge near Teton Pass, he dutifully stuck by me, racing a little ways ahead to explore. A week later, when we returned to bike the same route but going in the opposite direction, he paused behind me as we began up the switchbacks, wanting to smell something interesting. I kept going, grinding up the steep grade, and when I turned the next corner and looked back, he was nowhere to be seen. On I went, switchback after switchback through the deep forest: no Pukka.

I know some people who at this point, distressed at not being able to see their dog, would have begun calling for it and blowing a whistle, if the dog had been trained to respond to one. These people's inability to let a dog explore on its own is exasperating for the dog, who, in human terms, is reading. Have you ever tried to read a book and been with someone who interrupts you at every paragraph? That's what it's like for a dog whose person cannot bear its absence and is perpetually calling it to come. Eventually the dog—like a person kept from studying—learns less.

When I broke into the meadow near the ridge crest, there sat Pukka, directly on the trail, staring down its long final switchback to where I came out of the forest. Though he had run this trail but a single time, and despite the fact that he was now going the opposite way, he had nonetheless grasped the arrangement of its switchbacks. Cutting them all, and without being able to see me in the thick conifers, he had taken the shortest path to where I would emerge from the trees, his left brow cocked as I approached and his amused expression saying, "You'll have to go a lot faster than that to get ahead of me."

Naturally, we have to ask: Does a dog's having topographic knowledge really promote better health? In other words, do cartographers really live longer lives? As in so many things, it's not the goal that counts so much as what happens while you're achieving it. For dogs, as well as for us, having the ability to make our own decisions, at least some of the time, is the essence of autonomy, whether these decisions entail exploring fields and forests without interruption, those distant cliffs at the end of the dog beach, or those friendly dogs at the rear of the dog park rather than those at its entrance, where your human always prefers to stand and asks you to stand, too. As most of us will concede, we don't feel really good if there is not some portion of our lives in which we can lead rather than being led.

Allowing a dog to take the lead has yet another advantage: it lets the dog train itself, discovering amusements on its own. Pukka, coming from a long line of retrievers, would tirelessly use me to toss balls, sticks, and Frisbees, and to have some peace while hiking I soon enforced a no-throw rule until we reached the summit. Having learned the word "enough," he would carefully obey our uphill protocol when it came to sticks, but the first time he found a tennis ball after our no-throw agreement had been introduced, he trotted up to me, his eyes aglow with hope: "Look at this ball, Ted!" He laid it softly on the ground at my feet, sat, and gave me an imploring look. "It's not a stick, as you can see. Might you make an exception?"

We were halfway up Snow King Mountain, on the long middle switchback, and ignoring the ball, I said, "No thank you, Pukka, not till the top," and walked on. The catwalk was canted slightly toward the fall line, and the tennis ball, which had started to roll, picked up speed and went over the edge, bouncing down through the forest.

Pukka watched it disappear, turning his head this way and that as if trying to understand how a tennis ball, having not been thrown by me, was nevertheless moving away so rapidly. Suddenly, I saw a dawning realization go through his mind, the canine version of Newton seeing the apple fall: there is a force that makes balls roll downhill on their own!

Before the ball could vanish, Pukka leapt off the catwalk, hurtled down through the forest, and snagged it on the fly. He did not return directly. Instead, he ran an angling course through the trees and emerged on the catwalk about fifty yards uphill from me. Well before I reached him, he placed the ball on the edge of the catwalk and stared at me with a mischievous grin: "Look what I've discovered!" He then lowered his head and gave the ball a little push with the tip of his nose, sending it down the fall line once again. Giving me a laugh—"Hah! No-throw rule be damned!"—he hurtled down after it. After that, Pukka ignored me all the way to the summit, playing fetch with gravity as I called, "Well done!"

Like some inventors, he then applied his discovery to other fields.

As soon as the snow fell and buried all the readily available sticks, he took to pruning dead limbs from spruce trees until he found one that met his specifications — about two feet long and one inch in diameter. Running ahead of me as I skinned uphill, he would drop his stick in the powder, duck his head beneath it, balance the stick on the top of his snout, and fling it high into the air, leaping up to snag it. Occasionally, after an especially spectacular leap and catch, he'd pause and look back to me, wagging his tail — "Did you see that one!" — and I'd applaud.

Congratulating his play had its effect. Many a day while I was at my desk, I would hear the dog door slap, and I'd soon see Pukka, having found a ball or a stick, flinging it into the air and catching it, running back and forth among the aspen trees, diverting himself for an hour or so and getting exercise while I did not.

The only thing that worried me about his playing fetch solitaire was that he would sometimes get so engrossed in chasing his ball that he'd dash into the road after it. In Merle's day, such behavior wouldn't have given me a second thought, but since that time the village had doubled in size, a dozen new homes having been built, one of them being my own. Some of these new residents had had children, and the children had become teenagers who now drove. Most of these people also commuted to Jackson to work, since there's no public transportation between Kelly and Jackson, and like rural people nationwide, we shopped online, as the nearest truly complete shopping center was three hundred miles away in Salt Lake City. Online shopping meant UPS and FedEx deliveries. Adding to this traffic were the cars, trucks, and vans of the service people, whom an increasing number of Kelly's new residents hired to do what many of us used to do for ourselves — clean our homes, mow the grass, plow the snow, and paint and stain our structures.

Unfortunately, it wasn't only the amount of traffic that had increased, so too had its speed. Cars are a lot quieter than they used to be, and they have far more distractions in them — like good sound systems and cell phones — that take one's mind away from how fast one is going. Writing in my office, one window of which faces Kelly's main road, I could see this firsthand: cars reaching thirty, forty, and sometimes forty-five miles per hour as they zoomed down Kelly's long, straight, narrow stretch of blacktop between the cattle guard at the entrance to the village and the start of the gravel road by the bridge over the Gros Ventre River.

This, of course, was the road upon which Merle had lain, greeting incoming and outgoing cars, where Pukka chased his ball and sometimes also lay, waiting for me to return from a bicycle ride, and where A.J., Burley, Goo, and Buck played, lounged, and walked. It was also the road where other village dogs ambled, people rode their horses, mothers pushed their kids in strollers, old people tottered along on ski poles, and deer, elk, moose, and bison meandered, the latter having lived in Kelly long before it had a human name. Forty miles per hour doesn't seem fast, but when this much animal and human traffic is on a road, it's fast indeed, and there were some close calls.

One might say, as some motorists do, that "roads are for cars" and that consequently human and animal traffic should make way. And this is exactly what has happened the world over as pedestrian space has given way to vehicular space, with increasingly grave consequences to the health of both people and dogs, consequences that go far beyond being struck by a vehicle. As recent studies have found, when neighborhood walkability declines, the number of hours people spend in front of their TVs goes up, as does the amount of time they sit in automobiles, driving to places they once reached on foot. Many of us also spend our working lives deskbound, in front of computers, giving us about fourteen hours of sitting opportunities each and every workday. And while most of us are working at our desks, watching TV, or driving in our cars, it's safe to say that our dogs are not being exercised unless they have a dog walker, since most communities do not allow dogs to roam about on their own.

This amount of sitting and lying about is unprecedented in the evolutionary history of both people and dogs, and our bodies, strange as it may seem, object to this much rest, at least on a biochemical level. The muscle inactivity that sitting produces leads to elevated levels of several biomarkers—blood glucose levels, lipase, triglycerides, and C-reactive protein—all of which have been associated with an increased risk for diabetes, heart disease, and cancer.

Sitting also makes individuals fatter, and not merely because they aren't getting vigorous exercise. This is one of the more startling revelations of recent research on sedentary behavior: we can be getting our thirty minutes of vigorous exercise each day, as recommended by many governmental health agencies, and yet still be what researchers have begun to call "an active couch potato." During the rest of the day, while we sit, our blood vessels lose most of the enzyme that captures fat from the bloodstream so it can be burned up by muscle. And the longer we sit, the larger the accumulation of blood glucose, triglycerides, and inflammation. These findings have prompted exercise physiologists and governmental health agencies to recommend that everyone get up from their chairs for a couple of minutes every hour, in addition to their daily aerobic exercise, because the simple act of standing and moving around helps to lower all the previously mentioned biomarkers implicated in the development of chronic diseases.

Our dogs, though, haven't read these recommendations. They are snoozing at home while we stand up and stretch at our workstations, walk down to lunch and back up several flights of stairs, and then drive home to give them their short evening walks in neighborhoods that have become overwhelmed with cars, road noise, and exhaust fumes. Wanting to give our dogs more off-leash time without endangering their lives, some of us put our dogs into our cars and drive them to the dog park, where we stand around, talking with our friends while our dogs finally get real exercise.

Counterintuitively, people and dogs in urban neighborhoods may actually get more daily exercise than those in the suburbs, as urban people use cars less and have more shopping opportunities close at hand. Clearly, creating more dog- and people-friendly neighborhoods, which encourage walking and make it pleasurable, would go a long way toward improving the health of both people and dogs.

Kelly, of course, was still one of the more dog-friendly places on Earth, surrounded by oceans of open space. Nonetheless, a lot of people and dogs preferred to use its single road because it was convenient, especially in the winter when the surrounding open space became inaccessible for people who did not ski or snowshoe. I was therefore not thrilled to see our village's single road becoming dominated by cars, and so I called the sheriff's department, asking if they would enforce the speed limit. I was told that the speed limit could not be enforced since Kelly, being an unincorporated village, had no posted speed limit. If we got the Wyoming Department of Transportation to put up signs, fulfilling the legal requirement to tell motorists what the speed limit was, the sheriff's department would enforce it.

And so we got WYDOT to help us erect some signs, each of them saying fifteen miles per hour, with the well-recognized silhouettes of walking schoolchildren beneath the numerals. The signs did absolutely no good. People sped by them as if they weren't there, and the sheriffs, summoned to enforce the now-posted fifteen-mile-per-hour speed limit, had more pressing matters to deal with than to drive out to sleepy Kelly and sit in their cars with a radar gun.

Clearly, the problem we faced with these speeding drivers was similar to the one that I had faced with Pukka's chasing wildlife. There was no practical way to influence the speeding drivers when they were actually barreling down Kelly's narrow little road, their minds elsewhere. Many of these drivers had dogs and children of their own and would readily have acknowledged, if reminded, that they were going too fast. In fact, some of the most habitual offenders were mothers themselves. They would drop off their children at the Kelly elementary school, and a few minutes later — with a baby strapped in the car seat behind them and the dog grinning behind its grate — they would blast back out of Kelly, gabbing on their cell phones.

One day, as I sat typing on the upper deck of my house and watched the fifth soccer mom speed by, I thought, "They need e-collars." If I could only convince the speeding drivers to wear e-collars, I mused, I could sit up here and sting those who exceeded the fifteen-mile-per-hour speed limit. A luscious thought. And, a moment later, I saw how it could be done.

I walked down the main road and canvassed every homeowner who lived on it, asking them if they, too, were annoyed by the speeding drivers. Virtually every homeowner said that he or she was annoyed — "annoyed" being a much toned-down version of the words some of my neighbors used to describe how they felt about their dogs, children, horses, spouses, and themselves being endangered by the speeding drivers' thoughtlessness. Every single person agreed that e-collaring the drivers was a fabulous idea.

And that's exactly what we did: we erected three speed bumps along the main road, and the results were stunning. Overnight, cars that had been speeding along at thirty to forty miles per hour began to drive at fifteen miles per hour, just as posted by the signs. The drivers had not grown more observant or more considerate of pedestrians and animals. Going faster than fifteen miles per hour over the speed bumps caused their cars to buck like broncos. That was the "sting," the speed bumps proving—as they have done in communities around the world—to be one of the most inexpensive and maintenance-free ways of changing the behavior of speeding drivers and creating more dog- and people-friendly neighborhoods.

It's true that there are communities where speed bumps can't be installed. These neighborhoods have main thoroughfares going through them, commerce is important to all of us, and we're not going to return the entire world to the speed of dogs and horses. Yet even under these circumstances, dogs can be given more freedom than they have, as one reader near Philadelphia pointed out to me. He and his neighbors—living on completely fenced, half-acre properties—installed dog doors in the rear entrances of each of their homes as well as in the fences between their yards. Prior to the installation of the dog doors, each dog had to spend weekdays by itself. Now they could come and go as they wished, visiting their friends next door and beyond, traveling across several acres of communal fenced dogdom, swimming in one of the pools, going in and out of various homes, and conducting their own affairs—completely safe from nearby speeding traffic—while their people were at work.

This is a clever way to give dogs more room in suburban settings. Yet having several fenced properties connected by dog doors, while certainly better than a single fenced yard, still doesn't provide that much ground for an active healthy dog. That most iconic of dog names, Rover, it must be recalled, was not bestowed by accident.

How, then, might we give our dogs more room to rove? Communities whose roads have speed bumps and end in cul-de-sacs might consider fencing their entire neighborhood and then letting the dogs roam free, the fence protecting them from faster-moving traffic beyond the dog-friendly quarter. There are gated communities for golf lovers and horse lovers—why not gated communities devoted to dog lovers?

The short, practical, and litigious answer is that golfers and equestrians don't attack wildlife or people and packs of free-roaming dogs sometimes do. Well-publicized attacks on humans occurred in Sicily in 2009 and in the Navajo Nation in the southwestern United States in 2011. These incidents were tragic, but have to be put in perspective. The dogs involved in these attacks were either strays without a human home or the dogs of people who lacked the resources and inclination to teach their dogs good behavior—everything from being gentle with children to displaying politeness to other dogs, to not chasing cats, wildlife, livestock, or humans.

All of these behaviors can be instilled by people who have their dogs' welfare at heart and would like their dogs to enjoy more freedom. Such people take the time and effort to ensure that their dogs learn right behavior, which then becomes a long invisible leash, held by the dog itself. Moreover, as an increasing number of a community's dogs acquire such right behavior, the more such good behavior will be learned by dogs who haven't yet acquired it, for the simple reason that dogs learn by watching each other. Peer pressure — as when Pukka watched Buck and learned to bark — is amazingly powerful, in both humans and dogs.

One summer day I had the chance to witness such canine peer pressure, the positive kind, in action. I was typing at my desk and was startled to see the reflection of two running horses in my windows. Horses who have escaped their corrals are not a usual sight in Kelly, and so I went to the great room to investigate, only to find that our two guest dogs visiting from out of state — swift, compact mixed-breeds, one reddish-brown, the other golden — were chasing the pair of escaped horses across the lawn. On the deck sat Pukka, A.J., Burley, and Goo, soberly watching the chase unfold only twenty yards from them. As I came out of the door all four dogs turned their heads to me with looks that said, "Chasing horses is not allowed, is it?"

"No," I replied, "it's absolutely forbidden. No chasing horses."

Vindicated, and with stony faces, the four of them looked back to the two dogs nipping at the heels of the fleeing horses. A few moments later, the two visiting dogs cornered the horses against some nearby evergreens.

With huge grins, our two visitors glanced back to us, very pleased with themselves — "See what we did!" — and were met by our icy stares.

If two dogs ever wilted in their fur, those two dogs did. "Chance, Spencer," I called. "Come." They looked at the horses they had just captured; they stared back to me and the other dogs: was it possible that they were being reprimanded for having rounded up these huge magnificent beasts?

"Come," I called again, my tone saying, "I mean it." Reluctantly, they trotted to us, sat down on the deck, and looked from me, to the horses, and then to their four new dog friends, who glared daggers at them.

"*No . . . chasing . . . horses,*" I declared and walked inside.

Pukka, A.J., Burley, and Goo turned their backs on our two visitors and padded after me. A moment later, our two guests followed us into the house, walking with mincing steps, clearly embarrassed and puzzled. Strange as it seemed, here was a place where a dog could run free, yet dog speed was sometimes no speed at all.

CHAPTER EIGHTEEN

The Bad Good Death

C HANCE AND SPENCER, our two horse-chasing house-
guests, came to Kelly in a very roundabout way. I would not
have met either of them had I not remained troubled by having bought a dog from a breeder instead of adopting one from a shelter.
Hanging up the phone after getting another progress report on Abby's
pregnancy from Doug Radloff in Minnesota, I continued to wonder if
I had done the right thing.

The reassurances that I gave myself as I awaited Pukka's birth—my
two childhood dogs had come from shelters, Merle had been a stray,
and all four of my cats had been shelter cats or strays—didn't alleviate
what I felt to be a moral stone in my boot. All the animals to whom I
had given a home were long gone. What about those in the present?
I could keep walking on that stone or try to do something about it. I
was certain, however, that simply telling Doug that I didn't want one
of Abby's puppies, and then getting a shelter dog, was not a sufficient
response to these millions of needless deaths. Something more was
required. In light of the quest that I'd undertaken, could I really write
a book about longer-lived dogs and not try to understand the system
that killed so many of them young? And wouldn't all of us, even those
who have adopted a dog, like to know if there's a better way to reduce
these shelter deaths faster than one dog at a time?

It was with the hope of answering these questions that I set off for
southern California before Abby gave birth to Pukka. I chose southern
California because I had other dog-related research to do there, but
even had I gone to some other place in North America, I would have
found much the same story. The challenge faced by thousands of US

and Canadian shelters, both urban and rural, is the same: they receive more dogs and cats than they can place in new homes.

These animals are surrendered for two main reasons. First, people move and can't take their dogs with them. Second, people have no idea, financially or behaviorally, what caring for a dog entails — puppies and active breeds in particular. In more rural times, puppies had all the outdoors in which to do their business, and active breeds — herders, retrievers, and shepherds — could be left outside on their own. In today's urban world, puppies soil the house, and adult dogs, bored out of their minds for lack of exercise, bark and chew furniture, and the result is that their people — who may have started out with all the good intentions in the world — become disappointed, frustrated, and overwhelmed, in just about that order, and surrender their dogs, sometimes to the very shelter from which they were adopted.

The job of shelters is made even more challenging by feral cats and stray dogs. Never having lived with people, these animals are swept up by animal control agencies and then must be socialized, an often difficult task if they are beyond adolescence and set in their ways.

As we walked through the grounds of the Los Angeles County Downey Animal Care Center, John Embery, its manager, related these facts to me. John, a tall, silver-haired man with a small gray mustache, had been doing shelter work since 1984, and in his mild and informative voice he described the operation of the shelter, his tone pitched somewhere between that of a kindly headmaster giving a tour of his boarding school and a funeral director explaining the sad but necessary details that attend the end of life.

Here was the kennel building, a low-roofed yellow shed, one of several on the two-acre compound, labeled CAUTION: OBSERVATION DOGS (these were dogs who had bitten someone). Here was the kennel for SICK, INJURED, AND NURSING MOTHERS, here the one for STRAY MALE DOGS, and there the one for STRAY FEMALES. We passed several wheelbarrows laden with forty-pound bags of kibble waiting to be distributed, and finally came to the last building, this one for AVAILABLE ANIMALS — dogs who had passed the legally mandated five-day holding period during which an owner could claim them and who were now available for adoption.

All in all, there were about 450 dogs and cats at the shelter this sunny February day, along with some chickens, roosters, iguanas, and turtles. About ten thousand dogs and nine thousand cats came through the shelter in a year, and to make room in the cages for the daily new arrivals, those dogs and cats whose time had expired—at most about thirty days—were killed. In former times, this had amounted to about a hundred dogs and cats a day, but county-funded spay/neuter programs had brought these numbers down. Still, more dogs and cats came in than were adopted, and sometimes thirty of them were killed in a single morning. In fact, across North America, the single most important factor behind dogs dying young is that they are killed in the very facilities designed to shelter them.

As we walked by the buildings, dozens of dogs barked at us, raising their voices to be heard above their fellows—"Notice me! Take me! Here I am!"—a cacophony that increased markedly as we turned into the AVAILABLE ANIMALS building and walked down the wide concrete aisle between the two facing lines of cages. The dogs—pit bulls, many dogs resembling Chows, and mixed-breeds of every size, color, and shape imaginable except large purebred dogs—twirled, jumped, and put their paws on the chain-link fences of their cages, yipping, howling, baying, and barking, making conversation impossible. The lack of purebred dogs at Downey this morning was not unusual. Rescue organizations devoted to particular breeds visited the shelter and cherry-picked the purebred dogs, putting them up for adoption in facilities that didn't have the constant pressure of new arrivals.

Only one dog among the dozens remained silent: a young, trim, golden dog with the racy build of a Vizsla. He had a long snout and intelligent yellow eyes and stared at me silently. I couldn't help but gaze back as he stood so motionless and with such poise and dignity. His color, his steady, knowing eyes, and his collected air reminded me of Merle.

John was saying something I couldn't hear, and we walked on. Outside the shed, he repeated it for me: "By June or July, we can have up to six or seven hundred animals at the shelter. The cats are all having their babies, and dogs are out more during the summer, running."

"Must be noisy," I said.

He arched his eyebrows toward heaven, which I took to mean: "You wouldn't believe it."

We crossed a wide courtyard and reached the back of the complex where one last building stood, parallel to the administrative center at the front gate and, like it, perpendicular to the kennels, boxing them in and giving the shelter the air of a compound. One wing of this building

housed the veterinary facilities as well as a small photo room with a
green carpet upon which animals were photographed for the shelter's
website.

A good photo of a smiling dog markedly improved its chances of
adoption, John explained, and indeed, many were adopted every
day, but the shelter's balance sheet — more dogs admitted than were
adopted — inevitably led to the surplus being killed, particularly the
pit bulls. John's voice became resigned. These dogs — a grab bag of
American Pit Bull Terriers, Bull Terriers, and American and Stafford-
shire Terriers, as well as all the mixes that had been bred from these
breeds — had become the dog of choice for tough young men in America's inner cities. They weren't necessarily bad dogs, but they were
strong dogs, and when trained to be aggressive, they could do damage.
"We have a large population of pit bulls, and a good majority of those
aren't placeable," he said. "They've been used for fighting. They're not
ready to go into someone's home. We do have some rescue groups that
will take them, but the population is so high that they can't take all of
them."

We walked across an airy concrete foyer, lined with cages and with a
high ceiling, and stood before an unmarked door. A great many of the
pit bulls ended up right here — he reached out and opened the door to
the killing room, a white cinder-block cubicle without windows and lit
by overhead fluorescent lighting. A stainless steel gurney stood against
the adjacent wall; there was a drain in the floor; on a small table in the
corner were needles and syringes along with latex gloves and bottles
of "Fatal-Plus," the vivid blue solution of sodium pentobarbital that is
widely use to euthanize dogs, cats, and laboratory animals. There was
also a razor among the instruments, to shave the front leg of the dog or
cat so the vet tech could easily find a vein and insert the needle. Hanging on the other side of the door, and clipped to the wall, was a six-
foot-long pole with a padded wire loop at its end, called a Ketch-All,
employed, John said, to restrain dogs who were hard to handle. All the
dogs, no matter how small, were muzzled before they were killed. Behind the gurney was a second door, leading to a walk-in freezer where
the dead dogs and cats were stored until they could be picked up by the
rendering truck.

"That's it," said John.

We walked out, and he told me that he had to go back to his office.
I sat on a bench in the sunshine, just outside the door to the concrete

foyer, and waited for the animal control officers to lead the condemned dogs across the compound. As the line began, I followed the dogs in. The first to be killed was a white-and-brown pit bull, low-slung and with the rolling gait of a sailor. He was held by a tall, fit, African American man, who, with his chiseled, sober features and pressed khaki uniform, looked like a soldier doing an unpleasant but necessary job. Standing several feet from the door of the killing room, he ran a microchip scanner over the pit bull one final time. The dog didn't have one, and as the tall ACO led him on, the dog walked happily and with a big smile on his broad face: "Oh boy, taking a stroll at last!"

At the door he was met by one of the shelter's three registered veterinary technicians, each of whom rotated through the jobs of spaying and neutering, routine medical care, and killing the daily batch of dogs and cats. Today it was the turn of Ehab Gad, a dark-skinned man of medium height, with gelled black hair, his friendly grin showing widely spaced yellow teeth. He wore a hip-length blue smock and spoke with a Hispanic accent.

Making smooching noises with his tongue, Ehab petted the white-and-brown pit bull, gave him a visual once-over, and stepped aside so the ACO could lead him into the killing room. The door closed behind them — this was as far as I was allowed to observe — and outside the work of the shelter continued: laborers hosing down the cement runs between the cages and ferrying the wheelbarrows of kibble to the different kennels; in the parking lot a horse trailer was hitched to a pickup truck to fetch a horse escaped from its corral in a rural neighborhood; and above everything, the barks and howls and mournful bays of the hundreds of dogs.

The door opened. The pit bull lay motionless on the stainless steel gurney, covered by a blanket, from which its lower legs stuck out. No more than a few minutes had gone by. Another white-and-brown pit bull was led in by a very large, heavyset ACO, his head shaved and his face as somber as his colleague's. The dog was scanned and examined quickly, and, wagging his tail and panting happily, he trotted into the killing room.

The next dog, with a strong resemblance to a Beagle, seemed tense as he received his welcoming pat and visual once-over from Ehab. As the vet tech stepped aside so the tall ACO could lead him through the door, the Beagle raised his nose and sniffed the air. That was all he needed. He planted his front paws and tucked his tail between his legs.

Struggling, his claws scraping the concrete, he was dragged through the door.

On they came, led by the two male ACOs and a plump Latina, dressed in the same khaki uniform as her male colleagues, her young, kindly face framed by abundant black curls. While one dog was inside the room, she crouched by the adjacent sink with a white pit bull, a female whose ears had been chewed off and whose teats hung low, as if she had been recently nursing. The dog rubbed her head against the woman's chest, made a playful little yip, and rolled on her back. The woman rubbed her belly, and the dog pumped her paws joyfully in the air. I, too, reached down and stroked her belly.

The door opened, Ehab gave the white pit bull a quick glance and stepped aside so she could be led in. The heavyset ACO came into the foyer with the next dog, a handsome though mangy-looking fellow with the features of a Chow. I asked the ACO why the female pit bull, so recently nursing, hadn't been spared. "She's unplaceable," he said. "People just don't want dogs like that. And she's aggressive, unpredictable. She tried to bite me last week."

The procession continued: a matted sheepdog, shuffling along like an aristocrat fallen upon hard times, his black-and-white coat patchy and threadbare; several sprightly Chihuahuas, scampering into the killing room as if going to a ball; a handsome mastiff, who looked old but perfectly healthy; a sleek silver pit bull, young and strong and trembling violently as he ignored my petting, his eyes hanging upon the door—it opened and he was dragged inside; a Lab-shepherd cross, shaking convulsively and defecating; a piebald pit bull who, as the door opened, sent me an imploring gaze—"You just petted me, why don't you do something?"—before she, too, was dragged inside, fighting the whole way, her claws scraping the concrete.

After that I had to leave. I sat on the wooden bench and looked at the trees and the blue California sky while the enormity of what was happening inside that cinder-block room, and across LA County and in animal shelters throughout North America, sat upon me like a thunderhead of tears.

I blinked them away and walked back inside. A torn-up pit bull was brought in by the soldierly ACO and scanned. The man's face jumped in surprise—the wand displayed a microchip's number. Someone had actually implanted a microchip in this battered street dog. It was as if the dog's defense attorney had presented exculpatory evidence at the eleventh hour, and the pit bull was led back to his kennel, walking reluctantly — "Bummer, I just got outta my cage!" — his five-day clock restarted as the shelter began to trace the chip's data and attempt to locate his owner.

The heavyset ACO brought in a Chow-like dog with a long golden coat. She waited with the patient air of a well-socialized dog, and I glanced at the paperwork he held in his free hand. Her name was Lady, and she had been surrendered by her owner, who could no longer take care of her. Through the door she went — not merely in apparently perfect health, but also with a graceful and mannered walk, the leash hanging loosely in the ACO's hand — and a moment later the door opened and back out she came, not flustered in the least by her brush with death. "She's nice," Ehab explained to me, "and young and healthy, and she passed the temperament test."

"What is the temperament test?" I asked, suddenly realizing that one final step had been going on behind the closed door, one last thumbs-up or thumbs-down that I had not been able to witness.

"I open their mouths," said Ehab, "and see how they react."

Obviously, Lady had been a lady.

At last, the cats were brought in, all in their boxes, waiting patiently as cats do. One after the other they were taken into the cinder-block room and killed. And then it was over. Thirty-three dogs had come into the concrete foyer, nine had gone back to their cages for another chance to find a home. Seven cats were on the list to be killed; six had been dispatched.

Ehab Gad began to clean up his instrument table, and I asked him about the Chihuahuas. They were small dogs; LA was an urban place; they seemed perfectly suited for big-city adoptions. Why had they been killed?

"No one is going to adopt them," he said. "We have just too many."

"What about the pit bull," I asked, "who looked like she was nursing puppies?"

"Someone — a rescue group maybe — adopted the puppies already," he replied. And then he repeated what the heavyset ACO had told me. She was aggressive, and he didn't want to take a chance of her biting someone.

I thought of Michael Vick's dogs — the pit bulls the football star had used for fighting, had tortured, and who after his arrest had been deemed incapable of being rehabilitated by PETA (People for the Ethical Treatment of Animals). The organization stated that the dogs had suffered too much cruelty, could never lead normal lives, and would be better off dead. Others disagreed, including a team of animal behaviorists led by the ASPCA, who evaluated the dogs and found only one out of the fifty dogs too violent to be nurtured back to normal life. This dog was killed, and another was euthanized for medical reasons. Two more dogs died while waiting in shelters during the court proceedings. As for the rest, all forty-six of Michael Vick's pit bulls have now been placed in new homes and are living with families and children, or they're at animal sanctuaries on friendly terms with handlers they know and trust, some of the dogs working toward the day when they may be adopted. The major difference between Michael Vick's pit bulls and the thousands of pit bulls who are killed each year in American shelters is the fame of their person and the infamy of his deeds, both of which brought his dogs the care that shelters like Downey — with their ever-pressing number of new admissions and tight budgets — don't give their dogs.

"This must be very hard for you," I said to Ehab Gad as he finished cleaning up the instrument table and stowed the blue bottles of Fatal-Plus.

"Yeah," he replied. "I don't like it, but you know sometimes we have to do it. That's our job." He gave me his friendly gap-toothed grin.

I thanked him and walked outside, leaving the compound by its side service gate and finding a shady tree under which to sit and breathe some fresh air while I waited for the rendering truck to arrive. I sat, and I waited, and I watched the dogs in the AVAILABLE ANIMALS building through the chain-link fence. They had noticed me walk along the fence and sit down, and they had come forward in their cages and begun to bark at me, not confrontationally, but in the way all the dogs in the shelter barked at passersby: "Notice me!" All except one: the handsome golden dog who had caught my eye as John Embery and I walked through the kennel earlier that morning. Like Merle, he was a shape-shifter, and he now appeared to be more Ridgeback than Vizsla. He also seemed young, only ten or twelve months old, yet he held himself erect, cool and self-possessed amid the bedlam.

He had met my gaze before, and he did so again, his face and piercing yellow eyes glowing in the sun. We held each other's stare for several moments, and then he woofed at me, just once, very softly and politely, saying, "I see you over there." A moment later, he extended his forelegs and gave me a play-bow, wagging the tip of his raised tail: "I'd like it if you came over here and said hello."

I went back through the fence and walked down the aisle between the cages until I was even with his. He came through his dog door from the outside and approached me without rush, not wary, but decorous, leaning his body against the wire of the cage. I petted him as I could, just scratching his ruff through the chain-link fencing, and then I let him smell my fingers. He sniffed them delicately, giving them a soft lick.

"I'll be back," I told him and went to find John Embery.

The shelter manager was in his office, and I said, "Can I take the dog in cage 413 for a walk?" He said of course I could and got me a rope with a slip noose at its end, and together we walked back to the AVAIL-ABLE ANIMALS kennel.

The dog let me slip the noose over his head, and he followed me down the concrete aisle, stepping gingerly outside and looking around warily.

Only yesterday he had been led away and neutered, and I said, "Not to worry. We're just going for a walk."

I led him out the sliding gate and across the asphalt parking lot, and the instant his paws sank into the grassy berm he put his nose deep into the grass, took a lungful, and leapt high into the air, making a joyous clutching noise in his throat as if his heart would burst with happiness. Landing lightly, he gave another great leap, turned in mid-air, and kissed me on the mouth. We walked along the grass, and he smelled and smelled and smelled, as if drinking water that had been long denied him. Then he paused and gazed at the cars going by and the trees and the sky.

While he looked around, I knelt by him and put my nose into his ruff. He smelled of urine and some high-powered, antiseptic cleaner. Beneath those smells, however, was the smell of himself: dry and sweet and a little nutty.

John was watching me. I stood up, and we walked over to him, the dog walking by my side. "I don't want him killed," I said. "If no one adopts him, I'll come get him."

The three of us walked back inside the sliding gate, and I handed John the leash.

"I'll call you," said John, "before we do anything." He led the golden dog toward the kennel building, and as soon as the dog saw where he was going, he put out his front paws, slammed his tail between his legs, and began to struggle violently. John had to drag him through the door and all the way back to his cage.

Animal shelters like the one in Downey, California, are barely a century and a half old, the first having been created in London in 1860 by Mary Tealby. Called the Temporary Home for Lost and Starving Dogs, it was popularized by Charles Dickens and moved to its present location in Battersea, on the south side of the Thames, where it still shelters and rehomes dogs and cats today. America's first shelter for dogs and cats, Philadelphia's City Refuge for Lost and Suffering Animals, was founded by Caroline Earl White in 1874. She, too, had been inspired by the previous century's emancipatory spirit, embodied in the American and French Revolutions, the abolition of slavery throughout the British Empire in 1833, and the American Civil War.

It took little stretch of the imagination for intellectuals like her to apply the ideals of freedom and brotherhood to the care of animals. The Royal Society for the Prevention of Cruelty to Animals was founded in 1840 in London, and its American offshoot, the ASPCA, was established in 1866 in New York. Its creator, Henry Bergh, the scion of a shipping family, used his wealth and influence to champion the cause of animals, lobbying the state legislature to swiftly pass an anticruelty statute that gave the ASPCA the power to enforce it. He then roamed New York City with his staff of three, operating a horse ambulance, putting out drinking water for draft animals, and nabbing animal abusers.

Stray dogs did not fare as well. Despised because of their frequent barking and the rabies they might carry, they became the targets of roving bands of thugs who made their living as dog catchers — the city paid a bounty of fifty cents for every dog they captured. Even owned dogs were snatched on their morning strolls and taken to the Brooklyn pound, where they were kept in a rough-and-tumble shed by the East River. Each day all the unclaimed dogs were crammed into a large iron cage that was swung over the river by a boom and plunged into the water for six minutes.

This barbaric treatment of dogs was steadily outlawed as SPCAs and humane societies sprang up across the United States and helped to enact anticruelty laws in thirty-seven out of the thirty-eight states by 1888. Today the best-known of these organizations is the Humane

Society of the United States, but it's a relatively new arrival on the animal welfare scene, having been founded in 1954.

As these SPCAs became a recognized part of American society, many communities began to see them as a means of solving their stray dog problems. They contracted with local SPCAs or humane societies to do their animal control. Henry Bergh had not allowed the ASPCA to take on such duties, believing that collecting stray dogs and cats and then putting them to death would taint the organization's original mission of giving succor to animals. But six years after his death in 1888, the ASPCA accepted New York City's animal control contract and soon replaced the drowning of dogs and cats with what was considered the more humane method of the gas chamber. Eventually, asphyxiating dogs and cats was widely supplanted by killing them with an injection of sodium pentobarbital. Not surprisingly, and as Henry Bergh had feared, this dual mission created a confusion of aims that continues to trouble the animal welfare movement to this day, most notably in referring to the practice of killing healthy animals as "euthanasia."

Like many English words, the word *euthanasia* comes from the Greek and literally means "the good death." Historically, the term was narrowly applied to the practice of ending a life filled with pain or suffering, but during the latter part of the twentieth century the meaning of euthanasia was broadened to include the killing of healthy dogs and cats who had been surrendered to or collected by animal shelters.

The person most responsible for initiating and then encouraging this practice was Phyllis Wright, who worked for the Humane Society of the United States as its director for companion animal care from 1969 to 1991. A dog trainer for the US Army during the Korean War and a champion of spay/neuter programs, Wright published one of the most influential essays of the animal shelter movement in the summer of 1978. It appeared in *The Humane Society News*, a publication of HSUS, and was called "Why Must We Euthanize." In it Wright advanced the position that it was our duty to euthanize healthy animals so as to release them from suffering. "We know that death, humanely administered, is not an evil," she wrote, "but a blessing to animals that are of no comfort to themselves or to the world because they are unwanted and suffering in isolation." Her argument hinged on the notion of companionship. "Where does your dog and cat like to be?" she asked. "They like to be where you are," she answered. Without such companionship — confined to a small cage or chained on a porch — animals, she claimed, suffered. "Being dead is not a cruelty to animals," she therefore concluded, and she put her beliefs into practice with extraordinary zeal. As she stated in her essay, she had, at the time of its publication, personally euthanized seventy thousand animals.

Wright's argument was embraced by many shelter workers. She had the bully pulpit of HSUS behind her and, at first glance, her logic seemed sound: animals didn't like to be confined; there weren't enough homes for all the animals in shelters; therefore we had the moral obligation to alleviate the suffering of dogs and cats through a painless death. Wright was also widely admired as a tireless crusader. She testified at the local and state levels about the evils of the decompression chamber and the need to replace it with the more humane method of lethal injection. For several generations of shelter workers, she became a mentor and hero. As Martha Armstrong, one of HSUS's senior vice presidents, recalls, "She was known as 'Mother Wright.' We all learned at her knee."

Wright's star has faded — her essay can no longer be found through an Internet search, and her biography has been stripped from the HSUS website — yet killing healthy animals in North American shelters goes on, albeit not with the fervor with which it was once practiced. The number of dogs and cats killed in North American shelters has fallen — from about 23 million in 1970 to between 3 million and 4 million today — thanks in part to programs that Wright herself championed: mandating dog licenses and prohibiting free-roaming dogs; educating the public about what has been called "the pet overpopulation problem" and the concomitant need to spay and neuter dogs; and sterilizing all animals who come from shelters.

Important as these programs have been, they have failed to address the underlying assumption of Wright's day — in short, that killing dogs and cats was the most effective way to control the population of those animals who ended up in shelters. Nor have these programs addressed Wright's two other major premises: that dogs and cats suffer so much when confined that they prefer death to waiting for their freedom, a premise that effectively strips them of hope; and that they are always happiest by our sides, an assumption easily demolished by anyone who watches feral cats or who visits the developing world, where stray dogs revel in their own company.

It took three out-of-the-box thinkers to point out that homes could be found for the majority of animals who were being killed in shelters, if shelters changed how they did business. One of these men was Edward S. Duvin, a writer and founder of a variety of social welfare movements, whose 1989 essay "In the Name of Mercy" provided a comprehensive critique of how shelters were managed at that time and in many cases still are: without maintaining standards, without keeping statistics, and without screening employees.

Duvin's essay eventually became the cri de coeur of the shelter reform movement, but others had already been putting some of his ideas into practice. In 1976, Rich Avanzino—a California attorney, pharmacist, and lobbyist for the state's professional pharmacist association—was hired by the San Francisco SPCA to put the shelter on a sound financial footing.

Avanzino was a critical thinker, an affable networker, and a skilled manager. He was also an adherent of Henry Bergh's belief that shelters should in fact be sanctuaries, and he inaugurated protocols that have become widely adopted by shelters determined to reduce their kill rate. Instead of asking people to have their dogs and cats sterilized *after* adopting them, he had the animals sterilized *before* they left the shelter. For those who already had dogs and cats, he started inexpensive spay/neuter clinics so that low-income families would be more willing to sterilize their pets. (The first low-cost spay/neuter clinic had been established in Los Angeles in 1971.) He then initiated what proved to be a linchpin in reducing the kill rate of healthy animals: a foster care program that used community goodwill, in the form of a cadre of local volunteers, to house very young kittens and puppies until they were old enough, or healthy enough, to go to their long-term homes. In many shelters, young animals were typically killed immediately, and in many shelters they still are.

Avanzino's foster care program not only helped to advertise dogs and cats to people who wouldn't have normally come to the shelter; it also made the shelter money. The shelter no longer had to pay the costs of killing young animals and disposing of their bodies, and when they were placed directly from their foster homes, the shelter received the adoption fees.

Avanzino implemented two more programs that in retrospect seem so obvious that it's astonishing they weren't put into place before. First, he took the dogs and cats to the people instead of hoping that the people would come to the shelter. Loading dogs and cats in a van, he set up booths around the city and began off-site adoptions. Second, he kept the shelter open on evenings and weekends, when working people actually had the time to visit and adopt a pet. This strikingly simple move — opening the shelter at times that are convenient for the working public to visit — has still not been instituted by many shelters.

With revenues up as a result of increased adoptions and donations, he was able to bankroll two more expensive programs. He began to treat sick and injured animals, and he hired animal trainers to correct behavioral problems, so as to make animals who would have been deemed unplaceable attractive candidates for adoption.

By 1994 the deaths of healthy dogs and cats in the shelters of San Francisco fell to nearly zero, Avanzino having demonstrated in fewer than two decades that there was an alternative to killing millions of healthy animals. Most important, he had shown that what many shelters were calling "the pet overpopulation problem" was often a problem of marketing. Along the way he also proved that the public, long seen as the problem, was in fact a large part of the solution.

In 2001 his protégé at the San Francisco SPCA, Nathan Winograd, took these principles and exported them to Tompkins County in rural upstate New York. A former criminal prosecutor and corporate attorney, he wanted to show that what had occurred in a big liberal West Coast city could happen in Anywhere, USA. At the time, the Tompkins County shelter routinely killed animals when all its cages became full, and the day after Winograd arrived he was told by his staff that this was the situation now facing the shelter. A litter of six puppies had just been surrendered, there was no room at the inn, and he must decide which dogs were to be killed to free up some space.

After thinking it over, Winograd surprised his new coworkers by bringing horse troughs into the lobby, placing them next to the front desk, and then laying the puppies within them. As he said, "What better way to showcase those little gems, while simultaneously giving them much needed socialization?"

During the next three years, Winograd would use all the techniques that Avanzino and he had refined on the West Coast to reduce the kill rate of the Tompkins County shelter. In addition, he instituted a feral cat program known as TNR, that trapped, neutered, and released cats back to the wild, alive but unable to breed, and he fired those shelter workers whose default position was to kill animals instead of finding ways to save them. As a result, he brought the shelter's kill rate down to

7 percent of the animals admitted, terminating the lives of only those animals who were too ill or injured to be treated.

For their accomplishments, Avanzino and Winograd were not universally hailed. Their critics in the traditional shelter world claimed that their no-kill methods led to animals being left in small, filthy crates for long periods of time. Others alleged that no-kill shelters might work in wealthy urban centers, but not in poor rural America, despite what Winograd had shown in Tompkins County. Still other naysayers maintained that no-kill shelters could bill themselves as "no-kill" only because they turned away animals that the open-admission shelters of their communities were forced to take in. This, of course, had been disproved by the San Francisco SPCA, which took all comers.

Winograd left Tompkins County and in 2004 founded the No Kill Advocacy Center, dedicated to bringing about the day when no healthy or treatable animal would be killed in an American shelter. He then published a book, *Redemption: The Myth of Pet Overpopulation and the No Kill Revolution in America,* in which he put together an eleven-point program – the No Kill Equation. Highlighting the techniques that he and Avanzino had developed, the program was designed to help traditional shelters become no-kill ones, facilities that Winograd defined as taking in everyone who barked and meowed at the door and sending at least 90 percent of them back out to new homes. The most important measure that a community could take to reduce its shelter's kill rate, Winograd repeatedly emphasized, was to hire a compassionate director.

When I met him at the annual No Kill Conference in Washington, DC, in 2010 – a short man in a black polo shirt, comfortably unshaven, and with a winning grin – he told me that in order to speed the hiring of such compassionate shelter directors, he was proposing nationwide model legislation, the Companion Animal Protection Act, which would set basic standards of care and protection no matter who was running a shelter. Directors would have to meet these standards or be fired.

Over three hundred shelter workers were at the conference, hoping to learn how to transform their shelters into no-kill ones, and Nathan would soon tell them what he now told me: he was confident that a no-kill nation was just over the horizon. "Consider that 17 million people are looking for new animals each year," he said. "If we can convince just 20 percent of them to adopt from shelters, we could zero out the killing."

His old colleague Rich Avanzino, now the head of Maddie's Fund, a foundation that awards grants to organizations promoting no-kill strategies, was helping to make this happen. Maddie's was funding a massive ad campaign, called "The Shelter Pet Project," which would promote adoption to pet owners who were undecided about where to get their next dog or cat.

On one principle he would not budge. His smile faded, and he gave me a steady gaze. He refused to countenance the word *euthanasia* for the killing of healthy animals, even though he knew that his moral and semantic stance infuriated potential allies in the traditional shelter world. Some of these people continued to sanitize the deaths that happened in shelters with euphemisms. To illustrate what he meant, he played me a tape made at an HSUS workshop, where a euthanasia instructor had become incensed when one of her students brought up the subject of no-kill shelters. Exasperated, she told him, "What we have done is humanely destroy rather than *kill*. *Kill* is such a negative connotation. We're not *killing* them! We are taking their life. We're ending their life. We're giving them a good death. We're humanely destroy—whatever. But we're not *killing!* And that's why I cannot stand the term 'no-kill shelters!'"

Her attitude—not rare among shelter workers, as I discovered—is one of the reasons that a relatively small number of shelters have become no-kill: if shelter personnel believe that they're not killing dogs and cats, only giving them "a good death," there is less incentive to change how shelters operate. And in fact, as of 2012, only about two hundred US shelters could be called no-kill facilities, having met the widely accepted definition of being open-admission and saving 90 percent of the animals they receive. This is a small percentage of US shelters, which number roughly thirty-five hundred, and according to Nathan, it isn't only shelter workers defending the status quo that has slowed the pace of reform. It's also because the Humane Society of the United States, the largest and most powerful animal welfare organization in North America, hasn't supported a no-kill nation.

"How do you mean?" I asked him.

Quickly, he reeled off a list of accusations, the most significant of which included HSUS's support for shelter directors who killed animals in shocking numbers; its campaigns against TNR; its opposition to legislation that would make shelters work more efficiently; and its pessimistic estimate of the time needed to reform shelters. "Why," he asked me, "does HSUS believe that it will take until 2020 to create a no-kill nation?"

I walked the short half-mile up Twentieth Street, across Pennsylvania Avenue, and one block down L Street, where I stood in front of the glass-and-steel headquarters of the Humane Society of the United States. With 11 million members, $162 million in its coffers, and multiple campaigns to end animal cruelty and reform the livestock industries, it is one of the most influential animal welfare organizations in the world. Upstairs, I found Wayne Pacelle, HSUS's CEO, in his corner office, sitting at a large desk and dressed in a cool green summer suit, tall and closely shaved, with his cuffs shot, but without a tie in the muggy heat. After we exchanged pleasantries, I asked him what he thought of Nathan's charges.

Wayne shook his head in wounded anger. "I am the founder of the National Federation of Humane Societies," he said. "I felt that there needed to be a consortium of local humane organizations, its purpose to unite the animal welfare industry and to engage communities in homing every healthy and treatable animal entering an animal care facility nationwide by 2020. I don't know what more I can do to reform institutions than to get these institutions — the very ones that the Winograds of the world consider to be the problem — to embrace this goal."

He went on to say that he had been having discussions with his staff about the issue of no-kill, and he could categorically tell me that HSUS was moving decidedly in that direction. "A no-kill nation must be one of the greatest aspirations of this organization, but it can't be achieved overnight. There are complex social and political factors that have to be considered."

He ticked them off. Birders didn't like free-roaming cats and were backed by powerful wildlife organizations. Trapping, neutering, and releasing feral cats was therefore controversial in many communities, even though he and HSUS now stood firmly behind the concept, no matter what the organization's policy had been prior to his watch. There were also puppy mills. They were largely unregulated by the federal government and kept pumping dogs into the system, now more than ever via the Internet. Furthermore, simply firing ill-performing shelter directors, as some with whom I had been speaking proposed, would not immediately bring about the dawn of a no-kill age.

Leaning across his desk, he extended an open hand to me. "When I go to Jackson, Mississippi," he said, "and they're euthanizing 80 percent of the animals, my instinct is not to demonize these shelter workers. Rather, it is to teach them how to reduce their euthanasia rate through best management practices, through better fund-raising, through better marketing, and through better outreach."

"What about supporting legislation that removes such ill-performing shelter workers?" I asked.

"I'm a great believer in the law," he said quietly, sitting back in his chair. "However, the law doesn't have to speak in every situation." His face became contemplative, and he added, "There may be circumstances where you want your adversaries to turn into your allies down the road, and it might take five or ten years to bring them along that path."

To understand how these complex social and personal dynamics affected a shelter's operation, he suggested that I visit some shelters in the area, both good and bad, and see for myself.

CHAPTER NINETEEN

Shelters to Sanctuaries

I DROVE DOWN TO VIRGINIA, where Susanne Kogut, the director of the Charlottesville-Albemarle SPCA, had turned her facility into a no-kill one almost overnight by closely following Nathan Winograd's No Kill Equation. The shelter was newly built and looked like a gracious country inn with beige siding, a steep roof, and cozy gables overhung by shade trees. Susanne had the same air of welcoming hospitality. A slender woman in her early forties, she had an impish face, wry chocolate-brown eyes, and two long smile lines extending from her cheekbones to her jawline. She was seated at a conference table in her spacious office, her auburn hair falling on the shoulders of her black turtleneck. Gesturing with her twenty-ounce Starbucks cup toward three stray puppies playing in a corner, she said with a smile, "I take my work home with me."

Back in 2005, a group of local volunteers had wanted to find someone who would put an end to what they considered the shelter's unacceptable kill rate: 20 percent of the dogs and 53 percent of the cats who entered the facility were killed. Tired of corporate law, Susanne had applied and got the job.

Initially there had been hard times—very hard times, she conceded. "When I first came on," she told me, "the biggest barrier I had was the staff. They weren't open to change, and some of them tried to sabotage me by killing sick animals that I was determined to treat." Ignoring Wayne Pacelle's advice about turning recalcitrant staff members into allies over a span of five to ten years, she fired them directly. Almost as hard to deal with was the staff's unwillingness to try fostering out more young kittens and puppies, animals who had previously been put to death automatically.

She had overcome her staff's inertia through constant marketing. "Anything from putting out flyers," she told me, "to drafting a press release for the local paper, to putting our pleas on the TV and radio stations." Making her voice upbeat and sprightly, she said, "'We've got these kittens, and we want to save them; can someone put them in their house temporarily?'" And people came. "Mothers walked through the door," she recalled, "saying, 'My kids played with a litter of kittens at a friend's house. Can we have a litter of kittens, too?' Sure!"

Within eight months of taking over the helm at the Charlottesville-Albemarle SPCA, Susanne had tripled foster care placements. She and her crew now took in any animal who came to the door while saving 92 percent of the cats and 96 percent of the dogs, the remainder of them too ill, injured, or aggressive to be placed in a home.

Good media relations were only partially responsible for reducing the shelter's kill rate. Following Avanzino and Winograd's lead, she had gone directly to the community, throwing a party that brought in thousands of people. Fifty animals were adopted that very day. The now-annual Critter Ball had become a major fund-raising event. She and her staff also redesigned the shelter's website, enhancing it with bright friendly colors, and Sissy Spacek agreed to host a cheery promo video filled with happy children walking out of the shelter with adopted animals in their arms. Susanne partnered with a golf tournament, supported lavishly by local businesses, all the proceeds going to the SPCA. She put up links from the shelter's homepage to Facebook, to Twitter, to YouTube; she began to write a blog; and she kept the shelter open every day from noon to 6:00 P.M.

"Let's take a tour," she said.

She led me around the shelter—sparkling kennels, the dogs on raised beds to keep them off the concrete floor, a grassy quadrangle in the middle of the building where people could walk potential adoptees, and cats frisking in communal rooms with ladders and platforms. As we walked from hall to hall, we stepped into basins filled with towels soaked in disinfectant, a measure used by the shelter to stop the spread of disease. Suddenly, over the PA system, came a cheerleader's voice: "If you are currently walking Buster, could you please return him to the front desk? He's just been adopted and is ready to go home!"

Finally, we stood outside the back door, where dozens of plastic kennels were piled in stacks. Each could hold a medium-size dog, but they were empty, waiting for the surge of summertime cats who could easily overwhelm the facility's built-in cat quarters. Pointing to them, Susanne described how, soon after her arrival, several disgruntled employees had requested that the board fire her for housing the overflow of summertime cats in these large plastic pet transporters instead of killing them directly. They called such crating "inhumane." Shaking her head in disbelief, Susanne said, "What is the difference between a cage in the wall and a free-standing crate on the floor next to it? It's the same square footage. And why is it inhumane to put cats temporarily in a crate while they're awaiting adoption, but it's more humane to kill them instantly?" Again, she shook her head at what she had considered a simple, temporary, life-saving device and others considered cruel. Even when she had tried to help other shelters during busy times, she had been rebuffed.

Paulette Dean, the director of the Danville Area Humane Society—a facility in southern Virginia that killed 76 percent of the dogs and 96 percent of the cats who came under its care—had refused to send Susanne animals who were about to be killed, maintaining that Susanne was holding dogs in crates. Susanne had replied that although she temporarily kept cats in crates, she housed dogs in larger kennels, as most shelters did. She repeated her offer to take Paulette's dogs and offered to drive the 270 miles round-trip to pick them up. Susanne was still waiting for an answer. Hoping I could get one, while also seeing the challenges that stood in the way of a poor rural shelter bringing down its kill rate—Danville is far poorer than Charlottesville—I drove to southern Virginia, in fact almost to North Carolina.

Unlike Charlottesville's modern, bright, and welcoming building, set in an upscale neighborhood, the Danville shelter had been placed in a public works complex and was surrounded by a grubby landscape of dump trucks, parked school buses, and maintenance sheds. It was literally and psychologically an uphill journey to get to the shelter, a low cinder-block structure, creamy custard in color, with dogs, cats, chickens, rabbits, butterflies, and songbirds painted brightly on its outside walls. Despite its attempt at a cheerful exterior, the shelter was fighting its location and its age.

I entered a small run-down lobby, low-ceilinged and crowded with ferret and rabbit cages. A large white cockatoo perched above them, and another parrot, a Blue-and-Gold Macaw, sat on a perch in the hallway leading to the kennels. The smell was overpowering. A nose-stinging, throat-burning, eye-tearing mixture of urine, methane, and feces permeated the entire building.

Summoned by the receptionist, Paulette Dean came down the hall, a small, soundly built woman in her fifties, wearing a long black skirt and a smart blue jacket like those worn by equestrians. She had rosebud lips and sincere brown eyes, the plastic frames of her glasses matching the tints of henna in her short dark hair.

She had done secretarial work, she told me, and had been on the board of the shelter for many years. Finally, in 1991, she had become its director. As she related these personal details, she led me toward the kennels, and as we passed the Blue-and-Gold Macaw he took a ferocious swipe at my outstretched hand. I snatched it back just in time.

"We're bird people," she commented, "if you can't tell. And yes, he will take off your arm."

Opening a heavy glass-and-metal door into the cat area, she apologized for the odor, now far stronger than in the lobby. The smell was "a constant battle," she said, asking me to please keep in mind that it was a very old shelter with many problems. She was doing what she could to modernize it. With the help of donations, their small lobby was going to be renovated – it would have a cathedral ceiling – and a new no-kill wing would be built onto the present structure. In that wing, dogs who had a higher chance of being adopted would be housed without the risk of being killed to make room for others.

We visited the cats in stacked cages, and then the dogs, their kennels facing each other from either side of a cement floor. There were no raised dog beds here or cheery announcements on the loudspeaker. At times I couldn't hear what she was saying, so loud was the barking.

Our brief and deafening tour done, Paulette and I went to her office at the back of the shelter, a small cramped space, twelve feet by twelve feet, where once again she apologized, this time for the terrible mess. Her three cockatiels and her parrotlet came to work with her every day, she explained, and there were also shelter parakeets flying about. Almost every visible surface was covered with their poop. "You're welcome to sit there," she said, pointing to the one clean chair.

She then began to describe the hard realities of running her shelter on a budget of approximately $250,000, with which she had to deal with the 6,000-plus animals who had come into the shelter the previous year. By contrast, Charlottesville had a $2.5 million budget for 4,500 animals.

Daunting as that comparison appeared, some shelters in the United States spend only $1.50 per capita for the communities they serve, yet save 90 percent of their dogs and cats. Others spend as much as $6.30 per capita, but save only 60 percent of their admissions. There's no predictable pattern. At the time of my visit, the Danville area spent $4.69 per capita.

Many other factors needed to be considered besides the strict mathematics of funding, Paulette continued. For example, this was the rural South. "It's part of the United States," she told me, "but it's a different country, with different attitudes, priorities, and struggles, and these limit how effective a shelter like ours can be. This area is very uneducated and has the second- or third- highest unemployment rate in the state."

I agreed that she had some large challenges. I wondered, though, if she had tried some of the techniques that other shelters nationwide had put in place to reduce their kill rates. For example, did the shelter have an active foster care program?

"Oh my," she said, "we've tried!" The shelter had begun what she called "a semi-active foster care program," but she had soon discovered that the volunteers were lying to her, saying that the animals they took home had died when in fact they had been giving the animals away. She now did foster care on a case-by-case basis. She also put on occasional adoption fairs and took animals to PetSmart. I asked why the shelter wasn't open on weekends and at night, and she told me that they couldn't hire enough people to meet their insurance requirements.

"What if you closed one weekday," I suggested, "and opened on Saturday instead? More people might come."

"We've considered that," she replied, "and we haven't come to any conclusion."

"And wouldn't it help," I ventured, "when Charlottesville or another shelter with high adoption rates offers to take animals off your hands, that you would let them take them?"

"We do it on a case-by-case basis," she answered. In fact, she had to house animals that Charlottesville refused.

Surprised by this information, I said, "I thought Charlottesville admits all animals, just as you do."

"They consider themselves open-admission," Paulette replied, "but the animal control officers out in Albemarle County say that now when people call about unwanted cats, the philosophy of the shelter is to say that the cats are better off on the streets. I can't do that."

Before I could ask if the cats were feral and candidates for TNR or cats already living with people, she stood and said, "Let me get you some pictures."

She returned with a photo album full of color images of abused dogs and cats: dogs so long chained that their collars had grown into their necks; cats with grievous wounds and their fur burned off; starved dogs, mangy dogs, flea-bitten dogs; dogs so bloody, oozing, and hairless that they were on the point of death. Not only was she head of the Danville Area Humane Society, Paulette explained, she was also a "court-appointed humane investigator" and had witnessed this sort of cruelty and suffering repeatedly. In fact, she saw it all the time. She went into homes on raids, faced people with knives and guns, received death threats, and had once been told that her house would be torched because she wouldn't allow the release of neutered cats into the wild.

"It was the middle of the night when *that* man called," she elaborated, "and I told him, 'Sir, could you please come in the morning to burn my house down. I am very sleepy right now, and I don't think I could make it outside in time.' Of course, he never came."

I grinned at her pluck; she replied with a tiny smile. Her droll story was as much energy as she could expend on levity. I said, "It sounds like you don't have a trap, neuter, and release program here."

"No, we don't. There would be no one to feed and water the cats every day and monitor their health."

"They're feral cats," I replied. "They'd hunt."

"But how do you know they wouldn't be hit by cars or a fox wouldn't get them?" Her sincere brown eyes became pained behind her henna-tinted glasses. "I officially do not have a belief one way or the other about TNR, but let's say a certain area can support twelve cats, and the twelve cats keep the thirteenth cat out. What happens to the thirteenth cat?" She touched the photo album. "Where does that cat go? I know that's nature. I know that feral cats die. I know they starve. I know they get hit by cars. But I'm the one who has to see their suffering when people bring them in here, dying of starvation."

She took a breath and steadied herself. Speaking of the suffering that she saw every day, she had almost begun to cry. She took another breath and blinked back her tears. "Do I like our euthanasia numbers? No!" she exclaimed. "They are appalling! But what are we supposed to do? Can we say *no* to these animals? The answer has to be *no*. And at the end of the day, I feel good about what we do. The animals that come through our doors, doggone it, we'll make sure that their troubles are over. And if that means that the final act of mercy we give them is a kind death surrounded by employees who have fed them and watered them and cared for them, then maybe that is all we can do for them. Then maybe that is the end of their suffering." Putting her hands flat on her desk around the photo album, she lifted her head and pulled back her shoulders. "My religious beliefs help me in this."

I waited several moments, and when she didn't amplify, I asked, "How do you mean?"

"I don't believe that this is the end for them. I believe that they have eternal spirits and eternal lives. My church teaches that actually – I'm a Mormon." She tapped the last photo she had shown me. "This dog" – it was the terribly flea-bitten one – "she was an absolute skeleton. Her owner was on crack and looked twice my age. She left her dogs to die. And we intervened, got the fleas off this one, and got her on vitamins. But we just could not find this dog a home. I tried everything to get that dog a home, and we just couldn't, so we had to euthanize her. But she's in a better place now."

Driving away from the Danville Area Humane Society, I had much to think about. Paulette Dean had some large hurdles to face: a shabby, run-down building, a community with some ingrained ways of keeping dogs, and a limited budget with which to change both. Nonetheless, she had managed to pass an anti-tethering ordinance over the opposition of many locals and was providing free ten-by-ten-foot fenced enclosures to those who couldn't afford their $200 price. She was hoping that this program would help the community make the transition from chaining dogs to giving them some more off-leash time. By her own admission, this was hardly an ideal solution – a ten-by-ten-foot enclosure was not enough room for a dog – but it went some ways toward preventing embedded collars. She was also building a no-kill wing onto the existing building.

Yet, as I periodically checked back to the Danville Area Humane Society's website, which had been under construction at the time of my visit, I noticed a tone emerging that was a mirror of Paulette's concerns: the suffering of animals and the punishment of malefactors. There were photos of kittens left in a bag by the side of the road, of a puppy found in a Dumpster, and of an abused, scared-looking cat being held on a gurney, the captions mentioning rewards of up to $1,000 "for the information leading to the arrest and conviction of the person or persons. . . ." The sobering, cheerless images of abused animals continued in a repeating scroll, creating an atmosphere almost as grim and depressing as that of the shelter itself.

Granted, the Charlottesville-Albemarle SPCA has a lot more money to throw at its website, creating a bright, welcoming, and effervescent mood, but when I checked the website of the nearby Martinsville–Henry County SPCA — located in an area that, as Paulette had pointed out to me, had an even higher unemployment rate than Danville — I found pages full of happy-looking dogs and cats being held by smiling children and comely women. There was also a wonderfully catchy photo of an orange tabby looking at itself in a mirror, with the reflection of a great maned lion staring back, the caption reading, "Planned Giving — Leave a Legacy of Love."

Wanting to find out how a shelter in the same economically depressed area of the rural South — Martinsville is but a forty-minute drive west of Danville — managed to host such an appealing website, I spent an hour and a half visiting with its executive director, Leslie Hervey, a short blond woman in her early fifties, who had replaced the previous director in 2004 and had been hired because of her background in fund-raising. The shelter's board wanted her to mount a capital campaign to build a new shelter, and she had agreed on one condition: the shelter, which had been killing dogs and cats, had to become no-kill. Not wanting to lose her fund-raising talents, the board had agreed.

Those talents immediately showed as we spoke. In the honeyed tones of the Deep South, and using words like *relationship, partnership,* and *supporters,* she described how her shelter was given only $15,000 from the City of Martinsville and $7,000 from Henry County per year, yet she made up the balance of her $650,000 budget through active membership campaigns, planned giving, and reliance on what she called "a herd of volunteers." In fact, one of them had designed the shelter's website — with its signature orange tabby admiring itself as a great donational lion — for free.

The new shelter had playpens for puppies, glassed-in condos for the cats, and a sparkling-clean veterinary examination room. There were raised dog beds and dog blankets and dog toys, and the puppy rooms had in-floor heating. Leslie was as buffed as her shelter, wearing a black, midthigh power dress and black pumps, about which she said, "I always need to be ready to meet a major donor or be on a TV show." She grinned and added that she had just been cleaning the restrooms in these very clothes.

She went on to say that even though she took in all puppies who came her way, she could not claim to be running an open-admission facility. Once the shelter was full, she couldn't accommodate another dog until one had been adopted. The nearby Henry County pound "got stuck," as she said, "doing the dirty work for the whole community." If I added in the animals who were killed at that facility, I'd see that her geographic area killed 16 percent of the nearly three thousand dogs who entered their system every year. By contrast, the three shelters in the Danville area killed 69 percent of the thirty-one hundred dogs who came through their facilities.

I let these numbers sink in. Then I asked, "So how did you reduce the kill rates in your area when faced with the very same factors Danville is facing: deep local unemployment, the same cultural attitudes toward animals, and the same lack of funding from municipal and county authorities?"

"We have a relationship," she said — there was that word again — "with the North Shore Animal League on Long Island, New York. Each year North Shore takes a thousand of the thirteen hundred puppies we get." I had seen the North Shore Animal League's statistics. Created in 1944, it is the largest no-kill animal rescue and adoption organization in the world and has saved the lives of close to one million animals. "I've offered to take puppies from Paulette," Leslie continued. "I've told her I'd worm them, and vaccinate them, and send them up to Long Island for free. But she says that I'm just dumping our problems on Long Island and that every area should take care of its own."

In the months to come I often thought of these three shelters, as well as the one I had visited in Downey, California, wondering why some communities change the leadership of their shelters and others do not. After looking at the records of more than three dozen shelters, I decided that sometimes communities change the leadership of their shelters because a social tipping point is reached — enough community members become tired of their shelter's high kill rate and replace the old guard with more creative management. Sometimes a shelter becomes no-kill from within, an influential insider orchestrating the change. Occasionally, as Ryan Clinton, the attorney who helped to lead the no-kill initiative in Austin, told me, "An old shelter director sees the light."

Even though this transformation of shelters from kill to no-kill has occurred throughout the United States, a regional tilt toward high kill rates remains. Across the South, far more dogs are put to death than in the North, and one of the consequences of this disparity is the growing scarcity of adoptable dogs in the northeastern part of the United States and the upper Midwest. Shelters in these regions have proved so successful in finding homes for their dogs that they no longer have enough dogs for people who want an inexpensive pet. As a result, shelter dogs are increasingly imported from the South to meet this demand, as are street dogs from Latin America and Asia.

A vast network of volunteers, rescue workers, and pilots run these transportation lines, driving and flying these dogs hundreds and sometimes thousands of miles from shelters that kill dogs to those that won't. As these life-saving missions have grown more numerous — especially those embarking from Mexico and the Caribbean — the threat of transmitting parvo, distemper, and rabies to the resident dog population has increased. In August 2010, for instance, a cargo plane from Puerto Rico landed in Orlando, Florida, with 222 homeless dogs, heading to New York for an adoption event held by PetSmart and the ASPCA. Some of the puppies were incubating parvo and distemper, and they exposed all the dogs on the plane to the deadly viruses, causing the entire lot to be quarantined and a large rescue operation to be launched at a cost of $550,000, which did not include the time spent by local veterinarians who volunteered their services. Eighty-nine of the dogs died.

Parvo, distemper, and rabies aren't the only diseases that foreign dogs may carry. Adenovirus-1 is still prevalent to the south and north of the United States, as Dr. Ron Schultz related, and screwworm, the flesh-eating larvae of the New World screwworm fly, is still endemic on some Caribbean islands. The Centers for Disease Control, using data collected at US airports and border-crossing stations, has calculated that upwards of three hundred thousand dogs per year are imported into the United States, either for resale or as part of rescue operations. In light of these numbers and lax screening, the US Animal and Plant Health Inspection Service has proposed stricter importation regulations for dogs, requiring that an imported dog be at least six months old and be vaccinated for all major canid diseases. Whether there will be adequate funding to enforce such regulations at dozens of international air terminals and hundreds of land border crossings remains to be seen.

None of these immediate issues of canine epidemiology hint at what lies over the horizon: the day, perhaps around 2030, when adoption initiatives like the Shelter Pet Project have helped US and Canadian shelters reduce their kill rates and place all their dogs locally. Animal welfare leaders are already pondering this eventuality and wondering what it might mean for the future of animal shelters. As Dr. Stephen Zawistowski, the ASPCA's Science Advisor, told me, "If the metric of success has traditionally been how many dogs you adopted out, do you continue to use that measure by importing dogs from other regions or do you redefine your metric? For instance, defining it as the overall health of dogs in your community – do they have adequate nutrition, a warm dry place to sleep, and adequate veterinary care?"

Many shelter workers to whom I've related these rosy predictions have shaken their heads in disbelief and said, "The brains in New York and Washington have never worked in a shelter! There'll always be too many unwanted dogs."

It comes as a surprise then for some of these people to learn that western Europe has solved the problem of unwanted dogs. No healthy dogs are killed by law or practice in the shelters of Italy, Austria, Switzerland, Germany, Sweden, Norway, Finland, and Denmark. In France about eleven thousand dogs – healthy, ill, and aged – are killed each year, and in the United Kingdom about seven thousand healthy dogs are put to death annually. As percentages of the total canine population of these nations, these numbers represent, respectively, one-fifteenth and one-twenty-fourth the number of healthy dogs killed in the United States each year.

What makes these statistics so remarkable is the fact that cities in western Europe have not mounted spay/neuter campaigns, and most Europeans keep their dogs intact. How then can western Europe have such low kill rates in its shelters?

One assumption used to explain this large difference between the kill rates of Europe and North America is Europe's dense urbanization. Since intact dogs are perpetually leashed in these widespread urban areas, goes the argument, they are prevented from breeding and there are no stray dogs. This assumption is wrong. I've watched European dogs running freely under the voice command of their people in many of the parks of Europe's great cities. I've also seen dogs running off-leash on beaches, swimming in the ocean and in lakes, and I've hiked and skied with them in the mountains. Why, then, aren't there millions of puppies being born from these sexually intact, at-loose dogs, only to be put to death in European shelters?

The answer may seem startling to those of us who are used to controlling the dog population through spaying and neutering. Western Europeans have paid attention to one of the most fundamental aspects of canine biology: female dogs come into estrus but twice a year. If a female dog is sequestered during this time — in other words, kept in the house, in the barn, in the kennel, or carefully supervised on her leash, and not allowed to consort with intact male dogs — she won't get pregnant, and she cannot get pregnant the rest of the year, when she's not in heat. As a great many Europeans with whom I've spoken have told me, "I control my female dog when she's in season." By employing this strategy, a nation can have intact dogs, even free-roaming intact dogs, and not have a surplus of puppies.

Some who work in the US shelter system have pointed out to me that Americans will never be this responsible. But having now spoken with thousands of Americans who live with dogs, I have to wonder if this is truly the case.

What may be a far more important factor in determining how many healthy dogs a nation puts to death is not its people's responsibility, or lack of it, but their poverty. The United States, with the largest gross domestic product in the world, turns out to be a rather poor nation when it comes to measuring the well-being of its citizens. In fact, it ranks twenty-seventh among the thirty-one developed nations of the Organization for Economic Cooperation and Development when it comes to overall poverty, child poverty, the poverty of its senior citizens, and the amount of social justice its citizens enjoy.

The number of dogs put to death in the animal shelters of these nations tracks this ranking. The Scandinavian nations have the most comprehensive social welfare system, the least amount of poverty, and the lowest kill rates in their shelters – zero. The United Kingdom's social welfare system is not as extensive as Scandinavia's, and its kill rate is higher. Canada has a more robust social welfare system than the United States, but remains under the influence of its powerful neighbor to the south. It has modeled its animal shelters after those in the United States, and as a result Canada still kills more than 15 percent of the dogs and cats who enter its shelters. Last in line is the United States. Among all these developed nations, it has the thinnest social welfare system and the most widespread poverty, and it kills the most dogs each year.

Statistics at the local level mirror these national trends. John Embery, the manager of the Los Angeles Downey Animal Care Center, told me that if I drove just fifty miles across the city to the wealthier community of Agoura Hills, I wouldn't see anywhere near the number of dogs being turned in to its shelter as were being turned in to his. He was correct. Between 2008 and 2011, the Downey shelter, whose community has a median income of $60,000, took in eight times the number of dogs taken in by the Agoura shelter, whose community has a median income of $110,000. During those same three years, the Downey shelter killed 50 percent of the animals it housed, whereas Agoura killed 20 percent. A 2009 study of feline neutering rates, which was published in the *Journal of the American Veterinary Medical Association*, supports the idea that care of animals is related to income. Ninety-three percent of the cats in US households that earn more than $35,000 per year are neutered, as compared to only 51 percent of the cats in households earning less than $35,000.

Do these studies imply that people with lower incomes don't care about their dogs and cats? No. They suggest that when people are on the edge of surviving, they may choose to care for their children first. Frequently, the only way to do that is to surrender their animals, even if the dog or cat has been a longtime companion. One compelling study done at twelve US shelters illustrates these difficult choices: 63 percent of the people who relinquished their dogs for euthanasia had lived with their dog for more than six years. Nearly 20 percent of them had lived with their dog for between twelve and fourteen years. These were no slight partnerships being ended. Strikingly, nearly 60 percent of the dogs relinquished to shelters specifically for euthanasia because of old age or disease came from households that earned less than $35,000 a year.

Sobering as these economic predictors are, they can sometimes be turned around, even by a shelter director who has been at the helm of a poor shelter for decades. In the winter of 2012, Paulette Dean drove over to Martinsville, Virginia, and had a long talk with Leslie Hervey. A few months later, Paulette began to send her puppies, who would have been killed in her Danville shelter, to the North Shore Animal League on Long Island, New York.

CHAPTER TWENTY

Chance

A WEEK AFTER I returned to Wyoming from my visit to the Downey shelter, I still had not heard from John Embery, so I telephoned him and left a message, asking whether the golden dog who had caught my fancy had been adopted. John responded with a four-word e-mail: "Dog is still here."

In a couple of weeks I was leaving on a research trip, one that would take me back to Europe and then to India, where I would observe a project that trapped street dogs, sterilized them, vaccinated them against rabies, and returned them to their homes on the streets of Jaipur as a way to reduce the stray dog population and the incidence of rabies it transmitted to humans. The trip had been a year in the making — the people who were hosting me had narrow windows of time in which to show me their research — and it could not be postponed. I'd be gone for weeks, and it did not seem like the best of times to get a new dog, entrust it to a dog-sitter, and then return to take over its training.

Moreover, I wanted one of Abby's puppies. I loved Abby, I admired Taylor, and I could trace their healthy genes back for many generations. I believed that one of their puppies had a better-than-average chance of being both physically and mentally sound, and I wasn't about to forgo that hope for the dog in the Downey shelter. Nor was I prepared to let him die.

"Take them both," said a friend who had two dogs, both of whom were old and wise and well socialized. I thought about it. Had the Downey dog been more of a known quantity, already house-trained and with manners, I might have been more willing to follow her advice and give two dogs a try. I wasn't keen, though, on raising an infant puppy and what amounted to an adolescent unsocialized dog at the same time. With everything else on my plate, I didn't think I could give both of them their proper due.

After a few days of mulling things over and hoping that someone had adopted the handsome golden dog, I checked back with John Embery, only to learn that the dog remained in his kennel. As my departure drew closer, I imagined trying to get the dog out of his predicament — his clock winding down, his monthlong stay coming to an end — from deep within India, eleven time zones from Los Angeles, and with the sketchy phone and e-mail service at the Jaipur animal sanctuary.

Asking around, I was unable find anyone interested in taking on another dog. Everyone was content with the one or two they had. The days passed, and I felt the weight of the promise I had made to the dog growing heavier. Kneeling beside him outside the fence of the Downey shelter and putting my nose into his ruff, I had said, "I will get you out of here." Too many weeks had already gone by, and he was still in the equivalent of jail.

So I instituted a stopgap measure. I called a friend who lived a two-and-a-half-hour drive east of Los Angeles, explained the dilemma I was in, and very kindly, most kindly even for a dog lover, she agreed to drive down to LA, pick him up, and keep him temporarily, which earned her my everlasting thanks. She brought the dog, whom I had begun to call Chance — for the chance meeting that had brought us together — to her rather elegant ranch home, where he first soiled her rugs, then chewed them to shreds. He demolished her TV remote and destroyed her phone. He upset her small dogs, he infuriated her large cats, and he drove my friend, who was long over raising young children or young dogs, to distraction. She called and said, "He's lovely, but I can't do this."

I was shortly heading to the other side of the world.

At the time, one of the people whom I'd hired as a researcher was a woman from the Blue Ridge Mountains of Virginia named Vicki. She was a tireless coordinator of dog rescue and transportation, sending out thousands of cross-postings about dogs who were about to be killed and then driving some of these dogs hundreds of miles to shelters where they would get a reprieve. I now called her and asked if she knew of anyone who might be interested in adopting what I thought was a very nice dog, albeit a little rough in his manners. I sent her some of Chance's photos, one from his Petfinder profile and several that my California friend had taken with her cell phone, showing Chance — trim, golden, and smiling. Vicki said she'd put out the word.

A few hours later, she called back and said, "I'll take him."

"You have four dogs already," I reminded her, "and Lonnie" — that was her husband — "will kill you, and I don't want to have your murder on my hands."

"I asked him already," she said in her drawl, "and he's fine with it. Besides," she added, "Chance looks a bit like Merle."

The problem was how to get Chance across the continent, but I told Vicki I'd work on it. It took a day and a half before I found a solution: I hired a firm in Los Angeles called Pacific Pet Transport, which drove up to Palm Desert and retrieved Chance in an air-conditioned van. The driver then placed him in a large plastic dog crate, took him to LAX, and made sure that he got on his direct flight to Dulles International Airport, just west of Washington, DC, and a hundred-mile drive from where Vicki and Lonnie lived. They met him that afternoon and led him — a little dazed from his many moves and the long flight — out of his kennel. Then, giving him hugs and a stroll around the parking lot to restore his land legs, they put him in the back of their SUV and drove him over the mountains to home.

Whether it was being around Vicki and Lonnie's much larger dogs, having the freedom to roam up their wooded mountainside, the absence of cats, Vicki's doting on him, or some combination thereof, Chance did not chew their rugs, phones, or TV remotes, and he got along splendidly with his new housemates. He even began to sing, demonstrating an important point about dogs whose adoptions fail because of their bad behavior. In many cases that bad behavior may be nothing more than the dog saying what a human might say when forced to live with strangers: "These people are okay, but they're not my people."

Calling me in Wyoming, Vicki held the phone up to Chance, and I heard him break into a long, drawn-out, and contented "AwwRooo," which reminded me, clutch in my throat, of Merle.

Nearly two months later, upon my return from India, I finally saw Chance in person when I stopped in the nation's capital. Vicki, in her habitual canine work clothes — sweatpants, polo shirt, golden hair parted in the middle and falling onto her shoulders — drove him down to the city to say hello. I found him lying on his bed in her SUV, surrounded by some toys, his head resting shyly between his paws. "I am so happy to see you, Chance," I said. Here he was, nearly three thousand miles from where I had met him in the Downey shelter, just as gold, but a little more filled out, his keen yellow eyes staring into mine, but without any recognition of who I was—not really a surprise after what he had been through and how briefly we had met. I touched noses with him and said, "How about a walk?"

The spring twilight was warm, and we left my hotel and strolled over to the White House, I holding Chance on his leash, he looking around with a mix of curiosity and caution. He had just been running in the woods of the Blue Ridge Mountains, and the people and traffic now seemed to put him on guard. Perhaps they reminded him of LA.

When we reached the tall black fence that surrounds the president's mansion, Chance stuck his nose through the bars and looked at the great white building illuminated against the fading blue of the heaven. "I was hoping Bo would come out," I told him, referring to the Portuguese Water Dog whom the first family had gotten. "But I guess he's busy. Aren't you lucky, Chance, that you weren't adopted by the Obamas? Think of all those meetings you would have had to attend, those state dinners, and having to live behind this big black fence!" He gave his tail an acknowledging wag, and I gave him a hug before we walked back to the hotel.

Handing him over to Vicki, I said what I had said many times before: "Thank you for helping me get him out of there."

"He's always your dog," she answered.

"I appreciate that," I said, "but it seems he's got his family now."

She confessed that he really did and that she would find it hard, very hard, to let him go.

"He can come visit," I suggested, "and play with my new pup."

And so he did, Vicki and Lonnie driving west with him and his best buddy Spencer and arriving in early September when the aspen were still green. By this time, however, more than a year and a half had gone by, and Chance had come under Spencer's influence. A reddish Border Collie mix, Spencer had been badly beaten before Vicki rescued him, and he had turned into a bully as a way of protecting himself from further harm, barking at other dogs, pushing and shoulder-butting them, baring his teeth, and in general being a highly unpleasant fellow.

Chance had adopted all of Spencer's aggressive behavior, and the two of them double-teamed the privileged five—Pukka, A.J., Burley, Goo, and Buck—who initially gazed at them as if they were aliens from outer space ("Who are you guys?") and then started raising their hackles.

Watching the riotous scrum that unfolded between the seven dogs, Vicki shook her head in resignation at Spencer's and Chance's behavior. A blessed being when it came to rescuing dogs, she has been less successful at giving her own dogs boundaries. Sounding like Scarlett O'Hara, she said, "Those two dogs *do* manipulate me."

At this point I attempted to defuse the situation by bringing Spencer and Chance into the house. Pukka followed, and they immediately pinned him against the sliding glass doors, growling and baring their teeth. Pukka, his fur now raised like a hedgerow from neck to tail, gave me a look: "Are you going to take care of this or am I?"

I normally let dogs settle their differences on their own, but a dog fight seemed like a bad way to start a long-anticipated visit. I did not want one in my house. So I took Spencer and Chance by their collars—Spencer screaming and struggling, Chance going meekly—and led them into the hall, where I put Spencer into the bathroom and Chance into my office for a two-minute time-out. Pukka lay down in the middle of the great room and gave me a grateful look: "Thank you for taking care of those two goons."

His thanks were premature. The moment I released Spencer and Chance, they rushed him, barking at the top of their lungs. Back into the slammer they went, Spencer scratching wildly at the door and trying to tear it down with a mixture of desperation and rage.

Opening the door, I stepped inside, pointed a finger at him, and said firmly but very quietly, "Stop that, Spencer, or you won't get out." He backed up, panting hard. "Your choice," I said. He looked at me, his lips twitching upwards to expose his teeth. "Sit down, please," I said levelly, "and cut that out." I kept my finger pointing at him. He sat down and lowered his lips. I let a few seconds go by. "Very good," I told him. "Very good." I closed the door and waited. He did not scratch, and after another two minutes I released both of them.

They emerged very subdued and eyed Pukka warily, as if he might have been the cause of their confinement, but they made no move toward him.

"Excellent," I told them. "Well done."

They gave me a sober eye. Apparently, Kelly was not Tara.

This impression was further reinforced by our walks around the village, many other dogs joining our group of seven. Spencer and Chance initially growled and bumped aggressively into the other dogs, but were ignored. They became frustrated and barked wildly. No one reacted, which made them anxious. They whined at each other. Finally, they turned quiet and studied what was going on around them: Here were dogs pleasantly walking side by side and not vying for dominance. What a concept! Peer pressure spoke louder than old habits. They joined the line.

We strolled to the post office and got the mail; we played Frisbee in the sage; and we rode horses, Spencer and Chance discovering that horses had been created not to be chased, but so that dogs could lead them on long hikes. It wasn't that Chance and Spencer didn't get to do some of these things back in the Blue Ridge — it was that at Camp Kelly they had to do them with at least five other dogs and a human who wouldn't stand for their nonsense. Slowly, Chance left Spencer's wing.

One morning we went swimming in the Gros Ventre River, and he stood teetering on a rock across the channel from me, enviously watching the three retrievers, Pukka, A.J., and Burley, doing laps as they fetched the sticks I threw.

"You can do it, Chance," I called to him. "Jump in! Join us!"

Spencer, in the meantime, stood on the bridge and barked down at him, "Don't do it! Don't jump! You'll be sorry!" All the while Goo — wading in the shallows and maintaining his long-standing boycott against complete immersion — barked at the top of his lungs, "Nice catch! I'd join you if I could!"

Ignoring both of them, Chance kept his eyes on the retrievers, Kelly's Olympic synchronized swim team, circling in the river before me, bringing me their sticks and plunging back into the swift water the moment I cocked my arm.

"You can do it, Chance!" I called. "You can do it! I know you can. Come on, we're waiting for you. Jump right in!"

He crouched low over his paws, rocking back and forth, his slim golden face suddenly doubtful.

"Jump!" I encouraged him. "Jump!"

He leapt and disappeared for a long second. Surfacing, he thrashed wildly, trying to walk across the river instead of swim through it. But he kept going — sinking, rising, flailing — and soon discovered that staying low improved his progress. When he entered the strong central flow of the river, he swam downstream, copying perfectly what Pukka, A.J., and Burley were doing. But his upstream ferry was a little rough, and he was swept behind the bridge abutment, disappearing from sight.

"No worries, Chance!" I called. "Keep swimming! I'm waiting for you."

And there he appeared, on the opposite side of the abutment, still swimming hard. He gained a rock island, shook himself off, and dashed across an archipelago of rocks. He had to swim one more deep channel, and then he gained the shore, where he leapt from rock to rock, running toward me as I applauded and cheered him on. He raced up to me, and I crouched beside him, stroking his flanks and saying, "What a swimming dog you are, Sir!"

Seeing his friend on dry land, Spencer tore down from the bridge and smelled him from nose to tail, making sure that he was okay. Chance did not reciprocate Spencer's attention. Instead, he turned toward the river and gazed at the three retrievers — still doing their laps — with an enormous grin: "I did that! I just swam the river. I'm a water dog!"

Once all the good sticks were lost, we walked home, and the dogs had their bones and naps. Later, in the coolness of the afternoon, we hiked up the Red Hill overlooking Jackson Hole, the Tetons sprawled across the western sky and the aspen falling in verdant benches to the valley floor. Pukka and Spencer, now shoulder to shoulder and acting as scouts, raced ahead while Chance continued to double back, brushing his flank against my leg and laughing at me, his warm yellow eyes saying, "Oh, this is the life!"

Watching him race off to catch the other dogs, his rear legs kicking up in joy, I had two thoughts, the first perhaps a little disrespectful, the great immortal words applied to a dog. Yet I heard them clearly, ringing from the mountaintops, and in their canine version pealing from Chance's heart: "Free at last! Free at last! Thank God Almighty, I'm free at last!" I also couldn't help but think of all the dogs whom I had seen on that never-to-be-forgotten day in Los Angeles, the dogs whom I had watched walking into or being dragged into that cinder-block room, all those Sophie's choices, whom I had allowed to slip away.

CHAPTER TWENTY-ONE

The Flip Side of Spay/Neuter

CHANCE, OF COURSE, was neutered. As part of its strategy to reduce the number of dogs coming into its shelter, Downey had sterilized him, just as virtually every shelter in North America would have sterilized him before letting him go to his new home.

Pukka, on the other hand, remained intact. As I've mentioned, one of the reasons that I had gone to a breeder—besides the obvious one of not having initially fallen in love with a shelter dog—was my concern that a shelter dog would be automatically sterilized, lose its beneficial sex hormones, and thus be at increased risk of certain diseases. When I explained this concern to friends and acquaintances and they realized that I had acted upon it and not neutered Pukka, I received three reactions: puzzlement, disapproval, and anger.

One person, representative of dozens of puzzled individuals, said, "Don't all dogs have to be spayed and neutered?"

"Why?" I replied.

"For their health."

"Where did you hear that?" I asked.

"From my vet."

The second response, disapproval, most often came in the form of silence, best expressed one night when Pukka was ten months old and an acquaintance of mine wanted to meet him. We were attending a lecture in Jackson, and after it was over she and I walked to the parking lot, where I let Pukka out of the Subaru. He said hello to my acquaintance—wag-wag-wag went his tail, sniff-sniff-sniff went his nose—and then his politeness was overcome by his need to take a pee.

He trotted directly away from us to a nearby snowbank, and watching him move off, my acquaintance cried, "Oh my God, he's got balls!"

"He's a male dog," I said.

"When are you going to take them off?" she asked immediately.

"Probably never. If I don't have to. There's a lot of evidence showing that intact dogs are healthier." I went on to explain the evidence.

Dead silence.

And then there were the people who became angry, all of them from the shelter world. Upon learning from me that Pukka was intact, and neither fenced nor confined to a very short lead, they berated me for helping to add to the shelter population. When I pointed out to these people that Kelly was not a city, nor even a town, but a village with about a hundred people and thirty dogs – all the dogs spayed and neutered and all of them known to me – that it was surrounded by millions of acres of wilderness, that it was eight miles from the nearest other community and fifteen miles from the town of Jackson, and that Pukka did not go beyond the edge of the village and consequently the chances of his impregnating anyone were quite small, I was still taken to task for being irresponsible. The fact that I might someday like to breed Pukka – so as to have one of his puppies and pass on some of his good genes – was only seen as further proof of my irresponsibility. In fact, one woman told me that my intentions were as misguided as Michael Vick's.

Since I was and continue to be a financial supporter of my local shelters, as well as the founding contributor to the Jackson Hole Animal Adoption Center's low-cost, mobile spay/neuter program, I laughed out loud. However, having a nuanced discussion about the costs and benefits of spaying and neutering, and how these procedures can be wisely applied so as to decrease the health risks that they pose to our dogs, is sometimes impossible with people for whom spaying and neutering have taken on the strength of a commandment: "Thou shalt not have an intact dog." How could I question spaying and neutering, some of these people asked me, when millions of dogs were dying in shelters and spaying and neutering had proven so effective in reducing the grisly toll?

Here's how:

Spaying and neutering aren't the only ways to prevent canine pregnancies. A tubal ligation, a vasectomy, or a hysterectomy all serve the same end as spaying and neutering—no puppies—and preserve a dog's beneficial sex hormones. For obvious reasons, these alternative ways to address a dog's reproductive capability—including keeping dogs intact—aren't readily discussed in the shelter world, at least not publicly. The shelter world has been trying to decrease the killing of healthy animals in what it has believed to be the most efficient and cost-effective way at its disposal: getting as many people as possible to spay and neuter their dogs.

But the shelter world doesn't represent the entire canine world. In the late 2000s, about 20 percent of people in America adopted their dogs from a shelter, whereas about 80 percent of them got their dogs from a breeder, a pet store, a friend, a relative, or a newspaper advertisement, or bred them at home. One may anguish over this fact, but these demographics not only represent how people get their dogs; they also often reflect the traditions, nostalgia, and very texture of people's lifelong love affairs with dogs.

These dogs—tens of millions of them who have not gone through the shelter system—have the option of retaining their beneficial sex hormones. Their people deserve as much information as possible about a decision—to sterilize or not to sterilize—that will profoundly affect their dogs' lives. Once apprised of that information, they can then decide whether sterilization, some form of birth control, or keeping their dogs intact is the best option for their particular dogs and their particular lives.

Unfortunately, the veterinary profession has not done a good job at illuminating these options for its clients. Just as many veterinarians derive significant income from giving dogs annual vaccinations, so, too, do many veterinarians have a financial stake in continuing to spay and neuter dogs, since teaching and learning new procedures, such as vasectomies and tubal ligations, takes time and money. Moreover, veterinarians are cultural beings just like the rest of us. They are just as influenced by social custom—the North American spay-neuter mantra—as the average person who lives with a dog.

One has to go a long way to find a veterinarian who questions the universal need for spaying and neutering and who can cogently argue for alternatives that bring about the same end: no unwanted pregnancies. Many people have found this veterinarian—Dr. Karen Becker—on the Internet, where she runs a website called Mercola Healthy Pets, writing articles and presenting videos on every conceivable health-related topic concerning companion animals. I found her at her clinic, the Natural Pet Animal Hospital, in Bourbonnais, Illinois.

We had barely begun to take a tour of her clinic when she told me that she wanted to set the record straight: she didn't believe in breeding a dog unless it was going to contribute something positive to the gene pool. "I think that breeders are picking the most beautiful dogs to breed," she said, "rather than the most functional."

That noted, we passed upright, glass-fronted freezers containing raw food, shelves of grain-free kibble, a well-stocked pharmacy of herbal and allopathic remedies, and spacious examination rooms and surgeries, her clinic an advertisement for her belief in high-protein, low-carb nutrition for dogs and cats—what she calls "a species-appropriate diet"—as well as her practice of integrative medicine, the blending of modern medical techniques with acupuncture, chiropractic, and herbal supplements. Her own life had followed a similar integrative course. She had wanted to be a veterinarian since she had been an elementary school girl in Iowa and had worked at a local animal shelter. She had then become a federally licensed wildlife rehabilitator, working with raptors in Colorado. From there she went to the Berlin Zoo, studied in Australia, and graduated from the Iowa State School of Veterinary Medicine in 1997, adding certifications in veterinary acupuncture, veterinary homeopathy, and exotic animals.

We went to an examination room, and Karen, wearing a casual white blouse and pants, kicked off her sandals and sat cross-legged on a low couch. I took an armchair. She was tall, loose-limbed, with black hair and green eyes, and at breakneck speed she began to tell me about the alarming number of dogs whom she was treating for endocrine disorders.

"These conditions became rampant in my practice between 1999 and 2007," she said, "and hypothyroidism was the one I most commonly diagnosed. But after 2007 adrenal disease surpassed thyroid disease. I was seeing six cases a week."

She went on to explain that she also saw many ferrets, who are commonly desexed at three weeks of age. Ninety percent of these animals died of pancreatic tumors or adrenal disease, whereas those ferrets who were not desexed did not have anywhere near the same incidence of these conditions. She believed that a similar phenomenon was taking place in dogs.

She took a breath, a very short one. "So many factors play into this," she said excitedly. "I want you to see how all the pieces fall into place." She picked up a color diagram from the arm of the sofa and showed me how the pea-sized adrenal glands sit atop the kidneys and how they secrete cortisol when a mammal is stressed. For a dog that stress could come from being left in a crate for eight hours while its person was at work.

"You're supposed to chuck cortisol when being chased by a grizzly bear!" she exclaimed. "But only for a few seconds, not for eight hours. If you're constantly chucking cortisol, it creates adrenal burnout. Now this is going to bring it all into focus for you." She made her fingers into binoculars around her eyes. "This is so cool. Here's the kingpin." Pointing to the diagram, she described the function of each layer of the adrenal gland: the outside layer produced aldosterone, which balanced electrolytes like chloride, sodium, and potassium; the middle layer produced cortisol; and the inner layer produced a small amount of estrogen, progesterone, and testosterone.

"Now" — she put down her diagram and looked at me intently — "the majority of sex hormones are meant to come from the testes and ovaries. So we rip them out of dogs at four to six months of age, and in some shelters at six weeks of age, just like we do for young ferrets. The dogs become asexual, their testosterone, progesterone, and estrogen — three of the hormones that are vital for normal, healthy metabolic processes — taken away in an instant." She snapped her fingers. "Okay, Ted, this is a quiz. So where's the last remaining piece of tissue that can secrete sex hormones?"

Just like a good dog trainer, she had set me up for success.

"The adrenal glands," I said.

She sat back and smiled, but only for a moment. Leaning forward, she narrowed her eyes and asked me, "Is this metabolically stressful for the dog?" Before I could answer, she cried, "Uh-huh! The poor little adrenal glands are called upon to produce the sex hormones that the testes and ovaries are supposed to excrete: give us more, give us more, give us more. And the result is this."

Reaching for a sheaf of lab reports, she bounded off the couch and sat on the floor in front of me, leafing through the printouts of dogs sick with endocrine disease, their estrogen, progesterone, and testosterone levels all out of whack, the dogs fat, balding, and depressed, one, a male, with the estrogen levels of an intact female. "This is hormonally induced stress," she said, brandishing the lab reports, "caused by ripping out a dog's sex organs when we don't have to. And it's magnified by environmental stress! Everything from dogs being crated for long periods of time, to not getting enough exercise, to eating too many carbohydrates in the form of grain."

She laid down her sheaf of lab reports and said, "The grain breaks down into glucose, causing the pancreas to secrete insulin. The insulin lowers the blood glucose level, which prompts the adrenals to secrete cortisol to rebalance it. Is this stressful?" She opened her green eyes very wide and stared at me. "It's a yo-yo that leads to diabetes or Cushing's disease."

Having made her case—almost the same nutritional one that Dr. Ian Billinghurst had related to me—she paused, giving me a chance to play devil's advocate. "There are people," I said, "who would point out that without spaying and neutering, we'd have a lot more dogs on our hands. And some veterinarians recommend castration because it reduces roaming, marking, and aggression."

She gave me a look that said she was so disgusted with hearing this sort of nonsense from people who should know better. "I'll talk about behavior in a second," she said, "but let me first point out that it takes less time to do a tubal ligation, a vasectomy, or a hysterectomy than it does to neuter or spay, and dogs that have had their tubes tied, have had a vasectomy, or don't have a uterus cannot have puppies! It's impossible!" she cried. "Yet they still have their sex hormones! And no endocrine disease!"

"So have you completely changed over to these procedures?" I asked.

"In my practice I don't recommend spaying and neutering." She paused for effect. "Nor do I recommend vasectomies, tubal ligations, or hysterectomies."

Her delivery worked: she saw my surprise.

"Many of my clients are from Chicago," she explained. "They don't let their dogs run. These are very responsible people. Why do their dogs need to undergo an unnecessary surgery?" She cocked her head to the side, raised her eyebrows, and smiled sweetly at me, opening her hands. "If your dog is going to get humped at the end of its four-foot lead, I think"—she lowered her voice to a conspiratorial whisper—"you're going to know about it." Returning to the couch, she sat down, crossed her legs in a lotus position, and said, "Many of my clients' dogs are now intact. We're going Euro here. And I haven't had a single case of an unplanned pregnancy in my career."

The benefits of leaving a dog's sex hormones intact, she continued, went far beyond the avoidance of endocrine dysfunction. "Intact dogs look different," she said. "They have muscles. They're ripped. Those strong backs prevent intervertebral discs from rupturing. Sex hormones make for lean body tone and also keep a dog's back end from going out and cruciates from tearing."

As for behavioral issues like roaming, marking, and aggression, she pointed to the evidence demonstrating that castration didn't necessarily change these behaviors: many male dogs still roamed, still marked, and had the very same personalities after they had been neutered. As for humping people's legs, you could train a male dog not to do that, but people didn't want to put in the time it took to extinguish such behaviors.

For a moment, I recollected the day I had done exactly that with Pukka. Emmylou, a black Lab from the south side of Kelly, had come over to our house for the first time. Though she had been spayed years before, she must have still smelled attractive to Pukka. Becoming very excited, he tried to mount her as she lay on the living room floor. He wouldn't listen to my "leave it," so I pulled him away and led him to the bathroom, where I shut him in and gave him a two-minute time-out. When I released him, he immediately ran to Emmylou and tried to hump her. Back to the bathroom he went. Eventually I put him in the bathroom for a total of four time-outs. But upon emerging the last time, he looked at Emmylou, he looked at me, he looked back to Emmylou, and he sighed. Then he lay on the floor about six feet from her, his eyes fixed upon her, but he didn't make a move toward her.

"So how might the spay/neuter mind-set be changed?" I asked, returning to the discussion.

"You won't change the shelter system," she said. "We have to go back to the teaching institutions to change how things are done. But that's difficult because they don't want to change." She shook her head in a mix of despair and amusement. "'Why do you have to stir up the pot?' my colleagues tell me. 'Why do you have to get everyone's hackles up?' One of my best friends is a large animal vet from South Dakota." Opening the corner of her mouth, she pantomimed spitting tobacco juice. She deepened her voice and said, "'Karen. Disease trends will shift, so just treat the disease. You don't have to think about the whys, Karen. Just treat the disease.' God love him." She shook her head again. "But he represents a lot of my profession. No one is interested in the whys. If you want to talk to someone who is interested in the whys, you need to go see Jack Oliver."

Before flying to Knoxville, Tennessee, where Dr. Jack Oliver ran the endocrinology lab at the University of Tennessee's College of Veterinary Medicine, I spent several days reading the peer-reviewed studies that Karen Becker suggested I look at. I printed out a great stack of papers, close to a hundred of them, that examined the costs as well as the benefits of spaying and neutering. These two terms, even though widely used, are often misunderstood.

For example, during my travels I met half a dozen shelter workers who thought that there was no difference between spaying and neutering dogs and giving them tubal ligations and vasectomies. One volunteer at a well-known shelter actually told me that her shelter "never castrated dogs," only did "something harmless inside of them" to prevent them from having puppies. She was shocked to learn that her shelter's veterinarian removed the testicles of every male dog who came through the facility. Given the extent of these misapprehensions, it would be worthwhile to take a minute so as to describe the basics of spaying and neutering before we discuss their potential health effects.

Spaying and neutering are forms of sterilization. They remove a dog's gonads — either a female dog's ovaries or a male dog's testicles. Subsequent to sterilization, no more sperm or eggs can be produced, hence no puppies. The dog's production of sex hormones also ends. In North America spaying is most often done by removing both the ovaries and the uterus, a procedure called an ovariohysterectomy. Less invasive is to remove only the ovaries and preserve the uterus, termed an ovariectomy. A male dog is sterilized by having his testicles removed. The dog is said to be "castrated" or "neutered."

An intact dog, as the word implies, is sexually complete, and barring any physiological problems with its sperm or eggs, it will be able to reproduce if it copulates with a similarly intact dog. In some parts of the United States, intact dogs are called "uncut." In the United Kingdom, they are sometimes called "entire."

A tubal ligation, also called a ductal ligation, is performed on a female dog and prevents her eggs from leaving her ovaries. A vasectomy is done on a male dog, and it blocks or cuts his vas deferens and prevents sperm from being ejaculated. The result of these two procedures is the same: no puppies. A female dog can also be prevented from having puppies by the removal of her uterus, called a hysterectomy. Without a uterus, there is no place for a fetus to grow. However, none of these three surgical procedures stops the flow of a dog's sex hormones — estrogen and testosterone — because they don't touch the dog's ovaries or testicles.

Of the two common procedures used to sterilize dogs, spaying has more documented health benefits than neutering. It ends the production of estrogen, and without estrogen, a dog's risk of breast cancer decreases. In fact, spaying a dog before her first heat — in other words, before she reaches sexual maturity and has estrogen coursing through her body — reduces her relative risk of developing mammary cancer to 0.5 percent. Mammary cancer is the most common cancer of intact female dogs, with an overall incidence of 3.4 percent, and this is why so many veterinarians strongly endorse spaying.

But not all breeds have the same incidence of mammary cancer. One Swedish study put Springer Spaniels, Dobermans, and Boxers first, second, and third on a list that ranked the risk of mammary cancer in fifty-one breeds. German Shepherds were number nine, English Cocker Spaniels number thirteen, Jack Russell Terriers number twenty-six, Labrador Retrievers number twenty-eight, Bernese Mountain Dogs — well known for contracting other forms of cancer — number forty-one, and the Rough-Coated Collie number fifty-one. Norwegian and Czech studies showed similar findings, with Boxers and English Cocker Spaniels having a high risk.

Mammary cancer also takes many forms, from benign to extremely aggressive, and a dog's survival depends on which form of mammary cancer she has, the size of the tumor upon diagnosis, if it has metastasized, and, if metastasis has occurred, whether the cancer has spread to the lymph nodes. Depending on the character of the particular mammary cancer and the treatment initiated, a dog could live for only a few weeks, survive a year or more, or be completely cured. According to one Swedish study, the overall mortality rate for canine mammary cancer is about 6 percent.

Spaying a dog by removing her ovaries also eliminates the chance that she will ever develop pyometra, which literally means "pus in the uterus," since the disease is dependent on the production of progesterone. Pyometra can be treated with antibiotics, but is occasionally fatal. Just as is the case for mammary cancer, certain breeds have a greater risk of developing pyometra than others. About half of intact Bernese Mountain Dogs and Rottweilers will have a pyometra episode before the age of ten, as will 35 percent of Golden Retrievers and 22 percent of Labs, but only 10 percent of Beagles.

This sort of data demonstrates that a one-size-fits-all approach to spaying doesn't do justice to the differences found in individual breeds. For a moment, think of yourself as a savvy Bernese Mountain Dog wanting to live as long as possible. Since your risk of mammary cancer is very low, you may want to hold on to your ovaries, as they have protective effects against other cancers and diseases. On the other hand, if you don't wish to have puppies, you may elect to lose your uterus since you have a better than one-in-two chance of contracting pyometra by the time you're ten.

Most North American veterinarians do not use this kind of breed-specific approach to spaying. They recommend that all female dogs have their ovaries removed to prevent mammary cancer and pyometra. In a similar fashion, North American vets recommend that all male dogs be castrated to avoid testicular cancer. Once again we need to look at the risks.

Those dogs who keep their testicles have a very low incidence of the disease — only 0.09 percent — and their risk is dependent on their age: almost no dogs who are younger than six years old develop such tumors, whereas they are more common in dogs over the age of ten. Fortunately, metastasis is not often seen in testicular cancer: less than 15 percent of such tumors spread to other parts of the body. Testicular tumors are usually found when swelling is noticed by the dog's person or its vet, and treatment is straightforward: removal of the affected testicle. As is the case for human testicular cancer, the canine variety is one of the most treatable forms of cancer, even if it has metastasized. Survival rates with early detection are very high in both dogs and humans: between 90 and 100 percent.

The veterinary literature suggests that most intact male dogs over the age of six will show some degree of BPH (benign prostatic hyperplasia), an enlargement of the prostate gland, and some vets also recommend castrating a dog at a young age so as to preclude the development of this condition. Yet many dogs will not develop a serious case of BPH, nor have any symptoms, even if they do have an enlarged prostate gland. If the prostate does cause problems, dietary modification and herbal supplementation can put the condition into remission, just as with human males.

A large number of veterinarians with whom I spoke also told me that castration prevents prostate cancer, a contention that is not supported by numerous peer-reviewed studies in the veterinary literature. In fact, studies done in both the United States and Europe demonstrate the opposite: neutered dogs develop prostate cancer more frequently than intact dogs — their risk is two to four times higher — and the prostate cancer of neutered dogs is more prone to metastasize.

Many other downsides of spaying and neutering have been documented. Spayed female dogs have a 4 to 20 percent incidence of urinary incontinence (depending on the study) as compared to intact ones, who have an incidence of only 0.3 percent. Treatment for the condition with drugs is often lifelong. Spayed and neutered dogs are also more likely to have more adverse reactions to vaccines — 38 percent more likely for females, 27 percent more likely for males — and are also more prone to be obese, particularly spayed females, whose risk is twice that of intact female dogs.

Some of the most worrisome studies on spaying and neutering show that sterilized dogs have an increased risk of developing several forms of cancer. They have twice the risk for osteosarcoma — bone cancer — than intact dogs, large breeds like the Irish Wolfhound, the Saint Bernard, and the Great Dane having the highest risk of all. Spayed and neutered dogs are also two to four times more likely to develop bladder cancer, and spayed females have been found to have five times the risk of intact females for developing hemangiosarcoma, a cancer of the blood vessels. The risk for males is lower but is still 160 percent higher than in intact dogs. In North America, hemangiosarcoma is the leading cause of death for Golden Retrievers, a good reason to think carefully before spaying or neutering a dog from this breed.

Spayed and neutered dogs are also at greater risk than intact ones for orthopedic injuries. They have a higher incidence of both hip dysplasia and ACL injuries, a rupture of the anterior cruciate ligament of the knee. They may also be more prone to a weak rear end as they become older because their back muscles aren't as well developed as those of intact dogs.

As dogs age, some of them display symptoms similar to those of people with Alzheimer's disease. These dogs forget their human and canine companions and can't recall where their bed and bowls are. Research at UC Davis has shown that what is now being called "canine cognitive impairment" does not progress as rapidly in intact male dogs who have developed the disease as it does in neutered ones. The study couldn't draw any conclusions about female dogs since not enough were enrolled in the study. However, the primary researcher, Dr. Benjamin Hart, pointed out that both estrogen and testosterone have been shown to reduce the accumulation of β-amyloid. This peptide is present in the neural plaque that has been associated with the cognitive impairment seen in both humans and dogs.

In 2009 researchers did specifically look at the protective effects of ovaries. This groundbreaking study examined the lifetime medical histories of what it called "centenarian" Rottweilers, 119 dogs who had lived to thirteen years and beyond. Their histories were compared to those of 186 Rottweilers who had the usual longevity for the breed, nine years. The lead researcher, Dr. David Waters of the Gerald P. Murphy Cancer Foundation and Purdue University, found that most of the dogs who reached exceptional old age for the breed were females, just as is the case for human centenarians. But instead of simply putting the females into the categories of "spayed" and "unspayed," as previous researchers had done, Waters and his team analyzed their total years of ovary exposure. They then found that those females whose ovaries were removed before the age of four lost the survival advantage that they had held over males in terms of living to an exceptionally old age. Those Rottweilers who kept their ovaries until they were at least six years old were nearly five times more likely to reach exceptional longevity, living 30 percent longer than the average for the breed. In other words, the study found that holding on to one's ovaries is important for long canine life.

A human study using thirty thousand US nurses has corroborated this finding. Women who have their ovaries removed to prevent the development of ovarian cancer, or its metastasis, reduce their risk of dying from ovarian and breast cancer but increase their risk of all other cancers as well as heart disease.

The Rottweiler study provoked some immediate criticism from other veterinarians, specifically that family clustering accounted for the exceptional longevity in these dogs rather than the retention of their ovaries. In short, said the critics, if a dog's mother lived to a very old age, she, too, had a better chance of doing so. But Waters controlled for this variable and still found that longevity persisted in dogs who kept their ovaries even after family clustering had been factored in.

On the social front, many veterinarians with whom I spoke were also concerned that members of the public would take the information in the Rottweiler study as license to no longer spay or neuter their dogs, leading to more dogs dying in shelters. When I suggested to these veterinarians that a tubal ligation or vasectomy brought about the same end — no puppies — and conserved the dog's estrogen or testosterone, I would often be told that tubal ligations and vasectomies were untested fringe procedures.

These statements took me by surprise, for after speaking with Karen Becker, I had done a PubMed search for tubal ligations and vasectomies in the US National Library of Medicine. Within a few seconds, I found thirteen articles that spoke favorably of tubal ligations or vasectomies. One of the articles came to the same conclusion that Karen had expressed: the procedures were "easy, quick and safe." The oldest article, "Sterilization of Nursing Puppies," published in *Modern Veterinary Practice* in 1976, described both vasectomies and salpingectomies (the removal of the oviducts) as taking about ten minutes to complete, with complications rare.

Such quick and easy techniques could have wide application in animal shelters interested in reducing the costs of spaying and neutering. Yet not one of dozens of shelter workers and directors with whom I spoke, and almost none of the veterinarians whom I interviewed, had ever considered any method of canine birth control other than spaying and neutering, a testament to how the spay/neuter mind-set has overshadowed the teaching of other pregnancy-preventing methods in North American veterinary training centers. And "overshadowed" doesn't do justice to the omission.

In a telephone survey that I conducted in 2011, I discovered that not one of twenty-nine veterinary training hospitals in the United States taught its students how to do a vasectomy or a tubal ligation on a dog despite the fact that peer-reviewed literature had discussed the procedures for close to forty years. The College of Veterinary Medicine at the University of Illinois and the vet school at the Michigan State University replied that they would teach the procedures if a student asked to learn them. One Canadian veterinary teaching center, Atlantic Veterinary College at the University of Prince Edward Island, taught vasectomies, but not tubal ligations.

Also telling were the responses I received to my inquiries at the vet schools. They ranged from bemusement to mild hostility: was I somehow suggesting that spaying and neutering weren't in the best interest of dogs? Only one veterinarian, Dr. Robert McCarthy, a veterinary surgeon specializing in orthopedic and soft-tissue surgery at Tufts University's Cummings School of Veterinary Medicine, thought my inquiry an important one, and when I asked him why his and other veterinary training schools weren't teaching vasectomies and tubal ligations, he laughed, a bit ruefully. "The reason they're not being taught," he said, "is habit. Spaying and neutering were taught a hundred years ago, and so we continue to do it that way today. It's only recently that we've started to accumulate data showing that loss of hormonal function may have consequences."

For Dr. McCarthy, the evidence had become so compelling that he no longer recommended neutering. "If you have a male dog," he told me, "and you can prevent him from contacting intact female dogs, and he doesn't have a behavior problem, then I wouldn't castrate him. If you're worried about him inadvertently breeding with someone, then I'd strongly consider giving him a vasectomy." He paused, then added: "Vets could make just as much money on vasectomies as they do on castrations, so finances shouldn't be an issue. The real reason they're not doing vasectomies is education. The literature on the health concerns over neutering is very recent and has rarely been introduced into the veterinary curriculum."

Female dogs, he continued, were another matter. The issues for them were not as clear-cut. There was data supporting that intact female dogs were healthier, but the risk of breast cancer and pyometra rose if a dog kept her ovaries. In addition, repeated heat cycles and the vaginal bleeding associated with them were difficult for most owners to manage. Therefore, for him, the choice was often to remove the ovaries.

In light of Rob's observation, I went back to Karen Becker and asked her how her clients managed to deal with the bleeding of an intact female dog. Giving what amounted to an e-mail snort, she wrote, "Healthy human females manage this issue MONTHLY, not twice a year! My clients buy denim hot pants that Velcro on, put a sanitary napkin inside them, and go about their day. Or they gate the cycling female in a tiled kitchen where they can mop. We're talking spots, not a gallon of blood each day."

I also asked her how she dealt with the fact that intact dogs have an increased risk for mammary cancer and pyometra. "There isn't one cookie-cutter answer," she responded. "Each dog must be evaluated as an individual, based on its breed, environment, training, and its person's beliefs. What you have to keep in mind is that spaying before puberty dramatically reduces the risk of breast cancer and eliminates the possibility of pyometra, but it increases the risk of many other often fatal conditions." She then listed all the ones I've just described, adding that only 1 percent of intact females die of pyometra. Against this tiny risk must be weighed a spayed dog's greater risk of dying from several other cancers, endocrine disease, and orthopedic injuries. Individually and in combination, these risks far exceeded 1 percent for a spayed dog.

"How did my profession," she concluded, "end up preaching that because ovaries can cause two diseases, they should be automatically removed, even when the mortality rate for the two diseases they cause — pyometra and mammary cancer — is small? Have all the wet dog kisses licked away common sense?"

Veterinarians also counsel their clients to spay or neuter their dogs to change their behavior, especially if the dog is male. As Doctors Foster and Smith, the widely read Internet veterinarians and online marketers of pet supplies, put it, "Castration in young dogs prevents aggression, roaming, urine marking, and a variety of other unwanted male behaviors. The surgery is safe and relatively inexpensive, and in the long run saves the owner money."

What Doctors Foster and Smith neglect to mention is that behavior doesn't reliably change after neutering. At UC Davis, for example, fifty-seven dogs were neutered for their ongoing behavioral problems, then monitored for the next five years. Only 25 to 40 percent of the dogs showed any resolution of their habitual roaming, mounting, and urine marking in the house. As for aggression — one of the most frequently invoked reasons for castrating a dog — only 10 to 15 percent of the neutered dogs became more tractable. Similar findings came from a study of female German Shepherds done in Korea. The researchers found that all fourteen dogs who had been spayed were more reactive to the approach of an unfamiliar human walking with an unknown dog than were the intact dogs in the control group. Even the most positive study about sterilization's ability to change behavior still found that 40 percent of the Dutch dogs surveyed had no change in their roaming, mounting, urine-marking, and aggression after being sterilized.

Since I had easily found veterinarians willing to tell me that neutering a male dog made him better behaved, I started looking for vets who might have a different opinion about the universal efficacy of the procedure. One was Dr. Kim Henneman, the head of Animal Health Options in Park City, Utah, who told me that castration had very little effect on large dogs who had been bred to be tractable, for example, retrievers and herders who enjoyed working as a team with a person. They were biddable before castration and remained so afterward. Not so with those breeds she called "spoiled little lap dogs, like Shi Tzus, Malteses, and Lhasa Apsos." If you told an intact male dog from one of these breeds, "don't mark in the house," she said with a grin, "they might flip you the bird." With such willful dogs, castration might very well save a person's furniture.

Another vet with whom I spoke, Dr. Gary Weitzman, the veterinarian CEO of the Washington Animal Rescue League in Washington, DC, had seen thousands of dogs come through his shelter. He told me, "We don't feel that neutering a male dog has any effect on its ultimate behavior. Obviously, we can't have overpopulation, but there's got to be more humane and innovative ways to deal with it." He was intrigued by vasectomies and tubal ligations and wanted to study their applicability to shelters.

Dr. Bruce Fogle, the British veterinarian and author of many dog books, including *The Dog's Mind*, also noted the difference in cultural attitudes about castration between Europe and North America and the impact of these differences on a dog's long-term health and longevity. "I have 15 to 20 percent American clients," he told me, "all of whom ask me when they get a dog, 'When should my dog be castrated?' They take it as a given that this is what's done with dogs. But unlike with female dogs, in which you can eliminate the threat of mammary cancer and womb infections, there are far fewer good reasons to castrate a male dog."

My own experience with Merle and Pukka bears out what these studies and veterinarians have observed: sterilizing a dog doesn't always achieve the elimination of behaviors that some people find objectionable. For example, Merle, who came to me neutered, almost never spent the entire night in our house until he was on his deathbed. He simply had to take a midnight walk around the village and see what was happening outside. Intact Pukka, on the other hand, has never left the house at night for more than a quick evening pee. Merle, by the accounts of tourists who met him, wandered a couple of miles from the village. Pukka, by the account of his GPS collar, has not strayed beyond the edge of the village.

According to received wisdom, neutering diminishes aggression. Yet, nine of the ten altercations Pukka has had with other dogs on the trail or in the dog park — posturing, growling, hackles raised, and one outright attack — have been initiated by neutered dogs, not by him. Pukka's tenth fracas was started by another intact dog, but he was the only one out of seven intact dogs whom Pukka met during his first two years of life who wanted to fight. The other six intact dogs and Pukka got along famously.

Unlike Merle, Pukka often lies under my desk when I'm writing, with his head on my feet. Merle never did this. He had more important things to do outside. Yet readers who have corresponded with me on the pros and cons of spaying and neutering have pointed out to me that Merle's wonderfully loving personality and his deep attachment to me were a result of his having been neutered. What, then, am I to make of intact Pukka, who, if anything, is more affectionate than Merle and certainly more tractable?

With regard to appearance, Pukka is a more ripped dog than Merle ever was, having the sinewy muscles of a track star, and his physique often provokes comments about his not being a Labrador Retriever. When I ask people what they mean by this comment, they hesitate, then politely say, "Well, he's not . . . he's not . . . oh, you know, he's not bulky enough."

This particular physical difference between the two dogs certainly has to do with testosterone — Pukka has it, Merle did not. But their behavioral similarities and differences have far more to do with how they spent their early puppyhoods, and the subsequent atmosphere of the home in which they matured, than with the fact that one was neutered and the other was not. The truth of the matter is that Merle spent part of his puppyhood roaming, and Pukka spent most of his in my office and around our house. Although Pukka has freely circulating testosterone and that has influenced his musculature, other factors have influenced his personality: his mother and his uncle, the two adult dogs whom he knew as a puppy, are gentle; his breeder is a soft-spoken, gentle man; he was socialized in the company of gentle dogs, A.J.'s anomalous attack notwithstanding; and consequently, even with balls, Pukka's not an aggressive dog.

Nonetheless, many people in the dog world continue to propound the notion that intact male dogs are aggressive and that their behavior can be improved with a scalpel instead of nurture and training. Dog shows constantly disprove this notion. Dogs in most kennel club shows have to be intact in order to compete, and most of these dogs get along.

Some would object that show dogs are a special case: highly trained and with professional handlers. But John Rogerson, the world-renowned British dog trainer and behaviorist, pointed out to me that such training can easily be done by the average person, as he himself discovered during a course that he was teaching in Belgium. He had just begun a four-day training workshop — one of the dozens he teaches each year for organizations as wide-ranging as Guide Dogs for the Blind, the RSCPA, and the US Air Force — when a woman walked into the class with her female dog, who happened to be in estrus.

John immediately went to the course organizer, telling him in no uncertain terms that the student could not attend the workshop with her bitch as it would be a distraction for all of the male dogs in the class.

"His reply astounded me," John told me. "He said that this was a real-life situation and that this was exactly what dogs and their owners would have to deal with in the normal course of their lives, and so there was no reason to ask her to leave."

The woman and her dog remained, and all of the intact male dogs were initially distracted, but their owners soon learned to control them. "By the end of the fourth day," John said, "the bitch's presence made no difference to any of the male dogs. It was an eye-opener for me, and now I allow bitches in season in any of my classes. However, in the USA, it is rare to find any training class where even entire males are allowed through the door, never mind bitches in season."

One of the best summaries of all the above scientific material is "Long-Term Health Risks and Benefits Associated with Spay/Neuter in Dogs" by the science writer Laura Sanborn. It's available on the Internet. As the title suggests, her paper is an excellent primer for people and shelters trying to make an informed choice about whether to spay and neuter or use another birth control strategy.

These choices will only increase as nonsurgical chemical contraception is refined and developed. For instance, a zinc-based sterilant, Esterilsol/Neutersol, has been widely used in Mexico to sterilize street dogs quickly, efficiently, and inexpensively ($6 per dog). When injected into a dog's testicles, it causes them to wither. It's been approved by the FDA for use in the United States and could be used in shelters to reduce the cost of castration, though its long-term health effects are still unknown. Suprelorin, approved for use in Australia, New Zealand, and the European Union, is an implant that makes male dogs sterile for either six months or a year (two dosages are available), and GonaCon, a vaccine that has been tested on wildlife as well as feral dogs and cats, can be used on both sexes and gives two-and-a-half years of infertility from a single injection.

One male human contraceptive method that has been successfully used in India also holds promise for dogs. Called Vasalgel, it's a polymer that is injected into the vas deferens and kills sperm as they are ejaculated. It is currently being reviewed by the FDA for human use in the United States, and since Vasalgel's effects are reversible, it would provide a welcome tool for people who are looking to assess the genetic and behavioral merits of their potential breeding dogs as they mature over a period of several years, but who don't want to worry about their dogs becoming dads.

Hoping to spur such innovative contraceptive techniques, including vaccines and viruses that prevent pregnancies, Gary Michelson, a billionaire medical inventor who heads the nonprofit foundation Found Animals, has offered a $75 million prize to the team of researchers who invent a non-invasive, safe, cheap, and easy-to-administer chemical contraception for dogs and cats. If you would like to remain informed about the latest developments in pregnancy-preventing methods for companion animals, look at the website of the Alliance for Contraception in Cats & Dogs, which has been the lead organization on this front.

At last, one rainy spring day, I met Dr. Jack Oliver, the director of the endocrinology lab at the University of Tennessee's College of Veterinary Medicine. A cheerful man in his early seventies, with thinning gray hair and wearing a casual short-sleeved shirt and tie, he had held professorships at the colleges of veterinary medicine at Purdue, Texas A&M, and Ohio State University, and for thirty-five years had taught pharmacology and endocrinology at the University of Tennessee. With obvious pride, he showed me around his laboratory, lined with refrigerators holding test tubes filled with canine and ferret blood samples, banks of computer monitors, incubators that resembled giant kitchen sinks — these, too, filled with test tubes — and a large Packard Cobra II Auto Gamma Counter, which did the grunt work of calculating the hormonal concentration of each blood sample.

As we walked along I described what Karen Becker had told me about the amount of adrenal dysfunction she was seeing in her practice, and I wondered if that was unique to her client base or was he seeing similar test results from other veterinary practices.

"We are seeing thousands of cases of adrenal disease," he told me in his soft southern accent. "We'll do over six thousand dogs this year, and we get samples from all over the United States and Canada, and at least seventeen foreign countries. It's a problem. It's out there. And more and more people are recognizing it."

I asked him if spaying and neutering dogs, and the early sterilization of puppies in shelters when they were no more than infants, might be contributing to the large amount of adrenal dysfunction he was seeing.

"I think it could," he said, nodding his head. "I think it could, because it certainly occurs in ferrets when they're spayed and neutered at a very young age, probably younger than what's done for dogs in shelters." He grinned and held up a cautionary finger. "But the studies haven't been done, so you can't say for sure that spaying and neutering is the cause in dogs."

We went to his office, where he sat me in front of his computer monitor and led me through a long and complex discussion of adrenal pathways, using arrows and flowcharts. When we were done, I said, "You have tens of thousands of records here."

He gave a pleased nod.

"Does each record indicate whether the dog was spayed or neutered?"

"If the vet knew that information, yes, the records would indicate that."

"So what would it take to crunch the data that you have here at your lab and give us an answer?"

Leaning back in his chair, Jack smiled broadly. Crunching data was one of his favorite subjects. "If you saw 75 percent of the dogs that were spayed or neutered at one month of age showing up with adrenal disease," he said, "and those that were spayed or neutered above six months of age had it only 10 percent of the time, that would a strong indication that there was a connection." His smile clouded. "But none of our data is on a computer. It would probably take two workers a couple of years — going full-time at $30,000 a year — to crunch all the data. If someone gives me a $100,000 grant, then we'd have an answer."

Fourteen months after we spoke, on June 5, 2011, Dr. Jack Oliver passed away. His project remains unfunded; his data still sits in his lab; the lab has no plans to investigate his findings.

It would be wonderful to have Jack Oliver's data on the association between spaying and neutering and adrenal disease, but even without it there are enough studies in the veterinary literature to help people make an informed decision about their dogs' reproductive status. Unfortunately, people who get a dog from a shelter cannot make such a decision, as most shelters sterilize their dogs before they leave the premises.

What, then, can you do if you want a shelter dog and you'd like it to retain its full complement of beneficial sex hormones? You might offer to post a bond with the shelter, a substantial deposit certifying that you will have a veterinarian give the dog a vasectomy or a tubal ligation. You can then offer proof that this has been done so as to effect the return of your bond. Or you can urge your shelter to hire veterinarians willing to perform vasectomies and tubal ligations on-site. Since these procedures can be performed in about half the time it takes to spay or neuter, the shelter could save money and perhaps increase adoptions, as dogs who have had vasectomies and tubal ligations could be advertised as being pregnancy-proof while also having the benefits of their sex hormones. Such dogs could be given a small ear tattoo, signifying their reproductive status, in case they came back into the shelter system.

Some shelter personnel have pointed out to me that all this is good in theory, but the last thing they need is a bunch of aroused male dogs howling after females in estrus. This is a legitimate concern and can be addressed by spaying and neutering adult dogs while giving puppies tubal ligations and vasectomies. The puppies won't be displaying adult sexual behavior for months to come.

These are a few of the strategies that could help North Americans regain an accurate perspective about the behavior of intact dogs. However, restoring such a perspective will take time. Intact dogs have almost completely vanished from ordinary family life during the last four decades and can now only be seen on a regular basis at dog shows and field trials, in some inner-city neighborhoods, and on Indian reservations. This is not a representative sample of dogdom, either behaviorally or genetically. But when I've remarked to people in the animal welfare movement that we need to be concerned about the narrowing of the canid gene pool, and its consequences for the health of dogs as well as our understanding of them, I've been called an egghead. As one person told me, "I can't get exercised over long-term genetic effects when millions of dogs are dying in shelters."

This is certainly one way to look at it, but I believe that we can give our care to both ends of the canine population: the dogs who may die in shelters in the short term as well as all those generations of dogs yet to be born. There are millions of ground troops willing to help in this effort, legions of responsible people in cities, suburbs, and rural places who would like to get a dog, who would make their dogs into good canine citizens, and who would not let them breed indiscriminately. These are the very sort of people who, with a little encouragement and advice, would test their dogs for genetic diseases and assist in passing on the valuable genes that are steadily being culled from the dog population at large. After all, in the space of forty years, the shelter and veterinary professions convinced the majority of these people to spay and neuter their dogs. They could certainly do the opposite, with far-reaching effects.

Consider Golden Retrievers. One of the reasons that more than 60 percent of them die of cancer in North America is that the public has been browbeaten into believing that the average Golden has no business contributing to its gene pool. The dog next door and down the block, who still might have genetic diversity, is deemed unworthy of reproducing, while a handful of show dogs are permitted to pass on what has proved to be a fateful genetic legacy.

Regrettably, potentially upstanding dog keepers across North America continue to be dissuaded from breeding dogs. If they so much as think about letting their dogs have puppies, they're accused of being irresponsible, and if they do let their dogs have a litter, they are labeled "backyard breeders," the worst of the worst in today's dog world. Yet Merle was more than likely bred in a backyard, and so was Pukka.

The castigation of backyard breeders hasn't been limited to words. In many locales, merely having an intact dog has been criminalized by the passage of mandatory spay/neuter laws, which have been widely billed by their supporters as a key element in reducing the killing of innocent dogs in shelters. These laws haven't worked. Kill rates have either stayed the same, fallen more slowly, or actually risen after the introduction of such laws in cities and regions as widely separated as Aurora, Colorado, and the Australian Capital Territory. Los Angeles is a prime example. It passed a mandatory spay/neuter law in February 2008, and by the end of the year the number of dogs killed in the city's shelters had risen 24 percent — "stalling," as Los Angeles Animal Services wrote in its official report, "a long-standing trend of impressive annual double digit decreases." Over the next three years, the number of dogs killed in LA shelters continued to rise, despite the mandatory spay/neuter law. In addition, mandatory spay/neuter laws have driven otherwise law-abiding citizens underground. So as to shield their dogs from surveillance, they refuse to license and vaccinate them. The ASPCA is against mandatory spay/neuter laws, and so are the American Veterinary Medical Association, the Anti-Cruelty Society, the No Kill Advocacy Center, the Best Friends Animal Sanctuary, and many other animal welfare organizations.

Yet the spay/neuter drumbeat goes on, helping to make sure that all the wonderful, healthy, varied genes that have lived in the dog population at large — and historically have been passed on in backyards, on street corners, and in fields — will steadily vanish. Don't misunderstand me. I am not suggesting that we return to a time when stray dogs roamed at large and shelters killed far more millions of dogs than they kill today. I am suggesting that in our attempt to end these deaths by insisting that every dog is better off sterilized, we are creating a diminished canine landscape that we may come to regret.

CHAPTER TWENTY-TWO

Not Long Enough

TWO YEARS AFTER his arrival in Kelly, Pukka was still a very young dog, tireless and always ready to run and play, but those same two years had taken a toll on some of the privileged five. A.J., for one, had become noticeably stiffer as he entered his seventh year, adopting a rocking, rolling gait instead of a steady trot. He also became much more conversational, producing a stream of moans and groans and soft yips that seemed expressive of his disappointment in having to slow down rather than a complaint of severe pain. I would give him massages as he lay on the dedicated quadruped couch, saying as I rubbed, "Oh, let's do those shoulders, A.J., and the lower spine. How important is the lower spine to a dog?" And he would throw back his head, stretch to the tips of his toes, and groan melodramatically, "Awrraa, roooo, mmrrraah, a bit more toward the hips, please, yes, awrrrr, right there."

Whether it was a general mellowing, said to come with advancing age, or his becoming resigned to my living with Pukka, A.J. also grew very affectionate toward him during this time, giving him gentle kisses on the lips while tenderly wagging his tail: Darth Vader redeemed at last.

Buck, too, began to slow down as he approached his ninth year, hobbled by a partially torn anterior cruciate ligament in his right rear knee, the knee itself filled with bone spurs. His veterinary orthopedic specialist, after manipulating the joint and taking X-rays, recommended TPLO surgery (tibial plateau leveling osteotomy) to fix the problem. But Scott was not willing to put Buck through the surgery and the subsequent four to six months of recovery and rehabilitation. Instead, he consulted with Marybeth Minter. She gave Buck a homeopathic remedy, fish oil, and a combination of glucosamine, chondroitin, MSM (methylsulfonylmethane), and antioxidants, which slowed the degeneration in his knee. These were some of the very same age-delaying remedies that she had prescribed for Merle in his later years, also giving him acupuncture and chiropractic along with these supplements. Today an arthritic dog's care might also include injectable Adequan, a drug that has been shown to reduce joint pain and restore mobility.

Although the efficacy of some of these therapies remains debated, combinations of them, administered by a skilled veterinary practitioner, are worth considering by anyone with an ailing senior dog before ever making the very subjective judgment that the dog is no longer enjoying life and therefore should be put down. As one of the pioneers in integrative veterinary care, Allen Schoen, told me, "I look at these dogs, and I say, 'You're twelve. You have a few more years to go. Let's rebuild your health; let's rebuild your immune system; let's rebuild everything. There are great holistic approaches — nutrition, acupuncture, herbs, chiropractic — that will help rebuild you.'" And in Merle's case, these therapies gave him three more years of quality hiking, skiing, and enjoying his mayoral rounds.

Buck felt better after his treatments, but still limped if he did the five-mile ridge loop across the river from the village. Scott thought about putting him on Rimadyl, the popular canine nonsteroidal anti-inflammatory drug, but after doing some research he chose not to. Even though Rimadyl has been taken by about 15 million dogs with arthritis, it has been associated with more than thirteen thousand adverse reactions and more than three thousand deaths from liver damage, Labrador Retrievers being particularly sensitive. Scott reduced Buck's activity, and Buck had to readjust his notion of a good day out. I thought of how he, Pukka, and I had recently climbed to the top of the Jackson Hole Ski Area, over four thousand vertical feet, and skied back down, laughing and hooting through the deep powder. Buck would probably not be doing that with us again. Like many aging athletes, he would have to resign himself to swimming — no great hardship, since he loved the water.

Age, too, began to change Burley. He became wide and solid, and his coat grew ever thicker, longer, and shaggier. He looked like a little grizzly bear. But what he lost in speed, he gained in authority. Unable to beat Pukka to the ball, he would wait until I went inside, and then, as Pukka mouthed his ball in the shade of the aspens, Burley would lock jaws with him. Pulling, tugging, and wrestling, he'd finally wrench the ball from Pukka's grasp and run to the woodpile with it, where he would barricade himself between the split logs and the house, with the ball beneath his chest, so none of the other dogs could get it.

Pukka would dash into my office and stand on my desk stool with his front paws. Pressing his shoulder against mine, he'd look into my eyes with the greatest of urgency: "Burley's stolen the ball!" His rapidly beating tail would add, "Please help us!"

Behind him, A.J. and Goo would be wagging their tails in agreement: "Only you can get it back! Only you!"

Getting up, I'd go outside and call, "Burley, please bring the ball."

Instantly, he'd come out from behind the woodpile, shamble across the deck, and lay it at my feet. All four dogs would now be panting in glee, A.J. and Goo barking, "Let the game begin!" I'd throw the ball out into the sage, and off they'd race.

After a few tosses, I'd go inside and within another minute Pukka would be back in my office, standing on my desk stool and panting theatrically, "Burley's got the ball again! You've got to help us!"

Back outside I'd go, retrieving the ball from Burley and wondering why Pukka was allowing him to take it. After all, he didn't let Burley mouth-wrestle bones from him.

This exercise went on for several days, and then, after a long bout of fetching one warm afternoon, everyone came into my office except Burley. With his longer coat, he chose to lie in the coolness of the shadowed north bathroom. The three other dogs lay behind me, Pukka chewing on the ball with happy squeegee-ing noises. After a few minutes, the noises stopped, and from the corner of my eye I saw him walk out of my office, go through the hall, and enter the bathroom, whose door I could just see.

Getting up, I tiptoed across the room and peeked around the door jamb. Pukka had placed the ball on the floor in front of Burley's nose, but Burley wouldn't pick it up. He was hot and done playing. Pukka waited. Burley made no move toward the ball, so Pukka gripped it between his front canines and pressed it against Burley's lips. Burley still wouldn't take it, and Pukka nudged the ball against his mouth several times, until Burley grudgingly opened his mouth and took the ball.

Pukka stepped back, and Burley got to his feet. I raced back to my desk stool, sat down, and put my hands on the keyboard just as I heard the dog door slap and Burley leave.

An instant later, Pukka burst into my office. Standing on my bench, he earnestly lashed his tail. "Burley's stolen the ball! Only you can get it back!" He grinned wickedly.

I shook my finger playfully in front of his nose. "You faker," I told him. "I saw you give the ball to Burley. And you two." I turned to A.J. and Goo, who were standing behind Pukka, shoulder to shoulder, their tails beating in solidarity: "Burley's got the ball! Only you can get it back. Only you!"

I began to laugh, and they began to laugh, wagging their tails harder and harder.

"You're all in cahoots!" I cried.

"Ha-ha-ha!" they panted, tails lashing, "but isn't it such a great game!"

Even with my best efforts to preserve these valuable balls — collecting them at the end of the day and putting them atop the fridge — they steadily disappeared. They were lost on walks, they went into the river, they were left at other people's homes, and Burley, arch ball thief that he was, storehoused them around his own woodpile. However, he was unable to guard them constantly, and dogs from down the road would steal them. At last, by the end of the summer, we were down to one ball, and I ordered a dozen more. They came in two boxes, one containing the red, blue, and cream-colored balls that the dogs had been using, with raised continents on them, making them look like globes. The six other balls were made of the same material, but recycled, and they were smooth. Blue, black, and purple, they were much squishier.

I held both boxes under Pukka's nose so as to let him choose which one he wanted. He did a quick olfactory survey of the twelve balls, immediately ignoring those with the continents on them. Instead, he chose a black smooth one, the novelty of the new trumping his old favorites.

I clipped off its hang tag and handed it to him. He squeezed it a few times, his eyes growing euphoric at its pliant texture. Running around the room, he squirted the ball out of his mouth and caught it as it rebounded off the walls, doing a couple of laps before sitting before me and offering me the ball. I took it and squeezed it. "Magnificent," I agreed and tossed it high in the air. He leapt up and caught it. Carrying the two boxes to the guest room, I placed them on the desk and went back to work as I heard him throwing the ball against the log walls of the great room. For all of five minutes.

Then I heard the door to the guest room being unlatched and pushed open, something Pukka had learned to do so as to bid our guests good morning. I heard a soft scuffle, and he reappeared in my office, looking a little sheepish. In his mouth he held one of the balls with continents on it, a blue one, the hang tag still attached. Very gently, he laid the ball at my side, his eyes saying, "I think I like this one better."

"Okay," I said, "there's nothing wrong with tradition," and I clipped off the hang tag. I tossed him the ball, and he trotted off. Going to the guest room, I closed its door and went back to work. Pukka began to play fetch solitaire.

Shortly, I heard the door to the guest room opening once again, and a minute later there was Pukka, laying one of the smooth balls on my desk stool, this one purple.

"Sir," I said, "are you going to try all of them?"

A short wag of his tail: "Perhaps."

I clipped off the hang tag, tossed him the ball, and made sure the guest room door was closed before returning to work. However, I left the two boxes of balls on the desk, for I wanted to see what Pukka would do if I didn't limit his choices.

Three minutes later, he was bringing me yet another ball, this one a red one with continents on it.

"Pukka," I said, "I think you'll bring me every ball, just the way you used to bring me all the toys in your basket when you were a puppy."

"Huh-huh-huh," he panted. "The chances are good." Sitting before me, he grinned.

"Well, I think we should save them for later," I told him. "Otherwise, Burley will steal them all."

Under his inspection, I returned the ball to the box in the guest room, and then I extended a hand toward the door. He went out before me, and I picked up the purple ball with which he had been playing and tossed it to him.

He took it to his bed in the great room while I went to the kitchen and filled a glass with water. When I turned around, he was lying on his bed about twenty feet away, in sphinx position, his forelegs outstretched toward me, the blue ball with the continents centered between his paws, the black ball to his right, and the purple one to his left.

"My goodness, Sir," I said, "you are rich in balls."

He smiled softly: "That I am."

He waited until I put my glass down on the counter, then he nudged the continent ball toward me with the tip of his nose, rolling it across the wooden floor of the great room, past the woodstove, and into the kitchen.

I picked it up and tossed it lightly back to him. He caught it on the fly without rising off his belly.

Carefully, he placed the ball between his outstretched legs and a second later nudged it toward me with his nose. Scooping it up, I walked over to him, picked up the other two balls and took them back to the kitchen. It seemed that he had chosen the ball with the continents as his favorite, but I decided to do a test to see if he was organizing his balls deliberately or by chance. Standing at the sink, I tossed the black ball directly at him.

He moved his head to the side, letting the ball skim by his ear and ricochet off the couch behind him. He didn't even bother to look toward where it was bouncing, but kept his eyes on me. I tossed the purple ball at him. He ducked and the ball flew over his head. His eyes never left the blue ball in my hand.

I lobbed it at him, and he jumped up and caught it in midair. Landing, he did a twirl, shaking his head in delight: "Yes! My old favorite!"

"*Ah, monsieur,*" I told him warmly, as I had once told Merle, watching him excavate his outdoor beds with extraordinary care, "*tu es un chien vraiment méticuleux.*"

Pukka raised one brow and lowered the other, the ball bulging in his mouth: "Yes, I am a particular dog, especially when it comes to balls."

His actions over the next few months also proved that he was a loyal one, for he went to great lengths to retrieve a favorite ball once it had been put into play: belly crawling under the car; scaling the teetering sides of the woodpile and descending it in an avalanche of logs; and making acrobatic rescue leaps—into trees, off of cliffs, and onto counters—that left me admiring both his grace and his restraint.

One afternoon I remember in particular. After washing off one of the slobbered cream-colored balls that he, A.J., Burley, and Goo had been retrieving, I placed it on the windowsill behind the kitchen sink to dry. I also placed it there—far out of reach—because I was tired of being their caddy. I went to my office, but didn't hear the dogs go back outside.

Wondering what they might be doing, I sneaked through the hallway and peered around the fridge. All four dogs sat before the kitchen sink and gazed up at the ball with longing. Though in plain sight, it was so clearly unattainable. After a few more moments, A.J., Burley, and Goo turned and walked outside. There was obviously nothing to be done, said their resigned postures: Ted had gone back to work; the ball could not be rescued; they might as well try to find other ways to divert themselves.

Pukka didn't follow them. Standing on his hind legs, he placed his paws on the counter and stared at the ball resting beyond the deep moat of the sink. He cocked his head from side to side, considering its position and what lay in his path: the large stainless-steel compost bowl, a bottle of dish-washing detergent, a drinking glass, the swan-necked kitchen tap, and the water-filtration spigot.

After another moment of careful study, he dropped to all fours and coiled over his paws. Then, from a dead standstill, he leapt up, all seventy pounds of him, easily clearing the edge of the counter and landing precisely amid the clutter, like a cat. Without interrupting his forward motion, and without making a single sound, he plucked the ball off the windowsill, completed a fluid turn, and sprang lightly to the floor, where he dashed through the kitchen, arced around the woodstove, and pranced outside, bearing the ball aloft to his friends.

What impressed me about his leap was not merely its height and accuracy, but also the fact that there was a bag of almonds and a bunch of bananas on the counter, each a favorite of his, along with a baguette. He could easily have snatched them. Watching him take the ball and ignore the food also made me realize that he could have snatched elk and pheasant, salmon and cheese, vegetables and chocolate, along with countless other goodies, on many an occasion while I worked in my office or outside. But he never did.

I cannot explain his civil behavior—not taking food until it was offered—for it's not something that I trained overtly. It was simply an understanding that Pukka came to on his own, just as Merle had. Even if I left Merle for several hours in the back of the Subaru with a couple of haunches of elk, he'd never take a bite, a habit that Pukka has followed to the letter, the dogs themselves deciding to be mannerly. Perhaps they — keen observers of posture, tone, and gesture — accumulated the weight of my intent and turned it into their tradition.

These are a few of the many scenes that come to mind when I think of Pukka's first two years, as well as one more, my favorite and I know his: he at his chosen work, loping through the golden grass, trailing the spoor of running pheasants before boosting them into the air, tail feathers streaming and voices cackling. Shoulder-high in the grass, he gazes at them flying toward the blue horizon with the fondest of grins. At that moment, I wish we could live ten thousand years, so I could keep on watching him, young and strong and strikingly prime.

I know others feel exactly the same way about their dogs, and it's this desire — that they remain forever young or at least live as long as we do — that causes even sensible people to talk of cloning. After all, cloning promises that the beloved dog can be restored to its youth — with all its woofs and wags and smells — as if it had never departed this life, only taken a brief leave of absence. Some of these people have gone so far as to suggest that I exhume Merle, harvest some of his DNA, and reproduce him through bioengineering. Then, they've pointed out, I could have both Merle and Pukka by my side, and not merely the spirit Merle, but the flesh-and-blood dog himself.

I've not been as confident as they that this miracle can be pulled off, and it's not because I doubt that cloning works to duplicate a dog's physical being. The results are there for all of us to see. Since 2005, when the first dog was cloned in South Korea, an Afghan Hound named Snuppy, about forty dogs have been cloned. Nonetheless, cloning a dog remains a difficult technological feat, since a dog ovulates only twice a year, and her eggs — unlike those of the more commonly cloned farm animals, like cattle, pigs, and goats — are still immature while they're in the ovary. They must be harvested from the oviducts, which is a more demanding operation. Moreover, once they're released, their life span is short — only twenty-four to thirty-six hours.

Once these technological hurdles have been overcome and a viable egg has been harvested, its nucleus is replaced with the nucleus from a cell of the donor dog — in the case of Merle, perhaps a cell from one of his bones. The reconstructed egg is then treated chemically or electrically to stimulate cell division, and the resulting embryo is transferred to the uterus of a female dog, who, some two months later, gives birth, *voilà*, to Merle himself. Or so the theory goes.

Unknowns remain. Given the newness of the technology, we don't know how long these cloned dogs will live. The health of cloned farm animals, for instance, has not been as robust as that of those born from natural reproduction. Nor have the bioengineers been able to guarantee that a cloned dog will look exactly like the deceased one in all cases – no small disappointment for those who want the very same dog back by their side. There's also the cost of cloning to be considered: the biotech firms charge between $50,000 and $150,000 per dog, depending on the discount they have been willing to offer their customers. This price point has put cloned dogs out of the reach of most people who would like to have their departed dogs restored to life.

All these practical matters dissuaded me from exhuming Merle and then using a bit of his DNA to reproduce him in a far more tangible shape than the one I had re-created in words. Nor will I consider cloning Pukka when his time comes – a long way in the future, I hope – even if the technology becomes more reliable and its price falls.

What stands in my way is my doubt that the entirety of our life experience can be stored in a random single cell, which can then reproduce the totality of our mind, soul, and spirit, restoring our departed loved ones, dogs or otherwise, to our sides. How, for example, could Merle II and Pukka II be the unique dogs whom I had known, even if they looked exactly like their forebears? Merle II would not have spent his puppyhood on the Navajo Nation, gone down the San Juan River with a much younger Ted, and come to Wyoming when he and I were still young in country that was young to both of us. Pukka II would not have been born to a mother named Abby, with an uncle named Casey, in a litter of ten brothers and sisters, on a farm in Minnesota. He would not have driven home to Wyoming through Yellowstone and watched bison and bears with the middle-aged Ted who held him in his arms.

Not believing that cloning works on this level – reproducing the memories and soul of a dog as well as its body – has helped me to cherish each and every ball toss, each and every lope through the grass, each and every day. Living in the present has also helped me to turn my attention to something less chimerical than cloning and more immediate than anticipating the eternal toss and fetch of the hereafter:

the quest for a way to help dogs live longer than they currently do in the here and now. This search has been a lesson in gradualism.

Even if we select the parents of a dog wisely, keep the dog away from pollutants, provide the dog with fine nutrition, vaccinate the dog minimally, and take care of the dog's reproductive capabilities with an eye to its breed and gender, we may still add only a few years to its life span. It's a sobering prospect. Yet, advances in biotechnology and medicine are steadily brightening it, making our hopes for much-longer-lived dogs a reality instead of a dream.

For instance, at University College London, researchers have tagged endothelial progenitor cells — a type of stem cell that promotes vascular healing — with magnetic nanoparticles and then directed them to the site of arterial injuries, creating a template for organ repair. Nano-tagging could also be used to deliver anticarcinogenic antibodies and viruses precisely to tumors.

Other scientists at Wake Forest University School of Medicine in North Carolina have used autologous cells — cells that are taken from the patient — to culture and grow bioartificial organs that are then used to replace diseased ones. As of this writing, bioartificial bladders have been implanted in humans whose factory-issued ones are no longer functional, and bioartificial livers have been given to Beagles with acute liver failure. Both procedures have been successful in more than a dozen patients.

At the Albert Einstein College of Medicine in New York, researchers have also given aging mice a gene that allows the cells in their livers to digest and recycle proteins more efficiently. In effect, mice who were the equivalent of eighty-year-old humans have had their aging livers restored to the condition of mice a quarter their age.

These breakthroughs in human medicine will increasingly be applied to veterinary medicine and will extend the life spans of our dogs, especially if a master genetic switch, one that determines the rate of our aging, can be found and eventually turned off. What a welcome day that will be: no more stiff joints, no more graying hair, no more wrinkles, no more botox. Not eternal life, but one with more youth and less pain.

While the search for this master aging switch goes on, there is yet another way to produce longer-lived dogs, albeit one that may take some time. We can change how we breed them, selecting first for longevity instead of for coat color, height, or the shape of the skull. In this way we could reset the evolutionary clocks of dogs – the clocks of danger that we spoke of in chapter 2 – so that dogs no longer resemble their short-lived ancestor, the wolf.

The idea is the brainchild of Michael Rose, a professor of evolutionary biology at the University of California–Irvine. He used the humble fruit fly in his work, breeding only those fruit flies who had slightly longer life spans than what is average for the species. In this way Rose let natural selection cull some of the genetic defects from his population of flies, leaving the hardy survivors. Generation by generation, his flies lived slightly longer, and within three decades Rose managed to produce fruit flies who were living four times as long as the average life span for the species.

When I asked him if the same method could be applied to dogs, he replied, "Yes. The methods are completely general to any animal whose breeding you can control."

Hearing this, I became very excited, for it would mean that we could extend the life spans of large dogs to fifty years, while small ones could live into their eighties. And if these dogs were screened for genetically transmitted diseases, received enhanced nutrition, and were kept from environmental pollutants, another decade might be added to their life spans.

Then Dr. Rose reminded me that it would take one hundred to two hundred generations to accomplish this goal. Still, if a dog generation is about four years, I thought, we could have very long-lived dogs within four centuries. What are four centuries when one is talking about creating longer-lived dogs? After all, the people who laid the foundation of Cologne's cathedral in 1248 did not live to see its soaring completion six centuries later. Why not apply the same vision to dogs?

Dr. Rose once again checked my enthusiasm by reminding me that longevity has low heritability, about 10 to 20 percent, as compared to the high heritability of, say, coat color. In addition, the generation time of these steadily longer-lived dogs would grow ever longer, and therefore it might take as much as a thousand years to produce septuagenarian canines.

Despite how daunting this sounds, some breeders have already embarked on the key component of this scheme – selecting for longevity – in the hope that they can produce longer-lived dogs in the much shorter run. For instance, one kennel devoted to Golden Retrievers, Gaylan's Goldens in Cold Spring, New York, has proposed what it calls "The Rule of 6s." Gaylan's suggests choosing from a line of dogs that will produce litters whose coefficient of inbreeding is less than 6 percent. All the grandparents of these litters should have lived longer than six years, and one parent, typically the sire, must be at least six years old. Ideally, the sire would have been bred fewer than six times.

Many breeders would point out that such a program severely limits their ability to select for other traits. And they would be correct. However, that's why dogs don't live as long as they might: longevity has not been a trait high on the list of what most dog breeders want to see in a dog. For instance, in one of the most frequently cited references on dog breeding, Malcolm Willis's *Genetics of the Dog*, longevity is not even mentioned as an objective for which to strive, though Willis does say that "longevity is important in a working dog because the longer the dog can stay active the longer the period of time over which the costs of training can be spread." Not much here about trying to make dogs live longer because they're the companions of our heart.

Yet, how many of us would actually jump at the chance to have a really long-lived dog if presented with the opportunity? As Wayne Cavanaugh, the president of the United Kennel Club and one of our more progressive thinkers on canine matters, told me, "Would people want dogs if they knew that they would be a commitment of thirty to fifty years? What if dogs begin to outlive us? What then happens to these dogs?"

These are good questions, and everyone's answers will be different. But despite the unknowns, I told Wayne that I was willing to start pushing the boundaries of the normal canine life span, and there was no better place to start than with Pukka himself and his future puppies, whom I was certain wouldn't be conceived until the passing of a few more years had demonstrated his hardiness. Indeed, I might wait until he reached his sixth birthday.

Pukka, of course, disagrees with me on this matter. If his interest in two intact Springer Spaniels, whom he met in Seattle, can be trusted, he's ready to be a dad right now.

"Leave it," I said as he advanced upon them across their garden.

He gave me his "you have *got* to be kidding me" look.

"Patience, monsieur," I told him. *"Patience."*

Looking a bit deflated, he watched the two sweet-smelling spaniels trot across their lawn and into the trees. Then he looked down and saw the ball he had dropped and forgotten. Picking it up, he offered it to me. I tossed it in the opposite direction, and without a backward glance at the spaniels, he dashed after it. I smiled. Whether you're a dog or a human, when romance fails, there's always sport.

CHAPTER TWENTY-THREE

Forever Young

BY THE END of the summer, I had been at my desk for five long months with very little time off, and I needed a vacation. I thought that Pukka might need one as well, even though his life had been neither hard nor boring while I had been deskbound. He had eaten good food; he had enjoyed the latest veterinary care; he had the company of many canine and human friends; and he had come and gone through his own dog door, not to mention accompanying me to town and on daily walks and bike rides. But I could tell that there was something missing.

During Merle's lifetime, and now during Pukka's, I had noticed how they became different dogs — more invigorated, if that can be imagined, and more self-assured — after we broke from our daily routine and took a camping trip, culminating with a mountain summit and a grand view. Pukka had already climbed Crystal and Jackson Peaks in the Gros Ventre Mountains as well as the Sleeping Indian; he had scaled Mount Glory and Taylor Mountain in the Tetons; and he had come back to Kelly from each of these excursions glowing with health and accomplishment. It seemed the perfect time, as summer turned to fall, to climb another peak in one of my favorite ranges, and the one in which I had done my first backpacking trip with Merle, the Winds.

These mountains stretch for a hundred miles southeast of Jackson Hole and are officially known as the Wind River Mountains of Wyoming — named for the river that flows along their eastern flank — but for me, and for everyone who loves them, they'll always be "the Winds": a jagged rampart of pinnacles, turrets, and spires, their granite smooth to the touch, their basins full of turquoise lakes and wildflowers. The Continental Divide runs along the crest of the Winds, making it possible to wander between the Atlantic and Pacific sides of the continent, all the while gazing to sprawling faraway steppes and other ranges, the distant peaks appearing so close in the clear thin air that it seems you could walk to them in an hour.

Throwing together some lightweight food, I called out to Pukka, who was napping on the dedicated quadruped couch, "We're going to the Winds, Pukka! The Winds!"

He opened a sleepy eye and saw that I was doing something in the kitchen — always a promising sign. Descending from the couch with a languorous doggy bow, he padded across the great room and stood at my side as I placed bagels, dehydrated black bean spread, and freeze-dried dinners into a stuff sack. Not much of interest there for him. But when I went to the pantry and began to pour dehydrated elk chips into Ziploc bags, his tail shifted into high gear: "Now we're talking. Looks like I'm going someplace, too!"

"Not just someplace, Pukka. The Winds!"

Intrigued and having caught my excitement, he followed me to the shed. Seeing me take a backpack and a sleeping bag from their place on the wall, he gave his tail an acknowledging beat: "I know that gear. We're going to sleep outside. Excellent!"

"But this will be a different trip," I explained to him. "You've been a puppy and have gotten a free ride because you were too young to carry your own food. Now that you're a big dog, you'll have the pleasure of carrying it. Won't that be exciting!"

Responding to my happy tone, his tail beat a complementary tattoo: "I bet it will!"

I took down Merle's panniers and let Pukka smell them. His tail slowed; his dark amber eyes went reflective: "Ah, the dog whose smell still lives in the corners of the house."

A.J., Burley, and Goo, ever inquisitive, came bounding over, and I stepped out of the shed to let them have a smell of the panniers.

"Sit, please," I asked Pukka. Hearing "sit," all of them dutifully sat.

Gently, I placed the panniers over Pukka's back. He squirmed.

"Wait."

He waited, the others now eyeing him enviously. Pukka was obviously getting something they were not. They leaned forward, waiting their turn, and their interest made Pukka grow very still.

I buckled the chest strap, smoothed the fleece-lined shields along his flanks, and fastened the girth hitch.

"Oh," I cried in admiration. "You're a packin' dog now."

He stood, testing the sensation. Empty, the rig weighed only a few ounces. No burden there. He took a few steps. Nothing to it. Unlike Merle, who had sat rooted to the earth the first time I put on the panniers, Pukka took an exploratory stroll around the grass, making a half-circle and beginning to grin.

"Yes," I said, "you look splendid, Sir, and it's just your color." I gave him my fawning shopgirl's voice.

He threw back his shoulders, while the other dogs crowded around him, sniffing and pushing. This only made Pukka more aware that he had been singled out for special treatment. "Ha-ha-ha!" he panted. "Look what I have and you don't!"

A.J., Burley, and Goo stared at me plaintively: "You're always so fair. None for us? What gives?"

"I'm sorry, boys." I held out my hands, palms up, the well-understood sign for "no more." "I can't take all four of you."

Their faces fell.

"I'm sorry. I really am."

They turned and walked back across the field to their home, shoulders hunched, Burley, the most sensitive of the three to any affront, casting a look behind him that said, "I thought you were my friend!"

"Burls," I called, "don't be —"

Before I could finish, Pukka rubbed against my knee in triumph. In the endless toy wars between him and Burley, he had just scored a major victory. He was wearing the panniers and Burley was not. He gave a joyous leap: "You and me, Ted, and my panniers!"

"Yes," I agreed, "you and me. And let's get some weight in those panniers and see what you think of them then."

Taking the pack and sleeping bag, and grabbing a small tent, a sleeping pad, and a stove, I followed Pukka into the house to finish our packing. There, in the kitchen, his approbation of the panniers steadily rose as he watched me stow the Ziploc bags containing his dehydrated elk in them.

"Want to try the weight?" I asked him.

He stood rock-still as I placed the panniers over his shoulders, his tail now swishing with dawning comprehension: "I carry my food in the panniers, and then I get to eat it! What a terrific idea!"

"You got it," I said, taking off the panniers. "And what's more, you'll carry a bit of my gear as well, in return for my having carried all of yours." I added my camp sandals, a book, and tent stakes to his load, topping it off at six pounds, then laid the panniers aside and turned to the task of replenishing our joint human-canine first aid kit.

Once upon a time, in the early days when I was doing these back-country trips with Merle, our first aid kid consisted of a few Band-Aids, some gauze pads, and a roll of adhesive tape. Bare bones, to be sure, and fortunately, neither Merle nor I ever suffered any life-threatening trauma. These days — as medical expertise, technological sophistica-tion, and my own knowledge of canine health have increased — such a first aid kit seems inadequate and I bring more: stretchy vet wrap, also called "self-cling wrap," to keep gauze pads in place (it's far easier to deploy than adhesive tape, and it won't stick to fur); the antibiotic Clavamox for infected wounds; a small bottle of saline solution for eyes that become irritated with dust or grass seeds; Ascription (coated aspirin) for pain and swelling; and 3 percent solution of hydrogen per-oxide to induce vomiting if a dog has swallowed something toxic, one teaspoon per ten pounds of dog to a maximum of twelve teaspoons. The hydrogen peroxide also doubles as an antibacterial solution to cleanse wounds. Butterfly bandages are in my kit as well as Super Glue, which is great for repairing both cracked fingers and cracked paws.

I also bring along some homeopathic remedies that have been rec-ommended to me by the holistic veterinarians Marybeth Minter and Allen Schoen, the key ones being arnica for swelling, trauma, and shock; nux vomica for vomiting; arsenicum for poisoning; apis mel for stings; phosphorus for clotting; and aconitum for anxiety and fear.

Although homeopathic remedies remain much debated in both the veterinary and human medical professions, I've personally seen rapid improvement in Pukka when I've given them to him after he was stung by bees and on another occasion when he began to vomit after eating an unidentified red berry. I've also gotten positive results by using ar-nica on myself for soreness during long hikes.

That said, I fully realize that the efficacy of homeopathic remedies has not been medically proven. Yet they appear to work for many peo-ple and their dogs, either because they are working in some way we don't currently understand, or, as Professor Edzard Ernst of the Uni-versity of Exeter, a specialist in the analysis of clinical medical trials, has written, "the individualized, empathetic and time-intensive ap-proach most homeopaths adopt to healthcare yields good clinical results." So I continue to put the little vials of tiny white pills, weighing almost nothing, in my first aid kit alongside the allopathic drugs.

The last thing I put in my first aid kit is an updated knowledge of how to use it. Wanting to learn more about the particular first aid needs of our dogs, I enrolled in a seminar presented by Michelle Sevigny, the founder of DOGSAFE Canine First Aid, in Vancouver, British Columbia. We learned how to assess an injured dog's level of consciousness, give artificial respiration and CPR, stop bleeding, clear obstructed airways, attend to seizures, and splint broken limbs. It was one of the more worthwhile days I've spent, and details about these techniques are in the notes.

The sky was deep blue and the aspen were just turning gold as I dabbed sunscreen on my face and put on Pukka's panniers and my backpack. Up the trail we went, heading toward the Cirque of the Towers, ten miles distant. We didn't get more than half a mile before Pukka spied the Big Sandy River flowing to our right. Dashing through the long grass and the spruce, he plunged off the bank into the sun-glittered water, swam a small circle, and jumped back onto terra firma, shaking heartily and running up to me with a happy grin: "Oh, did that feel good!" I was glad that I'd placed my book and his food in double Ziploc bags. We were off to a good start.

Not for long.

As we crossed the first sidestream, two backpackers came from the opposite direction, and Pukka greeted them warmly, tail wagging.

"Great day!" I exclaimed.

"Fabulous!"

"Have a good one!"

"You too!"

We passed each other, and distracted by the camaraderie, the clear blue sky, and the fresh cool air — how wonderful it was to be away from my desk and hiking at last! — I stubbed my toe on a rock and catapulted forward. It happened so fast that I couldn't brace myself with my trekking poles. The weight of my pack drove me forward, and I crashed full-length on the trail, smashing my face in the dirt. Stunned by the blow, and my own clumsiness, I lay there, bleeding and seeing stars.

Pukka rushed to me in a dither and licked the blood off my face. His eyes were wide: "Are you okay? What can I do? Are you hurt bad?"

After having spent so much time thinking about first aid for my dog, this was an ironic start to the trip.

"Nothing but my pride," I assured him, putting an arm around his shoulders and picking myself up. My cheek ached where it had slammed into the ground, and wiping off the blood with the back of my hand, I thought, "Hmm, when have I done that before?"

I couldn't remember, and I said aloud, "Wow, Ted, you're really getting decrepit." Then, trying to be a little easier on myself, I recollected that it had been a long time since I had spent this many months at my keyboard, doing nothing in the way of exercise except ride my bike, swim, and hike with Pukka. Yet, not all that long ago, I had been able to throw on a big pack — no matter how many months I hadn't carried one — and scamper up trails like a mountain goat. Suddenly I heard Tennyson's line, spoken by the aging Ulysses: "We are not now that strength which in old days / Moved earth and heaven."

"So true, Uly, so true!" I thought. Then, brushing off my muddy knees, I laughed. Not five minutes down the trail, and I was already campin' dirty.

Pukka, hearing me laugh, jumped at my face and wagged his tail in relief: "You're okay, Ted! You're okay!"

"I am," I said. "I really am."

Up the trail we went, I placing my feet a little more carefully, and after a few hours we came to Big Sandy Lake. On its narrow berm of sand, I took off Pukka's panniers, sat on my pack, and ate a bagel. He brought me a stick, and I threw it far into the lake. He plunged in and swam sleekly through the turquoise water, looking like a golden otter, the tall gray peaks rising above him.

We went on through rocky glens, crossing tumbling little waterfalls and making our way over aprons of pale granite patched with orange lichen, the lodgepole and fir giving way to whitebark pine, their big cones crunching underfoot. The air was clear and warm, and there was not a thing to worry about: no e-mail, no phone calls, certainly no traffic. As for grizzly bears, I had a canister of pepper spray on my hip belt. Even that often-pressing concern of tourists the world over, where to find a restroom, was of no concern. Stepping off the trail, I took a pee. Pukka, coming quickly to my side, sniffed the bush — "Oh, excellent find, what a good spot!" — and cocking his leg, he aimed his stream inches from mine while giving me a complaisant look: "You and me, Ted, peeing together, like good friends should!"

On we went, up through small cliffs, and down into narrow valleys. At last we ascended the rutted trail to Jackass Pass, the going now so steep that we could only see sky ahead of us until we crested the Divide.

Shazam!

The great monolith of Pingora rose before us, soaring above Lonesome Lake, the mountain's upswept faces and sheer dark walls improbably Gothic in their sky-reaching grandeur.

Pukka stopped and stared.

Beyond Pingora, in a serried crown of turrets and fins, the Cirque of the Towers stood before us: Wolfs Head, Sharks Nose, Block Tower, Warrior, and War Bonnet. I stood, also rooted to the spot by the stupendous view. It had been a quarter of a century since I had crossed this portal and climbed those great faces. Pukka, with no history to make him nostalgic, walked to the sign marking Jackass Pass, raised his leg, and marked his arrival.

Since camping within a quarter of a mile of Lonesome Lake is no longer permitted (over the years too much human waste has flowed into its clear waters), Pukka and I angled away from the trail and strolled down the yellowing hillsides of tundra until we found a terrace with a perfectly flat spot for the tent, set to the leeward of large granite boulders and in a semicircle of whitebark pine. The site had a view to the lake and the Cirque above it, and there was a spring nearby.

"Could you ask for more?" I asked Pukka as I took off his panniers.

"Yes, I could!" he replied with a grateful pant and immediately threw himself on the grass, rubbing his back in ecstasy, his four paws massaging the sky. Leaping to his feet, he laughed at me: "Oh, I'm perfect now!"

"Let's get some water," I suggested, "and that'll make us feel even better."

We got our water at a little spring, and back at camp I commenced the old routine: pitch the tent, wrap the guylines around stakes and rocks . . . tighten the prusik knots . . . the familiar tasks comforting. People had been doing this for tens of thousands of years — making home behind a windbreak of trees and boulders — and it was, as it has always been for me, like returning to family.

Done, I took my power lounger (a fold-up chair of foam, Cordura, and webbing) and placed it in the last sun of the meadow behind camp, leaning its back against a pine tree. There I sat, admiring our little yellow tent and the peaks of the Cirque soaring above it.

Pukka, who had disappeared, came back with a stick. I threw it a few times, thinking that he would soon lie down and have a post-hike nap, as Merle would have done. But the ten-mile walk and the long climb with panniers had apparently done nothing to tire him out. I threw the stick some more, reminding myself that Merle at this young age wouldn't have lain down to take in the view, as he did when he became an older and more contemplative dog. As a young dog, he would immediately roll on his back when I took off his panniers, just as Pukka had, and then he would leave camp to scour the rock piles for marmots. So I couldn't be hard on Pukka, who was simply following his own star.

I threw the stick several more times, but at last grew weary of the game. Putting the stick down on the grass next to me, I said softly, "I'm going to sit here in the sun, Pukka, and write some notes, and then read, so enough."

His shoulders slumped at the dreaded word, ending all games, all hope, all good times, but, much to his credit, he lay down on his belly, his toes just touching his stick while he gazed from it to me.

"Thank you," I said and opened my notebook and began to write. He raised one brow and lowered the other — yes, the notebook was out — and he put his chin on his paws and closed his eyes.

I wrote; I looked at the peaks; Pukka dozed. Finishing my notes about our walk in, I simply gazed at the peaks, finding it hard to believe that I had once climbed their great vertical faces.

My eyes wandered up the fifteen-hundred-foot route that Frank and I had done on the east face of Pingora, starting at first light, reaching the summit after sunset, and rappelling off in the twilight, his faint call — "Off rappelllll!" — floating up to me as I stood alone on the summit, the heaven already darkening in the east. I waited a few more moments — taking it all in — then I clipped into the ropes and followed him down into the night.

Heroic days.

Laying a hand on Pukka's ruff, I felt his warm fur, lambent in the last sun. There had been no dogs back then — in the time of the great alpine faces and the extended hikes and floats across Alaska, the six-month-long trips to Nepal, Siberia, and Africa, the year-and-a-half-long journey to the tip of South America. No dogs in my life then, and no regrets, then or now, about their lack — the long hiatus between my childhood dogs and those of my adulthood. Sitting in the arms of the Cirque, with my hand on Pukka's ruff, I was glad that I had lived those journeys when I could.

I fed Pukka and ate my dinner; then we watched the stars come out before going to sleep. In the morning, we watched the stars dim, the peaks turn rosy, and the line of sun move down them. Without distractions, it was easy to follow the circle of the day.

I brewed some tea and sat in the door of the tent, my sleeping bag over my knees, for the air temperature was still below freezing. Mug of tea in hand and very comfy, I read an entertaining novel. Having had almost no downtime in the last five months, this was what I had come to do. Not so Pukka.

He had already made several walkabouts among the boulders, pines, and little meadows surrounding our camp, and he now came into the tent to sit by my side. His eyes, boring into mine, said, "Is *this* going to be our day? Sit here and *read?* I thought we were going hiking!"

"This is what camping's about, Pukka!" I said cheerfully. "Going nowhere for a while."

His face fell.

"Oh, don't worry," I consoled him, putting an arm around his shoulders. "We'll go on a climb later today, I promise, but for a while I'd like to read. It's my day off, and this is so much fun, just hanging out and reading a book, watching the sun rise."

I went back to my book, and he gave a huge sigh, collapsing next to me as if he were a balloon and I'd stuck a pin in him. Placing his head between his paws, his ears hanging over his forearms, he was the template of dejection. His eyes, however, continued to track outside, one brow going up, the other down, and before a minute went by, he jumped to his feet, gave a little snort — "You can waste the day, but I'm not" — and out the door he went, disappearing around the large boulder alongside of which we had pitched our tent.

After a while I got up and made another cup of tea, and Pukka reappeared, giving his tail a snappy little wag — "At last, you're up!"

"Shall we go meet the sun, Sir?" I asked him.

We walked away from camp — into the meadow behind our big boulder — and stood, waiting for the line of sun to reach us. One minute went by, then another, and as the line of sun crossed my body I felt its instant heat. "Mmm!" I said. Even Pukka raised his face to the golden cascade, his eyes closed.

"Pretty nice, eh?" I remarked.

He gave his tail three swishes, his eyes still closed: "Yes, very nice, I will admit."

Back at camp, I put out his breakfast and made my own, taking it and my power lounger to the smooth granite outcropping below our tent, so much like a veranda. Stands of whitebark pine, terraces of rock, and small lush meadows descended to the shore of Lonesome Lake, while the Cirque — spires and turrets and fins — rose above us.

I ate and soaked up the sun. Pukka, now resigned to the hopeless inactivity of the day, lay down just beyond the reach of my crossed feet, where, sphinxlike, he examined the basin below, studying it slowly from one end to the other. Occasionally, his ears pricked, his nose twitched, and he stiffened. Then he relaxed — "Nope, not what I thought" — and resumed his survey.

I read on, and in a little while Pukka turned on his side, placing his shoulders against the soles of my feet, shod only in socks. I pressed; he gave a deep sigh: "Yes, together." He stretched to the tip of his toes, pushed his back harder against my feet, and sighed again. The rock was warm, the morning now mild, and he was very comfortable, but there was more to his heartfelt sigh than our pleasant surroundings and the age-old, reassuring press of human foot against the back of a dog.

Out here, we lived on the same level: we slept on the ground; we ate on the ground; and we did our business on the ground, together. Camping was the great equalizer. At home, everything emphasized our difference in station: I ate at a table; I sat on a chair; I slept in a bed. Even though I frequently got down on the floor with him, he was most always below me. There were hundreds of different toys and balls I could buy Pukka, but I don't think there was any gift finer than that of going camping together and living with him at his height.

Sometime in the late morning, I finished reading and loaded a light day pack with our lunch and some extra clothing. I hung our food bags out of the reach of bears, and we set off for Jackass Pass. Studying the topographic map, I had decided to climb Dog Tooth Peak, for in all my trips into the Cirque I had never climbed to its 12,488-foot summit and I was excited about doing something new with Pukka. I also couldn't resist the nice overtones of Pukka's first mountain in the Winds being named Dog Tooth Peak.

We cruised along, I on the trail, Pukka coursing over the aprons of rock and into the forest, sometimes disappearing for five minutes, only to be waiting on the trail, far below me, when I came around a bend. I stopped for some water, and he trotted to my side, conducting the air with the happiness of his tail.

"Pukka," I said, "we're having too much fun." I gave him a rub on the shoulders, and he wriggled: "Yes, too much fun!"

Down we continued, backtracking our route of the previous day and emerging from the forest at North Lake. There we jumped its inlet and started uphill, going along a tumbling stream, bashing through willows, crossing stands of evergreens, and climbing through beautiful, salmon-colored shields of granite, the stone bordered by harebells and asters, their gentian petals fading with the coming fall.

Pukka began to act birdy, his tail beating faster and faster as he did figure eights through the grass, working out a scent trail: "I smell a bird! I smell a *bird!* I smell a *BIRD!*" And before I could say "blue grouse," he had one in the air, his face ecstatic.

The bird landed at the top of a pine tree and looked down at us from a swaying bough.

I gave the grouse a nod for entertaining my dog, and Pukka gave it a throaty "Huh! I'll see you on the way back."

Up we went, the evergreens giving way to yellowing tundra, Pukka gamboling ahead of me in the long tireless stride of a wolf. Occasionally, he'd glance back: "That way, no?"

"That's the way," I'd call, and off he'd lope.

The sun poured down upon us; the summit block of jumbled rock grew closer; Pukka bounded through the boulders, perching on their fins and staring down at me with a grin: "You're so slow. I'm so fast."

"You are!" I called.

As we climbed, galleons of cumulus clouds floated above us, and we could see Big Sandy Lake far below, as well as the tiny line of the trail upon which we had hiked. Behind it rose dark forested ridges, and beyond them lay sprawling yellow steppes, stretching away to distant ranges.

Ahead, the way became more jumbled and confused, and I wondered if I'd find a way through for Pukka. Rocky walls loomed above us, and here and there I began to need both hands and feet to scramble up. I needn't have worried. Pukka found the way, skimming up twelve-foot-high boulders, his paws finding purchase on nubbins and tiny hollows. Turning, he'd grin back at me, tongue lolling.

"Oh, you are a climbin' dog!" I called up to him.

"Huh-huh-huh," he panted. "It's nothing."

"Oh, I don't know about that!"

He gave me a big wag of his tail, turned, and continued upward, jumping across six-foot-wide trenches between the boulders, landing briefly on their narrow fins, and leaping on, his constant upward motion preventing him from falling. We had passed 12,000 feet and were now panting a bit. Soon, we found snow lying between the boulders, and Pukka, wearing his built-in crampons — his claws — dashed up the snow and ice as if it weren't there. I had to be a bit more careful.

We could see the summit above us, and driving himself over the last jumble of rocks, Pukka reached the top before me, a small flat rock with a cairn in its center. Standing next to it, he gazed all around, actually doing a 360-degree circle, his tail beating triumphantly as I came up to him.

"The very top, Sir!" I cried. "Congratulations! Your first Wind River peak!" Lean and gold, he stood above me, and as I climbed up to join him, he stepped forward and pushed his head against my chest. I lowered my face into his ruff and rubbed his shoulders.

"Well done, Pukka," I said quietly. "Well done."

I climbed onto the summit. He stood on his hind legs, put his paws on my shoulders, and licked my face. After our celebratory hug, we shared the view, he wandering around the summit to gaze in every direction, and I turning round the clock, the horizon more than a hundred miles away and taking in the states of Wyoming, Idaho, Utah, and Colorado. The Continental Divide went directly between my straddled legs, and playfully I spat on the cairn, imagining myself heading down to both the Atlantic and Pacific Oceans. I would soon be part of the continent and the bordering seas. Pukka came over, sniffed the cairn, raised his leg, and peed. He, too, was heading downstream.

We sat and ate: I an elk sandwich, Pukka several handfuls of elk jerky. We drank some water and then relaxed side by side. He leaned his flank against me — "Touch, together, the best!" — and I circled an arm around his shoulders and thought of our distant future, when he and I would be older and no longer able to do this sort of climbing. How on some winter day we might be sitting by the woodstove, and I'd remember when we were young and strong and climbed Dog Tooth Peak together. Perhaps he, too, would remember this September day, his paws twitching in his dreams as he became a pup once again, bounding over boulders and leading the way to the summit. I was glad that I had paid attention to my instincts, gone on this trip, and not stayed home to finish chores. Who, in their old age, will remember vacuuming the house over summiting Dog Tooth Peak in the Winds?

We lingered, and lingered some more, not wanting to give up this grand view.

"Oh, Pukka," I said, giving him a hug. "My heart is big with you."

He rubbed his head against my face: "And mine with you!"

I stood and picked up a handful of snow, casting it to the six directions — north, east, south, west, heaven, and earth — as I offered my thanks to the great blessings: health, home, love, dogs.

Finally, we descended. I wasn't worried about returning by headlamp, but it would be nice to watch the sunset from camp. Down, down, down we went, going off the northern side of the summit, which looked easier from above than the way we had come up. And so it proved, Pukka leading the way and disappearing into grassy passages between the boulders, only to return in a while and gaze up at me with a telling look that said, "This way goes, Ted. Trust me. It really does."

And every single time, it did.

Down we went — into the boulder fields, the willows, and the pines, Pukka finding and flushing the grouse once again. We crossed the head of North Lake, climbed back over Jackass Pass, and descended into camp.

There we found neighbors camped on the terrace several hundred yards above us, their tent obscured by large boulders and trees. It soon became apparent that it was a man and a woman with a dog on a long leash. The instant the dog spied us, it began to bark.

Pukka stood still, gazing up at the barking dog with his hackles raised, every muscle taut, a soft growl rumbling in his throat.

"Oh, Sir!" I told him. "Manners, please. You are not going to bark at that dog."

The dog, partially hidden by willows and evergreens, barked sharply at us: "Danger! Intruders! I see you down there!"

"Grrrr," Pukka replied softly.

"He can bark," I told him. "You cannot. This is non-negotiable. You know that."

He gave an annoyed snap of his tail: "I know that. And I'm not barking. I'm rumbling."

He had me there. Conceding his point, I said, "How about dinner?"

At the well-known word, Pukka's interest in the dog vanished. He followed me to a low flat rock where I set his bowl and poured out his dehydrated elk chips. Inhaling them, he wagged his tail inquiringly: "I could use another bowl of that."

"If you do," I told him, "you won't have any breakfast." His face, hearing my tone, took on a resigned expression: "Okay. I'll wait."

Sitting in my power lounger, I got my own dinner going, and when I looked up I noticed that Pukka had disappeared. I walked around the alcove of trees and spied him walking across the meadow toward the terrace above, where the dog was once again barking at him.

"Please leave that dog alone," I said.

Pukka wagged his tail. "I just want to see who it is."

What harm could come from that?

"All right," I said, motioning with my hand in our habitual "you can go" gesture. He waited, making sure he hadn't mistaken what I had signaled. "It's okay," I told him. "Go play."

He shot across the field, up through the rocks, and a moment later I could see his golden shape cavorting around the black shape of the dog. I returned to the stove, fixed some soup, and, mug in hand, walked to the camp above so as to make sure that Pukka wasn't making a nuisance of himself.

He and the dog, a large black fellow with Labrador features, were chasing each other round and round, even though the black dog was still on his long tether. The man and woman, both in their twenties, sat with their mugs and watched the dogs play. We exchanged small talk, and they said they didn't mind Pukka playing with their dog, whose name was Blue.

"If he becomes a problem, just give a shout," I said and went back to camp.

It grew dusky; the dogs played on. I whistled for Pukka, and when he didn't come, I went up and got him. Reluctantly, he accompanied me to camp, looking back all the while with a wistfully wagging tail: "That dog is so much fun to play with!"

"I know," I replied, "I know. But he's on a leash, which probably means that his people aren't comfortable with his coming down here. So maybe they don't want you up there."

I sat and ate my dinner while Pukka edged away from camp, slipping toward the meadow and back toward Blue.

"Uh-uh," I told him for the third time. "You don't want to wear out your welcome."

He sighed and came back to me, his nostrils twitching at the smell of my curry. A moment later, he walked to his bowl, lapped some water, and then, with a show of nonchalance so feigned that I had to stifle my laughter, he began to slowly meander along the edge of the pines as if he had developed a sudden interest in dendrology. He examined the resinous trunks, he sniffed the boughs, he poked at fallen pinecones with his snout, step by casual step edging ever closer to the meadow, where he would disappear from my sight.

I whistled. He turned and looked at me. I shook my head and said, "Leave it, Pukka. Please come back here."

Clearly unhappy, he came.

"Why don't you have a little rest?" I suggested. "It's almost dark. You climbed Dog Tooth Peak. You played with Blue for over an hour. We have a long walk ahead of us tomorrow, and you'll be carrying your panniers."

He gave me a miffed looked that said, "I'm not tired." I had a suspicion that there was more bravado than truth in his statement, and I said, "Why don't you lie down and enjoy this lovely evening? It's our last night in the Cirque." I gestured to the ground before me, and he elected not to contest the issue. He smelled the ground where I had gestured, but found it not to his liking. Wandering toward the tent, he sniffed its door and decided to go inside, where he began to push and prod my sleeping bag with his paws and snout, flinging it around, until it was just the right shape for him to nest in. Then, with an enormous sigh — "Oh, what's a dog to do? Here I am, prisoner of this taskmaster, I might as well make the best of things" — he settled onto my sleeping bag, closed his eyes, and was instantly asleep.

I watched Mars rise in the east, and then the Pleiades, the seven sisters, float above the peaks, a miniature Dipper set among the stony spires. The woman in the camp above laughed, her voice like the tinkle of a rill, and I remembered her flaxen hair coming out of her wool stocking cap. It was the same color as that of a woman who, not that long ago, I had wished to be mine. I gave a sigh as big as Pukka's and turned in.

The night was cold, well below freezing, and Pukka kept me awake, leaning against me, despite having a thick pad and my parka covering him. The wind began to blow, and I slept fitfully, not wanting to remember how much I had wanted to be with this woman, but doing so nonetheless.

She had been standing in line with nearly a hundred other people, waiting to have her book signed, a strong yet delicate figure in a low-cut T-shirt and Capri pants, very seaside, and not all that much younger than I. After I signed her book and we had talked about her dogs—one gone, the other still living—she said, not wanting to close down our brief conversation, "You and I have a lot in common. I ski, I hike, I kayak, I ride horses, and I bike." Her body looked like she was not making this up.

What could I say? If I was reading her correctly, she wanted more than her book signed, and I was interested. She had something . . . the word came to me right away: *spine*. It was in her erect posture and direct, open gaze, her self-assured blue eyes saying, "I am a force, and I think we could be a force together." All this in under three minutes. Bravely, touchingly, she had ventured out on a limb and now risked embarrassment.

I was still holding her book, and I could feel the line of people behind her growing impatient, their communal vibe saying, "Stop talking to that fox in the too-tight T-shirt and Capri pants and get back to what you're supposed to be doing: signing our books."

"That's great," I said lamely and handed her book back. She took it, nodded, and walked away. I watched her go and thought, "Get up and catch her. You will never know what might happen if you don't."

I sat right where I was and signed people's books for the next hour.

When I checked my webmail two days later, there was a note from her: "I'd love to talk to you, if you have the time while on the East Coast." She left a phone number.

I called her when I returned to Wyoming, and we talked for an hour and a half. Then we wrote, and we talked some more, eventually meeting in her city, at a seafood restaurant, where I found her sitting at a corner table. Not long into dinner, I knew that what I had surmised on the phone and through e-mails was true. She was one of the most intelligent and interesting people I'd ever met, opening horizons I hadn't seen, asking me questions I hadn't thought of.

However, I quickly discovered that her intelligence had its limitations, as did mine. She didn't say good-bye after dinner, and nor did I, despite our very busy lives and most of a continent standing between us. How could I? I was already in love with those limpid blue eyes, hanging on me, and how sleek and supple and pulled together she was: well read, conversational, as athletic as she had claimed, inventive in her kitchen, and devoted to her horses and dogs. Not only could I not say good-bye to her, I would have happily commuted to Antarctica to keep on seeing her. And so we saw each other for a while.

Then one of the things I admired about her — her cool logic — prevailed. She couldn't run her corporation from Jackson Hole, even via the Internet. She had ninety employees to think of, and she still wanted to shepherd the company she had created to greatness. I could appreciate her predicament. I couldn't move to the East Coast and write this book among crowds and cars and cities. Yet seeing each other long-distance, at monthlong intervals, was not what she wanted to do at this stage of her life. She wanted a man by her side. Had she been a dog, she would have stayed in the West. Had I been a dog, I would have followed her east. But we were not dogs. We were two people as much in love with our work as we were with each other.

Pukka shifted and snuggled against me, reminding me of the last time I had held her, and she had whispered in my ear, soft as starlight, "I wish we weren't breaking up, so I could keep on falling in love with you."

I put an arm over him, and he stuck his head into the opening of my sleeping bag and shivered. I pressed my nose into his ruff and smelled his clean, bamboolike odor, scented by the pines through which he had run and underlain by nutty lanolin. He bored deeper into my sleeping bag.

"Are you really a Labrador Retriever?" I asked him.

By way of an answer, he shivered again.

I unzipped the bag and put it over both of us, spooning him against me, my sweet young pup, his head under my chin, his back against my chest. I held him and thought, "How curiously things have turned out." Here I was — more than halfway through my allotted run — still without a human partner, but with this very fine dog, with whom I was spectacularly in love: alone on the great divide, but not.

Perhaps Pukka felt my restlessness. Rubbing his face against my jaw, he gave me a lick on the cheek. I pulled him closer and felt his heart beating against mine. Then he relaxed completely and let out a sigh: "Ah, that's better – touch, together, as we should be."

In the morning, I sat in my power lounger, watching the Cirque brighten from my veranda of granite. Blue and his people broke camp, and Pukka followed their departure with his eyes until they were out of sight over the top of Jackass Pass. As they disappeared, he looked at me and whined, "I had such a good time with that dog."

"I know," I said. "Maybe we'll see him on the way out."

"Hmmm." He made a soft noise in the back of his throat – expressing what? Doubt? Disappointment? Longing? It sounded like longing for the company he had had.

He padded across the rock apron and lay down alongside me, his back against my leg – "Touch, that's better" – and gazed down to Lonesome Lake and the Cirque rising above it.

Between Merle's death and meeting Pukka, nearly five years had gone by. It had now been two years since I had said good-bye to the woman who had hooked her long delicate finger into my heart and whose pull still beckoned.

Picking up my notebook, I wrote five lines from the poet Theodore Roethke, which had stood me in good stead before. I didn't need to write them down since I knew them by heart. But it was good to see them, staring me in the face:

> *A lively understandable spirit*
> *Once entertained you.*
> *It will come again.*
> *Be still.*
> *Wait.*

About midday, we climbed to Jackass Pass, where I spent a good minute looking back, sealing the view in my mind: Pingora's giant face, the long dorsal fin of arêtes and towers, stretching around the basin. Who knew when I might walk this way again?

We headed down the far side of the pass and when I turned for one more look, we had sunk the Cirque.

Pukka raced ahead of me and an hour later, at the inlet of North Lake, he picked up a stick and asked me to throw it into the water for him. "Let's keep going," I told him, "and I'll throw a stick for you at Big Sandy Lake." I motioned downvalley. "Come on, let's go. You can swim down there, where we stopped and ate lunch the other day."

He immediately dropped the stick and ran down the trail ahead of me, his blue panniers bouncing. After another hour of hiking, we came to the lake, and Pukka hurried along the shoreline trail, bypassing a dozen coves and beaches for nearly half a mile. He was a hundred yards ahead of me when he made a sharp left turn off the trail, ran to the water's edge, and stood upon the exact spot where we had eaten lunch two days before.

Staring at me, he wagged his tail: "This is the spot where you threw the stick and I swam, isn't it?"

"It is!" I exclaimed, impressed with his seeming comprehension of what I had told him back at North Lake. "Well done, Pukka! Well done!"

I didn't think, of course, that he had completely grasped the meaning of my sentences. Nonetheless, he had come directly here. Why not nurture any budding connections between his grammar and mine? After all, praise makes the promise bloom.

"Very well done!" I told him again.

I took off his panniers. He dashed away and found a suitable stick. I launched it across the water, and he leapt in. The summit of Dog Tooth Peak rose over the far end of the lake, high on the great divide where we had stood the day before, and Pukka swam toward it, paddling hard, a young dog following his heart, and I following mine, younger, far younger, for having gone into the mountains with him.

He came back to shore and shook himself at a polite distance, as we had agreed upon. Then, grinning hugely, he pranced up to me and tossed the stick into my waiting hand.

"Oh, you are a pukka dog!" I told him. "Do you know that?"

He beat his tail against his sides with joy.

With Great Thanks

To the many who helped me write this book:

April North, for her constant loving presence in Pukka's life and mine. April exercised Pukka with her own dogs – Kirah, Bruce, Asha, and Maggie – while I was tied to my desk, and she was there for both Pukka and me during medical emergencies and scary times. I also want to give my very special thanks to my longtime friend Kim Fadiman, for his ever-present ear, his astute readings of my drafts, his pitch-perfect advice on matters of style, and his fine companionship. I would be much the poorer writer and person without Kim.

Others contributed to this book by steadily feeding me information on environmental, medical, and veterinary issues as well as reviewing some or all of these chapters: Peter Vasilas, Irene and Nikolia Rallis, Elpis Kerasote, Anthony Platis, Doug Radloff, Allison von Maur, Suzanne W. Dixon, Richard Irwin, Dr. David Shlim, MD, and Dr. Debbie Hadlock, VMD.

Scottie Westfall, who writes the Retriever, Dog, & Wildlife Blog, helped me to navigate the world of purebred dogs, as did Wayne Cavanaugh, the president of the United Kennel Club. Wayne's insider perspective has been invaluable, and without it, I would have written a far less coherent book. Patti Strand, the director of the National Animal Interest Alliance, Susan LaCroix Hamil, on the board of directors of the AKC Canine Health Foundation, and Robin Hovan, the research facilitator for the Golden Retriever Club of America, were frequent sounding boards about canine health and kennel club politics. Dr. Marilyn Fender, the global communications coordinator of the Centronuclear Myopathy Project, gave me a highly detailed and critical reading of the initial drafts of the two genetics chapters, which put them on much sounder scientific footing. Without the careful reading of these chapters by the dog breeder and trainer Debby Kay, and the many hours she spent talking with me about canine health and longevity on her farm in West Virginia, this entire book would have been much less accurate. My thanks also go to Anne Fadiman for her enthusiastic input on fine grammatical points.

The Austrian canine geneticist Hellmuth Wachtel kindly opened his library and his years of knowledge to me, helping me to better understand the evolution of purebred dogs. Doug Smith, the leader of the Yellowstone Wolf Project, has been one of my longtime advisers on the biology and habits of wolves. Dina Sutin made two fine videos of Pukka for my website, Forrest McCarthy made another, and Jonathan Selkowitz went the extra mile to shoot the cover of this book. Barbara Larkin was an excellent guide to positive-reinforcement training and with her husband, Tim, helped to make Pukka a steadier bird hunter.

Dozens of veterinarians fielded my endless questions. My heartfelt thanks go to Marybeth Minter and Theo Schuff, not only for answering my questions about canine health, but also for taking such fine care of Merle and now continuing that tradition with Pukka. I'm also indebted to Dr. Heather Carlton, who saved Pukka's life when he was seriously injured and thus gave this book's main character the chance to become a longer-lived dog.

Dr. Bruce Fogle in the United Kingdom has been ever-gracious in sharing his knowledge of dogs and introducing me to a variety of colleagues, most notably Dr. Åke Hedhammar and Karin Drotz of the Swedish Kennel Club, whose help proved crucial in unfolding some of this book's arguments. Dr. Greg Ogilvie, of the Angel Care Cancer Center in Carlsbad, California, spent over two years discussing canine cancer with me and was extremely open in allowing me to see every aspect of his clinic's operation. I also want to extend my deep thanks to Greg's wife, Karla, who looked after Pukka while I was in southern California, allowing him to join Cocoa, Luna, and Dash at the Ogilvie homestead. Dr. Karen Becker has also been an ever-present resource on canine health and the latest advances in veterinary care.

Several other veterinarians were particularly generous with their time: Lisa Barber, Ian Billinghurst, Jeff Bryan, Jean Dodds, Erick Egger, Marty Goldstein, Kim Henneman, Laura Nafe, Jack Oliver, Allen Schoen, Kim Selting, Frances Smith, David Waters, and the immunologist Ron Schultz. My very special thanks go to Jack Reece, who helped me understand the stray dogs of India.

Many people in Europe were especially important in helping me to understand the differences between how dogs are raised in Europe and how they are raised in North America: in the United Kingdom, the dog trainer and behaviorist John Rogerson, the dog breeder and trainer Mary Ward, the webcaster Julie Hill, and Bill Lambert of the Kennel Club; in Ireland, the veterinarian Pete Wedderburn; in Switzerland, Lucia Kälin; in Italy, Serena Magano, Donatella Derchi, Cristina Pellegrini, Elisabetta Petrogalli, and the dog trainer Stefano Tansella; and in Russia, Kerry Irwin and Alexey Vereshchagin.

I'd also like to send my very warm thanks to Manfred, Huberta, Fritz, and Cato Barthel, who gave me my base camp in Austria and taught me much about how European dogs live. As well, I wish to express a special thank-you to the German dog writer Eva-Maria Krämer, who gave me a two-day-long tour of the German training, veterinary, and shelter worlds and who has answered a long stream of my e-mailed questions.

Several readers pointed me to interesting scientific findings (Michael Blott, Michele Mold, and Diana Roberts), did research for me (Greg Smalley), opened doors for me in the pet food industry (Anthony Bennie), gave me a guided tour of how stray dogs live in Los Angeles (Kat Thomas of the Los Angeles Police Department), or helped me to find Pukka (Jim Brown, Sharon Fanning, and Diane Lavett). The author Mark Derr kindly shared some of his insights into the problems of purebred dogs.

Many in the animal shelter world spent long hours discussing how to make shelters work better: Rich Avanzino, Cristina Bedini, Christophe Bellanger, Roberta Benini, Ryan Clinton, Brenda Comerford, Paulette Dean, Conor Dowling, John Embery, Rebecca Emeny, Maria Rosaria Esposito, Gianluca Felicetti, Lindsay Goldring, Sylvia Hemmerling, Leslie Hervey, Susanne Kogut, Andrea Kuhn, Natalia Merkurieva, Donal Moroney, Alessia Nervegna, Wayne Pacelle, Angela Petrovna, Andrew Rowan, Marcy Rydd, Robin Starr, Inge Welzig, Nathan Winograd, and Stephen Zawistowski. I'm particularly grateful to Ryan Clinton and Nathan Winograd for their critical review of the shelter chapters and for the candidness of Ryan Clinton and Stephen Zawistowski about many issues in the shelter world.

The interlibrary loan staff of the Teton County Library — Carol

Connors, Eva Dahlgren, Mike Windsor, and Jessica Johnson — processed hundreds of interlibrary loan requests with alacrity and ongoing interest. This book simply could not have been completed without their assistance. My researchers Maria Hayashida, Kate Hayden, Susan Scarlata, Jennifer Simon, Vicki Soles, and Morri Stewart spent many hundreds of hours tracking down hard-to-find information, and I would like to extend my very fond thanks to Jen for our many fine conversations, to Vicki and her husband Lonnie, whose care of Chance will never be forgotten, and to Kim Jones, to whom I shall be forever grateful for getting Chance out of the Downey shelter when I was leaving for India.

Russell Galen (my agent), Laurie Brown (the senior vice president of Houghton Mifflin Harcourt), and Andrea Schulz (HMH's editor in chief) — dog lovers all — have been great supporters of this book. Andrea's incisive ideas about restructuring the book proved instrumental in helping me get to the heart of the argument, and her friendship, humor, and advice have been of great comfort during the creation of this work, as has Russ's.

Several friends have been there for me during the long haul: the Landale Family, Bill Liske, Peter Vasilas, Baker and Diane Rawlings, Benj Sinclair, Steve and Sonja Sharkey, Susan and Mayo Lykes, Karen Wilbrecht, and Len Carlman and Anne Ladd. Of course, I could not have written this book without the support of my home mountains and the strength, peace, and energy they've given me as I completed this long task. Nor could I have done it without the counsel of the dogs themselves: A.J., Burley, Goo, and Buck; Kirah, Bruce, Asha, Maggie, and Hansie; Chance and Spencer; Pearly, June Bug, and Bailey, and my most constant companion Pukka, along with the spirits of Brower and Merle, still walking by our sides.

Notes

All quotations in the text that are not specifically cited below were recorded by me between October 2007 and May 2012, either in person, by phone, or by e-mail. The names of some people and dogs have been changed to protect their privacy.

2. The Clocks of Danger

8 **walkabout away from its pack:** Douglas W. Smith, Leader, Yellowstone Wolf Project, telephone interview with the author, July 5, 2007.

13 **jackal to the giant polar bear:** L. David Mech, *The Wolf* (Garden City, NY: Natural History Press, 1970), 21; Bruce Fogle, *The New Encyclopedia of the Dog* (London: Dorling Kindersley, 2000), 14; W. D. Mathew, "The Phylogeny Of Dogs," *Journal of Mammalogy* 11, no. 2 (May 1930): 117–38.

in as little as two months: Online at The Virtual Nature Trail at Penn State New Kensington, species page for the deer mouse; Frank H. Clark, "Age of Sexual Maturity in Mice of the Genus Peromyscus," *Journal of Mammalogy* 19 (1938): 230–34; W. J. Hamilton Jr., "Growth and Life Span of the Field Mouse," *The American Naturalist* 71, no. 736 (September-October 1937): 500–507.

14 **"r-selected" and "K-selected":** "r" and "K" were originally mathematical terms in an equation describing the driving forces of evolution, but today they are used generically to describe the traits of particular species. S. N. Austad, "Comparative Aging and Life Histories in Mammals," *Experimental Gerontology* 32 (1997): 23–38.

three or four years: Douglas W. Smith, Leader, Yellowstone Wolf Project, interview with the author, Mammoth Hot Springs, WY, March 18, 2005.

twelve to fourteen years: Online at International Wolf Center, "Frequently Asked Questions About Wolves."

survive to breed: Across North America the average wolf litter size is 5.4. See Todd K. Fuller et al., "Wolf Population Dynamics," in L. David Mech and Luigi Boitani, eds., *Wolves: Behavior, Ecology, and Conservation* (Chicago: University of Chicago Press, 2003), 175. In Yellowstone National Park, with its abundant prey, the average litter size is 7.8. See Paul Schullery, *The Yellowstone Wolf: A Guide and Sourcebook* (Worland, WY: High Plains Publishing Co., 1996), 130.

15 **one calf a year:** Richard D. Taber et al., "Population Characteristics," in Jack

Ward Thomas and Dale E. Toweill, eds., *Elk of North America: Ecology and Management* (Harrisburg, PA: Stackpole Books, 1982), 281–83.

their mating battles: Bruce Smith, former senior biologist, National Elk Refuge, Jackson Hole, WY, e-mail communication with the author, April 9, 2008.

the bigger you are: Alex Comfort, "The Life Span of Animals," *Scientific American* 205 (1961): 108–19.

extended our life span: Caleb E. Finch, *The Biology of Human Longevity* (Boston: Academic Press, 2007), 3.

the bigger your brain: Angelos C. Economos, "Brain–Life Span Conjecture: A Reevaluation of the Evidence," *Gerontology* 26 (1980): 82–89; João Pedro de Magalhães, "Comparative Biology of Aging," online at Senescence.info.

150 and 200 years: Online at San Diego Zoo, "Reptiles: Galápagos Tortoise."

sometimes even a century: Steve N. Austad and Kathleen E. Fischer, "Mammalian Aging, Metabolism, and Ecology: Evidence from the Bats and Marsupials," *Journal of Gerontology: Biological Sciences* 46 (1991): B47–53.

lives for forty years: Andrej J. Podlutsky et al., "A New Field Record for Bat Longevity," *Journals of Gerontology Series A: Biological Sciences and Medical Sciences* 60 (2005): 1366–68.

16 **half a century:** D. J. Holmes and M. A. Ottinger, "Birds as Long-Lived Animal Models for the Study of Aging," *Experimental Gerontology* 38 (2003): 1365–66.

17 **their nongliding counterparts:** Steve N. Austad and Kathleen E. Fischer, "Mammalian Aging, Metabolism, and Ecology: Evidence from the Bats and Marsupials," *Journal of Gerontology: Biological Sciences* 46 (1991): B52.

earthbound ostriches: Online at San Diego Zoo, "Ostrich."

live longer than soft-shell ones: Michael R. Rose, *The Long Tomorrow* (Oxford: Oxford University Press, 2005), 66; Kenneth K. Chew and Alex P. Ma, "Common Littleneck Clam," US Fish and Wildlife Service Biological Report 82(11.78) (August 1987); Barbara J. Abraham, "Softshell Clam," US Fish and Wildlife Service Biological Report 82(11.68) (August 1986).

the Methuselahs of nature: John C. George et al., "Age and Growth Estimates of Bowhead Whales (*Balaena mysticetus*) via Aspartic Acid Racemization," *Canadian Journal of Zoology* 77 (1999): 571–80.

18 **first American one in 1982:** Online at Embrace Pet Insurance Blog, "Where Was the First Pet Insured?" May 1, 2006.

began to use these insurance records: A. Egenvall et al., "Mortality in over 350,000 Insured Swedish Dogs from 1995–2000: II. Breed-Specific Age and Survival Patterns and Relative Risk for Causes of Death," *Acta Veterinaria Scandinavica* 46, no. 3 (2005): 121–36. About 70 percent of Sweden's dogs were insured at the time of the study — that figure has now gone up to 80 percent — and the researchers believed that Agria's database was a close representation of the Swedish dog population in general, though they did note that the study only covered dogs to the age of ten. See A. Egenvall et al., "Survey of the Swedish Dog Population: Age, Gender, Breed, Location, and Enrollment in Animal Insurance," *Acta Veterinaria Scandinavica* 40, no. 3 (1999): 231–40; and Brenda

Bonnet, "Breed Risks for Disease in Purebred Dogs," presentation at the conference "The Purebred Paradox," Washington, DC, April 28, 2011.

19 **only six and a half years:** G. Bernardi, "Longevity and Morbidity in the Irish Wolfhound in the United States – 1966–1986," *Harp and Hound* 1 (1988): 78–84. Cancer and heart disease took about an equal toll on Swedish Great Danes, but cancer kills most of those in the United States.

20 **giant breeds do not:** Nathan B. Sutter et al., "A Single *IGF1* Allele Is a Major Determinant of Small Size in Dogs," *Science* 316 (April 6, 2007): 112–15.

an organism's life span: Andrzej Bartke, "Insulin and Aging," *Cell Cycle* 7, no. 21 (November 2008): 3338–43; Cynthia Kenyon et al., "A *C. elegans* Mutant That Lives Twice as Long as Wild Type," *Nature* 366 (1993): 461–64; M. Tartar et al., "A Mutant *Drosophila* Insulin Receptor Homolog That Extends Life-Span and Impairs Neuroendocrine Function," *Science* 292, no. 107 (2001): 107–9; Matthias Blüher et al., "Extended Longevity in Mice Lacking the Insulin Receptor in Adipose Tissue," *Science* 299 (2003): 572–74; Cynthia J. Kenyon, "The Genetics of Aging," *Nature* 464, no. 25 (March 2010): 504–12.

its life span increases: Andrzej Bartke, "Insulin and Aging," *Cell Cycle* 7, no. 21 (November 2008): 3338–43.

centenarian populations around the world: Yousin Suh et al., "Functionally Significant Insulin-Like Growth Factor I Receptor Mutations in Centenarians," *Proceedings of the National Academy of Sciences* 105, no. 9 (2008): 3438–42; Ludmilla Pawlikowska et al., "Association of Common Genetic Variation in the Insulin/IGF1 Signaling Pathway with Human Longevity," *Aging Cell* 8, no. 4 (2009): 460–72; Y. Li et al., "Genetic Association of *FOXO1A* and *FOXO3A* with Longevity Trait in Han Chinese Populations," *Human Molecular Genetics* 18, no. 24 (December 15, 2009): 4897–4904; Bradley J. Wilcox et al., "*FOXO3A* Genotype Is Strongly Associated with Human Longevity," *Proceedings of the National Academy of Sciences* 105, no. 37 (September 16, 2008): 13987–92; Friederike Flaschsbart et al., "Association of *FOXO3A* Variation with Human Longevity Confirmed in German Centenarians," *Proceedings of the National Academy of Sciences* 106, no. 8 (February 24, 2009): 2700–2705.

zero incidence of cancer: Polly Dunbar, "'Immune' to Cancer: The Astonishing Dwarf Community in Ecuador Who Could Hold the Key to a Cure," *MailOnline*, August 16, 2008; Nicholas Wade, "Ecuadorian Villagers May Hold Secret to Longevity," *New York Times*, February 16, 2011.

cataloged in purebred dogs: W. Jean Dodds, DVM, "Guide to Hereditary and Congenital Diseases in Dogs," online at SiriusDog.com; C. A. Smith, "New Hope for Overcoming Canine Inherited Disease," *Journal of the American Veterinary Medical Association* 204, no. 1 (January 1994): 41–46.

60 million and 77.5 million dogs: For the estimate of 60 million dogs in the United States, see Andrew Rowan, president and CEO of Humane Society International, interview with the author, Washington, DC, April 28, 2011; for the estimate of 77.5 million dogs, see "Pet Ownership," in *2009/2010 National Pet Owners Survey,* online at American Pet Products Association.

in some European countries: Åke Hedhammar, interview with the author, Stockholm, Sweden, August 27, 2008.

22 **two of the most popular breeds:** US breed rankings are from the American Kennel Club website; breed rankings for the United Kingdom are from the Kennel Club website.

live up to 1.8 years longer: B. N. Bonnett et al., "Mortality in Insured Swedish Dogs: Rates and Causes of Death in Various Breeds," *The Veterinary Record* (July 12, 1997): 40–44; A. Egenvall et al., "Gender, Age, Breed, and Distribution of Morbidity and Mortality in Insured Dogs in Sweden During 1995 and 1996," *The Veterinary Record* (April 29, 2000): 519–25; P. D. McGreevy and F. W. Nicholas, "Some Practical Solutions to Welfare Problems in Dog Breeding," *Animal Welfare* 8 (1999): 329–41; G. J. Patronek et al., "Comparative Longevity of Pet Dogs and Humans: Implications for Gerontology Research," *Journal of Gerontology* 52A (1997): B171–78; H. F. Proschowsky et al., "Mortality of Purebred and Mixed-Breed Dogs in Denmark," *Preventive Veterinary Medicine* 58, nos. 1-2 (April 30, 2003): 63–74.

99.9 percent of the wolf's DNA: Kerstin Linblad-Toh et al., "Genome Sequence, Comparative Analysis, and Haplotype Structure of the Domestic Dog," *Nature* 438 (December 8, 2005): 803–19.

4. Houndy Labs

36 **1.5 million healthy dogs:** See the websites of the American Society for the Prevention of Cruelty to Animals (ASPCA) and the Humane Society of the United States (HSUS); Stephen Zawistowski, ASPCA Science Adviser, e-mail communication with the author, March 26, 2012.

compared to intact dogs: Online at Laura J. Sanborn, "Long-Term Health Risks and Benefits Associated with Spay/Neuter in Dogs," May 14, 2007.

live a year longer: Dr. Kelly M. Cassidy, "Conclusions," online at Dog Longevity, July 13, 2007.

39 **a love of roaming:** Ed Martley, *Blender: Colorado River Dog* (Rapid City, SD: Top Dog Publishing Co., 1997).

40 **in the early 1500s:** Richard Wolters, *The Labrador Retriever* (New York: Dutton Books, 1992), 1–60.

calling them "Labradors": Lord George Scott and Sir John Middleton, *The Labrador Dog* (London: H. F. & G. Witherby Ltd., 1936), 33.

contribute their genes: Online at faqs.com, "rec.pets.dogs: Labrador Retrievers Breed-FAQ," February 26, 2002. Initially, Labrador breeders, set on producing black dogs, had no use for light-colored pups and culled or gave them away. The dogs paid this human bias no mind and kept producing yellow pups out of black dogs, proving that the gene for a yellow coat in the Labrador Retriever was well established in the population and only needed the meeting of two recessive alleles for the color to express itself. See Helen Warwick, *The New Complete Labrador Retriever* (New York: Howell Book House, 1989), 85. In

1899 this happened once again, but someone was finally charmed by the result. Major C. E. Radclyffe's two black dogs, Neptune and Duchess, produced a litter with two yellow puppies, whom Radclyffe didn't discard. Instead, he named them Ben and Juno and registered them with the Kennel Club. Ben, now known as Ben of Hyde, went on to sire many yellow pups. See Richard Wolters, *The Labrador Retriever* (New York: Dutton Books, 1992), 154–55.

sheep protection act: For the Newfoundland sheep protection act, see Lord George Scott and Sir John Middleton, *The Labrador Dog* (London: H. F. & G. Witherby Ltd., 1936), 117. For Great Britain's rabies quarantine, information is available online at Orders in Council and Despatches, "Importation of Dogs Order of 1897," and "The Public General Statutes Passed in the Fifty-Seventh and Fifty-eighth Years of the Reign of Her Majesty Queen Victoria, 1894 with a List of the Local and Private Acts, Tables Showing the Effect of the Session's Legislation, and a Copious Index," vol. 31.

increasingly to Golden Retrievers: Jack Vanderwyk, "Labrador Typecasting," online at labradornet.com; Sharon Fanning, Cloverdale Labradors, e-mail communication with the author, February 6, 2008.

can still be seen in some Labs today: Not everyone was pleased with the results of these outcrossings. Another group of breeders believed that foxhounds brought "structural evils" into the Labrador line, turning the breed into something unrecognizable as the one that the Third Earl of Malmesbury and his contemporaries had worked so hard to perfect. See Lord George Scott and Sir John Middleton, *The Labrador Dog* (London: H. F. & G. Witherby Ltd., 1936), 117; see also Helen Warwick, *The New Complete Labrador Retriever* (New York: Howell Book House, 1989), 96.

named Ming: Dr. Bernard W. Ziessow, *The Official Book of the Labrador Retriever* (Lanham, MD: TFH Publications, 1995), 12.

5. Sifting the Genes

43 **"when two unrelated breeds are mated":** Online at The Goldendoodle & Labradoodle Website.

nonshedding coat of the Poodle: Ibid.; see also the Cockapoo Club of America website.

44 **mélange as "confusion":** Linda Orlando, "Crossing Culinary Boundaries with Fusion Cuisine," online at Buzzle.com.

"a purebred dog has to offer": Online at The Labrador Retriever Club, Inc., "Labradoodles."

scientific literature – genetic: D. H. Crews Jr. "Principles of Genetics I," online at Continental Kennel Club.

biological: Suzanne Edmands, "Heterosis and Outbreeding Depression in Interpopulation Crosses Spanning a Wide Range of Divergence," *Evolution* 53, no. 6 (1999): 1757–68.

veterinary: P. D. McGreevy and F. W. Nicholas, "Some Practical Solutions to

Welfare Problems in Dog Breeding," *Animal Welfare* 8 (1999): 329–41; Scott P. Greiner, "Crossbreeding Beef Cattle," May 1, 2009, online at Virginia Cooperative Extension.

horticultural: James A. Birchler et al., "In Search of the Molecular Basis of Heterosis," *The Plant Cell* 15 (October 2003): 2236–39.

are occasionally disappointed: Frances O. Smith, diplomate in the American College of Theriogenology and president of the Orthopedic Foundation for Animals, e-mail communication with the author, May 13, 2011.

a love of water: Online at Golden Retriever Club of America, "Brief History and Origin of the Golden Retriever."

scenting ability into the line: Online at American Kennel Club, "Golden Retriever History."

45 **getting systemic histiocytosis:** Patricia Long, "Histiocytic Diseases of the Bernese Mountain Dog," September 2001 (updated April 2009), online at The Bernese Mountain Dog Club of America, Inc.

if you're a Greyhound: Gail K. Smith, "Efficacy of Hip Dysplasia Screening: An Animal Welfare Imperative," presentation at the conference "The Purebred Paradox," Washington, DC, April 28, 2011.

5 percent of male Golden Retrievers: Federico C. F. Calboli et al., "Population Structure and Inbreeding from Pedigree Analysis of Purebred Dogs," *Genetics* 179, no. 1 (May 2008): 593–601.

"almost monstrous character": Charles Darwin, *The Variation of Animals and Plants Under Domestication* [1868], vol. 1 (Baltimore: John Hopkins University Press, 1998), 16.

scarcity and expense: Thorstein Veblen, *The Theory of the Leisure Class* [1899] (New York: New American Library, 1953), 103–4.

Numerous other critics: Mark Derr, "The Politics of Dogs," *The Atlantic Monthly*, March 1990, 50; Michael D. Lemonick, "A Terrible Beauty," *Time*, December 12, 1994, 64–70.

Pedigree Dogs Exposed: *Pedigree Dogs Exposed* can be seen on a variety of free websites.

46 **a parliamentary investigation:** Online at Associate Parliamentary Group for Animal Welfare, "A Healthier Future for Pedigree Dogs" (November 2009), 16; online at Nicola Rooney and David Sargan, "Pedigree Dog Breeding in the UK: A Major Welfare Concern? An Independent Scientific Report Commissioned by the RSPCA," 2008; online at Patrick Bateson, "Independent Inquiry into Dog Breeding," 2010, 1.

from closely related parents: Bill Lambert, health and breed services manager, Kennel Club, e-mail communication with the author, September 17, 2010.

penalized in shows: Online at Kennel Club, "Bulldog Breed Standard."

"Breeder of Merit": Online at American Kennel Club, "Breeder of Merit Program."

"Accredited Breeder Scheme": Online at Kennel Club, "Accredited Breeders Scheme."

recommended health screenings: Online at American Kennel Club, "AKC Breeder of Merit."

47 **sloping rear ends:** *100 Jahre Der Deutsche Schäferhund* (*100 Years of the German Shepherd Dog*), special issue of *SV-Zeitung* (April 1999): 76–77.

pelvis is abnormally formed: Doctors Foster and Smith Pet Education, "Hip Dysplasia in Dogs: Diagnosis, Treatment, and Prevention," online at drsfostersmith.com; H. A. W. Hazewinkel, "Are Hip Dysplasia and Elbow Dysplasia Hereditary Diseases?" Centennial Conference of the Dutch Kennel Club, Amsterdam, July 2, 2002.

20 percent chance: Jean Mueller, "Balance Problems with the American Show German Shepherd," online at Leerburg Video & Kennel; Gail K. Smith, "Efficacy of Hip Dysplasia Screening: An Animal Welfare Imperative," presentation at the conference "The Purebred Paradox," Washington, DC, April 28, 2011.

48 **might not be recognized:** Online at Tony Rosato, "Footprints in the Breed: The Aversham Pekingese," January 2007.

too long-nosed: Online at Shih Tzu Club, "Breed History."

49 **"a competitive edge":** Tony Rosato, "The Pekingese and the Happa Dog," online at Pekingese Club of America, "History of the Breed."

impeding the flow of air: Online at Claudia Nöller et al., "New Aspects of Brachycephalia in Dogs and Cats, Basics: Insights into Embryology, Anatomy, and Pathophysiology," University of Leipzig; Gerhard U. Oechtering et al., "Brachycephalic Airway Syndrome, Part 1: A New Understanding — It Is An Intranasal Problem!" and Gerhard U. Oechtering, "Brachycephalic Airway Syndrome, Part 2: Laser-Assisted Turbinectomy (Late) — A Novel Therapeutic Approach," presentation at NAVC conference, Orlando, FL, January 21, 2008.

through the nasal mucosa: Knut Schmidt-Nielsen et al., "Panting in Dogs: Unidirectional Air Flow over Evaporative Surfaces," *Science* 169 (September 11, 1970): 1102–4.

Later experiments: Marcia B. Goldberg et al., "Panting in Dogs: Paths of Air Flow in Response to Heat and Exercise," *Respiration Physiology* 43 (1981): 327–38.

50 **short-faced breeds:** Online at American Veterinary Medical Association (AVMA), "Frequently Asked Questions by Pet Owners About Short-Nosed Dogs and Air Travel."

52 **"mid and upper teens":** Online at Pug Dog Club of America, "Pug Health Guide."

"are no rarity": Online at Pug Club of the United Kingdom, "The Health of the Pug."

Morris Animal Foundation: Online at Morris Animal Foundation, "Golden Retriever Foundation Partners with MAF to Help Dogs Live Longer Healthier Lives."

between seven and eight years: Online at Berner-Garde Foundation.

repeated its surveys in 2000: Pat Long, Berner-Garde file manager, e-mail communication with the author, September 9, 2010.

55 **"less inbred and unsound":** The Hon. Mrs. Neville Lytton, *Toy Dogs and Their Ancestors* (London: Duckworth & Co., 1911), 87, 106–7.

"vanity of the breeder": Max von Stephanitz, *The German Shepherd Dog in Word and Picture* (Jena, Ger.: Anton Kampfe, 1925), 380.

56 **"injurious recessive genes":** John Paul Scott and John L. Fuller, *Genetics and the Social Behavior of the Dog* (Chicago: University of Chicago Press, 1965), 405.

95,539 registered descendants: Online at Performance Goldens, "Misty Morn's Sunset Descendants." By 2010, Cummings' Gold-Rush Charlie had 77,478 registered descendants, and Holway Barty had 22,854.

increases the chance of recessive genes: A. M. Oberbauer and J. Sampson, "Pedigree Analysis, Genotype Testing, and Genetic Counseling," in Anatoly Ruvinsky and Jeff Sampson, eds., *The Genetics of the Dog* (Oxon, U.K.: CABI Publishing, 2001), 462.

61.4 percent of Golden Retrievers: Online at Golden Retriever Club of America, "National Health Survey 1998–1999," 142.

might really be dying of: Rhonda Hovan, research facilitator for the Golden Retriever Club of America, telephone interview with the author, May 18, 2010.

57 **geneticist Sewall Wright:** James F. Crow, "Sewall Wright and Physiological Genetics," in James F. Crow and William F. Dove, "Anecdotal, Historical, and Critical Commentaries on Genetics," *Genetics* 115 (January 1987): 1–2.

that cost $11.59: Online at PedFast Technologies.

greater than 25 percent: John B. Armstrong, "Results of the Standard Poodle Longevity Study," online at NetPets.

58 **increasing numbers of dogs:** Online at Geonscoper, "DLA Diversity to Follow and Maintain Heterozygosity at MHC II Locus"; online at American Kennel Club Canine Health Foundation, "Major Histocompatibility Complex and Autoimmune Disease in Dogs"; J. M. Angelis et al., "Frequency and Distribution of Alleles of Canine MHC-II DLA-DQB1, DLA-DQA1 and DLA-DRB1 in 25 Representative American Kennel Club Breeds," *Tissue Antigens* 66, no. 3 (September 2005): 173–84; Barbara Bouyet, *Akita: Treasure of Japan*, vol. 2 (Thousand Oaks, CA: Magnum Publishing, 2002), 427–30.

60 **saved $2 million:** Lennart Swenson et al., "Prevalence and Inheritance of and Selection for Hip Dysplasia in Seven Breeds of Dogs in Sweden and Benefit:Cost Analysis of a Screening and Control Program," *Journal of the American Veterinary Medical Association* 210, no. 2 (January 15, 1997): 211.

stalled or been inconsistent: Minna Leppänen and Hannu Saloniemi, "Controlling Canine Hip Dysplasia in Finland," *Preventive Veterinary Medicine* 42 (1999): 121–31. Two breeds that showed declines in the incidence of hip dysplasia were the English Cocker Spaniel and the Rottweiler; the incidence in the Doberman and English Springer Spaniel remained unchanged.

still winning blue ribbons: see information online for Pointers at World Dog Show, Paris, July 7–10, 2011, http://www.cedia.fr/palmares/resultats .asp?expo=1765; for Pekingese, at "Västerås April 16, 2011," Kennel Drakedram; and http://www.drakedram.com/eng.html; for French Bulldogs, at Kennel

Ruffel & Bow: Black Pugs and French Bulldogs, http://ruffelnbow.webs.com/fbmales.htm.

tied registration to health certification: Niela Sback, Dansk Kennel Club, telephone interview with the author's researcher, Jennifer Simon, September 14, 2010; Astrid Indrebø, Norwegian veterinarian and president of FCI Breeding Commission, e-mail communication with the author's researcher, Jennifer Simon, September 22, 2010; Karin Drotz, Swedish Kennel Club, e-mail communication with the author, April 27, 2011.

breed clubs in Germany: Eva-Maria Krämer, German dog writer, trainer, and author of Infohund.de, e-mail communication with the author, September 18, 2010.

infused with new blood: Online at Kennel Club, "Pilot Scheme for Registering Dogs of Unverified Parentage."

"doggie dating service": Bill Lambert, health and breeder services manager, Kennel Club, telephone interview with the author, September 9, 2010; online at Kennel Club, "'Woof, He's Fit'—The New Doggie Dating Website That Puts Health First."

61 **identify canine diseases:** Online at American Kennel Club Canine Health Foundation, "Research."

"a dog breeding operation": Online at *Avenson v. Zegart,* 577F.Supp. 958 (Dist. Ct. Minn. 1984).

adherence to breed standards: Online at American Kennel Club, "Chairman's Report, September 2008."

to create healthier dogs: Lisa Peterson, Director of Communications, American Kennel Club, telephone interview with the author, September 21, 2010.

wishes were ignored: Online at United States Border Collie Club, "A Short History of the Border Collie and the AKC."

half its revenues: The AKC's tax returns show that about half of its income comes from dog registrations, more than twice the amount generated by dog shows and performance events. See American Kennel Club, 2008 tax return, Form 990, U.S. Department of the Treasury, Internal Revenue Service.

63 **looks over physical fitness:** Andrea Wood, "UKC Mission," in *United Kennel Club, 1898–1997, The First 100 Years* (Kalamazoo, MI: United Kennel Club, 1997), 3.

65 **introduced veterinary checks:** Online at Kennel Club, "Bulldog and Pekingese Fail Crufts Vet Checks," March 8, 2012.

"Could such disqualifications happen": Online at "Crufts' Campaign Against the Purebred Dog," *Best in Show Daily.*

"Never!!!": Online at *Dogs in Review,* Facebook post, March 13, 2012.

66 **"duty to the canine world":** Online at United Kennel Club, "United Kennel Club, Inc., Announces Major Revisions to Its Breed Standards."

mail supported Cavanaugh: Online at United Kennel Club, "Revised UKC GSD Breed Standard May 1ˢᵗ."

fallen 40 percent: Wayne Cavanaugh, e-mail communication with the author,

March 26, 2012; John Mandeville, *Dogs News* 27, no. 46 (November 19, 2010): 14.

6. On a Farm in Minnesota

67 **online data banks:** Some of these pedigree search engines are free and can be found by doing a search for the name of your chosen breed plus "pedigree search," as in "Labrador Retriever pedigree search." The AKC's search engine requires a fee for each pedigree. It was $12 when I did my searching.

71 **puppies handled from infancy:** Michael Fox, *Understanding Your Dog* (New York: Coward, McCann and Geoghegan, 1972), 99–102; Otto Weininger, "Physiological Damage Under Emotional Stress as a Function of Early Experience," *Science* 119, no. 3087 (February 26, 1954): 285–86; Seymour Levine, "Maternal and Environmental Influences on the Adrenocortical Response to Stress in Weanling Rats," *Science* 156, no. 3772 (April 14, 1967): 258–60; Robert Ader et al., "Attenuation of the Plasma Corticosterone Response to Handling and Electric Shock Stimulation in the Infant Rat," *Physiology and Behavior* 3, no. 2 (March 1968): 327–31; Seymour Levine, "Infantile Experience and Resistance to Physiological Stress," *Science* 126, no. 3270 (August 30, 1957): 405; Robert Ader and Stanford Friedman, "Differential Early Experiences and Susceptibility to Transplanted Tumor in the Rat," *Journal of Comparative and Physiological Psychology* 59, no. 3 (June 1965): 361–64; Carmen L. Battaglia, "Periods of Early Development and the Effects of Stimulation and Social Experiences in the Canine," *Journal of Veterinary Behavior* 4 (2009): 203–10; John C. Wright, "The Effects Of Differential Rearing on Exploratory Behavior in Puppies," *Applied Animal Ethology* 10 (1983): 27–34.

7. Duration of Immunity

75 **into young adulthood:** Robert W. Sears, *The Vaccine Book* (New York: Little, Brown and Co., 2007), 213.

    twelve years old: Online at Immunization Action Coalition; online at Netdoctor, "Childhood Vaccinations"; online at European Centre for Disease Prevention and Control.

    vomiting, fever, and thirst: Richard W. Nelson and C. Guillermo Couto, *Small Animal Internal Medicine,* 4th ed. (St. Louis, MO: Mosby Elsevier, 2009), 1315–17; online at "New Forms of Old Disease, Leptospirosis, Threatens Dogs in US," Cornell University Science News; online at Ron Hines, "Leptospirosis in Your Dog."

76 *International Vaccination Newsletter:* Online at healthy.net. *International Vaccination Newsletter.*

    "many anecdotes make a statistic": Hans Kruuk, *Hunter and Hunted* (Cambridge: Cambridge University Press, 2002), 55.

    vaccinated against rabies: Online at Barbara E. Kitchell, "Feline Vaccine–Associated Sarcomas," Thirtieth World Congress of the World Small Animal Veterinary Association.

given simultaneously at that location: Mattie Hendrick et al., "Postvaccinal Sarcomas in the Cat: Epidemiology and Electron Probe Microanalytical Identification of Aluminum," *Cancer Research* 52 (October 1, 1992): 5391–94. After one vaccination, the risk of cancer increased by 50 percent; after two, the risk went up to 127 percent; after three or four vaccines at the same location, the risk rose to 175 percent. See Gregory K. Ogilvie and Antony S. Moore, *Managing the Veterinary Cancer Patient* (Yardley, PA: Veterinary Learning Systems, 1997), 515–18.

injection-site sarcomas: D. W. Macy and M. J. Hendrick, "The Potential Role of Inflammation in the Development of Postvaccinal Sarcomas in Cats," *Veterinary Clinics of North America: Small Animal Practice* 26 (1996): 103–9.

number of afflicted cats: M. Vascellari et al., "Fibrosarcomas at Presumed Sites of Injection in Dogs: Characteristics and Comparison with Non-vaccination Site Fibrosarcomas and Feline Post-Vaccinal Fibrosarcomas," *Journal of Veterinary Medicine* 50, no. 6 (August 2003): 286–91.

laboratory mice and rats: Online at Katherine Albrecht, "Microchip-Induced Tumors in Laboratory Rodents and Dogs: A Review of the Literature, 1990–2006."

genetically susceptible individuals: D. W. Macy and M. J. Hendrick, "The Potential Role of Inflammation in the Development of Postvaccinal Sarcomas in Cats," *Veterinary Clinics of North America: Small Animal Practice* 26 (1996): 103–9; Hae Young Chung et al., "The Inflammation Hypothesis of Aging: Molecular Modification by Caloric Restriction," *Annals of the New York Academy of Sciences* 928 (2001): 327–35; L. F. Cherkas et al., "The Effects of Social Status on Biological Aging as Measured by White-Blood Cell Telomere Length," *Aging Cell* 5 (2006): 361–65; Online at Lasalle D. Lefall Jr. and Margaret L. Kripke, *Reducing Environmental Cancer Risk — What We Can Do Now: 2008–2009 Annual Report of the President's Cancer Panel*, 3.

77 **on the heels of vaccination:** Derek Duval and Urs Giger, "Vaccine-Associated Immune-Mediated Hemolytic Anemia in the Dog," *Journal of Veterinary Internal Medicine* 10, no. 5 (September-October 1996): 290–95; Harm Hogenesch et al., "Vaccine-Induced Autoimmunity in the Dog," *Advances in Veterinary Medicine* 41 (1999): 733–47; A. R. Allbritton, "Autoimmune Disease and Vaccination?" *Veterinary Allergy and Clinical Immunology* 4, no. 1 (1996): 16–17.

adverse reactions to the rabies vaccine: Keitaro Ohmori et al., "A Retrospective Study on Adverse Reactions to Canine Vaccines in Japan," *Journal of Veterinary Medical Science* 64, no. 9 (2002): 851–53; online at Rabies Challenge Fund, "About the Rabies Challenge Fund."

Center for Veterinary Biologics: Online at USDA Animal and Plant Health Inspection Service's Center for Veterinary Biologics.

vaccination caused the seizure: Robert W. Sears, *The Vaccine Book* (New York: Little Brown and Co., 2007), 57.

hundreds of millions of them: Timothy Frana et al., "Summary of Adverse Event Reports for Veterinary Biologic Products Received by the USDA from 1999 Through 2005," in "Veterinary Medicine Today Special Report," *Journal of the American Veterinary Medical Association* 229, no. 7 (October 1, 2006).

78 **between 2002 and 2004:** George E. Moore et al., "Adverse Events Diagnosed Within Three Days of Vaccine Administration in Dogs," *Journal of the American Veterinary Medical Association* 227, no. 7 (October 1, 2005): 1102–8.

safer forms of antigens: Robert Temple, *The Genius of China* (Rochester, VT: Inner Traditions, 1987), 149–51.

Adjuvants . . . are substances: Anne R. Spickler and James A. Roth, "Adjuvants in Veterinary Vaccines: Modes of Action and Adverse Effects," *Journal of Veterinary Internal Medicine* 17 (2003): 273–81; Dale R. Spriggs and Wayne C. Koff, *Topics in Vaccine Adjuvant Research* (Boca Raton, FL: CRC Press, 1991), introduction.

ill effects in both mice: M. S. Petrik et al., "Aluminum Adjuvant Linked to Gulf War Illness Induces Motor Neuron Death in Mice," *Neuromolecular Medicine* 9, no. 1 (2007): 83–100.

anemia, and bone disease: Committee on Nutrition, American Academy of Pediatrics, "Aluminum Toxicity in Infants and Children," *Pediatrics* 97 (1996): 413–16.

79 **no adjuvant at all:** Nilanjana Banerji et al., "Association of Germ-Line Polymorphisms in the Feline *p53* Gene with Genetic Predisposition to Vaccine-Associated Feline Sarcoma," *Journal of Heredity* 98, no. 5 (2007): 421–27.

this suite of genes: Derek Duval and Urs Giger, "Vaccine-Associated Immune-Mediated Hemolytic Anemia in the Dog," *Journal of Veterinary Internal Medicine* 10, no. 5 (September–October 1996): 290–95; Harm Hogenesch et al., "Vaccine-Induced Autoimmunity in the Dog" *Advances in Veterinary Medicine* 41 (1999): 733–47; A. R. Allbritton, "Autoimmune Disease and Vaccination?" *Veterinary Allergy and Clinical Immunology* 4, no. 1 (1996): 16–17.

"More lives have been saved": Marion C. Horzinek, "Vaccination: A Philosophical View," in Ronald D. Schultz, ed., *Advances in Veterinary Medicine*, vol. 41 (San Diego: Academic Press, 1999), 1–6.

eliminated by routine vaccination: Jeffrey B. Ulmer and Margaret A. Liu, "Ethical Issues for Vaccines and Immunization," *Nature Reviews* 2 (April 2002): 291–96; A. Himan, "Eradication of Vaccine-Preventable Diseases," *Annual Review of Public Health* 20 (May 1999): 211–29.

bear three children: Jack Larkin, "'No Force Can Death Resist': Reflections on Child and Infant Mortality in American History," research paper, online at Old Sturbridge Village, "Papers and Articles," 2000.

unremarkable part of daily life: George M. Baer, *The Natural History of Rabies*, 2nd ed. (Boca Raton, FL: CRC Press, 1991), 1–24.

80 **vaccinate all canines:** Ibid.; Timothy S. Frana et al., "Postmarketing Surveillance of Rabies Vaccines for Dogs to Evaluate Safety and Efficacy," in "Vet Med

Today: Special Report," *Journal of the American Veterinary Medical Association* 232, no. 7 (April 1, 2008).

required by law: George M. Baer, *The Natural History of Rabies,* 2nd ed. (Boca Raton, FL: CRC Press, 1991), 428–34.

in 2006, there were 71: Timothy S. Frana et al., "Postmarketing Surveillance of Rabies Vaccines for Dogs to Evaluate Safety and Efficacy," in "Vet Med Today: Special Report," *Journal of the American Veterinary Medical Association* 232, no. 7 (April 1, 2008); Jesse D. Dalton et al., "Rabies Surveillance in the United States During 2006," *Journal of the American Veterinary Medical Association* 231, no. 4 (August 15, 2007).

baits from airplanes: By 2002, the European Union had only 43 cases of rabies, all of them in two small areas of Germany and Austria, both bordering Slovenia, which is adjacent to Croatia, where rabies remains rampant. See J. Vitasek, "A Review of Rabies Elimination in Europe," *Veterinary Medicine – Czech* 5 (2004): 171–85.

except in bats: Online at World Health Organization, "Presence/Absence of Rabies in 2007."

dog population in 1974: Distemper has afflicted dogs for hundreds if not thousands of years and may have been brought from South America to Europe during the seventeenth century. Its scourge finally began to wane after a vaccine was developed in 1950. The response to canine parvovirus was far more rapid. The disease first appeared in Greece in 1974, and by 1978 it had swept through Europe, North America, and Australia. By 1980, it had affected millions of dogs worldwide, causing vomiting, diarrhea, and high mortality in puppies. A vaccine was formulated virtually overnight, and by 1981 new cases of parvovirus were already on the decline. See J. Blancou, "Dog Distemper: Imported into Europe from South America?" *Historia Medicinae Veterinariae* 29, no. 2 (2004): 35–41; online at Scientific Anti-Vivisectionism, "Canine Distemper Vaccine"; and L. E. Carmichael, "An Annotated Historical Account of Canine Parvovirus," *Journal of Veterinary Medicine* B52 (2005): 303–11.

81 **American Animal Hospital Association:** Online at Michael A. Paul et al., *Report of the American Animal Hospital Association (AAHA) Canine Vaccine Task Force: 2003 Canine Vaccine Guidelines, Recommendations, and Supporting Literature,* 17.

Baker himself: Online at Cornell University College of Veterinary Medicine, Baker Institute for Animal Health, Baker Institute/Public Information, "History."

"as a routine safety measure": James Baker, "Message from the Director," *The Institute Report* (Veterinary Virus Research Institute, Cornell University) 9 (October 1959).

82 **substantial duration of immunity:** Ronald D. Schultz, "Duration of Immunity for Canine and Feline Vaccines: A Review," *Veterinary Microbiology* 117 (2006): 75–79; Online at Michael A. Paul et al., *Report of the American Animal Hospital Association (AAHA) Canine Vaccine Task Force: 2003 Canine Vaccine Guide-*

lines, Recommendations, and Supporting Literature; and online at Michael A.
Paul et al., *2006 AAHA Canine Vaccine Guidelines, Revised.*

83 **fetal bovine serum:** Lisa Rodier, "Vaccinations 101," *Whole Dog Journal* (August 14, 2008).

expose dogs to unnecessary risks: Donald J. Klingborg et al., "AVMA Council
on Biologic and Therapeutic Agents' Report on Cat and Dog Vaccines," *Journal of the American Veterinary Medical Association* 221, no. 10 (November 15,
2002): 1401–7.

84 **Rabies Challenge Fund:** Online at Rabies Challenge Fund, "About the Rabies
Challenge Fund."

as French research: M. F. A. Aubert, "Practical Significance of Rabies Antibodies in Cats and Dogs," *Scientific and Technical Review of the Office International
des Epizooties* 11, no. 3 (1992): 735–60.

from Ron's own work: Ronald D. Schultz, "Duration of Immunity for Canine
and Feline Vaccines: A Review," *Veterinary Microbiology* 117 (2006): 75–79.

once every seven years: Online at Rabies Challenge Fund.

85 **see the notes for her recommendations:** Jean Dodds recommends giving a
puppy three rounds of parvo and distemper vaccines: one round at nine to ten
weeks of age, another at fourteen weeks, and the last round at sixteen to eighteen weeks, followed by a rabies vaccine no sooner than twenty weeks of age. At
one year, she boosts all three vaccines.

86 **In fourteen states:** Alabama, California, Colorado, Connecticut, Florida,
Maine, Massachusetts, New Hampshire, New Jersey, New York, Oregon, Vermont, Virginia, and Wisconsin.

88 **did not recommend vaccinating dogs against Lyme disease:** Meryl P. Littman et al., "ACVIM Small Animal Consensus Statement on Lyme Disease in
Dogs: Diagnosis, Treatment, and Prevention," *Journal of Veterinary Internal
Medicine* 20 (2006): 422–34.

the deer tick: Vincent Lo Re III et al., "Identifying the Vector of Lyme Disease,"
American Family Physician 69, no. 8 (April 15, 2004): 1935–37.

adverse reactions to spot-on treatments: Online at EPA, "Pesticides, Health,
and Safety"; online at "Flea, Tick Products Draw EPA Scrutiny," *Veterinary Practice News;* online at Healthy Pets with Dr. Karen Becker, "NEW! EPA Alerts Pet
Owners to Dangers of Flea/Tick Products."

asking for public commentary: Online at EPA, "EPA to Increase Restrictions
on Flea and Tick Products."

possible adverse effects: Online at EPA, "Response to Comments on the
Docket ID: EPA-HQ-OPP-2010-0229, Pet Spot-on Analysis and Mitigation
Plan," September 30, 2011.

89 **sprinkled with cedar oil:** Online at Pestigator.

food-grade diatomaceous earth: Online at Wolf Creek Ranch, "Buy Food
Grade Diatomaceous Earth."

according to the USDA: Online at USDA, "Insect Management in Food Processing Facilities with Heat and Diatomaceous Earth."

starting the cycle anew: Online at American Heartworm Society, "What Is Heartworm Disease?"

cycle of the heartworm is broken: Online at Washington State University College of Veterinary Medicine, "Recent Spokane Valley Heartworm Reports Discussed."

treat dogs every month: Online at American Heartworm Society, "Current Canine Guidelines."

monthly heartworm treatments: Online at American Heartworm Society, "Sponsors."

90 **"protection to their clients":** D. H. Knight and J. B. Lok, "Seasonality of Heartworm Infection and Implications for Chemoprophylaxis," *Clinical Techniques in Small Animal Practice* 13, no. 2 (1998): 77–82.

91 **exercise-induced collapse:** Online at University of Minnesota, Veterinary Diagnostic Laboratory, "EIC Information."

8. At Our Start

95 **begin a puppy's bonding:** Clarence J. Pfaffenberger, *The New Knowledge of Dog Behavior* (New York: Howell Book House, 1963); John Paul Scott and John L. Fuller, *Genetics and the Social Behavior of the Dog* (Chicago: University of Chicago Press, 1965); The Monks of New Skete, *The Art of Raising a Puppy* (New York: Little, Brown and Co., 1991).

96 **Wendy Volhard:** Online at Volhard.com, "Choosing Your Puppy (PAT)."

98 **like a weather forecast:** Patricia McConnell, *For the Love of a Dog* (New York: Ballantine Books, 2005), 188.

106 **raised by a human keeper:** Eniko Kubinyi et al., "Comparative Social Cognition: From Wolf and Dog to Humans," *Comparative Cognition and Behavior Reviews* 2 (2007): 26–46; Zsófia Virányi et al., "Comprehension of Human Pointing Gestures in Young Human-Reared Wolves (*Canis lupus*) and Dogs (*Canis familiaris*)," *Animal Cognition* 11 (2008): 373–87; Ádám Miklósi, *Dog Behavior, Evolution, and Cognition* (Oxford: Oxford University Press, 2007), 31–33.

110 **another brainy dog:** Juliane Kaminski et al., "Word Learning in a Domestic Dog: Evidence for 'Fast Mapping,'" *Science* 304 (June 11, 2004): 1682–83; Paul Bloom, "Can a Dog Learn a Word?" *Science* 304 (June 11, 2004): 1605–6; John W. Pilley and Alliston K. Reid, "Border Collie Comprehends Object Names as Verbal Referents," *Behavioral Processes* 86 (2011): 184–95; Nicholas Wade, "Sit. Stay. Parse. Good Girl!" *New York Times*, January 17, 2011.

9. Outward Bound

114 **school called Outward Bound:** H. Röhrs and H. Tunstall-Behrens, eds., *Kurt Hahn: A Life Span in Education and Politics* (London: Routledge and Kegan Paul, 1970); W. A. C. Stewart, "The Slackening Tide: The Thirties and Gordonstoun," in W. A. C. Stewart, *Progressives and Radicals in English Education,*

1750–1970 (Clifton, NJ: Augustus M. Kelley, 1972); G. Templin and P. Baldwin, "The Evolution and Adaptation of Outward Bound, 1920–1966," unpublished paper, Colorado Outward Bound School, 1976.

116 **A laid-back attitude:** Elizabeth Marshall Thomas, *The Social Lives of Dogs* (New York: Pocket Books, 2000), 238–40.

"**Allowing a single housesoiling mistake**": Ian Dunbar, *Before and After Getting Your Puppy* (Novato, CA: New World Library, 2004), 3–6.

118 **people underestimated the time:** Gary J. Patronek et al., "Risk Factors for Relinquishment of Dogs to an Animal Shelter," *Journal of the American Veterinary Medical Association* 209, no. 3 (August 1996): 572–81.

119 **can carry bacterial contamination:** Nicholas Dodman, ed., *Puppy's First Steps* (Boston: Houghton Mifflin, 2007), 90.

120 **afflicted with periodontal disease:** B. Colmery and P. Frost, "Periodontal Disease (Etiology and Pathogenesis)," *Veterinary Clinics of North America: Small Animal Practice* 16, no. 5 (September 1986): 817–33; M. Kyllar and K. Witter, "Prevalence of Dental Disorders in Pet Dogs," *Journal of Veterinary Medicine – Czech* 50, no. 11 (2005): 496–505.

diseases that can follow upon its heels: Lawrence T. Glickman et al., "Evaluation of the Risk of Endocarditis and Other Cardiovascular Events on the Basis of the Severity of Periodontal Disease in Dogs," *Journal of the American Veterinary Medical Association* 234, no. 4 (February 15, 2009).

periodontal disease at bay: C. Gorrel and J. M. Rawlings, "The Role of Tooth-Brushing and Diet in the Maintenance of Periodontal Health in Dogs," *Journal Veterinary Dentistry* 13, no. 4 (December 1996): 139–43; Colin E. Harvey et al., "Correlation of Diet, Other Chewing Activities, and Periodontal Disease in North American Client-Owned Dogs," *Journal of Veterinary Dentistry* 13, no. 3 (September 1996): 101–5.

121 **act like doggy dental floss:** Dr. Karen Becker, interview with the author, Bourbonnais, IL, April 7, 2010; Dr. Kim Henneman, interview with the author, Park City, UT, August 12, 2010.

Waltham's veterinarians recommend brushing: C. Gorrel and J. M. Rawlings, "The Role of Tooth-Brushing and Diet in the Maintenance of Periodontal Health in Dogs," *Journal of Veterinary Dentistry* 13, no. 4 (1996): 139–43.

123 **scarred for life:** Steven R. Lindsay, *Handbook of Applied Dog Behavior and Training*, vol. 1, *Adaptation and Learning* (Ames, IA: Blackwell Publishing, 2000), 62.

10. Building the Dikes

139 **spray it to death:** Online at D. G. Knochel and T. R. Seastedt, "Sustainable Control of Spotted Knapweed (*Centaurea stoebe*)."

140 **the Dow brochure:** Online at Dow AgroSciences, "Milestone Fact Sheet."

increased incidence of non-Hodgkin's lymphoma: Sheila K. Hoar et al., "Agricultural Herbicide Use and Risk of Lymphoma and Soft-Tissue Sarcoma,"

Journal of the American Medical Association 256, no. 9 (September 5, 1986): 1141–47; L. Hardell et al., "Malignant Lymphoma and Exposure to Chemicals, Especially Organic Solvents, Chlorophenols, and Phenoxy Acids: A Case-Control Study," *British Journal of Cancer* 43 (1981): 169–76; Kenneth P. Cantor, "Farming and Mortality from Non-Hodgkin's Lymphoma: A Case-Control Study," *International Journal of Cancer* 29, no. 3: 239–47; L. F. Burmeister et al., "Selected Cancer Mortality and Farm Practices in Iowa," *American Journal of Epidemiology* 188, no. 1 (July 1983): 72–77; Lennart Hardell and Mikael Eriksson, "A Case-Control Study of Non-Hodgkin Lymphoma and Exposure to Pesticides," *Cancer* 83, no. 6 (March 15, 1999): 1353–60.

kills dogs the world over: Online at University of Minnesota, Modiano Lab, "Non-Hodgkin Lymphoma."

Milestone label itself: Online at Dow AgroSciences, "Milestone Herbicide: Material Safety Data Sheet"; online at Dow AgroSciences, "Milestone Specimen Label."

141 **Virginia veterinary clinic:** Online at Olga Naidenko et al., "Polluted Pets: High Levels of Toxic Industrial Chemicals Contaminate Cats and Dogs," Environmental Working Group, April 2008.

eighty thousand synthetic chemicals: LaSalle D. Leffall and Margaret L. Kripke, *Reducing Environmental Cancer Risk: What We Can Do Now* (Washington, DC: US Department of Health and Human Services, National Cancer Institute, 2010), 20–22.

142 **only five of these chemicals:** The five chemicals are: polychlorinated biphenyls (PCBs), used as coolants and lubricants in electrical equipment; dioxins, a by-product of industrial processes such as bleaching paper; asbestos, used for fireproofing and brake linings (the EPA ban was overturned, however, by federal courts); hexavalent chromium, a paint additive; and halogenated chlorofluoroalkanes, which are used in propellants and have been implicated in the destruction of the ozone layer.

carcinogens, neurotoxins, and endocrine disruptors: Michael Shapiro, *Exposed: The Toxic Chemistry of Everyday Products and What's at Stake For American Power* (White River Junction, Vermont: Chelsea Green Publishing, 2007).

143 **"more potent in rapidly growing animals":** *Pesticides in the Diets of Infants and Children* (Washington, DC: National Academies Press, 1993), 29, 35, 55, 60–61, 78, 88.

grease-proof lining: PFCs have been shown to cause organ damage and delayed growth in lab animals, and children exposed to PFCs have increased odds of developing ADHD, attention deficit/hyperactivity disorder, which in dogs may express itself as excessive chewing, barking, and separation anxiety. Online at Minnesota Department of Health, "Perfluorochemicals and Health, May 2009"; Kate Hoffman et al., "Exposure to Polyfluoroalkyl Chemicals and Attention Deficit/Hyperactivity Disorder in US Children, 12–15 Years of Age," *Environmental Health Perspectives* 118, no. 12 (December 2010): 1762–67.

85 percent of America's corn: Online at Environmental Protection Agency, 40 CFR Part 180, [EPA-HQ-OPP-2010-0938; FRL-8872-6], Glyphosate; Pesticide Tolerance; online at FAO Document Repository, "Pesticide Residues in Food — 2005, 4.10 Glyphosate (158), Residue and Analytical Aspects."

lawns, and gardens: Online at EPA, "Interim Reregistration Eligibility Decision for Atrazine," April 6, 2006, 12.

disruption of endocrine systems: Jennifer Beth Sass and Aaron Colangelo, "European Union Bans Atrazine, While the United States Negotiates Continued Use," *International Journal of Occupational and Environmental Health* 12, no. 3 (July–September): 260–67.

abnormalities in fish: Online at US Geological Survey (USGS) Newsroom, "Commonly Used Atrazine Herbicide Adversely Affects Fish Reproduction," May 19, 2010.

non-Hodgkin's lymphoma in farmers: A. J. De Roos et al., "Integrative Assessment of Multiple Pesticides as Risk Factors for Non-Hodgkin's Lymphoma Among Men," *Occupational Environmental Medicine* 62 (2006): 597–607.

144 **without allowing any public representation:** Jennifer Beth Sass and Aaron Colangelo, "European Union Bans Atrazine, While the United States Negotiates Continued Use," *International Journal of Occupational and Environmental Health* 12, no. 3 (July–September 2006): 260–67.

to lack transparency: US Government Accountability Office, "Scientific Integrity: EPA's Efforts to Enhance the Credibility and Transparency of Its Scientific Process," GAO-09-773T, June 2009, 9; online at GAO, "Transforming EPA's Process for Assessing and Controlling Toxic Chemicals." The controversy over atrazine continues. See online at Toxipedia, "Atrazine Regulation in Europe and the United States."

So pervasive is BPA: Antonia M. Calafat et al., "Exposure to the US Population to Bisphenol A and 4-Tertiary-Octylphenol: 2003–2004," *Environmental Health Perspectives* 116, no. 1 (January 2008): 39–44.

BPA negatively alters: Frederick S. vom Saal and Wade V. Welshons, "Large Effects from Small Exposures. II. The Importance of Positive Controls in Low-Dose Research on Bisphenol A," *Environmental Research* 100 (2006): 50–76.

turned on and off: Ruth A. Keri et al., "An Evaluation of Evidence for the Carcinogenic Activity of Bisphenol A," *Reproductive Toxicology* 24 (2007): 240–52.

N-nitroso compounds: William Lijinsky, "The Significance of N-Nitroso Compounds as Environmental Carcinogens," *Journal of Environmental Science and Health* C4, no. 1 (1986): 1–45.

145 **Phthalates are used:** Y. Guo and K. Kannan, "Comparative Assessment of Human Exposure to Phthalate Esters from House Dust in China and the United States," *Environmental Science and Technology* 45, no. 8 (2011): 3788–94; D. Konieck et al., "Phthalates in Cosmetic and Personal Care Products: Concentrations and Possible Dermal Exposure," *Environmental Research* 111, no. 3 (2011): 329–36; H. J. Koo and B. M. Lee, "Estimated Exposure to Phthalates in Cosmet-

ics and Risk Assessment," *Journal of Toxicology and Environmental Health: Part A* 67, nos. 23-24 (2004): 1901–1014.

dizzying array of health problems: Barbara Kolarik et al., "The Concentrations of Phthalates in Settled Dust in Bulgarian Homes in Relation to Building Characteristics and Cleaning Habits in the Family," *Atmospheric Environment* 42, no. 37 (December 2008): 8553–59; Hirohisa Takano et al., "Di-(2-Ethylhexyl) Phthalate Enhances Atopic Dermatitis-Like Skin Lesions in Mice," *Environmental Health Perspectives* 114 (May 15, 2006): 1266–69; Susan M. Duty et al., "Phthalate Exposure and Human Semen Parameters," *Epidemiology* 14, no. 3 (May 2003): 269–77; online at "Chemical in Common Consumer Products (Phthalates) May Play a Role in Pre-Term Births," *Science Daily* (July 7, 2009); C. G. Ohlson and L. Hardell, "Testicular Cancer and Occupational Exposures with a Focus on Xenoestrogens in Polyvinyl Chloride Plastics," *Chemosphere* 40. nos. 9-11 (May-June 2000): 1277–82; Bung-Nyun Kim et al., "Phthalates Exposure and Attention-Deficit/Hyperactivity Disorder in School-Age Children," *Biological Psychiatry* 66, no. 10 (November 15, 2009): 958–63.

Research from around the world: Paula F. Baillie-Hamilton, "Chemical Toxins: A Hypothesis to Explain the Global Obesity Epidemic," *Journal of Alternative and Complimentary Medicine* 8, no. 2 (2002): 185–92; Béatrice Desvergne et al., "PRAR-Mediated Activity of Phthalates: A Link to the Obesity Epidemic?" *Molecular and Cellular Endocrinology* 304 (2009): 43–48; Felix Grün and Bruce Blumberg, "Environmental Obesogens: Organotins and Endocrine Disruption via Nuclear Receptor Signaling," *Endocrinology* 147, no. 6 (2006): S50–55; Felix Grün and Bruce Blumberg, "Minireview: The Case for Obesogens," *Molecular Endocrinology* 23, no. 8 (2009): 1127–34; S. W. Keith et al., "Putative Contributors to the Secular Increase in Obesity: Exploring the Roads Less Traveled," *International Journal of Obesity* 30, no. 11 (June 27, 2006): 1585–95; Retha R. Newbold, "Impact of Environmental Endocrine Disrupting Chemicals on the Development of Obesity," *Hormones* 9, no. 3 (2010): 206–17; Retha R. Newbold et al., "Perinatal Exposure to Environmental Estrogens and the Development of Obesity," *Molecular Nutrition and Food Research* 51 (2007): 912–17.

laying down of fat: Stephen D. Hursting et al., "Calorie Restriction, Aging, and Cancer Prevention: Mechanisms of Action and Applicability to Humans," *Annual Review of Medicine* 54 (2003): 131–52.

window of fetal development: Frederick S. vom Saal and Wade V. Welshons, "Large Effects from Small Exposures. II. The Importance of Positive Controls in Low-Dose Research on Bisphenol A," *Environmental Research* 100 (2006): 50–76.

bright or not so bright: A landmark study done at Columbia University's Center for Children's Environmental Health showed that children who had higher umbilical cord blood concentrations of fire-retardant PBDEs scored lower on tests measuring mental and physical development. By the time the children were six years old, those children who had had the highest exposure to PBDEs had IQs that were eight points lower than those of the children with the lower exposure. See Julie B. Herbstman et al., "Prenatal Exposure to PBDEs and Neurodevelopment," *Environmental Health Perspectives* 118 (2010): 712–19.

seventeen times higher in the bodies of North Americans: Heather M. Stapleton, "Polybrominated Diphenyl Ethers in House Dust and Clothes Dryer Lint," *Environmental Science and Technology* 39, no. 4 (2006): 925–31.

long-term sinks: Marcia G. Nishioka et al., "Measuring Transport of Lawn-Applied Herbicide Acids from Turf to Home: Correlation of Dislodgeable 2,4-D Turf Residues with Carpet Dust and Carpet Surface Residues," *Environmental Science and Technology* 30, no. 11 (1996): 3313–20.

146 **2,4-D and non-Hodgkin's lymphoma:** Sheila K. Hoar et al., "Agricultural Herbicide Use and Risk of Lymphoma and Soft-Tissue Sarcoma," *Journal of the American Medical Association* 256, no. 9 (September 5, 1986): 1141–47; L. F. Burmeister, "Selected Cancer Mortality and Farm Practices in Iowa," *American Journal of Epidemiology* 118, no. 1 (July 1983): 72–77; Kenneth P. Cantor, "Farming and Mortality from Non-Hodgkin's Lymphoma: A Case-Control Study," *International Journal of Cancer* 29, no. 3 (March 15, 1982): 239–47; P. Kristensen, "Birth Defects Among Offspring of Norwegian Farmers, 1967–1991," *Epidemiology* 8, no. 5 (September 1997): 537–44; Lennart Hardell and Mikael Eriksson, "A Case-Control Study of Non-Hodgkin Lymphoma and Exposure to Pesticides," *Cancer* 83, no. 6 (March 15, 1999): 1353–60; Dina M. Schreinemachers, "Cancer Mortality in Four Northern Wheat-Producing States," *Environmental Health Perspectives* 108, no. 9 (September 2000): 873–71. In addition, birth defects in Minnesota, North Dakota, South Dakota, and Montana increased along with the amount of acreage devoted to wheat that was treated with 2,4-D and its related herbicides. See Dina M. Schreinemachers, "Birth Malformations and Other Adverse Perinatal Outcomes in Four US Wheat-Producing States," *Environmental Health Perspectives* 111, no. 9 (July 2003): 1259–64. The incidence of birth defects also increased for those babies conceived in the spring, when most of the herbicides were being applied to the new spring wheat crop. These two studies helped to validate what a previous Minnesota study had shown: there were more birth defects in the western part of the state, devoted to wheat growing, than in the urban and forested portions of the state. Not only did the non-agricultural parts of Minnesota have lower birth defect rates, but they also showed no seasonal pulse for birth abnormalities in children conceived in the spring. In other words, there was a strong association between pesticide exposure and one's increased risk of bearing a child with birth defects. See Vincent F. Garry et al., "Pesticide Appliers, Biocides, and Birth Defects in Rural Minnesota," *Environmental Health Perspectives* 104, no. 4 (April 1996): 394–99; Vincent F. Garry et al., "Birth Defects, Season of Conception, and Sex of Children Born to Pesticide Applicators Living in the Red River Valley of Minnesota, USA," *Environmental Health Perspectives* 110, supplement 3 (June 2002): 441–49.

similar risk for dogs: Howard M. Hayes et al., "On the Association of Canine

Malignant Lymphoma and Opportunity for Exposure to 2,4-Dichorophenoxy-acetic Acid," *Environmental Research* 70 (1995): 119–25. These authors write: "Until additional studies of home exposure to pesticides are undertaken ... the higher risk we found in dogs whose owners personally apply 2,4-D in addition to employing a commercial lawn-care company would, at the very least, argue for prudence in the pursuit of the perfect lawn."

the dogs themselves: Marcia G. Nishioka et al., "Transport of Lawn-Applied 2,4-D from Turf to Home: Assessing the Relative Importance of Transport Mechanisms and Exposure Pathways," EPA, National Exposure Research Laboratory, March 1999.

the household's dog: Marcia G. Nishioka et al., "Distribution of 2,4-D in Air and on Surfaces Inside Residences After Lawn Applications: Comparing Exposure Estimates from Various Media for Young Children," *Environmental Health Perspectives* 109, no. 11 (November 2001): 1185–91.

off-gassing formaldehyde: Online at World Health Organization (WHO) International Agency for Research on Cancer (IARC), *IARC Monographs on the Evaluation of Carcinogenic Risks to Humans: Formaldehyde, 2-Butoxyethanol, and 1-tert-Butoxypropan-2-ol,* vol. 88 (2006); Gardiner Harris, "Government Says Two Common Materials Pose Risk of Cancer," *New York Times,* June 10, 2011.

147 **twenty-five common, fragranced products:** A. C. Steinemann et al., "Fragranced Consumer Products: Chemicals Emitted, Ingredients Unlisted," *Environmental Impact Assessment Review* 31, no. 3 (April 2011): 328–33.
to disclose the ingredients: Ibid.
mandated that the labels: Online at "Regulation (EC) No 648/2004 Of The European Parliament and of the Council of 31 March 2004 on Detergents." The EU has also created a category of products that bear its Ecolabel, emblazoned with a flower. Such products are certified to generate less severe environmental impacts and to have fewer hazardous ingredients than comparable conventional products. See online at European Commission Environment, "EU Ecolabel."
program called REACH: Online at European Commission Environment Directorate General, "REACH," October 2007.

148 **bladder cancer in dogs increased:** Lawrence T. Glickman et al., "Herbicide Exposure and the Risk of Transitional Cell Carcinoma of the Urinary Bladder in Scottish Terriers," *Journal of the American Veterinary Medical Association* 224, no. 8 (April 15, 2004).
an increased risk of lung cancer: John S. Reif et al., "Passive Smoking and Canine Lung Cancer," *American Journal of Epidemiology* 135, no. 3 (1992): 234–39; John S. Reif et al., "Cancer of the Nasal Cavity and Paranasal Sinuses and Exposure to Environmental Tobacco Smoke in Pet Dogs," *American Journal of Epidemiology* 147, no. 5 (1998): 488–92; Elizabeth R. Bertone, "Environmental Tobacco Smoke and Risk of Malignant Lymphoma in Pet Cats," *American Journal of Epidemiology* 156, no. 3 (2002): 268–73.

149 **German dog toys:** Online at ÖkoTest eMedien, "Tierspielzeug" ("Toys").

US Consumer Product Safety Improvement Act: Online at US Consumer Product Safety Commission, Consumer Product Safety Improvement Act, "Section 101: Children's Products Containing Lead; Lead Paint Rule" and "Section 108: Products Containing Certain Phthalates."

profound and irreversible effects: Sofie Christiansen et al., "Low-Dose Perinatal Exposure to Di(2-Ethylhexyl) Phthalate Induces Anti-Androgenic Effects in Male Rats," *Reproductive Toxicology* 30, no. 2 (September 2010): 313–21; Anderson Joel Martino-Andrade and Ibrahim Chahoud, "Reproductive Toxicity of Phthalate Esters," *Molecular Nutrition and Food Research* 54 (2010): 148–57.

DINP has been banned: Online at US Consumer Product Safety Commission, Consumer Product Safety Improvement Act, "Section 108: Products Containing Certain Phthalates."

antimony, a suspected carcinogen: Online at WHO, IARC, "Antimony Trioxide and Antimony Trisulfide," in *IARC Monographs on the Evaluation of Carcinogenic Risks to Humans: Some Organic Solvents, Resin Monomers and Related Compounds, Pigments and Occupational Exposures in Paint Manufacture and Painting*, vol. 47 (1989); online at US Department of Labor, Occupational Safety and Health Administration, "Antimony and Compounds (as Sb)"; "Carcinogen Antimony Found in Fruit Juices," *Daily Telegraph*, March 1, 2010.

150 **production of polyester yarns:** William Shotyk et al., "Contamination of Canadian and European Bottled Waters with Antimony from Pet Containers," *Journal of Environmental Monitoring* 8 (2006): 2880–92.

20 parts per billion: Ibid.

used to create tennis balls: Online at International Tennis Federation, "Manufacture of Tennis Balls."

151 **Material safety data sheets for DPG and CBS:** Online at Merchem, "Mercure DPG" and "Mercure CBS."

reduced nutrient intake: Richard D. Irwin, "1,3-Diphenylguanidine Administered in Feed to F344/N Rats and B6C3F$_1$ Mice," NIH Publication 95-3933, September 1995.

153 **begin to appear in stressed animals:** Warren P. Porter et al., "Endocrine, Immune, and Behavioral Effects of Aldicarb (Carbamate), Atrazine (Triazine) and Nitrate (Fertilizer) Mixtures at Groundwater Concentrations," *Toxicology and Industrial Health* 15 (1999): 133–50.

in the absence of these toxins: David Crews et al., "Epigenetic Transgenerational Inheritance of Altered Stress Responses," *Proceedings of the National Academy of Sciences*, doi/10.1073/pnas.1118514109; M. K. Skinner et al., "Transgenerational Epigenetic Programming of the Brain Transcriptome and Anxiety Behavior," *PloS ONE* 3, no. 11: e3745.

three generations in animals: Michael Skinner, "Environmental Epigenetic Transgenerational Inheritance and Somatic Epigenetic Mitotic Stability," *Epigenetics* 6, no. 7 (July 2011): 838–842.

for 250 generations: Pilar Cubas et al., "An Epigenetic Mutation Responsible for Natural Variation in Foral Symmetry," *Nature* 401, no. 9 (September 9, 1999): 157–161.

they may in fact be permanent: Online at TV.Natural News, "Interview with Dr. David Crews, University of Texas, Austin, author of Epigenetic Transgenerational Inheritance Paper"; Dr. David Crews, telephone interview with author, August 2, 2012.

mice who form social bonds: A. C. DeVries et al., "Social Influences on Stress Responses and Health," *Psychoneuroendocrinology* 32, no. 6 (July 2007): 587–603.

154 **"anti-progress ideologues":** Online at Gilbert Ross, "Junk Science Week: Toxic Terrorists Ignore Organic Food Threat," American Council on Science and Health, June 16, 2011; Gilbert Ross, "Dr. Ross Talks About BPA's Safety on KCTV5," American Council on Science and Health, November 4, 2010.

list galvanized steel: Online at US Department of Health and Human Services (DHHS), Food and Drug Administration (FDA), "FDA 1997 Food Code Chapter 4: Equipment, Utensils, and Linens, Section 4-101.15 Galvanized Metal, Use Limitations."

155 **chlorine react with organic matter:** LaSalle D. Leffall and Margaret L. Kripke, *Reducing Environmental Cancer Risk: What We Can Do Now* (Washington, DC: US Department of Health and Human Services, National Cancer Institute, 2010), 55.

156 **development of resistant bacteria:** Online at Stuart B. Levy, "Antibacterial Household Products: Cause for Concern," in *Emerging Infectious Diseases* (CDC) 7, no. 3 supplement (June 2001).

eighth largest economy in the world: Online at EconPost, "California Economy Ranking in the World," February 3, 2011.

157 **foods grown without pesticides:** LaSalle D. Leffall and Margaret L. Kripke, *Reducing Environmental Cancer Risk: What We Can Do Now* (Washington, DC: US Department of Health and Human Services, National Cancer Institute, 2010).

11. In the Time of the Big Light

167 **observing other dogs:** Leonore Loeb Adler and Helmut E. Adler, "Ontogeny of Observational Learning in the Dog (*Canis familiaris*)," *Developmental Psychobiology* 10 (1977): 267–71.

12. Carnivore to Monovore

177 **None of these grains existed:** Dolores R. Piperno et al., "Starch Grain and Phytolith Evidence for Ninth Millennium B.P. Maize from Central Balsas River Valley, Mexico," *Proceedings of the National Academy of Sciences* 105, no. 13 (March 31, 2009): 5019–24; Moshe Feldman and Mordechai Kislev, "Domestication of Emmer Wheat and Evolution of Free-Threshing Teraploid Wheat," *Israel Jour-*

nal Of Plant Sciences 55, nos. 3-4 (2007): 207-21; Frea Itzstein-Davey et al., "Wild and Domesticated Forms of Rice (*Oryza* sp.) in Early Agriculture at Qingpu, Lower Yangtze, China: Evidence from Phytoliths," *Journal of Archaeological Science* 34, no. 12 (December 2007): 2101-8; William Shurtleff et al., *The Encyclopedia of Seeds: Science, Technology, and Uses* (Oxfordshire, UK: Cabi, 2006), 447; online at SoyInfo Center, "The Soybean Plant: Botany, Nomenclature, Taxonomy, Domestication, and Dissemination," 2007; A. Badr et al., "On the Origin and Domestication History of Barley (*Hordeum vulgare*)," *Molecular Biology and Evolution* 17, no. 4 (1999): 499-510.

by at most 0.1 percent: Kerstin Linblad-Toh et al., "Genome Sequence, Comparative Analysis, and Haplotype Structure of the Domestic Dog," *Nature* 438 (December 8, 2005): 803-19.

178 **a finding corroborated by:** L. David Mech, *The Wolf* (Garden City, NY: Natural History Press, 1970), 186. Michael Somers, from the University of Pretoria's Centre for Wildlife Management and the editor of the *South African Journal of Wildlife Research*, also told me that African Wild Dogs do not eat the stomach contents of their prey and in fact leave the stomach behind.

"98 percent carnivore": See also Daniel R. Stahler, Douglas W. Smith, and Debra S. Guernsey, "Foraging and Feeding Ecology of the Gray Wolf (*Canis lupus*): Lessons from Yellowstone National Park, Wyoming, USA," *Journal of Nutrition* 136 (2006): 1923S-26S.

about thirty-three thousand years ago: Meitje Germonpré et al., "Fossil Dogs and Wolves from Paleolithic Sites in Belgium, the Ukraine, and Russia: Osteometry, Ancient DNA, and Stable Isotopes," *Journal of Archaeological Science* 365 (2009): 473-90; Nikolai D. Ovodov et al., "A 33,000-Year-Old Incipient Dog from the Altai Mountains of Siberia: Evidence of the Earliest Domestication Disrupted by the Last Glacial Maximum," *PloS ONE* 6, no. 7 (July 2011): e22821; Mark Derr, *How the Dog Became the Dog* (New York: Overlook Press, 2011).

sixteen thousand years ago: Jun-Feng Pang et al., "mtDNA Data Indicate a Single Origin for Dogs South of Yangtze River, Less Than 16,300 Years Ago, from Numerous Wolves," *Molecular Biology and Evolution* 26, no. 12 (2009): 2849-64.

twelve thousand years ago: Bridgett M. von Holdt et al., "Genome-Wide SNP and Haplotype Analyses Reveal a Rich History Underlying Dog Domestication," *Nature* 464 (April 8, 2010).

ten thousand years ago in China: Chen Xingcan, "On the Earliest Evidence for Rice Cultivation in China," *Indo-Pacific Prehistory Association Bulletin* 18 (Melaka Papers, vol. 2, 1999): 81-93.

179 **carnivorous wolves began their journey:** Jun-Feng Pang et al., "mtDNA Data Indicate a Single Origin for Dogs South of Yangtze River, Less Than 16,300 Years Ago, from Numerous Wolves," *Molecular Biology and Evolution* 26, no. 12 (2009): 2849-64.

Attracted to refuse dumps: Raymond and Lorna Coppinger, *Dogs: A New Un-*

derstanding of Canine Origin, Behavior, and Evolution (Chicago: University of Chicago Press, 2001), 60–61.

The Wolves of Mount McKinley: Adolph Murie, *The Wolves of Mount McKinley* (Washington, DC: US Government Printing Office, 1944), 59.

Italian wolf biologist Luigi Boitani: Luigi Boitani, "Wolf Management in Intensively Used Areas of Italy," in Fred H. Harrington and Paul C. Paquet, eds., *Wolves of the World* (Park Ridge, NJ: Noyes Publications, 1982), 161.

179 **fed stews of fresh vegetables:** Mary Elizabeth Thurston, *The Lost History of the Canine Race* (Kansas City, MO: Andrews and McMeel, 1996), 234.

180 **Dr. William Gordon Stables:** Gordon Stables, *Our Friend the Dog* (London: Deand and Son, c. 1884–96), 34–36.

The American Farmer: John S. Skinner, ed., *The American Farmer* 8, no. 47 (February 9, 1827): 373–74.

"scratching themselves to pieces": James Watson, *The Dog Book — Part 1* (New York: Doubleday Page & Co., 1905), 47.

in the late 1850s: Katherine C. Grier, *Pets in America* (Orlando, FL: Harcourt, 2006), 367–68; Mary Elizabeth Thurston, *The Lost History of the Canine Race* (Kansas City, MO: Andrews and McMeel, 1996), 235–36.

England during the 1820s: Skinner, *The American Farmer*, 373–74; Nimrod, *The Sporting Magazine* 22, N.S., no. 128 (May 1828): 250.

181 **"praise it so enthusiastically":** Advertisement for Spratt's dog food, *Saturday Evening Post*, February 26, 1927, as reproduced in Katherine C. Grier, *Pets in America* (Orlando, FL: Harcourt, 2006), 371.

Kennel Club's journal: *The American Kennel Gazette* 1, no. 1 (January 1889).

specialized dog foods: Katherine C. Grier, *Pets in America* (Orlando, FL: Harcourt, 2006), 369.

Orphan Puppy Food: *Spratt's Hints on the Care and Feed of Dogs* (Newark, NJ: Spratt's Patent Limited, c. 1920), 10–19.

Milk-Bone in 1908: Online at Del Monte Foods, "The Milk-Bone Story."

182 **"Where purity is paramount":** Online at Nestlé Purina, "History/Timeline of Ralston Purina Company."

Ralston preached: Janet Six, "Hidden History of Ralston Heights: The Story of New Jersey's Failed 'Garden of Eden,'" *Archaeology* (May-June 2004): 30–35; Edmund Shaftesbury, *Book of General Membership of the Ralston Health Club* (Washington, DC: Martin College Press Association, 1898), 5.

Mark L. Morris Sr.: Online at Hill's Pet Nutrition, "The Story of Hill's Pet Nutrition."

183 **bargain for consumers:** Michael Pollan, *The Omnivore's Dilemma* (New York: Penguin Books, 2006), 51–108.

Earl Butz: Online at NNDB, "Earl Butz"; Richard Goldstein, "Earl L. Butz, Secretary Felled by Racial Remark, Is Dead at 98," *New York Times*, February 4, 2008.

called it Science Diet: Online at Hill's Pet Nutrition, "Dr. Mark Morris, Jr."

"the most widely used source": Online at Hill's Pet Nutrition, "Dr. Mark Morris, Jr."

Seven of them work: Kathy L. Gross et al., "Macronutrients," in Michael S. Hand et al., eds., *Small Animal Clinical Nutrition*, 5th ed. (Topeka, KS: Mark Morris Institute, 2010), 71.

184   **Purina, IAMS, and Eukanuba:** Malia Bergknut and Josh Throne, fourth-year veterinary students at Colorado State University College of Veterinary Medicine and Biomedical Sciences, interview with the author, June 8, 2010; Juli Newton, graduate of the University of Tennessee College of Veterinary Medicine, interview with the author, October 24, 2010.

Hill's funds scholarships: Luce Rubio, Corporate Communications Associate Director, Hill's Pet Nutrition, e-mail communication with author, August 2, 2010.

again without charge: Online at Mark Morris Institute.

Nine of these veterinarians: Online at Mark Morris Institute, "Faculty."

185   **generous and meritorious act:** Telephone survey of 150 shelters around the United States (three per state) conducted by the author's researcher, Susan Scarlata, during November 2009.

Science Diet Shelter Nutrition Program: Luce Rubio, corporate communications associate director, Hill's Pet Nutrition, e-mail communication with the author, August 2, 2010.

Zing-yang Kuo: Zing-yang Kuo, *The Dynamics of Behavior Development* (New York: Random House, 1967), 66–72.

"Or by human beings": Ibid., 71.

13. Should a Wolf Eat Corn?

187   **"enough protein is given":** National Research Council of the National Academy of Sciences, *Nutrient Requirements of Dogs and Cats* (Washington, DC: National Academies Press, 2006), 292.

189   **One of the most revelatory:** Dennis F. Lawler et al., "Influence of Lifetime Food Restriction on Causes, Time, and Predictors of Death in Dogs," *Journal of the American Veterinary Medical Association* 226, no. 2 (January 15, 2005): 225–31.

extraordinary differences: Dennis F. Lawler et al., "Diet Restriction and Ageing in the Dog: Major Observations over Two Decades," *British Journal of Nutrition* 99 (2008): 793–805.

190   **have similarly protective effects:** Alan W. Barclay, "Glycemic Index, Glycemic Load, and Chronic Disease Risk: A Meta-Analysis of Observational Studies," *American Journal of Clinical Nutrition* 87, no. 3 (March 2008): 627–37. For a cautionary view of hyperinsulinemia and insulin resistance being the unique contributors to metabolic syndrome, see J. S. Yudkin, "Insulin Resistance and the Metabolic Syndrome — or the Pitfalls of Epidemiology," *Diabetologia* 50 (2007): 1576–86.

reducing the amount of starch: Patrick Nguyen et al., "Glycemic and Insulinemic Responses After Ingestion of Commercial Foods in Healthy Dogs: Influence of Food Composition," *Journal Of Nutrition* 128 (1998): 2654S–58S.

191 **risk of developing bladder cancer:** Malathi Raghavan et al., "Evaluation of the Effect of Dietary Vegetable Consumption on Reducing Risk of Transitional Cell Carcinoma of the Urinary Bladder in Scottish Terriers," *Journal of the American Veterinary Medical Association* 227, no. 1 (July 1, 2005).

people who eat vegetables: Rui Hai Liu, "Potential Synergy of Phytochemicals in Cancer Prevention: Mechanism of Action," *Journal of Nutrition* 134 (December 2004): 3479S–85S.

sled dogs as subjects: D. S. Kronfeld, "Diet and the Performance of Racing Sled Dogs," *Journal of the American Veterinary Medical Association* 162, no. 63 (March 15, 1973): 470–73; D. S. Kronfeld et al., "Hematological and Metabolic Responses to Training in Racing Sled Dogs Fed Diets Containing Medium, Low, or Zero Carbohydrate," *American Journal of Clinical Nutrition* (March 30, 1977): 419–30; Arleigh J. Reynolds et al., "Effect of Diet and Training on Muscle Glycogen Storage and Utilization in Sled Dogs," *Journal of Applied Physiology* 79, no. 5 (November 1995): 1601–7; Arleigh J. Reynolds et al., "Effect of Protein Intake During Training on Biochemical and Performance Variables in Sled Dogs," *American Journal of Veterinary Research* 60, no. 7 (July 1999): 789–96; Elaine P. Hammel et al., "Metabolic Responses to Exhaustive Exercise in Racing Sled Dogs Fed Diets Containing Medium, Low, or Zero Carbohydrate," *American Journal of Clinical Nutrition* (March 30, 1997): 409–18.

192 **eliminated the dogs' coprophagy:** W. R. McCuistion, "Coprophagy: A Quest for Digestive Enzymes," *Veterinary Medicine/Small Animal Clinician* (May 1966): 445–67.

Beagles running on treadmills: R. I. Downey et al., "Diet of Beagles Affects Stamina," *Journal of the American Animal Hospital Association* 16 (March–April 1980): 273–77.

hunting quail in Georgia: Gary M. Davenport et al., "Effect of Diet on Hunting Performance of English Pointers," *Veterinary Therapeutics* 2, no. 1 (Winter 2001): 10–23.

even when they were untrained: The only time when carbohydrates may help a dog's performance, one study found, is during multiple sprinting events separated by four to six hours. Fed carbs between these periods of intense exercise, Alaskan sled dogs recovered their glycogen stores more quickly than if fed fat and protein alone. See A. J. Reynolds et al., "Effect of Postexercise Carbohydrate Supplementation on Muscle Glycogen Repletion in Trained Sled Dogs," *American Journal of Veterinary Research* 58, no. 11 (November 1997): 1252–56.

dogs on the high-fat diet: Arleigh J. Reynolds et al., "Lipid Metabolite Responses to Diet and Training in Sled Dogs," *Journal of Nutrition* 124 (1994): 2754S–59S.

lessening their aggressive protection: Nicholas Dodman, *The Well-Adjusted Dog* (Boston: Houghton Mifflin, 2008), 19–22.

sweet potatoes have a low glycemic load: B. Ludvig et al., "Improved Metabolic Control by *Ipomoea batatas* (Caiapo) Is Associated with Increased Adiponectin and Decreased Fibrinogen Levels in Type 2 Diabetic Subjects," *Diabetes, Obesity, and Metabolism* 10, no. 7 (July 2008): 596–92; D. Craig Willcox et al., "The Okinawan Diet: Health Implications of a Low-Calorie, Nutrient-Dense, Antioxidant-Rich Dietary Pattern Low in Glycemic Load," *Journal of the American College of Nutrition* 28, no. 4 (2009): 500S–516S; online at the Okinawa Centenarian Study; Michael Booth, "Finding Eternal Youth in Japan," *The (London) Sunday Times,* June 7, 2009.

193 **carcinogenicity of BHA:** Online at IARC, "Summaries and Evaluations."
Ethoxyquin: Online at EPA, "EPA R.E.D. Facts: Ethoxyquin."
"**mixed tocopherols**": Online at PatentStorm, "High Purity Carnosic Acid from Rosemary and Sage Extracts by pH-Controlled Precipitation."
one-third of all agricultural pesticides: Online at Robert J. Gilliom et al., "Pesticides in the Nation's Streams and Ground Water, 1992–2001," US Geological Survey, Circular 1291, March 2006, 23.
have been genetically engineered: Online at GMO Compass.
they also contain the residues: Online at Environmental Protection Agency, 40 CFR Part 180, [EPA-HQ-OPP-2010-0938; FRL-8872-6], Glyphosate; Pesticide Tolerance; online at FAO Document Repository, "Pesticide Residues in Food – 2005, 4.10 Glyphosate (158), Residue and Analytical Aspects"; M. C. Arregui et al., "Monitoring Glyphosate Residues in Transgenic Glyphosate-resistant soybean," *Pest Management Science* 60, no. 2 (February 2004): 163–6.

194 **Roundup Ready:** Online at Jorge Fernandez-Cornejo and William D. McBride, "Adoption of Bioengineered Crops," Agricultural Economic Report 810, US Department of Agriculture, May 2002.
recommended ... studies of up to two years: Joël Spiroux de Vendômois et al., "A Comparison of the Effects of Three GM Corn Varieties on Mammalian Health," *International Journal of Biological Sciences* 5 (2009): 706–29.
and biodiesel fuels: Online at West Coast Reduction, "The Rendering Process," and National Renderers Association, "The Rendering Process."

195 **Fido is eating Rover:** John Eckhouse, "How Dogs and Cats Get Recycled into Pet Food," *San Francisco Chronicle,* February 19, 1990; Van Smith, "What's Cookin'?" *Baltimore City Paper,* September 27, 1995.
decided to investigate: Online at FDA, CVM, "Report on the Risk from Pentobarbital in Dog Food."
found to contain sodium pentobarbital: Online at FDA, "Dog Food Survey Results – Survey #1, Qualitative Analyses for Pentobarbital Residue."
(**HACCP) monitoring:** Online at FDA, "Hazard Analysis and Critical Control Point Principles and Application Guidelines."
Hill's Pet Nutrition confirmed: Luce Rubio, Corporate Communications Associate Director, Hill's Pet Nutrition, e-mail communication with the author, July 19, 2010.

196 **handling this many carcasses:** Online at County of Los Angeles, Department of Animal Care and Control, "Contract – D&D Disposal, Inc.," internal memo

from Marcia Mayeda to supervisors, August 21, 2008; online at Los Angeles County Animal Shelters, "Disposal (Rendering) of Deceased Animals from Los Angeles County Animal Shelters," Animal Rendering Fact Sheet.

199 **free from animal pathogens:** Prions, those notoriously difficult-to-kill protein-like particles that cause mad cow disease, can survive the high heat of the rendering process. Fortunately, prion infection of rendered products hasn't proven a serious public health threat. As of 2011, only three cases of mad cow disease have been identified in the United States and nineteen in Canada. See online at Centers for Disease Control and Prevention (CDC), "BSE (Bovine Spongiform Encephalopathy, or Mad Cow Disease)."

200 **It is *impossible*:** John Eckhouse ("How Dogs and Cats Get Recycled into Pet Food," *San Francisco Chronicle*, February 19, 1990) points out that in fact mix-ups between rendered products occur. Sacramento Rendering was cited five times between 1988 and 1990 for product-labeling violations, and a load of 52,280 pounds of rendered product labeled "meat and bone meal" and shipped from West Coast Rendering to Sacramento Rendering was found by the California Department of Food and Agriculture to be dry rendered tankage. In 2011 I contacted the CDFA and asked if any such violations had occurred since 1990. None had. Annette Whiteford, Director, CDFA Animal Health and Food Safety Services, e-mail communication with the author, May 6, 2011.

205 **legend, literature, or anecdote:** Cats were first domesticated ten thousand years ago in what is now Israel because they liked to eat the mice who had found a new and appealing niche in the first stores of wild grain that humans were collecting. See Carlos A. Driscoll et al., "Taming of the Cat," *Scientific American* (June 2009): 68–75.

"**level of renal function**": Richard W. Nelson and C. Guillermo Couto, *Small Animal Internal Medicine,* 4th ed. (St. Louis, MO: Mosby Elsevier, 2009), 645–59.

aerobic performance improves when dogs eat fat: Arleigh J. Reynolds et al., "Lipid Metabolite Responses to Diet and Training in Sled Dogs," *Journal of Nutrition* 124 (1994): 2754S–59S.

207 **studies in the anthropological and medical literature:** V. L. Boyce and B. A. Swinburn, "The Traditional Pima Indian Diet: Composition and Adaptation for Use in a Dietary Intervention Study," *Diabetes Care* 16, no. 1 (January 1993): 369–71; L. Cordain et al., "The Paradoxical Nature of Hunter-Gatherer Diets: Meat-Based, yet Non-atherogenic," *European Journal of Clinical Nutrition* 56, supp. 1 (2002): S42–52; E. Couto et al., "Mediterranean Dietary Pattern and Cancer Risk in the EPIC Cohort," *British Journal of Cancer* 104 (April 26, 2011): 1493–99; Katherine Esposito et al., "Long-Term Effect of Mediterranean-Style Diet and Calorie Restriction on Biomarkers of Longevity and Oxidative Stress in Overweight Men," *Cardiology Research and Practice* 2011 (2011), article ID 293916; Frank G. Hesse, "A Dietary Study of the Pima Indian," *American Journal of Clinical Nutrition* 7 (September-October 1959): 532–37; B. Hollander, "Freedom of Negro Races from Cancer," *British Medical Journal* 2, no. 3262 (July

7, 1923): 46; Ales Hrdlicka, "Physiological and Medical Observations Among the Indians of Southwestern United States and Northern Mexico" (Washington, DC: US Government Printing Office, 1908); F. P. Fouche, "Freedom of Negro Races from Cancer," *British Medical Journal* 1, no. 3261 (June 30, 1923): 1116; R. Fortuine, "Characteristics of Cancer in the Eskimos of Southwestern Alaska," *Cancer* 23, no. 2 (February 1969): 468–74; Trefor Jenkins et al., "Public Health and Genetic Constitution of the San ('Bushmen'): Carbohydrate Metabolism and Acetylator Status of the !Kung of Tsumkwe in the North-Western Kalahari," *British Medical Journal* 2 (April 6, 1974): 23–26; Robert McCarrison, "An Address on Faulty Food in Relation to Gastro-Intestinal Disorder," *The Lancet* 199, no. 5136 (February 4, 1969): 207–12; P. N. Mitrou et al., "Mediterranean Dietary Pattern and Prediction of All-Cause Mortality in a US Population: Results from the NIH-AARP Diet and Health Study," *Archives of Internal Medicine* 22 (December 10, 2007): 2461–68; John Murdoch, *Ethnological Results of the Point Barrow Expedition* (Washington, DC: Smithsonian Institution Press, 1988), 39; A. J. Orenstein, "Freedom of Negro Races from Cancer," *British Medical Journal* 2, no. 3269 (August 25, 1923): 342; George Prentice, "Cancer Among Negroes," *British Medical Journal* 2, no. 3285 (December 15, 1923): 1181; O. Schaefer et al., "The Changing Pattern of Neoplastic Disease in Canadian Eskimos," *Canadian Medical Association Journal* 112, no. 12 (June 21, 1975): 1399–1400; Albert Schweitzer, "Preface," in Alexander Berglas, *Cancer: Nature, Cause, and Cure* (Paris: Institute Pasteur, 1957), ix; Vilhjalmur Stefansson, *Cancer: Disease of Civilization?* (New York: Hill and Wang, 1960); Gary Taube, *Good Calories, Bad Calories* (New York: Alfred A. Knopf, 2007), 89–99; G. Tognon et al., "Does the Mediterranean Diet Predict Longevity in the Elderly? A Swedish Perspective," *Age* (Dordrecht, Netherlands) (November 26, 2010); A. S. Truswell, "Diet and Nutrition of Hunter-Gatherers," *Ciba Foundation Symposium* 49 (1977): 213–21.

14. Real Food, Many Forms

213 **nearly twice as much water:** Pat Willmer et al., *Environmental Physiology of Animals* (Oxford: Blackwell Science, 2000), 119.

217 **a dangerous fad:** Online at CVMA, "Raw Food Diets for Pets – Canadian Veterinary Medical Association and Public Health Agency of Canada Joint Position Statement."
    At least the AVMA: Online at AVMA, "*JAVMA* Report Offers Tips to Protect Pets from *Salmonella* – Raw Food, Bulk-Bin Treats Discouraged," June 21, 2011.
    some commonsense procedures: Online at AVMA, "Frequently Asked Questions About Dry Pet Foods and *Salmonella*."
    dozens of popular varieties of kibble: Online at IAMS, "P&G Expands Voluntary Limited Recall of Specialized Dry Pet Foods Due to Possible Health Risk"; online at AVMA, "Animal Health: Kroger Co. Recalls 10 Varieties of Pet Foods Sold in 19 States"; C. B. Behravesh et al., "Human Salmonella Infections Linked

to Contaminated Dry Dog and Cat Food, 2006–2008," *Pediatrics* 126, no. 3 (September 2010): 477–83; online at FDA, "2011 Recalls and Safety Alerts."

218 **third-party suppliers:** Marion Nestle, *Pet Food Politics* (Berkeley: University of California Press, 2008), fig. 4, p. 98.

219 **sequestered in the bones:** David J. Hoffman et al., *Handbook of Ecotoxicology*, 2nd ed. (Boca Raton, FL: CRC Press LLC, 2003), 381–84.

    in the top one inch of soil: Online at Subhuti Dharmananda, "Lead Content of Soil, Plants, Foods, Air, and Chinese Herb Formulas," Institute for Traditional Medicine.

    Global Environmental Monitoring System/Food Network: World Health Organization (WHO), International Agency for Research on Cancer (IARC), *IARC Monographs on the Evaluation of Carcinogenic Risks to Humans: Inorganic and Organic Lead Compounds*, vol. 87 (2006), 105.

    concentrations of lead in meat and grain: WHO, IARC, *IARC Monographs on the Evaluation of Carcinogenic Risks to Humans: Inorganic and Organic Lead Compounds.* The EPA found 2–83 micrograms of lead per kilogram in meats, and 2–84 micrograms per kilogram in grains.

220 **set at zero by the EPA:** Online at EPA, "Basic Information About Arsenic in Drinking Water."

    found to have anticarcinogenic properties: Online at California Veterinary Specialists Angel Care Cancer Center, "DHA – Docosahexaenoic Acid in Cancer Prevention and Therapy: The Silver Bullet?"; online at University of Maryland Medical Center, "Omega-3 Fatty Acids."

221 **salmon poisoning:** Cornelius B. Philip et al., "Studies on Salmon Poisoning Disease of Canines: I. The Rickettsial Relationships and Pathogenicity of *Neorickettsia helmintheca*," *Experimental Parasitology* 3, no. 4 (July 1954): 336–50; online at Washington State University, College of Veterinary Medicine, "Salmon Poisoning Disease."

    Xylitol: Frederick W. Oehme and William R. Hare, "Urban Legends of Toxicology: Facts and Fiction," in John D. Bonagura and David C. Twedt, eds., *Kirk's Current Veterinary Therapy XIV* (St. Louis, MO: Saunders Elsevier, 2009), 109–11.

222 **feeding dogs avocados:** Online at ASPCA, "People Foods to Avoid Feeding Your Pets."

    nutrigenomics uses genetic tests: Online at W. Jean Dodds, DVM, "Nutrigenomics for Companion Animals."

    "Nutriscan": Online at Hemopet/Hemolife, "Nutriscan Diagnostics."

    $229 per year: Online at American Pet Products Association, "Industry Statistics and Trends."

15. Whom Shall We Eat?

224 **begin the discipline of catching:** Jane Packard, "Wolf Behavior: Reproductive, Social, and Intelligent," in L. David Mech and Luigi Boitani, eds., *Wolves:*

Behavior, Ecology, and Conservation (Chicago: University of Chicago Press, 2003), 51–52.

235 *ineluctabilis:* Charlton T. Lewis and Charles Short, *A Latin Dictionary* (Oxford: Oxford University Press, 1975), 939.

236 **augmented with fish emulsion:** Michael Pollan, *The Omnivore's Dilemma* (New York: Penguin Books, 2006), 134–84.

two hundred other major spills: Online at International Tanker Owners Pollution Federation Ltd.

40 to 60 percent of a deer's diet: Richard Nelson, *Heart and Blood: Living with Deer in America* (New York: Alfred A. Knopf, 1997), 289–311.

237 **help me calculate:** Ted Kerasote, *Bloodties* (New York: Random House, 1993), 230–41.

3,900,000 kilocalories of fossil fuel: It takes 26,035 kilocalories to produce a pound of beef. See online at University of Washington, School of Oceanography, "Energy in Natural Processes and Human Consumption – Some Numbers." This number was calculated as follows:

- 1 barrel of oil (42 gallons) = 6.1×10^9 joules

  6.1×10^9 joules/42 gallons = 145,238,095 joules per gallon of oil

  1 calorie (lower-case "c") = 4.184 joules

  1 food Calorie (upper-case "C," or 1 kilocalorie) = 1,000 calories

  4.184 joules/1 calorie × 1,000 calories/1 Calorie = 4,184 joules/1 Calorie

  So, 1 Calorie = 4,184 joules, and 1 gallon of oil provides 145,238,095 joules.

  1 Calorie/4,184 joules × 145,238,095 joules/gallon = 34,713 Calorie/gallon

  34,713 Calories × 0.75 = 26,035 Calories per 0.75 gallons of oil

  Therefore, 1 pound of beef, which requires 0.75 gallons of oil to produce, requires 26,035 Calories to produce. Hence, 150 pounds of beef costs planet Earth 3,905,250 Calories.

238 **addition to the world's greenhouse gases:** Michael Pollan, "Power Steer," *New York Times Magazine*, March 31, 2002; online at UN News Center, "Rearing Cattle Produces More Greenhouse Gases Than Driving Cars, UN Report Warns"; UN Food and Agriculture Organization, *Livestock's Long Shadow*, 2006.

full of omega-3 fatty acids: L. Cordain et al., "Fatty Acid Analysis of Wild Ruminant Tissues: Evolutionary Implications for Reducing Diet-Related Chronic Disease," *European Journal of Clinical Nutrition* 56 (2002): 181–91.

good for one's heart and memory: Online at University of Maryland Medical Center, "Omega-3 Fatty Acids."

conjugated linoleic acid: S. F. Chin et al., "Dietary Sources of Conjugated Dienoic Isomers of Linoleic Acid, a Newly Recognized Class of Anticarcinogens," *Journal of Food Composition and Analysis* 5, no. 3 (September 1992): 185–97.

three times the amount: L. Cordain et al., "Fatty Acid Analysis of Wild Ruminant Tissues: Evolutionary Implications for Reducing Diet-Related Chronic Disease," *European Journal of Clinical Nutrition* 56 (2002): 181–91.

239 **"properly constructed vegetarian diet":** Ian Billinghurst, *Give Your Dog a Bone* (Bathurst, AU: Warrigal Publishing, 1993), 178.
positively stimulates its immune system: Ibid., 126–27.

16. The Worst Word in the World

246 **Morris Animal Foundation cancer survey:** Morris Animal Foundation, "Animal Health Survey Fiscal Year 1998," 1998, 14.

250 **can't measure morbidity or mortality:** The other notable confounder is that the 7 million records of the VMDB all come from US veterinary teaching hospitals, whose patients are the illest of the ill and not representative of the dog population at large. In addition, pet insurance providers don't require that health statistics for animals be tracked, as do human medical insurance providers. See John S. Reif, "The Epidemiology and Incidence of Cancer," in Stephen J. Withrow and David M. Vail, eds., *Small Animal Clinical Oncology*, 4th ed. (St. Louis, MO: Saunders Elsevier, 2007), 68–73.

252 **"The word cancer is as dark":** California Veterinary Specialists Angel Care Cancer Center, client handout, March 2006.

255 **can be found in the notes:** For North America, type "search for a specialist—American college of veterinary internal medicine" into your online search engine. This will take you to one of the webpages of the American College of Veterinary Internal Medicine, where you can use the drop-down menu to find a board-certified oncologist in your area. In the United Kingdom, type in "animal cancer trust specialist in oncology" and you will get a listing of specialists certified by the Royal College of Veterinary Surgeons and/or the European College of Veterinary Internal Medicine. The Animal Cancer Trust list may not be complete. Here are some other recognized oncology specialists in the United Kingdom: Animal Health Trust, Newmarket, Suffolk, www.ahtreferrals.co.uk; Dick White Referrals, Suffolk, www.dickwhitereferrals.com; London Veterinary Specialists, London, www.londonvetspecialists.com; Davies Veterinary Specialists, Hertfordshire, www.vetspecialists.co.uk; VetsNow Referrals, Glasgow, Glasgow.enquiries@vets-now.com; Pet Cancer Vet, North Yorkshire, www.petcancervet.co.uk; Fitzpatrick Referrals, Surrey, www.fitzpatrickreferrals.co.uk; Cave Veterinary Specialists, Wellington, Somerset, www.cave-vet-specialists.co.uk.

256 **the Wisconsin Protocol:** For a complete discussion of the Wisconsin Protocol, see online at Gregory K. Ogilvie, "Canine Lymphoma: Protocols for 2004," 29th World Congress of the World Small Animal Veterinary Association.
similar drugs were used: The fifteen-week course is the CHOP protocol, so-called because it treats non-Hodgkin's lymphoma with the following four drugs:

Cyclophosphamide, hydroxydoxorubicin (doxorubicin), Oncovin (vincristine), and prednisone.

Dogs with B-cell lymphoma: Online at "Canine Lymphoma," *Merck Veterinary Manual.*

257 **began to offer bone marrow transplants:** Online at North Carolina State University, College of Veterinary Medicine, "Canine Bone Marrow Transplant."

258 **Veterinary Pet Insurance:** Online at VPI Pet Insurance, "VPI Major Medical Plan for Dogs."

found at veterinary training centers: Radiology Oncology Systems, telephone interview with the author, November 23, 2011.

259 **cancer cells do not metabolize fats:** R. Kaaks and A. Lukanova, "Energy Balance and Cancer: The Role of Insulin and Insulin-Like Growth Factor-1," *Proceedings of the Nutrition Society* 60 (2001): 91–106; World Cancer Research Fund/American Institute for Cancer Research (AICR), *Food, Nutrition, Physical Activity, and the Prevention of Cancer: A Global Perspective* (Washington, DC: AICR, 2007).

a long list of scientific papers: Online at California Veterinary Specialists, Angel Care Cancer Center, "DHA – Docosahexaenoic Acid in Cancer Prevention and Therapy: The Silver Bullet?"; and University of Maryland Medical Center, "Omega-3 Fatty Acids."

260 **EGCG, epigallocatechin gallate:** N. G. Chen et al., "Proteomic Approaches to Study Epigallocatechin Gallate–Provoked Apoptosis of TSGH-8301 Human Urinary Bladder Carcinoma Cells: Roles of AKT and Heat Shock Protein 27-Modulated Intrinsic Apoptotic Pathways," *Oncology Reports,* July 4, 2011.

American Holistic Veterinary Medical Association: Online at AHVMA, "Directory."

promising immunotherapeutic agents: For a review of these compounds, see John Boik, *Natural Compounds in Cancer Therapy* (Princeton, MN: Oregon Medical Press, 2001).

PSK, polysaccharide K: Online at American Cancer Society, "Coriolus Versicolor."

shiitake mushrooms: J. Li et al., "Immunoregulatory and Anti-Tumor Effects of Polysaccharopeptide and Astragalus Polysaccharides on Tumor-Bearing Mice," *Immunopharmacology and Immunotoxicology* 30, no. 4 (2009): 771–82; C. Garrido, "Immunotherapy Eradicates Metastases with Reversible Defects in MHC Class I Expression," *Cancer Immunology, Immunotherapy,* May 8, 2001; N. Isoda et al., "Clinical Efficacy of Superfine Dispersed Lentinan (Beta-1,3-Glucan) in Patients with Hepatocellular Carcinoma," *Hepatogastroenterology* 56, no. 90 (March-April 2009): 437–41; online at T. F. Liu and W. C. Xue, "Clinical Implications of PSP in Oncology," in Cancer Research Group, *Recent Advances in Cancer,* Chinese University of Hong Kong, 1989, 57–62; K. Shimizu et al., "Efficacy of Oral Administered Superfine Dispersed Lentinan for Advanced Pancreatic Cancer," *Hepatogastroenterology* 56, no. 89 (January-February 2009): 240–44; P. Yang et al., "Clinical Application of a Combination Therapy of Lentinan, Multi-Electrode RFA and TACE in HCC," *Advances in Therapy* 25, no. 8 (August 2008): 787–94.

Avemar: Online at PubMed, which displays over thirty peer-reviewed articles on the beneficial effects of Avemar in treating cancer patients.

261 **"driver genes" ... "tumor suppressor genes":** Michael R. Stratoon et al., "The Cancer Genome," *Nature* 458 (April 9, 2009): 719–24; online at National Cancer Institute, "Tumor Suppressor Gene," in *Dictionary of Cancer Terms;* Amy Hardon, "A Roller Coaster Chase for a Cure," *New York Times,* February 22, 2010.

265 **"extent to which environmental exposures":** LaSalle D. Leffall and Margaret L. Kripke, *Reducing Environmental Cancer Risk: What We Can Do Now* (Washington, DC: US Department of Health and Human Services, National Cancer Institute, 2010), 4.

17. Dog Speed

269 **B. F. Skinner ... Karen Pryor:** B. F. Skinner, "How to Teach Animals," *Scientific American* 185 (1951): 26–29; Karen Pryor, *Don't Shoot the Dog* (New York: Bantam Books, 1999).

272 **"keeping my dog on a leash":** Online comment by Schmoo at Dogwise, March 25, 2007.

274 **child psychologist Dan Kindlon:** Dan Kindlon, *Too Much of a Good Thing* (New York: Hyperion, 2001), 77.

277 **ability to solve problems:** J. Topål et al., "Dog-Human Relationship Affects Problem Solving Behavior in the Dog," *Anthrozoös* 10, no. 4 (1997): 214–24.

mice who exercise: P. J. Clark et al., "New Neurons Generated from Running Are Broadly Recruited into Neuronal Activation Associated with Three Different Hippocampus-Involved Tasks," *Hippocampus* (March 30, 2012); Gretchen Reynolds, "How Exercise Could Lead to a Better Brain," *New York Times Magazine,* April 18, 2012.

delay the cognitive impairment: R. A. Kohman et al., "Voluntary Wheel Running Reverses Age-Induced Changes in Hippocampal Gene Expression," *PLoS One* 6, no. 8 (2011).

the inability to make one's own decisions: Online at World Health Organization, "The World Health Report 2002: Reducing Risks, Promoting Healthy Life"; Michael Marmot, *The Status Syndrome* (New York: Henry Holt and Co., 2004); Robert M. Sapolsky, *Why Zebras Don't Get Ulcers* (New York: Henry Holt and Co., 2004).

the lower your station: Robert M. Sapolsky, "The Influence of Social Hierarchy on Primate Health," *Science* 308, no. 5722 (2005): 648–52; Michael Marmot, "Social Determinants of Health Inequalities," *The Lancet* 365 (March 19, 2005): 1099–1104.

accumulating stress hormones: Online at Colorado State Education, "Glucocorticoids."

when constantly secreted: D. H. Abbott, "Are Subordinates Always Stressed? A Comparative Analysis of Rank Differences in Cortisol Levels Among Primates," *Hormones and Behavior* 43 (2003): 67–82.

278 **being treated unfairly:** Friederike Range et al., "The Absence of Reward Induces Inequity Aversion in Dogs," *Proceedings of the National Academy of Sciences* 106, no. 1 (January 6, 2009): 340–45.

twins of lower socioeconomic status: L. F. Cherkas et al., "The Effects of Social Status on Biological Aging as Measured by White-Blood-Cell Telomere Length," *Aging Cell* 5 (2006): 361–65.

stressed regardless of our economic well-being: Online at University of Utah, Genetic Science Learning Center, "Are Telomeres the Key to Aging and Cancer?"

279 **biologically nine to seventeen years older:** Elissa S. Epel et al., "Accelerated Telomere Shortening in Response to Life Stress," *Proceedings of the National Academy of Sciences* 101, no. 49 (December 7, 2004): 17312–15.

The physically more active twin: Lynn F. Cherkas et al., "The Association Between Physical Activity in Leisure Time and Leukocyte Telomere Length," *Archives of Internal Medicine* 168, no. 2 (January 28, 2008): 154–58.

In captive wolf packs: Scott Creel, "Social Dominance and Stress Hormones," *Trends in Ecology and Evolution* 16, no. 9 (2001): 491–97; Peter J. McLeod et al., "The Relation Between Urinary Cortisol Levels and Social Behaviour in Captive Timber Wolves," *Canadian Journal of Zoology* 74 (1996): 209–16.

in wolf packs living in the wild: L. David Mech, "Alpha Status, Dominance, and Division of Labor in Wolf Packs," *Canadian Journal of Zoology* 77 (1999): 1197; Rolf O. Peterson et al., "Leadership Behavior in Relation to Dominance and Reproductive Status in Gray Wolves, *Canis lupus*," *Canadian Journal of Zoology* 80 (2002): 1405–12; Douglas W. Smith, Leader, Yellowstone Wolf Project, interview with the author, Mammoth Hot Springs, WY, March 18, 2005; Douglas W. Smith, e-mail communication with the author, February 7, 2005; Jane M. Packard, "Wolf Behavior: Reproductive, Social, and Intelligent," in L. David Mech and Luigi Boitani, eds., *Wolves: Behavior, Ecology, and Conservation* (Chicago: University of Chicago Press, 2003), 57; Constance Perin, "Dogs as Symbols in Human Development," in Bruce Fogle, ed., *Interrelations Between People and Pets* (Springfield, IL: Charles C. Thomas, 1981), 80.

without the influence of their parents: Douglas W. Smith, Leader, Yellowstone Wolf Project, telephone interview with the author, July 5, 2007.

they who do most of the pack's hunting: Daniel R. MacNulty et al., "Predatory Senescence in Ageing Wolves," *Ecology Letters* 12, no. 12 (December 2009): 1347–56.

young wolves who often get to eat first: Brett French, "Old Wolves Need Younger Hunters to Thrive," *Billings Gazette*, October 6, 2009; Douglas W. Smith, Leader, Yellowstone Wolf Project, interview with the author, Mammoth Hot Springs, WY, March 18, 2005.

noticeable physiological effect: Jennifer Sands and Scott Creel, "Social Dominance, Aggression, and Faecal Glucocorticoid Levels in a Wild Population of Wolves, *Canis lupus*," *Animal Behaviour* 67, no. 3 (March 2004): 387–96.

285 **when neighborhood walkability declines:** T. Sugiyama et al., "Neighborhood Walkability and TV Viewing Among Australian Adults," *American Journal of Preventative Medicine* 33, no. 6 (December 2007): 444–49. Curiously, in Ghent, Belgium, as neighborhood walkability increased, self-reported overall sitting time increased. See D. Van Dyck et al., "Associations of Neighborhood Walkability with Sedentary Time in Belgian Adults," *American Journal of Preventative Medicine* 39, no. 1 (2010): 25–32.

they once reached on foot: For an overview of this phenomenon, see Neville Owen et al., "Adults' Sedentary Behavior: Determinants and Interventions," *American Journal of Preventative Medicine* 41, no. 2 (2011): 189–96. For particulars, see A. M. Bento et al., "The Effects of Urban Spatial Structure on Travel Demand in the US," *Review of Economics and Statistics* 83, no. 3 (2005): 466–78; X. Y. Cao, "Disentangling the Influence of Neighborhood Type and Self-Selection on Driving Behavior: An Application of Sample Selection Model," *Transportation* 36, no. 2 (2009): 207–22; R. Cervero and J. Murakami, "Effects of Built Environments on Vehicle Miles Traveled: Evidence from 370 US Urbanized Areas," *Environment and Planning A*, 42, no. 2 (2010): 400–418; L. D. Frank et al., "Obesity Relationships with Community Design, Physical Activity, and Time Spent in Cars," *American Journal of Preventative Medicine* 227, no. 2 (2004): 87–96; L. D. Frank et al., "Stepping Towards Causation: Do Built Environments or Neighborhood and Travel Preferences Explain Physical Activity, Driving, and Obesity?" *Social Sciences and Medicine* 65, no. 9 (2007): 898–914.

fourteen hours of sitting opportunities: David W. Dunstan et al., "'Too Much Sitting' and Metabolic Risk – Has Modern Technology Caught Up with Us?" *US Endocrinology* 5 (2009): 29–33. The chart in this article shows 15.5 hours of sitting opportunities, but the authors made an error in their addition: it is actually 14.25 hours of sitting opportunities. Neville Owen, e-mail communication with the author, December 4, 2011.

leads to elevated levels of several biomarkers: Marc T. Hamilton et al., "Role of Low Energy Expenditure and Sitting in Obesity, Metabolic Syndrome, Type 2 Diabetes, and Cardiovascular Disease," *Diabetes* 56, no. 11 (November 2007): 2655–67; Marc T. Hamilton et al., "Too Little Exercise and Too Much Sitting: Inactivity Physiology and the Need for New Recommendations on Sedentary Behavior," *Current Cardiovascular Risk Reports* 2 (2008): 292–98; Genevieve N. Healy et al., "Sedentary Time and Cardio-Metabolic Biomarkers in US Adults: NHANES 2003–2006," *European Heart Journal* 32, no. 5 (March 2011): 590–97, 667.

286 **lose most of the enzyme:** T. W. Zderic et al., "Physical Inactivity Amplifies the Sensitivity of Skeletal Muscle to the Lipid-Induced Downregulation of Lipoprotein Lipase Activity," *Journal of Applied Physiology* 100 (2006): 249–57.

the larger the accumulation: L. Bey at al., "Patterns of Global Gene Expression in Rat Skeletal Muscle During Unloading and Low-Intensity Ambulatory Activity," *Physiological Genomics* 13 (2003): 157–67; L. Bey and M. T. Hamilton, "Suppression of Skeletal Muscle Lipoprotein Lipase Activity During Physical Inactivity: A Molecular Reason to Maintain Daily Low-Intensity Activity," *Journal of Physiology* 551, pt. 2 (2003): 673–82; M. T. Hamilton et al., "Plasma Triglyceride Metabolism in Humans and Rats During Aging and Physical Inactivity," *International Journal of Sport Nutrition and Exercise Metabolism* 11 (supp., 2001): S97–104; M. T. Hamilton et al., "Role of Local Contractile Activity and Muscle Fiber Type on LPL Regulation During Exercise," *American Journal of Physiology* 275, no. 6, pt. 1 (1998): E1016–22; T. W. Zderic et al., "Physical Inactivity Amplifies the Sensitivity of Skeletal Muscle to the Lipid-Induced Downregulation of Lipoprotein Lipase Activity," *Journal of Applied Physiology* 100 (2006): 249–57.

get up from their chairs: Neville Owen, Baker IDI Heart and Diabetes Institute, data presented at the American Institute of Cancer Research conference, Washington, DC, November 4, 2011; online at Centers for Disease Control and Prevention, "Physical Activity for Everyone."

the simple act of standing: Marc T. Hamilton et al., "Too Little Exercise and Too Much Sitting: Inactivity Physiology and the Need for New Recommendations on Sedentary Behavior," *Current Cardiovascular Risk Reports* 2 (2008): 292–98.

urban people use cars less: Neville Owen et al., "Adults' Sedentary Behavior: Determinants and Interventions," *American Journal of Preventative Medicine* 41, no. 2 (2011): 189–96.

creating more dog- and people-friendly neighborhoods: To see how this is being done, see online at Active Living By Design.

288 **packs of free-roaming dogs:** Online at "Killer Dogs Sow Terror in Sicily," *BBC News,* March 17, 2009; and Jeri Clausing, "Reservation Dogs Roam Unchecked; Attacks Common," Associated Press/MSNBC.

18. The Bad Good Death

293 **are killed in the very facilities:** P. N. Olson et al., "Pet Overpopulation: A Challenge for Companion Animal Veterinarians in the 1990s," *Journal of the American Veterinary Medical Association* 198, no. 7 (April 1, 1991): 1151–52; Gary J. Patronek et al., "Risk Factors for Relinquishment of Dogs to an Animal Shelter," *Journal of the American Veterinary Medical Association* 209, no. 3 (August 1, 1996): 572–81.

298 **Michael Vick's pit bulls:** Jim Gorant, "Happy New Year," *Sports Illustrated,* February 29, 2008, 72–77.

300 **the Temporary Home for Lost and Starving Dogs:** Arthur W. Moss, *Valiant Crusade: The History of the RSPCA* (London: Cassell & Co., 1961), 198–99; online at Battersea Dogs and Cats Home, "Our History."

Philadelphia's City Refuge for Lost and Suffering Animals: Lila Miller and

Stephen Zawistowski, *Shelter Medicine for Veterinarians and Staff* (Ames, IA: Blackwell Publishing, 2004), 3–9.

founded in 1840: Online at Michigan State University College of Law, Animal Legal and Historical Center, "The History of the RSPCA"; and RSPCA, "Our Heritage."

the power to enforce it: Online at ASPCA, "History"; and Learning to Give, "Bergh, Henry"; Marion S. Lane and Stephen L. Zawistowski, *Heritage of Care* (Westport, CT: Praeger Publishers, 2008), 19.

unclaimed dogs were crammed: Stephen Zawistowski, *Companion Animals in Society* (Florence, KY: Cengage Learning, 2008), 72.

thirty-eight states by 1888: Online at ASPCA, "History."

301 **founded in 1954:** Online at HSUS, "About Us: Overview."

injection of sodium pentobarbital: Lila Miller and Stephen Zawistowski, *Shelter Medicine for Veterinarians and Staff* (Ames, IA: Blackwell Publishing, 2004), 3–9.

Phyllis Wright: Online at Sheila Walsh, "Phyllis Wright: The Woman Who Gave Shelters and Their Animals More Dignity," Humane Society of the United States (accessed March 14, 2010). The biography seems to be no longer available on the organization's website.

"Why Must We Euthanize": Phyllis Wright, "Why Must We Euthanize," *The Humane Society News* (Summer 1978): 24–25.

302 **"learned at her knee":** Online at Sheila Walsh, "Phyllis Wright: The Woman Who Gave Shelters and Their Animals More Dignity," Humane Society of the United States (accessed March 14, 2010).

3 million and 4 million today: Andrew N. Rowan and Jeff Williams, "The Success of Companion Animal Management Programs: A Review," *Anthrozoös* 1, no. 2 (1987): 110–22; Andrew Rowan, "Companion Animal Statistics," HSUS internal paper, May 2008; Wayne Pacelle, CEO of HSUS, interview with the author, July 30, 2010.

Wright herself championed: Elizabeth A. Clancy and Andrew N. Rowan, "Companion Animal Demographics in the United States: A Historical Perspective," in Andrew N. Rowan and Deborah J. Salem, eds., *The State of the Animals II: 2003* (Washington, DC: Humane Society Press, 2003), 14.

303 **"In the Name of Mercy":** Edward S. Duvin, "In the Name of Mercy," originally published in *animalines*, 1989, online at Best Friends Animal Society.

hired by the San Francisco SPCA: The section about Rich Avanzino's reformation of the San Francisco SPCA is taken from Nathan J. Winograd, *Redemption* (Los Angeles: Almaden Books, 2007), 37–50, and from Rich Avanzino, telephone communication with the author, September 20, 2011.

first low-cost spay/neuter clinic: Andrew N. Rowan, "Animal Sheltering Trends in the US," online at Humane Society of the United States.

304 **fell to nearly zero:** According to Dr. Jeffrey Bryan, DVM, who volunteered his veterinary services at San Francisco Animal Care and Control during the years when Rich Avanzino was reforming the city's SPCA, many animals with minor

illnesses – kittens, for instance, who had ear mites and who could have been easily treated – were not taken in by the SPCA and continued to be put to death at Animal Care and Control. Interview with the author, Columbia, MO, October 5, 2011.

Nathan Winograd: Background on Nathan Winograd is taken from his book *Redemption* (Los Angeles: Almaden Books, 2007), as well as from interviews with the author, Washington, DC, May 2–3, 2009, and July 31–August 1, 2010.

305 **small, filthy crates:** Nancy Lawson and Carrie Allan, "What Would It Take?" *Animal Sheltering* (January-February 2002).

they turned away animals: Christine Arnold, "Open-Door Versus No-Kill Shelters: The Facts," *Humane Society of Santa Clara Valley News* (Spring 1995); Ronnette Fish, "Parting Thoughts on No-Kill Delusion," *NACA News* (November-December 2004): 38.

the No Kill Equation: Online at No Kill Advocacy Center, "The No Kill Equation."

Companion Animal Protection Act: Online at Nathan J. Winograd, "Companion Animal Protection Act."

306 **only about two hundred US shelters:** Nathan Winograd, e-mail communication with the author, May 29, 2012.

number roughly thirty-five hundred: Wayne Pacelle, interview with the author, Washington, DC, July 30, 2010.

307 **$162 million in its coffers:** Online at Humane Watch, HSUS federal tax return for 2008.

19. Shelters to Sanctuaries

313 **$4.69 per capita:** This spending rate was calculated as follows: According to the US Census Bureau, 109,000 people live in Danville, Virginia, and Pittsylvania County, Virginia. At its meeting on November 16, 2010, the Danville Budget Committee voted on a FY2011 budget with $11,316 for animal control; on May 18, 2010, Pittsylvania County adopted a budget for FY 2010–2011 that included $250,329 for animal control. These funds, added to the Danville Area Humane Society budget of $250,000, bring the total expenditure for animal control in Danville City and Pittsylvania County to $511,635, which, divided by 109,000 people, equals $4.69 per capita for animal control.

316 **sobering, cheerless images:** Online at Danville Area Humane Society (images viewed August 19, 2011).

welcoming, and effervescent mood: Online at Charlottesville-Albemarle SPCA (images viewed August 19, 2011).

higher unemployment rate than Danville: The actual numbers for 2010 were 19.2 percent unemployment for Martinsville and 13.4 percent for Danville. Online at US Department of Labor, Bureau of Labor Statistics, "Unemployment Rates by County in Virginia, June 2011."

"Leave a Legacy of Love": Online at Martinsville–Henry County SPCA (images viewed August 19, 2011).

318 **increasingly imported from the South:** Stephen Zawistowski, science adviser, ASPCA, telephone interview with the author, July 28, 2011; Michael Schaffer, *One Nation Under Dog* (New York: Henry Holt and Co., 2009), 123.

a large rescue operation: Ronnie N. Graves, president, Sumter Disaster Animal Response Team, e-mail communication with the author, September 14–26, 2011; Larry Clifton, "Dogs Quarantined; many die," *Sumter County Times*, September 29, 2010.

New World screwworm fly: Online at California Department of Food and Agriculture, "Screwworm Fact Sheet, October 2007"; John H. Wyss, "Screwworm Eradication in the Americas," *Annals of the New York Academy of Sciences* 916 (2000): 186–93.

three hundred thousand dogs per year: J. H. McQuistion et al., "Importation of Dogs into the United States: Risks from Rabies and Other Zoonotic Disease," *Zoonoses and Public Health* 55 (October 2008): 421–26.

319 **proposed stricter importation regulations:** Online at USDA Animal and Plant Health Inspection Service, "USDA Proposes to Strengthen Health Requirements for Imported Dogs," "Importation of Pets and Other Animals into the United States," and "Bringing a Dog into the United States."

No healthy dogs are killed: Gianluca Felicetti, president, Lega Anti Vivisezione, interview with the author, Rome, Italy, September 10, 2008; Heinz Lienhard, president, Swiss Animal Protection, letter to the author's Swiss researcher, Lucia Kälin, May 3, 2010; Sylvia Hemmerling, press officer, Cologne Dog Shelter, interview with the author, Cologne, Germany, September 22, 2008; Inge Welzig, head of the Tierschutzverein, North Tirol, Austria Animal Home, interview with the author, North Tirol, Austria, April 16, 2010; Helena Skarp, Swedish Kennel Club, e-mail communication with the author, August 19, 2011; Astrid Indrebø, Norwegian Kennel Club, Department of Companion Animal Clinical Sciences, Norwegian School of Veterinary Science, e-mail communication with the author, August 25, 2011; Kaija Unhola, Finnish Kennel Club, telephone communication with the author's researcher, Kate Hayden, September 9, 2011; Lotte Brink, Dyrenes Beskyttelse (Animal Protection), e-mail communication with the author's researcher, Kate Hayden, September 9, 2011.

In France: Christophe Bellanger, Director, Société Protectrice des Animaux (shelter), La Ville de Gennevilliers, Paris, France, interview with the author, Paris, September 17, 2008.

and in the United Kingdom: Bruce Fogle, e-mail communication with the author, March 20, 2010.

320 **The United States, with the largest:** Online at "Strong Variations in Social Justice Within the OECD," *Bertelsmann Stiftung*, October 27, 2011; and "Bottom of the Heap," *New York Times*, October 29, 2011.

321 **Canada still kills:** Online at Canadian Federation of Humane Societies, "Shelter Animal Statistics," and "National Shelter Statistics 2010."

median income of Agoura: Online at City-Dat.com.

Downey shelter killed 50 percent: Agoura and Downey Animal Care Center statistics provided by Evelina Villa, Outreach/Media/Press Relations, Los Angeles County Department of Animal Care and Control, e-mail communication with the author, December 21, 2011.

study of feline neutering rates: Karyen Chu et al., "Population Characteristics and Neuter Status of Cats Living in Households in the United States," *Journal of the American Veterinary Medical Association* 234, no. 8 (April 15, 2009): 1023–30.

care for their children first: In one study, households that had an annual income of less than $20,000 were at the greatest risk for relinquishing their dog to a shelter. See Gary J. Patronek et al., "Risk Factors for Relinquishment of Dogs to an Animal Shelter," *Journal of the American Veterinary Medical Association* 209, no. 3 (August 1996): 572–81.

illustrates these difficult choices: Philip H. Kass et al., "Understanding Animal Companion Surplus in the United States: Relinquishment of Nonadoptables to Animal Shelters for Euthanasia," *Journal of Applied Animal Welfare Science* 4, no. 4 (2001): 237–48.

20. Chance

329 **"Free at last":** "Free at Last," the traditional Negro spiritual quoted by Martin Luther King Jr. in his "I Have a Dream" speech, delivered August 28, 1963 at the Lincoln Memorial in Washington, DC.

21. The Flip Side of Spay/Neuter

332 **80 percent . . . got their dogs:** American Pet Products Association statistics for 2009: adopted pet superstore (1 percent), adopted shelter (19 percent), breeder (27 percent), friend/relative (33 percent), gift (5 percent), Internet (1 percent), newspaper/private party (13 percent), pet store (6 percent), pet superstore (7 percent), bred/born at home (3 percent), rescue group (4 percent), stray (8 percent), veterinarian (1 percent). The percentages add up to more than 100 percent, meaning that there is overlap in the categories. In addition, the pet superstore category, which amounts to 7 percent of the total, is erroneous, since neither PetSmart nor PetCo sell dogs. They display shelter dogs for adoptions.

338 **without estrogen, a dog's risk:** William H. Parker et al., "Ovarian Conservation at the Time of Hysterectomy and Long-Term Health Outcomes in the Nurses' Health Study," *Obstetrics and Gynecology* 113, no. 5 (May 2009): 1027–37.

the most common cancer of intact female dogs: Robert Schneider et al., "Factors Influencing Canine Mammary Cancer Development and Postsurgical

Survival," *Journal of the National Cancer Institute* 48, no. 6 (December 1969): 1249–61.

incidence of 3.4 percent: I. J. Fidler and R. S. Brodey, "The Biological Behavior of Canine Mammary Neoplasms," *Journal of the American Veterinary Medical Association* 15, no. 10 (November 15, 1967): 1311–18.

One Swedish study: Agneta Egenvall et al., "Incidence of and Survival After Mammary Tumors in a Population of over 80,000 Insured Female Dogs in Sweden from 1995 to 2002," *Preventive Veterinary Medicine* 69 (2005): 109–27.

Norwegian and Czech studies: K. Arnesen et al., "The Norwegian Canine Cancer Register 1990–1998. Report from the project 'Cancer in the Dog,'" *European Journal of Companion Animal Practice* XI, no. 2 (October 2001): 159–69. J. Zatloukal et al., "Breed and Age as Risk Factors for Canine Mammary Tumors," *Acta Veterinaria Brno* 74 (2005): 103–9.

character of the particular mammary cancer: Stephen J. Withrow and David M. Vail, *Small Animal Clinical Oncology,* 4th ed. (St. Louis, MO: Saunders Elsevier, 2007), 626–28.

about 6 percent: Egenvall et al., "Incidence of and Survival After Mammary Tumors in a Population of over 80,000 Insured Female Dogs."

339 **pyometra:** Frances O. Smith, "Canine Pyometra," *Theriogenology* 66 (2006): 610–12.

10 percent of Beagles: Online at R. Hagman, "New Aspects of Canine Pyometra," doctoral thesis, Swedish University of Agricultural Sciences, Uppsala, 2004.

only 0.09 percent: Margaret V. Root Kustritz, "Determining the Optimal Age for Gonadectomy of Dogs and Cats," *Journal of the American Veterinary Medical Association* 231, no. 11 (December 1, 2007): 1665–75.

over the age of ten: Richard W. Nelson and C. Guillermo Couto, *Small Animal Internal Medicine,* 4th ed. (St. Louis, MO: Mosby Elsevier, 2009), 971.

Survival rates with early detection: R. S. Dhaliwal et al., "Treatment of Aggressive Testicular Tumors in Four Dogs," *Journal of the American Animal Hospital Association* 35, no. 4 (July-August 1999): 311–18; Stephen J. Withrow and David M. Vail, *Small Animal Clinical Oncology,* 4th ed. (St. Louis, MO: Saunders Elsevier, 2007), 638–41; online at American Cancer Society, "Testicular Cancer Overview."

benign prostatic hyperplasia: Richard W. Nelson and C. Guillermo Couto, *Small Animal Internal Medicine,* 4th ed. (St. Louis, MO: Mosby Elsevier, 2009), 976–77.

340 **herbal supplementation:** Kim Henneman, DVM, e-mail communication with the author, September 12, 2011; Marybeth Minter, DVM, e-mail communication with the author, September 16, 2011.

neutered dogs develop prostate cancer more frequently: F. W. Bell et al., "Clinical and Pathologic Features of Prostatic Adenocarcinoma in Sexually Intact and Castrated Dogs: 31 Cases (1970–1987)," *Journal of the American Vet-*

erinary Medical Association 199, no. 11 (December 1, 1991): 1623–30; Jeffrey N. Bryan, "A Population Study of Neutering Status as a Risk Factor for Canine Prostate Cancer," *The Prostate* 67, no. 11 (August 2007): 1174–81; Karen K. Cornell et al., "Clinical and Pathologic Aspects of Spontaneous Canine Prostate Carcinoma: A Retrospective Analysis of 76 Cases," *The Prostate* 45, no. 1 (October 2000): 173–83; Joyce Obradovich et al., "The Influence of Castration on the Development of Prostatic Carcinoma in the Dog, 43 Cases (1978–1985)," *Journal of Veterinary Internal Medicine* 1, no. 4 (1987): 183–87; E. Teske et al., "Canine Prostate Carcinoma: Epidemiological Evidence of an Increased Risk in Castrated Dogs," *Molecular and Cellular Endocrinology* 197 (2002): 251–55.

urinary incontinence: S. Arnold et al., "Urinary Incontinence in Spayed Bitches: Prevalence and Breed Predisposition," *Schweiz Arch Tierheilk* 131 (1989): 259–63; Dennis J. Chew and Stephen P. DiBartola, "Urinary Incontinence in Dogs – Diagnosis and Treatment," *Proceedings of the World Small Animal Veterinary Association* (Sydney, AU), 2007; P. E. Holt, "Urinary Incontinence in Dogs," *The Veterinary Record* (October 6, 1990): 347–50; N. M. Stöcklin-Gautschi et al., "The Relationship of Urinary Incontinence to Early Spaying in Bitches," *Journal of Reproductive and Fertility* 57 (supp., 2001): 233–36; M. V. Thrusfield et al., "Acquired Urinary Incontinence in Bitches: Its Incidence and Relationship to Neutering Practices," *Journal of Small Animal Practice* 39 (December 1998): 559–66.

more adverse reactions to vaccines: George E. Moore et al., "Adverse Events Diagnosed Within Three Days of Vaccine Administration in Dogs," *Journal of the American Veterinary Medical Association* 227, no. 7 (October 1, 2005): 1102–8.

more prone to be obese: A. T. B. Edney and P. M. Smith, "Study of Obesity in Dogs Visiting Veterinary Practices in the United Kingdom," *Veterinary Record* 118 (1986): 391–96; P. O. McGreevy et al., "Prevalence of Obesity in Dogs Examined by Australian Veterinary Practices and the Risk Factors Involved," *Veterinary Record* 156 (2005): 695–702. Obese dogs are at greater risk for musculoskeletal disorders, cardiovascular problems, diabetes, and cancer. See Elizabeth M. Lund et al., "Prevalence and Risk Factors for Obesity in Adult Dogs from Private US Veterinary Practices," *International Journal of Applied Research in Veterinary Medicine* 4, no. 2 (2006): 177–86.

twice the risk for osteosarcoma: G. Ru et al., "Host Related Risk Factors for Canine Osteosarcoma," *Veterinary Journal* 156 (1998): 31–29.

more likely to develop bladder cancer: Deborah W. Knapp et al., "Naturally-Occurring Canine Transitional Cell Carcinoma of the Urinary Bladder: A Relevant Model of Human Invasive Bladder Cancer," *Urologic Oncology* 5 (2000): 47–59.

160 percent higher: Wendy A. Ware and David L. Hopper, "Cardiac Tumors in Dogs: 1982–1995," *Journal of Veterinary Internal Medicine* 13, no. 2 (1999): 95–103. Although hemangiosarcoma is the most common cardiac tumor found in dogs, its overall incidence is quite low: 0.19 percent. However, some breeds are more predisposed than others to developing such tumors, including Bulldogs, Flat-Coated and Golden Retrievers, Boxers, English Setters, Boston Terriers, and German Shepherds. See C. Prymak et al., "Epidemiologic, Clinical, Pathologic, and Prognostic Characteristics of Splenic Hemangiosarcoma and Splenic Hematoma in Dogs: 217 Cases (1985)," *Journal of the American Veterinary Medical Association* 193, no. 6 (September 15, 1988): 706–12.

leading cause of death for Golden Retrievers: Online at Golden Retriever Club of America, "National Health Survey 1998–1999," 135.

for orthopedic injuries: Martin Silberberg and Ruth Silberberg, "Steroid Hormones and Bone," in Geoffrey H. Bourne, *The Biochemistry and Physiology of Bone*, 2nd ed., vol. 3 (New York: Academic Press, 1971), 401–84. Sterilized dogs have higher incidences of orthopedic injuries either because they're heavier than intact dogs, putting more stress on their joints, or because the ends of their long bones take longer to close than in intact dogs.

hip dysplasia: C. Victor Spain, "Long-Term Risks and Benefits of Early-Age Gonadectomy in Dogs," *Journal of the American Veterinary Medical Association* 224, no. 3 (February 1, 2004): 380–87.

ACL injuries: Julie M. Duval et al., "Breed, Sex, and Body Weight as Risk Factors for Rupture of the Cranial Cruciate Ligament in Young Dogs," *Journal of the American Veterinary Medical Association* 215, no. 6 (September 15, 1999): 811–14; online at American Kennel Club, Canine Health Foundation, "Health Implications of Spay and Neuter: Golden Retriever and Labrador Retriever," grant 01488-A for project by Dr. Benjamin Hart, UC Davis, July 1, 2010–June 30, 2011; J. R. Slauterbeck et al., "Canine Ovariohysterectomy and Orchiectomy Increases the Prevalence of ACL Injury," *Clinical Orthopaedics and Related Research* 429 (2004): 301–5; Jon G. Whitehair et al., "Epidemiology of Cranial Cruciate Ligament Rupture in Dogs," *Journal of the American Veterinary Medical Association* 203, no. 7 (October 1, 1993): 1016–19.

341 **canine cognitive impairment:** Benjamin L. Hart, "Effect of Gonadectomy on Subsequent Development of Age-Related Cognitive Impairment in Dogs," *Journal of the American Veterinary Medical Association* 219, no. 1 (July 1, 2001): 51–56.

"centenarian" Rottweilers: David J. Waters et al., "Exploring Mechanisms of Sex Differences in Longevity: Lifetime Ovary Exposure and Exceptional Longevity in Dogs," *Aging Cell* (2009): 1–4.

"spayed" and "unspayed": R. T. Bronson, "Variation in Age at Death of Dogs of Different Sexes and Breeds," *American Journal of Veterinary Research* 43, no. 11 (November 1982): 2057–59; A. R. Michell, "Longevity of British Breeds of Dog and Its Relationship with Sex, Size, Cardiovascular Variables, and Disease," *Veterinary Record* 145 (1999): 625–29. For a more nuanced view of spaying, see D. J. Waters et al., "Probing the Perils of Dichotomous Binning: How Categorizing Female Dogs as Spayed or Intact Can Misinform Our Assumptions About the Lifelong Health Consequences of Ovariohysterectomy," *Theriogenology* 76 (2011): 1496–1500.

thirty thousand US nurses: William H. Parker et al., "Ovarian Conservation at the Time of Hysterectomy and Long-Term Outcomes in the Nurses' Health Study," *Obstetrics and Gynecology* 113, no. 5 (May 2009): 1027–37. A rodent study revealed similar findings. The ovaries of young mice were transplanted into postmenopausal mice. These aged mice then resumed normal reproductive behavior, mating and having offspring. They also lived 40 percent longer than the control group of aging mice who had not received a pair of new ovaries. Online at European Society of Human Reproduction and Embryology, "Ovarian Transplantation Restores Fertility to Old Mice and Also Lengthens Their Lives," June 29, 2010.

provoked some immediate criticism: The primary methodological shortcoming cited by critics of the Rottweiler longevity study was that the researchers had preselected two groups that had particular outcomes (usual longevity versus exceptional longevity) instead of using the entire database of Rottweilers. This observation is accurate. See Paula Kislak, "Sees Limitations to Longevity Study of Rottweilers," *Journal of the American Veterinary Medical Association* 236, no. 10 (May 15, 2010): 1061. But supplemental data that Waters published in the original report speaks directly to this supposed shortcoming. In a separate study population of 237 female Rottweilers who died at a range of ages (not separated into groups), the retention of ovaries for at least 4.5 years was associated with a 37 percent reduction in mortality. This translated on average into living 1.4 years longer. Another concern—failing to account for a genetic component to the dogs' exceptional longevity—was also addressed in the tables and text of the original study (David J. Waters et al., "Exploring Mechanisms of Sex Differences in Longevity: Lifetime Ovary Exposure and Exceptional Longevity in Dogs," *Aging Cell* (2009): 1–4). Among the females who reached exceptional longevity, 22 percent had mothers who also reached exceptional longevity. In contrast, only 3 percent of females in the usual longevity group had exceptionally long-lived mothers. Could this apparent familial clustering of longevity overshadow the importance of ovaries? Here, too, the critics appeared not to have read the results of Waters's original study carefully. In their paper, Waters and his team conducted a multivariable statistical analysis that controlled for the familial clustering of exceptional longevity seen in the Rottweilers, and they reported that the strong association between keeping ovaries longer and living longer persisted even after familial clustering was taken into account. Another concern commonly raised was that the findings of the Rottweiler study might not be generalizable to all breeds, but Waters never said that they could be. See also David J. Waters, "In Search of a Strategic Disturbance: Some Thoughts on the Timing of Spaying," *Clinical Theriogenology* 3 (2011): 433–37; online at David J. Waters, "Ovaries and Longevity."

342 **"easy, quick and safe":** L. D. M. Silva, "Laparoscopic Vasectomy in the Male Dog," *Journal of Reproduction and Fertility* 47 (supp., 1993): 399–401.

"Sterilization of Nursing Puppies": D. F. Rice and C. G. Dewell, "Sterilization of Nursing Puppies," *Modern Veterinary Practice* 57, no. 10 (1976): 821–22.

344 **As Doctors Foster and Smith:** Online at Doctors Foster and Smith, "Testicular Cancer in Dogs."

behavior doesn't reliably change after neutering: J. C. Neilson et al., "Effects of Castration on Problem Behaviors in Male Dogs with Reference to Age and Duration of Behavior," *Journal of the American Veterinary Medical Association* 15, no. 211 (July 1997): 180–82.

German Shepherds done in Korea: H. H. Kim, "Effects of Ovariohysterectomy on Reactivity in German Shepherd Dogs," *Veterinary Journal* 172, no. 1 (July 2006): 154–59.

345 **Dutch dogs:** R. J. Maarschalkerweerd, "Influence of Orchiectomy on Canine Behavior," *Veterinary Record* 140, no. 24 (June 14, 1997): 617–19.

348 **Suprelorin . . . GonaCon:** For information on all these products, see online at "About Alliance for Contraception in Cats & Dogs."

Called Vasalgel: Online at Male Contraception Information Project, "RISUG/ Vasalgel"; Bill Gifford, "The Revolutionary New Birth Control Method for Men," *Wired* (May 2011).

viruses that prevent pregnancies: Vaccines and viruses are also being tested that could prevent pregnancies by blocking a sperm's entry into the egg or de-activating conception once it has taken place, all without affecting a dog's sex hormones. See David Grimm, "A Cure for Euthanasia?" *Science* 325 (September 18, 2009): 1490–93.

$75 million prize: Online at Found Animals, "Michelson Prize."

lead organization on this front: Online at Alliance for Contraception in Cats & Dogs, "Resources."

350 **no plans to investigate his findings:** Dr. Kellie Fecteau, Clinical Endocrinology Service director, University of Tennessee Veterinary Medical Center, e-mail communication with the author, September 22, 2011.

352 **Kill rates have either stayed the same:** Online at Australian Veterinary Association, Center for Companion Animals in the Community, "Mandatory Desexing."

Los Angeles is a prime example: Online at DogChannel.com, "Los Angeles Approves Mandatory Spay-Neuter."

"double digit decreases": Online at Los Angeles Animal Services, "2008 Statistical Report," 12.

despite the mandatory spay/neuter law: Online at "LA Animal Services Outcome Totals for Dogs from 11/1/06 to 10/31/11."

The ASPCA is against mandatory spay/neuter: Online at ASPCA, "Position Statement on Mandatory Spay/Neuter Laws."

American Veterinary Medical Association: Online at "AVMA: Mandatory Spay/Neuter a Bad Idea," *Journal of the American Veterinary Medical Association.*

the Anti-Cruelty Society: Online at Anti-Cruelty Society, "Frequently Asked

Questions About Mandatory Spay/Neuter"; online at No Kill Advocacy Center, "The Dark Side of Punitive Legislation"; online at Best Friends Animal Society, "Proposed Mandatory Spay-Neuter Ordinance Has Serious Flaws."

22. Not Long Enough

354 **Rimadyl:** Julie Schmit, "Even Painkillers for Dogs Have Serious Risks," *USA Today,* April 1, 2005; online at FDA, "Update on Rimadyl," December 1, 1999.

Labrador Retrievers being particularly sensitive: Online at Pfizer Animal Health, "Rimadyl (Carprofen)" (prescription instructions), December 2007.

360 **First dog was cloned in South Korea:** Byeong Chun Lee et al., "Dogs Cloned from Adult Somatic Cells," *Nature* 436 (August 2005): 641; Gina Kolata, "Beating Hurdles, Scientists Clone a Dog for a First," *New York Times,* August 4, 2005; Brandon Keim, "Cloned Puppies: Sure, They're Cute, but at What Cost?" *Wired* (August 19, 2008).

a more demanding operation: Online at FDA, "Animal Cloning."

Dr. Frances O. Smith, DVM, PhD, Diplomate American College of Theriogenology, e-mail communication with the author, May 29, 2012.

The reconstructed egg: Online at Human Genome Project Information, "Cloning Fact Sheet."

361 **born from natural reproduction:** Online at Human Genome Project Information, "Cloning Fact Sheet."

a cloned dog will look exactly: These anomalies have occurred because some of the clone's genetic material comes from the mitochondria in the surrogate mother's egg, whose nucleus is replaced by DNA donated by the organism to be cloned. Since mitochondria contain their own DNA, there is the potential for the surrogate mother to influence the characteristics of the cloned organism. See Taeyoung Shin et al., "Cell Biology: A Cat Cloned by Nuclear Transplantation," *Nature* 415 (February 21, 2002): 849; online at National Human Genome Research Institute, "Rainbow and 'CC,' the World's First Cloned Cat: Genetics of Tortoiseshell and Calico Cats" and "Cloning." In the case of dogs, the cloned puppies of Trakr, the search-and-rescue German Shepherd who was credited with finding the last survivor in the rubble of Ground Zero after the 9/11 attack on the Twin Towers, have different coat markings from their father. See Amy Jameson, "Five Puppies Cloned from 9/11 Hero Dog," *People,* June 17, 2009.

362 **the site of arterial injuries:** Panagiotis G. Kyrtatos et al., "Magnetic Tagging Increases Delivery of Circulating Progenitors in Vascular Injury," *Journal of the American College of Cardiology: Cardiovascular Interventions* 2 (2009): 794–802; online at Nanowerk, "Nano-Magnets Guide Stem Cells for Damaged Tissue Repair," August 17, 2009.

bioartificial bladders: Anthony Atala et al., "Tissue-Engineered Autologous Bladders for Patients Needing Cystoplasty," *The Lancet* 15, no. 367 (April 15, 2006): 1241–46.

bioartificial livers: Y. Zhang et al., "Immunosafety Evaluation of a Multilayer Flat-Plate Bioartificial Liver," *American Journal of Medical Sciences* 343, no. 6 (June 2012): 429–34.

given aging mice a gene: Online at Albert Einstein College of Medicine, "In Scientific First, Researchers Correct Decline in Organ Function Associated with Old Age," August 10, 2008.

363 **dog generation is about four years:** Malcolm B. Willis, *Genetics of the Dog* (New York: Howell Book House, 1989), 298.

Cologne's cathedral: Online at Der Kölner Dom, "History of the Building."

364 **"The Rule of 6s":** Online at Gaylan's Goldens, "Reversing the Trend: Proposing the Rule of 6s."

364 **"the longer the dog can stay active":** Malcolm B. Willis, *Genetics of the Dog* (New York: Howell Book House, 1989), 305, 361.

23. Forever Young

369 **"the individualized, empathetic and time-intensive approach":** E. Ernst, "A Systematic Review of Systematic Reviews of Homeopathy," *British Journal Clinical Pharmacology* 54, no. 6 (December 2002): 577–82.

370 **details about these techniques:** Michelle Sevigny, *DogSafe Canine First Aid* (North Vancouver, BC: DOGTIME Canine Recreation Co., 2008). Information about the course can be found online at Dogsafe Canine First Aid. Here are some of the basics of Sevigny's canine first aid course:

- Know your dog's baseline pulse and respiration rate. If your dog is injured, you then have a reference point.
- You can find your dog's pulse on the left side of its chest, at the femoral artery on the inside of its rear legs, and at its wrists. Toy dogs have a pulse rate of 100 to 160 beats per minute, large dogs 60 to 120 beats per minute, and puppies can have a heart rate of up to 200 beats per minute. Just as in people, the more athletic the dog, the slower its heart rate.
- Dogs respire at fifteen to thirty breaths per minute. Bigger dogs breathe more slowly than smaller dogs.
- You can check your dog's healthy circulation by pressing a finger on the pink area of its gum, removing your finger, and then noting how long it takes for the white gum to return to pink. One to two seconds is normal.
- To give an unconscious dog artificial respiration, close the dog's mouth and put your mouth over the dog's nostrils and blow in a breath every two to three seconds. CPR is done on the dog's left side. Kneel behind it, place your palms, one over the other, on the dog's left flank, just behind the elbow. If you're alone, give five compressions in a row, followed by one breath. If you have a companion who is doing the artificial respiration, give three compressions in a row, followed by one breath.
- For a dog who has collapsed, you can try an acupuncture resus-

citation. Place a sharp object (a pencil, a needle, or a fingernail) halfway down the vertical crease that runs between a dog's nose and its upper lip, then push and wiggle the sharp object hard into the crease — in fact, right down to the bone. This pinpoint pressure releases natural adrenaline, which might restore both heartbeat and breathing.

- To stop bleeding, apply pressure to the wound with a gauze pad, a bandanna, or your palm.
- If your dog has a seizure, don't put anything in its mouth. Keep the dog cool, since seizures burn up calories and the dog can overheat. Maintain a quiet environment and dim lighting. Unlike in the case of traumatic injuries, where soothing talk can be helpful, don't talk to a dog who is having a seizure, nor even touch it, as that stimulates the brain and might prolong the seizure.
- If your dog has swallowed a foreign object, use gravity to help remove it. For a small dog, hold it by its upper thighs, head down, and swing it through your legs. For big dogs, lift the rear limbs and hold the dog up like a wheelbarrow. If these techniques fail to remove the inhaled object, step behind the dog and put your arms around its waist. Using two fists against its abdomen, just below the ribs, thrust in and toward its head with two quick motions, repeating up to five times.
- For poisoning, induce vomiting by using 3 percent hydrogen peroxide, one teaspoon per ten pounds of dog, up to twelve teaspoons. A turkey baster is an easy way to administer it. For specific antidotes, contact the North American Pet Poison Helpline (800-213-6680). A similar service is operated in the United Kingdom by Toxcall (0203 368 6298).

371 **"We are not now":** Alfred, Lord Tennyson, "Ulysses," in M. H. Abrams, ed., *The Norton Anthology of English Literature* (New York: W. W. Norton & Co., 1968), 841–43.

383 **"A lively understandable spirit":** Theodore Roethke, "It Was Beginning Winter," in *The Collected Poems of Theodore Roethke* (Garden City, NY: Anchor Books, 1975), 55.

384 **praise makes the promise bloom:** Many researchers have noted this phenomenon: act as if students are smart and they'll return the expectation; act as if they're slow and they'll be so. See Robert Rosenthal and Lenore Jacobson, "Teachers' Expectancies: Determinates of Pupils' IQ Gains," *Psychological Reports* 19 (1966): 115–18; Robert Rosenthal, "Covert Communication in Classrooms, Clinics, Courtrooms, and Cubicles," *American Psychologist* 57, no. 11 (November 2002): 839–48; Herman H. Spitz, "Beleaguered *Pygmalion:* A History of the Controversy over Claims That Teacher Expectancy Raises Intelligence," *Intelligence* 27, no. 3 (September 1999): 199–234.

Index

Page references in italics refer to text graphics.